TAXATION AND DEBT IN
THE EARLY MODERN CITY

T0323162

FINANCIAL HISTORY

Series Editor: Robert E. Wright

Forthcoming Titles

TAXATION AND DEBT IN THE EARLY MODERN CITY

EDITED BY

José Ignacio Andrés Ucendo and Michael Limberger

LONDON AND NEW YORK

First published 2012 by Pickering & Chatto (Publishers) Limited

Published 2016 by Routledge
2 Park Square, Milton Park, Abingdon, Oxfordshire OX14 4RN
711 Third Avenue, New York, NY 10017, USA

First issued in paperback 2015

Routledge is an imprint of the Taylor & Francis Group, an informa business

BRITISH LIBRARY CATALOGUING IN PUBLICATION DATA

Taxation and debt in the early modern city. – (Financial history)
1. Intergovernmental fiscal relations –Europe – History. 2. Europe – Economic
conditions.
I. Series II. Andres Ucendo, Jose Ignacio. III. Limberger, Michael.
336.2'0144'0903-dc23

ISBN-13: 978-1-138-66160-8 (pbk)
ISBN-13: 978-1-8489-3185-5 (hbk)

Typeset by Pickering & Chatto (Publishers) Limited

CONTENTS

ACKNOWLEDGEMENTS

This volume is the result of the collective work of many people and institutions. We would like to express our deep gratitude to the contributing editors, Fausto Piola Caselli and Karel Davids, who have been a continuous source of encouragement and inspiration during the whole process leading to the publication of this book. Both organized and co-chaired with us the session on Urban Fiscal Systems and Economic Growth in Europe during the Sixteenth and Eighteenth Centuries of the World Economic History Congress held in Utrecht in 2009. Most of the essays included in this volume were presented to that session, and we would like to thank all those who attended for their remarks during the stimulating debate which took place on a sunny August evening in the unforgettable environment provided by the Utrecht University. Lastly, we would also like to thank the Spanish Ministry of Science, which has contributed to the publication of this book through the research projects 'Fisco y mercado: fiscalidad, derechos de propiedad y cambio institucional en la España del siglo XVII', HAR 2008-05425 and 'Niveles de vida y desigualdad. Aproximación social y regional en la España preindustrial', HAR2008-04078/HIS.

LIST OF CONTRIBUTORS

José Ignacio Andrés Ucendo: Lecturer of Economic History at the University of the Basque Country. His line of research is focused on the fiscal and financial history of Castile and Madrid during the seventeenth century. He is author of 'Castile's Tax System in the Seventeenth Century', *Journal of European Economic History*, 30:3 (2001), pp. 597–616 and 'Government Policies and the Development of the Financial Markets: The Case of Madrid in the Seventeenth Century', in F. Piola Caselli (ed.), *Government Debts and Financial Markets in Europe* (London: Pickering & Chatto, 2008), pp. 67–80.

Giuseppe Bognetti: Full Professor of Finances at the University of Milan. He has worked on the study of urban finances in northern Italian cities since the eighteenth century.

Alessandra Bulgarelli Lukacs: Associate Professor of Economic History at the University of Naples Federico II. She is an expert on the economic and social history of the kingdom of Naples during the early modern period. A substantial part of her research is focused on the fiscal and financial history of the kingdom. She is author of *L'imposta diretta nel regno di Napoli* (Milano: Franco Angeli, 1993) and 'The Fiscal System in the Kingdom of Naples: Tools for Comparison with the European Reality (13th–18th Centuries)' in S. Cavaciocchi (ed.) *La fiscalità nell'economia europea Secc. XIII–XVIII. Fiscal Systems in the European Economy from the 13th to the 18th Centuries* (Florence: Olschki, 2008), pp. 241–57.

Giuseppe De Luca: Associate Professor of Economic History at the University of Milan. His research field is focused on the history of the Milanese economy during the early modern period. He is author of *Commercio del denaro e crescita economica a Milano tra Cinquecento e Seicento* (Milano: Il Polifilo, 1996) and 'Government Debt and Financial Markets: Exploring Pro-Cycle Effects in Northern Italy during the Sixteenth and the Seventeenth Centuries', in F. Piola Caselli (ed.), *Government Debts and Financial Markets in Europe* (London: Pickering & Chatto, 2008), pp. 45–66.

Nadia Fernández de Pinedo Echevarría: Associate Lecturer of Economic History at the Universidad Autónoma de Madrid. She has worked on Spanish colonial trade during the nineteenth century. She is author of *Comercio exterior y fiscalidad: Cuba, 1794–1860* (Lejona: Universidad del País Vasco, 2002).

Bernd Fuhrmann: Professor of Medieval and Early Modern History at the University of Siegen. He is the author of 'Die Bedeutung direkter und indirekter Steuern in ausgewählten Städten im Deutschen Reich (Römischen Reich) vom 14. bis ins 17. Jahrhundert', in S. Cavaciocchi (ed.), *La Fiscalità nell'Economia Europea Secc. XIII–XVIII: Fiscal Systems in the European Economy from the 13th to the 18th Centuries* (Florence: Olschki, 2008), pp. 801–17.

Ramón Lanza García: Lecturer of Economic History at the Universidad Autónoma de Madrid. His research field is focused on different aspects of the Castilian economic and social history during the early modern period. He is the author of *La población y el crecimiento económico de Cantabria en el Antiguo Régimen* (Madrid: Universidad Autónoma, 1991) and *Miseria, cambio y progreso en el Antiguo Régimen. Cantabria, siglos XVI–XVIII* (Santander: Universidad, 2010).

Michael Limberger: Lecturer at the department of Early Modern History at the University of Gent. His research is on social and economic history of the early modern period. His works and articles include *Sixteenth Century Antwerp and Its Rural Surroundings: Social and Economic Changes in the Hinterland of a Commercial Metropolis (ca. 1450–1750)* (Turnhout, 2008); 'No Town in the World Provides More Advantages: Economies of Agglomeration and the Golden Age of Antwerp', in P. O'Brien (ed.), *Urban Achievement in Early Modern Europe: Golden Ages in Antwerp, Amsterdam and London* (Cambridge: Cambridge University Press, 2001), pp. 39–62 and 'Merchant Capitalism and the Countryside: Antwerp and the West of the Duchy of Brabant (15th–18th Centuries)', in P. Hoppenbrouwers and J. L. van Zanden (eds), *Peasants into Farmers? The Transformation of the Rural Economy and Society in the Low Countries in the Light of the Brenner Debate* (Turnhout, 2001), pp. 158–78.

José Antonio Mateos Royo: Lecturer of Economic History at the University of Zaragoza. He has worked on the economic and social history of the kingdom of Aragón during the early modern period. He is author of 'The Making of a New Landscape: Town Councils and Water in the Kingdom of Aragon during the Sixteenth Century', *Rural History*, 9:2 (1998), pp. 123–39 and 'Municipal Politics and Corporate Protectionism: Town Councils and Guilds in the Kingdom of Aragon during the Sixteenth and Seventeenth Centuries', in B. Blondé, E. Vanhaute and M. Galand (eds), *Labour and Labour Markets between Town and Countryside (Middle Ages–Nineteenth Century)* (Turnhout: Brepols, 2001), pp. 178–97.

Fausto Piola Caselli: Full Professor of Economic History at the University of Cassino. He is an expert on the social and economic history of Rome and the Papal States during the early modern period, and was editor of the volume *Government Debts and Financial Markets in Europe* (London: Pickering & Chatto, 2008).

Andrea Pühringer: Independent Historian. Author of the book *Contributionale, Oeconomicum und Politicum. Die Finanzen der landesfürstlichen Städte Nieder- und Oberösterreichs in der Frühneuzeit* (Munich: Oldenbourg, 2002).

Guy Saupin: History Professor at the University of Nantes. He is an expert on the history of the French cities during the early modern period. He is author of *Les villes en France's l'époque moderne* (Paris: Belin, 2002) and *Le pouvoir urbain dans les villes d'Europe atlantique* (Nantes: Ouest Editions, 2002).

Manon van der Heijden: Associate Professor of Economic and Social History at the University of Leiden. She is an expert on the economic and social history of the Dutch Republic in the seventeenth century. She is author of 'Renteniers and the Public Debt of Dordrecht (1555–1572)', in M. Boone, K. Davids and P. Janssens (eds), *Urban Public Debts: Urban Government and the Market for Annuities in Western Europe (14th–18th Centuries)* (Turnhout: Brepols, 2003), pp. 183–96 and 'State Formation and Urban Finances in Sixteenth and Seventeenth-Century Holland', *Journal of Urban History*, 32:3 (2006), pp. 429–50.

Martijn van der Burg: Lecturer of History at the University of Amsterdam. He has worked on the financial history of the Dutch cities during the early modern period. He is author (together with Marjolein 't Hart) of 'Renteniers and the Recovery of Amsterdam's Credit (1578–1605)', in M. Boone, K. Davids and P. Janssens (eds), *Urban Public Debts. Urban Government and the Market for Annuities in Western Europe (14th–18th Centuries)* (Turnhout: Brepols, 2003), pp. 197–218.

LIST OF FIGURES AND TABLES

INTRODUCTION

José Ignacio Andrés Ucendo and Michael Limberger

The course of the European history of the early modern period was shaped by the process of state formation. The rise of the fiscal state being one of the best manifestations of this trend, the study of the fiscal and financial systems created by the European polities of the period has attracted the interest of the researchers for a long time.[1] The nascent European states of the time developed fiscal systems at an early stage to raise the incomes with which to fund their progressively more expensive activities. As those revenues were not sufficient to pay their spending, the states supplemented them with income coming from short- and long-term public debt. Hence, the study of the fiscal state has unavoidably become closely intertwined with the analysis of advances in the European finances brought by the expansion of that same state.

Recent research has emphasized the continuities between the fiscal and financial history of towns and states and now it is widely acknowledged that the systems of public credit developed by the monarchies and republics of the early modern period were modelled on the example set by European cities during the last centuries of the Middle Ages.[2] At least since the thirteenth and fourteenth centuries a group of Aragonese, Italian and Low Countries towns began to issue annuities funded through taxation. This led to the development of notions of collective responsibility and set the basis for the implementation of the first systems of public debt in sixteenth-century Holland and other polities of the time, such as Castile and many Italian states.[3] Historians have devoted a large part of their effort to the study of urban debts, and, more recently, they have also become interested in the analysis of urban spending. It is commonly admitted that the supply of public services is one of the main tasks of the state, but things were very different before the contemporary period. The greatest part of the revenues obtained by the European states through finance and taxation was devoted to pay their expensive foreign policy, so the provision of public services was carried out by other institutions, such as the Church, guilds or towns. Recently, a number of works has begun to address this issue.[4]

It may be said, therefore, that at the present stage we have a good knowledge of the financial systems set up by the towns of the Continent, and that we begin to realize that urban centres were responsible for the development of at least part of the infrastructure required in any process of economic growth. Perhaps surprisingly, the study of the tax systems which enabled the cities to raise the revenues needed to fund such functions has tended to be consigned to a somewhat secondary place in the literature. The objective of this book is to fill in this gap and to offer an overview of the fiscal systems of the most important urban areas of the continent during the early modern period. As the trajectory of urban taxation was heavily conditioned by the simultaneous growth of the urban debts, which reflected the influence of state formation on the fiscal and financial stability of the European towns, the book also deals with the evolution of the financial systems in the urban world and its links with state finance.

The evidence included in the essays of the book points to the existence of a fiscal model which appears to have prevailed in most European cities. Leaving aside the case of the small Austrian towns described by Andrea Pühringer, most cities of our essays turned to indirect taxes to obtain a substantial part of their fiscal revenues. The reliance on indirect taxes, frequently levied on basic commodities such as wine, beer, meat, wheat or bread, must be accounted for by the fact that they enabled the oligarchies who ruled the European towns to relegate direct taxation to a secondary place, transferring a substantial part of the fiscal burden on the shoulders of the numerically predominant middle and lower sorts of urban populations. Another motive behind this preference can be seen in the idea that, as indirect taxes were supported by the whole of the urban population, they were also paid by visitors and foreigners.[5] The revenues obtained from indirect taxes only funded part of the urban spending and were supplemented by incomes raised through a growing urban debt, the expansion of which seems to have been common to most European towns of the period. Loans were used to fund the provision of public infrastructures and, especially, to raise the sums granted to the state by nearly every town of the period through subsidies, loans and gifts. The unrelenting growth of the resulting urban debt conditioned the structure of urban spending, compelling most cities to invest a substantial part of their tax revenues in the payment of the interests of the annuities issued by them.

City annuities seem to have exerted a lasting influence on the course of the fiscal and financial history of the European urban world, showing the close links between the fiscal systems of the cities and state formation. Although it is undeniable that the way the urban fiscal and financial systems evolved was affected by local circumstances, the essays of the book suggest that the influence of the state appears to have been of major importance. The wealth accumulated in the early modern city as a result of the development of trade and manufacture attracted the interest of the state, which saw the urban centres as a welcome source of apparently unending tax and financial revenues. The essays of the book deal with some of the methods used by the European governments to obtain income from their cities from the point of view of the latter.[6]

Given the administrative shortcomings of the states of the time and the vast reserve of fiscal and financial expertise accumulated in the European urban centres, the state resorted to the cities as intermediaries in the fiscal field. This trend is visible in nearly all the essays of the book. In the Neapolitan cities and Milan, for example, local councils collected an important part of the taxes which were due to the central government. In other cases the cities were more than simple intermediaries and they transferred part of their own revenues to the state, as in some towns of the Holy Roman Empire such as Marburg and Munich. This last trend is also present in the cases of Dusseldorf and Coblenz, where some indirect taxes, originally controlled by the municipal treasuries, became included in the list of state taxes at the end of the seventeenth century. Another good example of this trend may be found in Rome, where the papacy collected all the taxes levied in the city through its financial department (the Apostolic Chamber) and then allocated the amount deemed appropriate to fund the ordinary expenditures of the municipal administration to the town council.

The examples just mentioned indicate that very frequently the limits between state and municipal taxes were blurred and that many of the latter funded the central government. In other cases, however, there was a clear difference between those taxes collected by the Royal Treasury and those levied by town councils, although in practical terms such difference was less clear than one might think at first sight. This is particularly evident in seventeenth century Madrid. The Castilian capital offered substantial funds to the Royal Treasury between 1629 and 1679 through many gifts ('*donativos*'). To obtain the sums granted to the Crown in such gifts Madrid followed the same method used by many other European cities. It raised its municipal debt by issuing annuities whose interests were paid with the revenues obtained from the indirect taxes collected by the town council. From this perspective, then, such taxes really funded, although indirectly, the needs of the state rather than those of the town and could be described as a kind of royal taxes whose collection was deferred in time.

The essays of the book show that the early modern period deserves to be considered as the golden age of indirect taxation in the European urban world. The fiscal history of Madrid, Rome, Milan, Antwerp and the Neapolitan, Aragonese and German towns of the time was characterized by the continuous introduction of a broad range of indirect taxes, a fact that could not fail to influence the views of their contemporaries, also aware that the states were resorting to the same kind of taxes. It is perhaps not by chance that the Castilian and Italian economic commentators of the seventeenth and eighteenth centuries invested big part of their time and effort in the study of the relations between indirect taxation and price and wage levels.[7] Doing so, they laid the basis for a theory later developed by the classic economists who saw in the proliferation of indirect taxes one potential cause of rises in production costs with damaging consequences for manufacture and industry. This point was concisely expressed by Adam Smith in a paragraph of the fourth book of his *Wealth of Nations*: if price levels, driven by indirect taxation, grow more than nominal wages, then real wages will tend to fall. However, if nominal wages rise above price levels, the subsequent increase of real wages will prompt a simultaneous increase of productive costs.[8]

This view is often invoked to describe the decadence of the urban economies in seventeenth century Italy and Castile and it will also sound familiar to all those readers interested in the vast literature about the Dutch economic decline. Its main problem, though, is that up until now this theory has been more asserted than proven.[9] Any study of the impact of indirect taxation on prices and wages levels in the European cities during the early modern period faces difficulties which seem almost insurmountable.[10] To some extent, this is due to the limitations of our price data. Although during the last decades there has been an upsurge in the interest on the study of price and wage levels in the European urban world during the early modern period, our price data include bulk prices which do not reflect the incidence of the indirect taxes levied by the state and the local councils on the commodities sold in the cities. To solve this problem and to measure the real incidence of indirect taxation on urban price and wage levels, the compilation of good retail price series in the different European cities would be required. This is out of the scope of the present book, although, nonetheless, the papers on Madrid, Rome, Milan, Antwerp and the Aragonese and German provide some evidence to suggest that the consequences of indirect taxation on urban economies economy might well have been rather less damaging than what is often assumed.

At the end of the seventeenth century indirect taxation raised price levels in Madrid around 15–25 per cent, reducing the real wages earned by a building worker in the same measure. This rise was driven by the heavy fiscal burden which fell on a narrow group of commodities such as wine, meat and, in some phases, coal, particularly well represented in the consumption patterns of the inhabitants of the Castilian capital. During this period taxes amounted to 60–65 per cent of the retail price of cheap wine and to 30–35 per cent of that of mutton. The role of municipal taxes in both examples was basic, and the Madrid experience may be considered as supporting the traditional view about the influence of indirect taxes on price and wage levels. If we also consider that during the same period the salt tax was levied at Leiden at a rate of 100 per cent on value and beer at 60 per cent and that in Venice taxes represented 42 per cent of the price of high quality cloth, the Castilian capital could be included in the group of European towns where indirect taxation seems to have exerted a relevant influence on price and wage levels.[11]

However, other works show that the incidence of taxation on the costs of the silk and woollen fabrics in well-known Italian manufacturing centres such as Genoa (silk) and Florence and Milan (woollens) could hardly be considered heavy, never surpassing 5–6 per cent. This notion is strengthened by the evidence included in the essays of our book, pointing to the possibility, which would deserve further research, that the case of Madrid (and Leiden and Venice) might well have been less common than what is often thought.[12] The fiscal burden which fell on the consumption and sales of basic foodstuffs was much heavier in the Castilian capital than in Rome, Antwerp, Milan and the German cities and, as Nadia Fernández de Pinedo explains in her essay on eighteenth century Madrid, it was not until the first half of the eighteenth century that the first steps were taken to reverse this course and the Crown decided to increase the taxes levied on those products consumed by the members of the middle and upper classes living in the city.

To some extent, the difference between Madrid and the other towns of our essays could be considered the result of the specific way the levying of indirect taxes was arranged by every other city. While the most profitable taxes levied by the town council and the Crown on cheap wine in Madrid were excises proportional to its retail price and their effect on prices tended to rise with inflation, excises seem to have been relatively infrequent in other cases, such as Milan and Rome. In Milan, as recalled by Giuseppe De Luca and Giuseppe Bognetti, the stability in price and wage levels during the seventeenth century suggests that the effects of indirect taxes should have been rather less important than what has been traditionally considered. This was due, in part, to the fact that the indirect taxes levied in the capital of Lombardy were always fixed, so their incidence tended to fall during inflationary phases whereas in Rome, as Fausto Piola Caselli reminds us, wine and other foodstuffs were taxed on quantities. To this it should be added that the fiscal burden which weighed on wine and meat in seventeenth century Madrid appears to have been high from a comparative perspective. As Bernd Fuhrmann states in his essay, at the beginning of the sixteenth century indirect taxes were 20–22 per cent of the retail price of wine in Nördlingen and 33 per cent in Nuremberg. The same author reminds us that the fiscal burden which fell on most commodities was more moderate, in line with seventeenth century Rome, where, as Piola shows, taxes amounted to a moderate 10–12 per cent of the retail price of wine. Lastly, the difference between the effects of indirect taxes on price and wage levels in Madrid and the other cities of our essays should be also accounted for by the existence among the ruling oligarchies of the latter of an awareness of the potentially damaging effects of this kind of taxation which seems to have been virtually absent in the Castilian capital. In the case of Rome, in other centres such as Antwerp, and the Aragonese cities, as described by Michael Limberger and José Antonio Mateos Royo respectively, local councils promoted measures to dampen the worst effects of indirect taxation, levying, by example, heavier duties on middle and higher quality wines (in Rome) and beer (in Antwerp), and reducing the fiscal burden on wine and meat (in the Aragonese cities), whereas nothing like this seems to have existed in the fiscal and financial system set up by the local authorities in seventeenth century Madrid. Much of this awareness was related to the fear of public unrest. The seventeenth and eighteenth centuries saw frequent urban riots against fiscal measures. In order to avoid public protest, town councils in the Low Countries and some places in Switzerland or Germany tried to introduce social tariffs for taxation and had the town accounts controlled by representatives of the citizens or read in public.[13]

The indirect taxes collected by European cities allowed the local governments to raise the revenues needed to fund their growing debts. As the cases of many German cities and, especially, Milan, Madrid and Antwerp suggest, the payment of the interests of the annuities issued by the city treasuries was the most important urban expenditure, and this had lasting consequences on the financial evolution of those centres.

Recent research is showing an awareness of the relation between public services and economic growth.[14] Today it is commonly admitted that the supply of public services in education, health and infrastructures is one of the most important tasks of any state, but this idea would have sound alien to the kings and rulers of the sixteenth and seventeenth centuries, focused on the fulfilment of their foreign policy agendas. As a result, the supply of public services was carried out by other institutions and corporations, such as the guilds, the Church and the cities, but the capacity of the latter to offer such services seems to have been reduced as a consequence of their heavy indebtedness. In cases such as those of Madrid and Antwerp, the payment of the interests of the municipal debt, very frequently a result of the need of funding the state through the granting of subsidies and gifts, drew most part of their fiscal revenues and reduced their capacity to offer public services. This problem was aggravated by the fact that very frequently the urban financial systems were pervaded by a marked redistributive character, which stimulated wide tax evasion and depressed tax morale, as it may be seen in Milan, Madrid and the Aragonese and Neapolitan cities. The revenues obtained from indirect taxation were used to pay their interests to the buyers of the urban annuities who frequently belonged to the small oligarchies ruling the town councils.[15] Rather understandably, the main objective of this group was to ensure the payment of the interests of their debt, so the buyers of urban annuities and the creditors of the European cities acted as a pressure group which, as the case of Milan and the Neapolitan cities suggest, influenced the fiscal and financial life of the European towns, promoting those policies deemed more convenient for the fulfilment of their objectives. After 1658 the Bank of *Santo Ambrogio*, the main creditor of Milan, received the control of the most important indirect taxes levied in the city, whereas the pressure exerted by the owners of urban annuities was one of the main factors behind the compilation of a new and updated cadastre in the kingdom of Naples in 1740. This goes a long way to explain how in cities such as Antwerp or Madrid, where the value of the municipal debt was nearly twenty times that of its yearly fiscal revenues, the town councils refused to redeem the principals of the urban debt and decided to focus on the regular payment of the interests of the annuities issued during the sixteenth and seventeenth centuries. In what deserves to be considered as a textbook case of path dependency, which illustrates the consequences brought by the growing influence of the owners of the municipal debt on the financial life of European towns, this also makes some sense of why Madrid was still paying the interest on the '*efectos*' issued between 1629 and 1679 at such an advanced date as the beginning of the twentieth century.

But the expansion of urban debt had very different consequences in other cases, as the Dutch cities of Dordrecht, Haarlem and Rotterdam analysed by Manon van der Heijden and Martijn van der Burg. The economic expansion of the Dutch economy during its golden age enabled the cities of the Republic to set up complex systems of urban debt whose consequences seem to have been very different from those found in Madrid or the Neapolitan cities. The rise of trade and manufacture in these towns not only ensured the growth of the revenues obtained from the indirect taxes which funded the urban debts but also provided a broad range of social groups with incomes to buy those annuities, and soon a free annuity market in which the ownership of urban long- and short-term bonds was dispersed among a relatively high number of investors emerged. This trend had relevant consequences for the financial and economic stability of the Dutch cities because it helped to prevent the disadvantages of an excessive reliance on a narrow and enclosed group of investors and it also reduced the worst redistributive effects of the urban debts, enabling broad sections of the urban populations of the Republic to obtain additional sources of income which might help them to cope with times of hardship, old age, sickness and disability, as had already happened during the sixteenth century in other cities of the Low Countries such as 's-Hertogenbosch.[16]

As the reader will soon discover, the book does not include a chapter on any English cities. This is particularly regrettable because the fiscal and financial history of the English towns of the early modern phase seems to have evolved very differently from that of the European cities analysed in the book, at least judged from the standpoint of its capital, London. Although there were broad similarities, probably the most significant difference lies in the fact that the English capital did not resort to the expansion of its urban debt, at least to the same extent found in the rest of the European urban world.

Like the other European urban centres, English cities soon became an important source of fiscal and financial revenues for the Crown. During the Middle Ages the government raised substantial incomes from ordinary and extraordinary taxation from English towns. The former consisted of revenues, which included tolls and a broad range of other incomes coming from trade, profits of jurisdiction, rents, houses and lands in the royal domain, whereas the latter were occasionally collected to fund special needs such as warfare or royal weddings through the levying of tallages (also known as aids or gifts). Although it is difficult to estimate the urban contribution to the tax revenues of the English state on account of the problems posed by the documentary sources, it has been recently estimated that in 1327 and 1332 towns contributed about 10 per cent to Crown income and customs about 30 per cent.[17]

The fiscal relevance of London was already visible during the Middle Ages, when the city was known as 'the king's chamber' and acted as a kind of reserve for funding the English state.[18] This trend also prevailed during the Tudor and Stuart eras, when the English capital provided the central government with a substantial part of the sums it collected from direct and indirect taxation, in the form of parliamentary subsidies assessed on wealth and customs respectively, and made of the English capital one of the most important sources of fiscal revenues for the English state.[19]

There appears to have been more similarities between English and other European cities. As was normal in early modern Europe, the history of Tudor and Stuart England in the fiscal field was characterized by the development of a trend towards the devolution of responsibility to local communities and individuals, acting as intermediaries between the requirements of central government and tax payers, especially in the collection of funds for the defence of the realm through taxes assessed and raised locally which paid an important part of the military expenditures of the Crown.[20] Again, such processes were particularly prominent in sixteenth-century London.[21] During this period the city raised troops and paid the training of its militia through the corporate resources of the livery companies and local assessments. The funds invested by the city to such ends were substantial, especially during the last two decades of the century, and they helped to mitigate the consequences brought about by the declining yields of other sources of fiscal revenues of the Crown in the capital, such as parliamentary subsidies assessed on wealth.

Apart from providing tax revenues, the English cities also supplied the English Crown with substantial financial resources and once more the role of London seems to have been especially relevant since the Middle Ages. At the end of the fifteenth century, for example, the withdrawal of the financial services of the merchants of London played an important role in the fall of the Lancastrian regime and this trend continued during the greater part of the sixteenth century and the Stuart period.[22] During the first half of the sixteenth century the Crown borrowed in London from wealthy merchants and the corporation. It is well known that between 1544 and 1574 the Crown made an effort to raise loans in Antwerp, but this attempt was soon abandoned. Since 1575, and especially since the start of the Stuart period, the government resorted to the more traditional method of using the financial services provided by its capital.[23]

Here lies the most remarkable particularity of the English case from a comparative perspective. In the cities included in our essays the granting of subsidies and loans to the state led to the expansion of urban debt and the simultaneous rise of the fiscal revenues at the disposal of the local councils. To give an idea, between 1654 and 1679 Madrid's debt rose from 2 million ducats to 19 million and in the same period the tax revenues also grew, in real terms, from an index 100 to nearly 250.[24] Nothing like this seems to have happened in the English towns and London. During the sixteenth and seventeenth centuries the ordinary revenues of the English capital derived from property, city tolls, apprenticeship and freedom.[25] Although reduced, such revenues sufficed to fund the daily activities of the urban government, and in case of need they were supplemented by other methods, being particularly remarkable that the city authorities always showed a marked reluctance to the introduction of special taxes for civic purposes and to the expansion of the city debt. This reluctance can perhaps be explained as a result of some considerations which might have been prominent in the minds of the city's aldermen. Given their small value, the ordinary revenues of the town could have hardly been used as collateral to fund its debt. To achieve this objective it would have been necessary to expand the tax resources of the capital, but the problem here was that the fiscal burden which fell on the Londoners for the payment of local and royal taxes, the tithe and a group of rates among which the most important was the poor rate was far from negligible. Aware of this, the town authorities shared the prevailing 'low tax' philosophy which saw in an excessive fiscal burden one cause of rebellion, especially in the troubled circumstances of the revolutionary and Restoration periods, and refused the possibility of expanding a debt which would have required the simultaneous expansion of the tax base of the city, presumably through the introduction of indirect taxes and excises.[26]

This reluctance should have been strengthened by the fact that, as it has been emphasized by Vanessa Harding, London found in the administration of the Orphans' fund a welcome source of revenue which provided the local council with substantial incomes during the seventeenth century. Hence, the corporation avoided the need of reforming its finances and arrived to the last years of the century with an antiquated fiscal system whose incomes came from property, city tolls, apprenticeship and freedom fees.[27]

Lastly, the refusal to develop an urban debt system along continental lines might well have been reinforced for another reason. Unlike the norm prevailing in most European cities, the Crown raised loans in London but not from London, and this difference appears to have been crucial. The loans raised by the government in its capital were granted by wealthy individuals and the livery companies, who mobilized their own private funds in such operations, whereas in cities such as Madrid or Antwerp it was the towns themselves, through their local councils, which granted loans, subsidies and gifts to the central government by way of methods involving, as may be seen in the essays of the book, the expansion of the urban debt, the issue of annuities and the introduction of indirect taxes to fund such debt. The fact that the raising of loans by the Crown in sixteenth- and seventeenth-century London was to a great extent a private or nearly semi-private activity between the government and wealthy individuals and livery companies of the city helps to understand better why the local authorities did not feel compelled to resort to a long-term debt system funded by indirect taxes.

The differences between the fiscal and financial systems set up in London and the other European towns, then, seem clear and this raises the problem of analysing how such systems might have affected the course of the later economic and social history of the English and European economies. Although the answer to this question would require further research, we may advance some suggestions here. It has traditionally been emphasized that one of the main contributions of urbanization to economic growth lies in the role of cities as promoters of the division of labour and the advance of markets. To this it should be added that we are beginning to realize that during the early modern period European towns also fulfilled the function of providing at least part of the public services and infrastructures required in any process of economic growth. The evidence included in the essays of this book suggests that it would be impossible to understand the capacity of European cities to fulfil this last purpose without considering the state of urban finances and shows that the existence of advanced systems of public debt did not seem to have guaranteed 'per se' the achievement of economic success. Antwerp, Madrid and the Aragonese and Neapolitan cities seem to have developed relatively complex and refined debt systems, although they had to devote the greatest part of their revenues to the payment of the interest owed to the owners of local annuities. This curtailed the capacity of the city councils to provide public services and infrastructures, something compounded in the case of Madrid by the presence of a regressive fiscal and financial system. Something different seems to have happened in the Dutch cities. Although the fiscal and financial system set up in such centres was essentially very similar to that of the other cities of the book, the growth of the Dutch economy during its golden age ensured the yields of the indirect taxes collected in such centres and also provided a broad range of social groups with incomes to buy the annuities issued by such cities. The ownership of urban annuities was relatively widespread among members of the low and middle sorts of the urban populations of the Dutch cities, who saw in these assets a good investment for old age and times of sickness and disability. This contributed to reduce the extent of the regressive effects which seem to have prevailed in the fiscal and financial life of the Mediterranean cities.

The differences we have just mentioned indicate the absence of a clear connection between the development of complex tax and financial systems and the capacity of towns to promote economic growth through the supplying of public works and infrastructures and suggest that everything depended on the specific circumstances prevailing in each case. From this point of view, then, it would be interesting to consider the, at first sight, rather surprising possibility that the absence of advances in urban finances visible in the English case could have been a blessing in disguise. Unlike in Madrid or Antwerp, the tax revenues of London did not increase appreciably during the sixteenth and seventeenth centuries, but there are reasons to suggest that this did not hamper the supply of public works and services which promoted the advance of the economic life in the English capital. The rich sources of private capital accumulated by the local merchants funded the development and continuous improvements of the city port during the Middle Ages up until the eighteenth century. To this it should be added that, as in the rest of the kingdom, the inhabitants of the city paid the poor rates which made the basis of the poor-relief system thanks to which modern England enjoyed the benefits of probably the best system of social relief in early modern Europe.[28] It might be argued that the capacity of London's merchants and tax payers to provide such services could have been hampered by the presence of a fiscal and financial system following the European lines. Under such a system, the greater part of the growing tax revenues of the capital would have funded the city debt and would have probably exerted a rather regressive role. From this point of view, then, it could be stated that the backwardness still prevailing in the fiscal and financial life of the English capital at the end of the seventeenth century, in a period when other European cities such as Madrid, Antwerp and the Dutch and Italian cities had set up complex systems of urban debts, offered, quite unexpectedly, some relevant advantages which should not be overlooked and that would deserve further consideration.

1 FROM PRIVATE TO PUBLIC MANAGEMENT: TAX FARMING AND CUSTOMS DUTIES IN ROME (1630–1700)

Fausto Piola Caselli

The Urban Tax System[1]

The first steady settlements of Roman duty offices date back to the second half of twelfth century.[2] The town was at that time reduced to a scant population, but still showed off a proud municipal autonomy. All commodities brought into town were subject to the Dogana, a customs toll on traded goods of nearly 10 per cent.[3] Goods reached Rome by land, through one of the many gates still open in the ancient Roman walls, where a preliminary small amount was paid. Then they were carried on to the central warehouse near St Eustachius Church, where they were charged with final duties before going to retail. Merchandise arriving by sea on the River Tiber from the South was discharged at the Ripa Grande Harbour – near the Trastevere district. When shipped from Northern areas, goods landed at the minor Ripetta Harbour. In any case, considering the many active city checkpoints, the whole system was quite large and required strong management in terms of buildings, staff and controls. In the mid-fifteenth century the *Dogane* registered tax accounts reached an average of 4,500 records per year. The town budget did not need important financial contributions, and taxation was in fact then kept at very low levels, at nearly an average 5 per cent of declared goods value.[4]

However, in a few decades, policy faced new scenarios. Back from Avignon, the papal court landed in Rome with an ambitious programme to enlarge and consolidate the state. This was quite clear at least after the 1527 sack, when the Reformation sped up the whole process. Given that contributions from northern Europe were plummeting, the Apostolic Chamber – a sort of Treasury ministry – had only two financial choices left: public debt and taxation. Both of them were exploited, yet with different timing. At the very beginning the Chamber drove the lever of public debt, which registered a huge increase over the period from 1550 to 1650. High interest rates were offered to encourage investors, and capital inflow burst out towards the attractive Chamber cashier's windows.[5] Later on the debt was settled, at 3 per cent only.[6] Fiscal manoeuvres then followed, after a number of political outcomes which allowed the state periphery to be financially self-supporting, thanks to a strong regional treasurers' network. The wealthy Roman consumption markets then became the target of a new dynamic tax policy, by which town control was considered an absolute priority. The Chamber managed to deprive Rome of its glorious political and financial autonomy, running all the major town businesses directly. Even local taxes on meat were first cashed in by the Chamber, and then given graciously back to the Capitol administration to pay interests on city loans, which in turn had been imposed by the Chamber itself.[7] After many humiliations, in 1586 Sixtus V scornfully informed the town administrators that, given their absolute incompetence, he was forced to exclude them also from the Roman *annona*, the important food-supply department. They would be left only with the role of executing the Pontiff's decisions and little more.[8] From a financial point of view, this was a concrete threat. In the 1630s the Capitoline treasury still received a 50 per cent return from the tax farmers' contract fees, but in 1685 the percentage had been lowered to 15 per cent and from 1685 Rome was denied any earnings whatsoever. Custom fees were collected totally by the Chamber, and went to repay the interest on state public debt.[9]

Taxes in Rome were usually levied on consumption only. In times of emergency occasional amounts were drawn as compulsory gifts, as happened in 1708, when Roman guilds and citizens were asked to contribute in a generous way.[10] Taxation on real estate or on trade profits was unknown. In some cases the capital was even temporarily cleared from excises levied throughout the entire state territory, as it was for the second quattrino on every pound of meat sold by retail. (A quattrino being one-fifth of a baiocco, which in turn is one-hundredth of a scudo). Furthermore, the town area was still settled within the ancient Roman walls, which in glorious times had been conceived to protect a population of more than one million inhabitants. And now, with 50,000 people only during the mid-sixteenth century, there was enough room for cultivable pieces of land, small vineyards and private kitchen gardens or *orti*.[11] Therefore, poor families had good chances of providing for daily life through their own duty-free vegetables and poultry. Customs trade was mainly provided for by the rich courts, the religious orders' general houses and the Papal Curia staff. Poor relief and assistance was granted by a wide network of hospices, hospitals and charitable institutions, which contributed to a reasonable standard of living.[12] In 1629, according to the Venetian Ambassador Paolo Paruta, the Roman population was still used to the *tranquillo et abbondante tempo passato* (the quiet and abundant old days).[13] He could not have known that a fifty-year period of increasing taxation was close at hand, starting in the years 1642–4, owing to Urban VIII's wars against the Farnese family in Castro. Nonetheless, during the whole seventeenth century, papal authorities were able to keep the social climate in Rome peaceful.[14]

However, taxation growth was levied reasonably, and it was easily soaked up by the market. As a matter of fact, consumption grew dramatically from the early sixteenth century onwards.[15] The town was crowded with ambassadors, cardinal courts, local aristocracy and foreign aristocrats fighting for higher curial ranks and spending accordingly. A wide charity network set up by hospices, hospitals and confraternities was generously financed as well to provide poor people with assistance. Even if local production was poor, taxes on trade – mainly on foodstuffs – could secure good income for the Chamber. According to tradition, bankers and representatives from the most distinguished families got into the business as tax farmers, under the official name of customs officer.[16] They drew up a contract for a standard period of nine years and paid a yearly fee. Then bankers were allowed to cash duties by means of their own managing organization, in full autonomy. Most customs officers belonged to major Florentine firms such as Strozzi, Altoviti, Ceuli, Guicciardini and others, alternating with some Genoese families.[17] This position was undoubtedly very influential in the Roman financial world. However, the most attractive business was not tax farming itself, rather the additional financial services which it could secure, such as the management of public debt treasuries, or granting short-term loans at high interest rates. Special price discounts or *diffalchi* were established by the Chamber to compensate trade decline in times of war, or when the papal court had to settle far away from Rome for a long period, as occurred in 1543.[18] Nevertheless, yearly contract fees paid by bankers to exploit Roman customs – which reflected revenue – rose unceasingly. Amounts doubled in the second half of the sixteenth century, increasing at a parallel rate with the town population growth. Later on the trend improved quite remarkably, with a particular spurt between 1640 and 1670. All in all, from the beginning of the seventeenth century to its end, yearly amounts earned from customs duties tripled, at the least, while in the same period the registered town population increase was 35 per cent.[19] Roman trades did not suffer from tax increases and consumption markets stayed at high levels from the Renaissance period.[20]

This sketch outlines the scope and the timing of the customs business. It also clarifies why the Chamber, in spite of the great freedom previously granted to bankers, soon started to press hard upon customs management with rigid auditing. In 1689, customs were granted to Leonardo Libri, a high Chamber officer, *finché piacerà al papa* (as long as the Pope wanted).[21] The Libri contract did not mention any price to be paid, and the revenue went to the payment of the interest on the public debt. Customs administration was fully kept under the public governmental wing, even if it was still shaped within the formalities of a private one. From 1698 the customs system was run directly by the Chamber, with an ad hoc bureaucracy.

The *dogane generali* contracts included most of the duties paid in Rome on goods and foodstuffs, but not all of them. Salt duty was sold separately to other bankers, and the same happened with flour for a long time. The Castelli wine duty was always sold separately as well, at least up to the Leonardi Libri period. The wine duty was very profitable, granting a huge benefit to the contract owner, and the Chamber probably gave out all of its most profitable contracts according to its specific conveniences or interests. Almost all of the documentation of separate contracts has been lost, but prices paid for them may be known by the yearly state balance-sheet series, where such amounts are registered as an income from the Rome area.

All decisions concerning customs tariffs were strictly kept to the Chamber. Taxing citizens was a mere political affair and private bankers had no discretionary power over this issue. Contract prices were usually decided on the basis of the previous yearly tax yield, so that in principle there should be a full balance between the yearly amount paid by bankers for the contract and their alleged revenue.[22] Contracts were ceremoniously signed by the treasurer, after an official tender *alla candela* (for the time it took for a candle to burn). In theory the tender should have dealt with open offers on the rise coming from many competitors, ending when the candle flame reached a notch, but as a matter of fact the contractor's name with price and all conditions had been previously agreed in private. The general customs of Rome included a variety of important and less important tolls, from that of very fruitful meat, to quality wine, grain and all sorts of goods and minor trades. The main tolls were run as an autonomous department, each of them requiring separate staff, bureau, accountancy and cash. However head offices and warehouses were often physically located in the same building, as was the case for the land customs of St Eustachius. Consequently, the final contract price was the sum of many prices, each of them referring to a single toll, which in turn could be resold with a subcontract. Still, a considerable amount of duty-free wine for the Papal palace was included in the contract. Other duty-free goods could go beyond customs by order of the Chamber, on the condition they be refunded later on.

As a matter of fact, prices were fixed for a period of nine years, while consumption was expected to grow incessantly and profits should have therefore come from trade increase. Prices were not paid in cash to the Chamber, rather they were lodged to reward public debt interests, according to maturities and moneys marked in a *tavola* (bill book) annexed to each contract, which left bankers with great flexibility. It was therefore a mere cash transfer, but in times of money shortage customs officers could always enjoy a fresh cash flow to manage with. Eventually, when tolls were laid with reference to values and not to quantities, customs officers were given the power to estimate them according to the market value. In turn, if the merchants were not satisfied, they could pay taxes in kind and not in money.

All management costs were at the customs officers' expense, including *le solite mancie alli Signori Camerali* (the usual tips to main Chamber staff). Officers had to provide the salaries, premises and material of all kinds: paper for book-keeping, office furniture and coal for heating. They were in charge of everything, including armed patrolmen – with only one shot in the barrel – boatmen on the Tiber and cavalrymen across the town. Nevertheless, the Roman tolls adminis-trative system was continuously expanding, far beyond the sixteenth century. In 1650 there were sixteen garrisoned gates along the Roman walls, plus six active customs-bureau barriers inside the town, each one with its own admin-istration and accountancy, with a total staff of fifty-five. Everything included, yearly customs management cost nearly 12,000 silver scudi, that is, 4.3 per cent of the contract price.[23] Forty years later figures had considerably increased: nine barriers, seventeen wall gates, and 135 workers plus twenty-five apprentices in training, for a total amount of 27,000 silver scudi, still representing nearly 5 per cent of the contract price. However, documentation reports of many sentry posts near the seashore and in the Lazio countryside. Top salaries were growing as well: a governor in the post of the major land customs could earn a monthly wage of 20 scudi in 1650 and 30 scudi in 1689. However, people working at lower levels got a monthly amount of 5–10 silver scudi, without any meaningful increase in the whole period.[24] At last, the visible growth of trades and income during the second half of the seventeenth century made the old St Eustachio headquarters inadequate. At the end of the century, Innocent XII ordered the well-known architect, Carlo Fontana, to erect a new customs seat on the ruins of the ancient Hadrianeum.[25] The building – which may still be admired in a famous Piranesi printing – was ready in a few years, and the central Roman cus-toms administration remained there up until 1874.

Profits and Losses

The documentation concerning major contracts from 1630 onwards is helpful in drawing an image of both the increase of duties in Rome and that of the rela-tionship between tax farmers and the Chamber. The Rivaldi firm was in charge from 1630 to 1639, cashing nearly 330,000 silver scudi per year.[26] The Rivaldis were a well-known wealthy Roman family, holding very important positions in the hierarchy. After a promising start, the Rivaldi administration met with some difficulties and was forcefully ended by the Chamber at end of March 1639, five months before the natural conclusion of its term, due to a severe dispute. The Rivaldis had claimed price compensation starting from 1633, owing to the 1630–2 plague which hit Italy, highly reducing trade; however, they were paid off only with a loan. Unsatisfied, the Rivaldis dared to bring a lawsuit against the Chamber with disastrous results. In the Roman Curia's never-ending internal fights, the whole affair had soon taken a political turn. The Rivaldi properties were seized, their customs accountancy was confiscated and put in a sack by a Chamber notary – who immediately lost it. As a consequence the whole family was soon forced to take shelter in Tuscany. The litigation was settled only in 1656, with the approval by Pope Alessandro VII, after a brief accountancy reconstruction. The Rivaldis were acknowledged as Chamber creditors of a huge amount, but given that many hidden amounts of money and other privileges already had been granted to them, the final verdict was that they broke even. Many amounts had been probably reconstructed later for the litigation, as they showed standard figures year after year. In any case, the whole Rivaldi controversy proved that – at least in principle – customs contracts were no longer conceived by discretionary terms, and this was true for both parties. The Chamber did not exert supreme power, neither were the bankers/customs officers supposed to make immense profits nor suffer big losses.

The Genoese Ravenna family came after the Rivaldis, for the unusual period of 15 years, from 1640 to 1654. The basic original contract price was gradually encumbered with a 25 per cent increase, mainly due to a new burden on meat and to a further 2 per cent decided by Urban VIII as a general tax increase. The return to Roman Capitoline administration was still moderate, given that the meat increase was considered as pertaining to the Chamber only. The total yield, after a first remarkable increase in 1645, soon went back again to the usual standards of the period, producing a meagre 10 per cent increase in twenty years.[27]

As usual, yearly official accounts were in the red, mainly in the last two-year period. In 1647 a new controversy was brought against the Chamber. Ravenna was claiming to be paid back 110,000 scudi for the Castro war, which had remarkably reduced trades. An enormous amount of documentation was produced before the Chamber court, with comparisons between the income of *fertile* and *sterile* years.[28] The litigation brought no results, rather, only the promise of a contract renewal. Then a second lawsuit with new complaints started in 1652 or 1653, when it was clear that the Chamber was negotiating with a new banker firm. The customs officer again asked for a huge repayment because of the Roman increase of local handicraft production, which had depressed imports. According to Ravenna, this mainly concerned clothes, silks, trimmings, caps and glassware. Surprisingly, the Chamber set up an accurate inquiry, concluding that the Ravenna demands were well-grounded, hence offering the outgoing Ravennas a financial compensation, on the basis of an average tax rate of 9 per cent. Documentation however does not allow us to know how the whole affair was finally settled. Eventually the banker did not get any contract renewal.

The Tuscan Baldinotti firm from Pistoia was the next to be appointed, starting from 1 September 1654. It was granted a nine-year term contract, followed by a second one of fifteen years, thus totalling twenty-four years of continuous service to Roman customs.[29] Since the beginning, the price was increased with the flour tax, which became even heavier in 1662. Adding a new high profit toll in the general contract was a clear sign of favour and of good relationships with the Chamber.

In September 1656 a new plague hit the population. Accountancy for that year was therefore split in two separate periods: nine months from 1 September 1655, *prima del contagio* (before the plague hit) and three months starting 1 June 1656, *in tempo di contagio* (during the plague). The 1657 and 1658 fiscal years were officially considered periods of plague as well, just to show how big the depression was, in view of a future claim for damages; and finally the 1659 accountancy was identified as being *dopo il contagio* (post-plague). As a matter of fact, 1657–8 figures show a highly negative balance, while during other years, losses are quite close to zero. Average per year receipts were close to 470,000 silver scudi.

Figures also show that allowances to the Capitol were again reduced: 85,000 silver scudi, paid only with 83,544 silver coins, considering that the Jewish community had to pay an additional 1,456 scudi fee. All things considered, in thirty years the Roman customs yield had achieved almost a 40 per cent increase. In the final year of 1663, the loss was due, according to documentation, to the threat of war which probably made reference to the fierce dispute between the French and papal soldiers in August 1662, and the humiliating apologies presented by Alessandro VII to Louis XIV.

Unfortunately, the bookkeeping of the second Baldinotti contract has been lost, but a series of books of sworn accounts provides at least two important facts of information.[30] From 1645, the new item 'other receipts' was included to record all the amounts cashed by the customs officer for various issues not related to Roman customs, such as payments from other towns, from religious orders or for taxes coming from the state periphery. The 'other receipts' item soon reached high financial levels, proving that the customs officer was now covering a new, additional and meaningful service to the Chamber.

The yearly balance was often in the red, but the matter was settled quickly, as evidence of a new cooperative climate. On 17 November, a few months after the 1667 fiscal year was ended, the sworn accounts were presented to the Chamber. The same day they received its signature of approval by the general treasurer, in addition to that of one of the four Chamber clerks and other authorities. The negative balance was recognized as being correct and a bill of 17,161 scudi to the Chamber Cashier was signed on 29 November by the treasurer, in favour of Cesare and Zenobio Baldinotti.[31] No claim was produced from either part to break the contract. At this stage, tax farming had almost become a semi-public business, with no risks for all bankers who had duly followed all Chamber instructions and had been positively audited.

After the long Baldinotti period, the next contract was assigned for six years to the brothers Giuseppe and Domenico Petrosini. Their accounts were actually lost. Then a new contract was given jointly to Marchese Filippo Nerli, Antonio Nerli and Gio Francesco Fantoni. The Nerlis belonged to a very well-known and powerful financial family. Filippo Nerli was also at the time holding the role of Chamber cashier or *Depositario Generale*, therefore covering two important positions. From his customs management records there is only one bookkeeping year left (1684–5), in red. Nonetheless, apparently upon request by Nerli himself, the Pope decided to rescind the contract after only five years and three months, under the pretext he was holding both posts at the same time.

However, it was simply one further step on the long road towards public customs administration. The Nerli contract was in fact the last one managed by a private banker. Starting from 1 November 1689, the customs administration changed quite a lot. The new appointed officer was now Leonardo Libri, an esteemed member of the Chamber staff. Libri was given the customs not with a contract but, rather, through a papal grant, giving him full guarantees *in caso le riscossioni non bastino* (in case tax collection were not sufficient).[32] Any possible loss was fully covered by the Chamber, even if managing expenses were still formally put in the customs officer's charge. The papal decree only mentioned prices already paid in past times, however as a matter of fact, there was no real contract price and the sole obligation for Libri was to dispense customs yields to cover the dividends on public debt, following the Chamber's instructions as usual. The length of the contract was not mentioned and was left to at the Pope's discretion. The Libri management was therefore the last step before a full and official Chamber administration, under the direct responsibility of the general treasurer. This started on 21 May 1698, when the Rome customs officer's position was deleted after many centuries of fruitful and controversial services.[33]

According to bookkeeping records, the total yearly gross yield doubled from 1631 to 1701, increasing from an average 300,000 to 600,000 scudi and more, seventy years later. However, fees to the Chamber plus managing costs were just as high, and fiscal years mostly ended in the red for the whole private management period. A light silver scudo debasement in 1684, from 2.94 to 2.91 grams, did not produce a meaningful decrease of real values.[34]

It is quite difficult to assert whether private bankers' accounts were truthful or not. The history of *diffalchi* (discounts) and of litigations with the Chamber suggests that if official accounts were formally in good order, the daily customs management perhaps was not, at least during the Rivaldi and Ravenna years

(1630–54). From the Baldinotti contract onwards – except for a 1657 negative peak due to the plague period – the situation became smoother with acceptable final results, even if Chamber controls over accountancy had become quite rigorous. Figure 1.1 shows profits of revenue in percentage.[35] It suggests that in the 1660s, the job had become stable and profitable. This should have certainly supported the Chamber's plans to take over the management from private bankers.

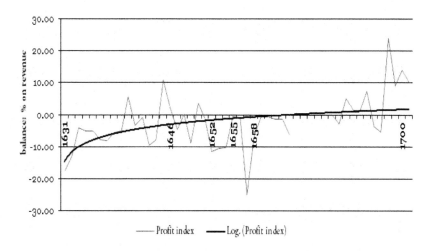

Figure 1.1: Profit index (1630–1701) of Rome's customs.

By the very end of the century, nothing could better prove that the shift to Chamber's administration had been an excellent choice both from a political and economic point of view than positive results, emphasized by a huge revenue peak in the 1700 jubilee year. In the same period, public debt was kept under strict control. Interest paid was lowering and general expenditure was directed towards a declining trend.[36] There was no state of alarm for papal public finances, as has been supposed.[37]

Per Capita Taxation

While all customs' contracts included a large number of tolls, some tolls were excluded. The Chamber's yearly state balance sheets report that salt and saltpetre – for instance – were regularly kept out from the general customs contract.[38] They were managed separately, with a contract which often included not only the town of Rome, but the whole Latium region, that is, a population three times greater than Rome alone. From 1669 salt was no longer sold anymore, probably because its production was not profitable and its yield was partially replaced by a flour increase and by small tolls such as soap, tobacco and spirits. Wine which produced good profits was sold separately as well. The Castelli wine, which was produced in the district vineyards and gave excellent fiscal returns, was included in the general customs contract only from 1689. Figure 1.2 has therefore been drawn up taking into account all the duties cashed by customs officers according to the previous tables, plus the salt price – in this case only one third – and the Castelli wine prices, in addition to some minor tolls through separate contracts as mentioned by bal-ance-sheet books, assuming that prices were very close to the total amount yielded.

The figure makes reference to demographic data as well: the Roman popula-tion increased slowly during the seventeenth century, from nearly 100,000 to 135,000 people, with only one deep but short fall in the 1656–7 plague period.[39] From 1633 to 1690, the per capita yearly gross yield grew regularly, from 3.5 sil-ver scudi to 5.2 scudi, totalling an almost 50 per cent increase. Average revenue was around 3.5 scudi in the period 1630–43, then rose to 4 scudi in the years 1644–57 as a result of the fiscal policy of Urban VIII. During the following forty years, starting from the first Baldinotti contract, per capita taxation yield grew additionally, mainly because of the rich flour tax which alone was able to yield 1 scudo per capita. A slight decline began only from the beginning of the eighteenth century (see Figure 1.2).

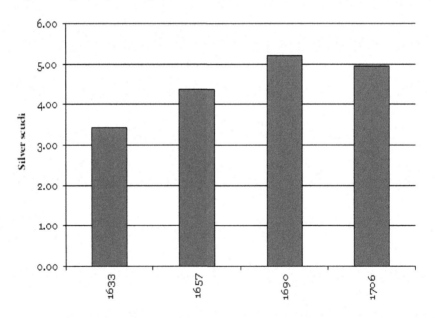

Figure 1.2: Per capita gross yield of Rome's customs.

As far as the cost of life in town is concerned, after the sharp growth of the late sixteenth century, prices remained fairly stable from 1610–20 onwards.[40] The *annona* had no great problems to face with grain supply for the town.[41] Grain was sold on the free market at an average price fluctuating from 6 to 7 scudi per *rubbio*, and in the late 1600s grain crops were abundant. Prices were cheap up to 1764.[42] Therefore, the tax increase shown in Figure 1.2 is not a result of inflation, rather it simply represents a real fiscal burden increase. In terms of sterling silver, considering the slight debasement of the scudo, the per capita increase grew from 10 g to 14.5 g.

Foodstuffs played a leading role, particularly in the second half of the century. They were taxed on their quantities, while other goods passing through Roman customs had usually to pay on value. The St Eustachius land customs or *Rome customs*, charged goods in the 1500s at a very low rate. It was more or less the same 3 per cent long established, plus an additional 1 per cent imposed by Sixtus V, totalling a very reasonable 4 per cent on declared or estimated value.[43] Later on, by 1632, the rate had considerably increased, with a net difference between the land and the river customs. According to documentation, the St Eustachius percentage on goods was raised to 7 per cent while the Ripa Grande river customs was 10 per cent. A few years later, Urban VIII added one per cent point in 1641 and one further point in 1643. Finally, under the pretext of *mettere un freno alla morbidezza ed esorbitantissimo lusso* (discouraging laxity and luxurious life) an additional 3 per cent was imposed in 1674 only on goods imported from abroad, while a similar reduction was granted for domestic goods.[44] Rates in Ripa Grande river harbour were therefore settled at 15 per cent for foreign goods and at 9 per cent for those coming from the Church state, while the St Eustachius rates were respectively 12 per cent and 6 per cent.[45] A new customs tariff was printed up, and officers from both customs were asked to meet monthly to appraise the value of all those goods not mentioned within it. The sea harbour of Civitavecchia, north of Rome, was considered as a free port and exemptions were allowed in Rome for goods in transit towards a final destination of over 40 miles, with a written statement. As far as concerns exports, indeed very scant, the bookkeeping has no records of exported goods. A few notes, at the beginning of the eighteenth century, mention a generic rate of 3 per cent.[46]

As bookkeeping records are quite detailed, revenues from tolls on foodstuffs and those yielded from other goods coming into Rome can be shown separately, according to all customs officers' terms (see Figure 1.3).[47]

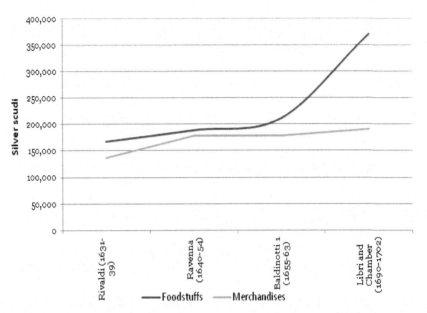

Figure 1.3: Foodstuffs and merchandise revenue according tax farmers' terms.

In Figure 1.3 the two curves are well balanced and seem to grow following a similar trend. Then, from the 1660s, paralleling a relevant population increase, foodstuffs figures suddenly increase, doubling their values in forty years, while other goods' duties remain stable. This proves how rigid the foodstuffs demand was, mainly that of flour, meat and wine. Yet it is easy to guess how carefully the Chamber was looking after Customs figures.

Flour

The very unpopular flour duty was not levied in Rome up until 1643.[48] Rather, most likely, for a long time flour paid a giulio per *rubbio* only at the wall gates (a giulio being one-tenth of a scudo; a *rubbio* being an average person's yearly grain consumption, around 200 kg). It was a matter of policy to maintain a low fixed price for a loaf, even in times of famine, when the Roman food department or *annona* made good work buying grains on the European market. Heavy taxation on flour started in 1643 at the rate of 2 giulii per *rubbio*.[49] It went quickly up to 6 giulii in 1652, when the contract price was agreed upon for 71,500 scudi: very close to a yearly *rubbio* per capita appraised consumption. Yet during this period the flour duty did not produce high profits. Eleven years later duties on salt were abolished, and in compensation the toll on flour was raised to 8 giulii per *rubbio*, with a proportional price increase for the bankers of 23,833 scudi, and soon produced high stable profits.[50] Adding one giulio per *rubbio* already paid at the gates, tax on the retail price was nearly 12 per cent, given that the price of flour on the free market was around 7 scudi per *rubbio*. Flour duty was abolished in 1697, in a period of good grain harvests, but for a very short while only because, after all, it produced more than 20 per cent of all yields. Other cereals like barley or forage paid much less.

Meat

Meat represented a huge toll as well. In the Chamber's staffs, the supervision of the roman *grascia* (oil and grease) was considered as a very promising position.[51] The *grascia* customs was in charge of cheese, olive oil and meat. Meat was first taxed at each *scannatura* (throat-cutting), with different precise tariffs according to the various animals, from 260 baiocchi for a cow down to 20 baiocchi for a lamb or small pork. However, the greatest revenue came from duties on retail meat sales, by means of a tax rate which was often increased between the sixteenth and the seventeenth centuries. It started with only 1 quattrino per pound in 1552, graciously left for the use of the Roman Capitoline administration. Then the tax gradually grew to 6 quattrini per pound in 1644, after which no further increase was levied. Eventually in 1674 the town of Rome was excluded from the meat return, which went directly to the Chamber.[52]

Figures show how variable the demand for the two main foodstuffs was with relation to tax increase. In seventy years, duties on meat had modestly increased from 4 to 6 quattrini, while that on flour had soared from 1 to 8. As a consequence, the two main foodstuffs evolved in a different way. Flour consumption did not drop rather it always remained at steady levels, even growing with a 10 per cent per capita quantity increase. On the contrary, meat declined nearly 30 per cent. Flour was definitely the most profitable duty and the framework of the customs system.

Wine

Wine tolls had a very peculiar history. Low quality local wine, *romanesco* or *dell'agro romano* coming from the vineyards within a 10-mile range in the territory around Rome was duty-free because of an old popular and appreciated tradition. The wine coming from the Castelli area – nearly forty miles from Rome – named as *forastiero* was much better and was taxed according to an old tradition too. In 1432 Eugene IV founded the University of Rome – *studium urbis* – financing professors and general expenses with the *forastiero* wine, through a rather complicated toll system: it was taxed according to its retail sale price, which innkeepers had to previously declare to customs. There were therefore multiple tariffs from 5, 6, 8, 10 and 12.5 baiocchi for each barrel.[53] The contract price of this toll soon increased from 33,000 to 43,000 scudi, given partly to town administration and partly to the Chamber. Considering the good financial results, Castelli wine was hit by a further toll for the Chamber, consisting of one additional giulio par barrel. Taxation on wine thus reached a good 10–12 per cent of the retail price, and its contract price increased from 22,000 to 38,000 scudi per year. Furthermore, good quality wine coming through the Ripa Harbour was also taxed with 4 or 6 giulii per *botte* (a barrel of 520 litres) and was regularly included in the general customs contracts. On the contrary, up to 1689 the more popular Castelli wine was always sold separately from the general customs, probably because of its high return. Excises levied on Castelli and quality wines brought in large amounts to Roman customs. In spite of free wine, quality wine was good business, given that at the end of the seventeenth century there were 110 taverns officially registered in Rome, eleven of which were managed by Jewish innkeepers.[54] But Rome was thick with wine merchants, one for every 174 inhabitants.[55]

Nevertheless, in spite of severe controls, wines were largely smuggled. An undated Chamber report – which was presumably written immediately after Innocent XII's pontificate, that is, at the very beginning of the eighteenth century – suggested a few proposals to improve customs yield.[56] Among the good advice about general management, a survey of smuggled foodstuffs is reported as well. The estimate on flour smuggling was close to 33,000 *rubbia*, nearly 10 per cent of the official taxed amount, while contraband on meat was calculated at 800,000 lb, only 8 per cent of the total regularly traded. Wine smuggling on the contrary was at very high levels. With regard to the Castelli wine only, the Chamber's calculation mentioned a yearly 450,000 barrel consumption, nearly 200 litres per capita, 35 per cent of which was introduced into town fraudulently.

Public Management versus Private

Customs officers' accounts registered continuous yearly losses. We presume that bankers had applied for tax farming in search of a good return, of course, but their available bookkeeping does not really suggest a final stand on this issue. At least for the first two contracts, profit derived from a variety of major and minor advantages, many of which would have probably been rather roguish and tricky. According to the Chamber claims prepared on the occasion of lawsuits, the Rivaldi bankers were accused of stealing daily from the customs cashier, and making no record.[57] They were also charged for compelling merchants to pay in kind, again without ever recording anything. During the Ravenna period, large amounts recorded under the title of *regaglie* (gifts to the Chamber high officers) were just camouflaging annual gifts to the customs officer himself of 10,000 scudi, the amount of which came to light only after thorough accountancy analysis. Halfway through the century, beginning with the Baldinotti period, there was more transparency. Tax farmers collected additional services for the Chamber, bringing in new money. The fresh money cash flow coming in daily to the customs cashiers was undoubtedly an important privilege. The Nerli books recorded in 1685 the amount of 2,300 scudi as a net profit 'per godimento di scudi 75,000 o 80,000 in circa che si puol calcolare al 3 per cento' (for available funds of 75,000 or 80,000 scudi, to be calculated at an average 3 per cent), given that 3 per cent was just the official interest rate on bonds at the time.[58] In the same year, the Chamber claimed 50 per cent of all flour revenue exceeding the amount of 108,660 scudi 'as had occurred with the previous banker'. Given that the flour price was fixed at 95,333 scudi, it was a good 14 per cent envisaged profit. Flour toll and Castelli wine always produced good yields and were able to compensate losses. Other contracts gave scant returns, as had happened to the costly *stadera* (steelyard balance) duty on all weights exceeding 50 pounds: to avoid it, merchants simply packed up goods in several light bags.

The 1689 shift from private to public management was carried out in times of revenue increase, because the Chamber was well aware of the Roman population's high consumption. Very pragmatically, in times of economic decline, the town riches still represented a huge source of revenue, and it was time to shut bankers out of the business. Furthermore, from a political point of view, a period of sharp institutional reforms had started, mainly under Innocent XI by the Odescalchi family (1676–89). By this time the Papal State was fully consolidated, and it was still unimaginable to put into private hands a public matter such as tax farming, which in Rome alone gathered a good 20 per cent of the state's yearly budget. Both economic and political issues converged to give rise to the change.

The Chamber was therefore eager to demonstrate that its own administration was producing good results much better than before, when the whole business was held by private bankers.[59] A Chamber accountancy prospectus concerning the Libri period from 1689 to 1698 calculated an average yearly gross income of 565,000 scudi, and a net one of 483,000, with a good 10 per cent increase on the previous average contracts.[60] Then, just to celebrate the treasurer Gian Francesco Albani, later elected as Clemente XI in 1701, an additional Chamber calculation for the three-year period from 1698 to 1701 demonstrated that gross income had until then reached the average level of 623,000 scudi, and a net one of 531,000, with an additional 10 per cent prodigious increase in a few years.[61] It still represented something very close to 5 silver scudi per capita. The Chamber staff was therefore arguing that a careful public administration could obtain better results than a fraudulent private one. This was perhaps true, taking into account all the embezzlement that had been carried out by private customs officers in the past.

However, a few years later the revenue curve kept sliding. In order to highlight the new preoccupation with the decreasing income, an additional summary made in 1719 by the Chamber accountancy department concerning a period of just over seventeen and a half years, between 1701 and 1719, estimated that Roman customs had produced a 9,448,113 silver scudi gross yield, with a gross yearly average of 538,268, partially counterbalanced by a 25 per cent general expenses fall. It represented nearly 4 silver scudi per capita only, with a clear tendency towards decline. Yet the most relevant aspect was that managing expenses were then yearly totalling 69,830 scudi, that is, more than two times as much as it was during the old private bankers' period. Then the Chamber once again turned to private management and in 1729 asked the Roman bankers Girolamo Belloni and then Nicola Pierantoni to take the position of customs officers, with poor outcomes.

In fifty years per capita taxation had lost 1.5 silver scudi, going back to the same levels as in 1630. Considering that managing expenses had remarkably increased under public rule, it was not a brilliant result. However, in times of deep economic depression, the harsh auditing of accounts and a fierce battle against smuggling flattened out the inevitable customs yield decline. As a matter of fact, Roman consumption still provided for the Chamber. In 1753, during the progressive papacy of Benedict XIV, Roman customs went back again to the Chamber. Then a new tax system at the state border was envisaged. It became operative in 1786, and produced a few better results.

2 FROM TAXATION TO INDEBTEDNESS: THE URBAN FISCAL SYSTEM OF MILAN DURING THE AUSTRIAS DOMINATION (1535–1706)

Giuseppe Bognetti and Giuseppe De Luca[1]

With the establishment of Spanish domination, the city of Milan, as well as the state of which it was the capital, entered a period of intense transformation. The geopolitical context was changing radically and its involvement in the imperial strategy of the Austrias now required, from the whole Duchy, a substantial participation in terms of resources.

Although most of the costs of the military maintenance of the dominion at the centre of the Po Valley was ultimately sustained thanks to the financial support of other Spanish territories, like Castile and the Kingdom of Naples, the pressure on the Milan state revenues increased as never in the past. For a considerable time, the interest of historians has been directed towards the accompanying rise in the burden of taxation which has been regarded as one of the main causes of the economic decline of Lombardy during the Spanish age and one of the primary components of the related *leyenda negra*.

This prevailing paradigm – based chiefly on complaints manifest in contemporary sources and heavily influenced by a negative consensus reached in the nineteenth century[2] – has been called into question over the last three decades. Due to source-based studies, the attention on the state financial and fiscal system in the Duchy under the Austrias is progressively losing its historiographical bias and is broadening, shedding light on all the effects and deep interrelations with social, political and economic aspects. Thus public finance is turning out to be a crucial element of the state-building process, not eclipsed by foreign domination; it entails far-reaching changes in the administrative machinery, in the equilibrium of social groups, in the balance between town and country and in the relationships between central authority and local communities.[3] Similarly, the nexus with economy is showing a wide array of interactions; the approach concentrated on overemphasizing fiscal effects hampering economic growth is being replaced by an outlook aimed at encompassing the varied linkage between the manifold components of the state finance and all the forces, protagonists and variables of economic life. This allows us to delve into the real consequences on the whole productive and trade world; increased fiscal pressure appears at present more as an evenly balanced burden between town and country than as a factor that boosts production costs; expanded public debt seems to be a multifunctional opportunity of investments for a large plurality of subjects rather than a useless consumption of capitals; and the collection and management of taxes look like the training ground for the local providers of financial services.[4]

Yet the renewed perspective has still hardly engaged local finance during the Spanish domination, either the finance of the towns or of the communities. Despite there being only a few scattered sources, local fiscal systems appear to be the focal point of the many-sided interactions between the Spanish centre and the Lombard periphery, between the exercise of power and the multifaceted local societies, between the strategic needs of what was considered the 'llave de Italia' (the key to Italy) and one of the richest European economies of the sixteenth to seventeenth centuries.

In particular, the fiscal system of Milan, by far the largest city in the Duchy, represents an important point of observation to grasp in depth the complete intricate interplay revolving around public finance.

I.

As with all the territorial entities forming the state, the urban fiscal system of the capital – all taxes and debts imposed, collected, issued and managed by the city on its own – was a part of the larger fiscal organization of the Duchy, with which it was strictly interrelated.

The structure of the fiscal system that Charles V inherited in November 1535 from the Sforzas was that of a top-down taxation (a cascade taxation system), employed also in other regional states. In this scheme the overall charge (the *contingente*) to be paid by the Duchy of Milan was decided on the basis of the needs of Madrid and of the local government, and then apportioned among the nine provinces of the state on the basis of their supposed wealth or population or both. In the course of decades these criteria had become more and more complex both for the build-up of new taxes and for the several changes introduced by the central power.

The amount assigned to each province was subsequently divided among the towns and their *contadi* (rural territories subject to urban jurisdiction) according to parameters often challenged by the rural population because they kept the trace of ancient privileges of city dwellers; the most hated was the different treatment of the land owned by inhabitants of rural areas (taxed as *perticato rurale*) and that owned by the citizens (taxed as *perticato civile* with more favourable rates or frequently exempt). The unfairness was amplified by the fact that, having established the quota of the city and of the *contado*'s, its composition and the methods used to extract it were quite different.

Using the distinction between direct and indirect taxes, which are functional for our understanding but can only be applied with great caution since these categories were unknown at that time and tended easily to turn one into the other, we can state that the towns raised their share of fiscal burden mostly from indirect taxation: excises, duties and tariffs on goods, especially of widespread consumption. Direct taxation on land had only a subsidiary function: a tax on city dwellers' land was levied only for the amount uncovered by tariffs. Sometimes the local governments were allowed by the state Governor to substitute or decrease the direct tax with an increase in tariffs or through debt; thus, as in the other Spanish province in Italy, the Kingdom of Naples, the system allowed and always produced a tax shift into the indirect form.[5] Aristocrats and merchants were called into taxation mainly during tough years when fiscal charges visibly increased and it was impossible to get additional money in the other way.

Conversely, in the rural communities the load due was chiefly collected by means of direct taxation (in open spaces, that is, not enclosed by walls, levying taxes was obviously difficult), such as: the salt tax (which, in the tradition of the old forced levy on salt, implied the paying of a fixed sum for the quantities of salt assigned to rural communities, regardless of actual consumption); the *tasso dei cavalli* (horse tax, depending on the military lodging that rural communities were obliged to provide since 1493); the *perticato* (a land tax determined on the basis of the value of land owned); the *imbottato* (a tax on agriculture products such as wine and wheat); and the *testatico* (a poll tax paid by rural dwellers for themselves and for their family members). Furthermore what made the fiscal contribution really intolerable and glaringly iniquitous for the countryside population was the frequent obligation of providing lodging for troops, while the towns and the land of the citizens (the already mentioned *perticato civile*) were exempt.[6]

At every level – state, towns and rural communities – tax collection was not managed directly by the central government but farmed out to contractors endowed with all relevant powers and rights set against the obligation to pay a fixed annual sum, determined generally every three years. The tax farmers' profit came from the difference between the amount paid and the actual revenues they were able to get from collection; in public budgets you could not find the real yield, but only the lump sum paid by the winning contractor to the administration for that specific fiscal source. The fiscal burden for the Duchy inhabitants and the actual revenues for government therefore did not tally;[7] according to this practice, broadly common in other European countries, the state was insured against the risks of negative economic cycles, which were only partially acknowledged in favour of the tax farmer, but would have not benefited from the possible growth of the yield.

The organizational model of the system was based on functions which had already arisen during the Sforza period, such as a general management body, an accountancy body and a central treasury office. The *Magistrato ordinario* (Regular Judiciary) was in charge of the administration of tax and revenue, beside issuing provisions regarding economic and monetary policy; it drew up the general balance of revenue and expenditure of the state. Its president was assisted by a staff consisting of six councillors and several officers, among which a prominent role was played by the two *ragionati* (accountants), who acted as a kind of accountancy bureau and recorded income and expenditure. The Regular Judiciary was coupled with the *Magistrato Straordinario* (Special Judiciary), who governed the sovereign's estate and decided over fiefs, smuggling and confiscations.[8] However, the vital nerve centre of the Duchy public finance machinery was, undoubtedly until 1640, the general treasury, which had a civil and a military section (merged between 1570 and 1615) and was responsible for tax collection and for the payment and transfer of all funds.[9]

Within this complicated architecture, the urban fiscal system of Milan, as well as those of the other towns of the Duchy, had thus a double function: as a centre for receiving taxes owed to the state, which flowed towards the central treasury office, and as a centre for deciding and collecting taxes for the local community's necessity. The financial troubles of the central government had an immediate impact on the budgets of the cities and created unending problems for the local authorities confronting the nobility, the merchants and the urban population. When the Spanish took over, the state capital was by far the wealthiest and most dynamic centre of the Po plain; its inhabitants had grown from 60,000 in 1540 to 117,000 in 1575 and, adding the residents of its rural district, made up a third of the state population and covered slightly less than a half of the whole Duchy territory;[10] by the middle of the sixteenth century the city contributed more than 25 per cent of the state revenues[11] and had consequently a fundamental role in the fiscal (and financial) bargaining arising between the huge needs of the Spanish Empire and the various bodies and territorial entities in the Dominion.

II.

On the basis of this system for apportioning taxation, Charles V imposed on his new subjects the *mensuale*, an extraordinary direct tax to be paid monthly (hence its name), which, regardless of this, survived until the end of the Spanish domination. After a few years of fluctuation, in 1547 the amount of the new tax was definitely determined in 300,000 scudi (in 12 monthly payments of 25,000 scudi), the equivalent of 1,650,000 lire[12] and became the most important entry item in the government revenues.[13] The unease for the sudden and unexpected introduction of this new tax, the understanding that it would actually be maintained as an ordinary tax (in 1552 the notary Simone da Pozzo wrote 'Extraordinariamente: hoc vocabulo utuntur in consolatione populorum' ('Extraordinary: this word is used for the consolation of the common people'),[14] the panic over its heavy burden coupled with a disorderly and inequitable collecting system had a strong negative impact on the taxpayers; from everywhere in the Duchy rose a wave of protest and complaints, but also suggestions and demands for a new taxation system based on fairer criteria. This was happening in other parts of Charles V's empire as well; the war costs of its geopolitical strategy was sharply increasing, due to innovation in military technology, and was reflected in an increase in fiscal burden, which could not be borne without a more equitable arrangement of distribution; the same need to design something new or to overhaul the system initiated an intense but not always orderly research along the same lines.[15] No city in the State of Milan thought it had lesser rights than any other in demanding a new *estimo* (assessment), and if hope could be raised for some relief everyone thought it could plead with good cause.

Thus, in 1543, the wish to augment fiscal revenues while avoiding a dangerous impact only on rural communities, led the Emperor to order – as a means of distributing the new tax, the *mensuale* – a new general census (or cadastre) of the state: not limited, however, as in the past to land ownership only, but including also the *mercimonio*, that is, income accruing from 'traffichi, mercanzie, banchi e cambi' ('commerce, goods, banks and financial activities'); from his instructions, besides, one could detect the intention of separating the fiscal administration of cities and *contadi*, removing the latter from the undeniable domination of towns. The Emperor was quite aware that this would displease the cities and the merchant and banking class because it would abolish all their privileges in a single stroke.

The *estimo* of land and of commercial activities followed two separate paths because of greater difficulties to be faced in evaluating the latter. By 1564 the operations for the land *estimo* were over and the new cadastre was enacted in 1568, with an increase in registered land from 8 million to 16 million *pertiche*.[16] The dispute on the *estimo mercimoniale* (the assessment of income from trade and banking) was settled only at the end of the century after drawn out and messy disagreements; the cities, and especially Milan, engaged in a hard fight to reduce their share of taxation, with town and rural residents, nobility and merchants on opposite sides to delay or correct the new system. The defence of the different interest groups was organized in many ways. A Congregation of the state was created, including representatives of the nine cities (Milan, Pavia, Como, Lodi, Cremona, Novara, Alessandria, Vigevano, Tortona) and of their rural territories, but soon it came to voice only the requests of the towns. Between 1560 and 1570, single congregations (*Congregazioni del contado*) developed autonomously in every rural territory; members of the congregations were mayors and agents elected by each community (with no interference by the cities); they were recognized by state authorities as the appropriate bodies for fiscal affairs, responsible for taxes collection on rural assets (the mayors had to be natives of the territory, at least three-quarters of their properties were to be taxed as *perticato rurale*, and they had to pay personal taxation in the community). The accepted government compromise between the Austrias Monarchy and the local ruling class began to be undermined by events related to the new census; in the marked dialectic between towns and rural communities, Madrid assumed a judicial mediation rather than a direct control on the various institutional bodies; not by chance, almost all the disputes found an end in the court of the Capital of Spain, where the cities, the rural districts and the same state Governor had an agent.[17]

Among the cities Milan played a decisive role in delaying the new system, well aware of the privileges it had always enjoyed; the smaller cities, instead, saw in the new system a kind of redressing of previous unfair conditions. The Duchy capital also contested the higher charge which fell on its real estate because of the higher values in the capital city compared to those in other towns; its endeavours suggested that the census operations starting in 1565 should consider not the current trade but that of the years 1548 and 1549.[18]

By the end of the century the conditions for completing the census of trade income were in place following a progressive shift of the economic centre of the state from urban production to manufactures and financial investment involving the rural territories. Since the 1570s the merchant class in Milan, as well as in other towns, had been progressively losing the central economic role it had acquired in the economic ascendance after the end of the French–Spanish wars. The production of urban guilds was decreasing in favour of transformation activities spreading to the countryside and directed essentially to the production of semi-finished silk goods; the interests of the principal economic actors were thus increasingly moving to the rural districts, aligning themselves in many cases with those of the landed nobility and merging with them.[19]

In this restructuring of the economic arrangements of the ruling classes, the new cadastre, finally addressing the ancient old imbalance between town and country, found room for approval. The ultimate result represented a compromise between the original purpose of charging each subject in proportion to his wealth and the resistance of the privileged classes. However the process of a more distributed taxation and of political representation of country classes, with the creation of the rural congregations, achieved important results.[20]

A new political negotiation concerning the sharing and collection of taxation took shape: in 1571 the Senate decided that the *tasso d'ambo le cavallerie* (a tax for cavalry, introduced in 1561 and paid only by the rural territories) had to be apportioned one-third to the countryside only and two-thirds to the whole state, citizens included; in 1572 it was decided that city judges could not intervene in proceedings between towns and rural districts; in 1593 it was established that lands acquired after 1573 by city dwellers had to be registered as *perticato rurale*, contributing to the *mensuale* and to the lodging tax: in other words, the condition of citizens could no more entail one of the oldest and most coveted privileges in the state. Four years later a provision was adopted for general equality in extraordinary lodgings, allowing fiscal adjustments to compensate communities for expenses incurred in the year for troops. Finally, in 1604, city residents were requested to contribute to lodging expenses a share of 50 per cent of the rural districts' quota.[21]

Taxation was gradually moving from subjects to objects, from taxation on individuals to goods. Almost inadvertently, under Charles V and Philip II, the fiscal system of the Duchy underwent three remarkable transformations: the importance of collecting the charge through direct taxes arose; trade income came to bear a part of the total fiscal load; and the predominance of cities on rural territories progressively decreased, also as a consequence of the changing political and economic context on which the fiscal system was based. These were the first outcomes of an important development concerning the balance of power in society, between Milan and the subordinate cities, between urban and rural elites.

Yet as soon as the sharing of the *estimo mercimoniale* was published in 1594, bargaining commenced for adjustments and in 1599 Milan received a reduction of 64 per cent and its territory of 45 per cent for a total of 17,000 scudi, which in this way became an additional burden for urban and rural real estate owners.[22] The capital succeeded, as had already happened for the census of landed property (whose quota was lowered from 40 per cent to 36.6 per cent),[23] in wielding all of its power and of its privileged relations with the government and with the ruling class to limit the erosion of old advantages. Either way, according to the new general *estimo*, Milan and its rural territory ended up paying two-fifths of the total fiscal charge of the state and more than 660,000 lire for the monthly tax only. A ruling of the Gran Cancelliere and of the President of the Senate diminished the quota of *mensuale* apportioned to the countryside surrounding the capital from 258,000 to 198,000 lire, but the city did not submit and managed to maintain what had previously been fixed, giving in change to its *contado* the revenues of the Monza duty.[24]

III.

Against the background of the progressive shrinking of the relief role played by the *contado* and of the rising requests by Madrid, the city of Milan's quota of fiscal load (as well as that of other urban centres in the Duchy) grew due to the state coffers. To answer the out of ordinary contribution enforced by the central government, the capital reacted first of all by increasing the indirect taxes which were under its jurisdiction and by enlarging the range of these kinds of levies.

Even if we do not yet have enough data for a comprehensive view of the city finances in the first forty years of Spanish domination, this tendency is evident. In 1548, after the state Governor's decision to provide the Duchy capital with new walls, the city was allowed to levy a tariff on incoming wine to which not even the clergy were to be let off: the *datio del vino proprio della città di Milano* was in this way fixed at 2 soldi and 6 denari for each *brenta* brought in by land and in 3 soldi and 6 denari for each one brought in by water.[25] But the endless military needs were by and large the main municipal expense during these years; on a single occasion in 1556, to sustain the artillery of the state, the extraordinary load imposed on the city amounted to 684,000 lire;[26] between 1561 and 1573, the town had to pay for military purpose more than 2,467,000 lire;[27] and we know that in 1559 Milan was permitted to levy an excise (named *bollino*) on wine sold within the walls, amounting to 5 soldi on each *brenta*; ten years later – again on the occasion of an extraordinary request – the excise was increased by another 5 soldi; in 1576 the city of Milan began collecting a tax (*dazio della carne*) of 6 denari for each pound of any type of meat sold at the slaughterhouses located in the town. To these taxes were added to the *prestini* (bakers) duties paid on white bread, of 50 soldi for each *moggio*[28] of flour used, and the tariff on the *macina ordinaria* (millstone), of 2 soldi for each *moggio* of flour, but applied also to wood, fish, prawns, straw and lime mortar. The overall picture of the municipal tax structure was finally completed by a series of direct taxes: the *tre perticati* tax (paid in this period on real estate registered as citizens' property), established in 1549, and the *tassa sulle case* (a home, shops and mills property and use tax, paid for one unit by the owner and for one half-unit by the occupant), started in 1557.[29]

Concerning the capability of city revenues to match its expenditures during the first four decades of Spanish rule, we only register repeated complaints, often expressed in hackneyed sentences and hyperbolic expressions, by the Milanese officials sent to Madrid to describe the capital's faltering conditions, always depicted on the verge of collapse.[30]

In the following period, when we start to have more complete and uninterrupted data, the status and the quality of the sources are a serious hindrance to a certain and full reconstruction of the conditions of Milan's public finances; the total destruction of entire collections of archival records, the dispersal of reports in unexpected documents and the semantic variability of definitions make the comparison of information and figures – often heterogeneous – difficult and unsound. It is hard, sometimes even impossible, for example, to distinguish – in the balance sheets of the city – between revenues and expenditures that belong to Milan and the ones that are due to the state treasury; sometimes (e.g. in 1578, 1586, 1587 and 1592, see Table 2.1) revenues are recorded net of exemptions and of the sums paid directly to the buyers to whom the incomes had been sold in advance (this was the form, long-term debt assumed in the Duchy and elsewhere) and hence they represent what has effectively been cashed by the city; in other budgets those figures are included and accounts are therefore more complete. In some others there is a sort of footnote indicating sums from past tax-farmings that the city still has to receive by the contractor. Until we have an uninterrupted series of balance sheets with a sufficient degree of analytic data it is impossible to understand whether the share of *mensuale* which the Governor asked the city to encash in advance each year, mostly from the end of the sixteenth century, was registered in a separate account or included in the town budget in the course of the fiscal year.

Table 2.1: Revenues, expenditures and deficit of the city of Milan (current value in lire).

Year	Revenue	Expenditure	Deficit
1574	749,224	764,633	15,149
1576	–	–	163,980
1577	–	–	398,659
1578*	540,509	711,526	171,017
1586*	244,872	506,109	261,236
1587*	317,373	686,496	369,123
1590*	104,137	935,763	831,625
1591	164,481	1,216,096	1,051,615
1592*	366,620	690,168	323,547
1600	1,030,154	1,308,399	278,243
1604	590,556	2,759,610	2,169,054
1605	1,247,221	1,458,555	211,334
1611	–	–	256,226
1612	1,142,500	2,248,782	1,106,282
1633	1,603,600	2,195,482	591,882
1638	1,794,054	2,542,416	748,362
1641	–	–	641,708
1658	1,773,792	3,400,005	1,626,212
1690	708,015	1,087,404	379,388
1703	933,951	1,831,740	897,789

*   the data of these years don't include the sold revenues.

All the figures are rounded down since the indications of soldi and denari have been eliminated to provide room and ease of reading.

Sources: 1574: ASCM, dicasteri, cart.15, f. 5; 1578: Archivo General de Simancas (hereafter AGS), estado, leg. 1247 (from here the deficit of 1576–7 is gleaned); 1586–1587– 1590–1591–1592: ASM, belgiojoso, cart, 238, fasc. II, ff. 38, 42–60; 1600, 1611, 1641: Pugliese, *Condizioni economiche e finanziarie della Lombardia*, p. 432–4; 1604–1605: ASM, miscellanea lombarda, IX, p. 56; 1612: ASM, miscellanea lombarda, VIII, p. 29; 1633: ASM, censo parte antica (hereafter pa), b. 1522; 1638: ASM, belgiojoso, cart, 238, fasc. II, ff. 157–8; 1658: ASM, commercio pa, b. 65; 1690: ASCM, dicasteri, b. 63; 1703: Agnoletto, *Lo Stato di Milano al principio del* Settecento, p. 196. The budgets of 1574, 1592, 1612, 1633, 1658 and 1690 have been already published in Cova, *Il Banco di S. Ambrogio*, pp. 164–77.

The data which, up to now, we have been able to collect in a comparable way, and other sporadic information show in any case that, after the hard period of the passage from Charles II to his son, the budgets of Milan had not been required to withstand excessive perturbations until the plague of 1576. To face the so-called epidemic of St Charles Borromeo, which produced heavy but not catastrophic losses, Milan sold in advance revenues backed by the wine duty cashing about 1.5 million lire;[31] but this was not sufficient and the effect was to deteriorate the relative equilibrium that the budget held up to that time (see Table 2.1). In the last quarter of the century, mounting central military requests – both as a greater share of the *contingente* and as extraordinary contributions – were sustained relying on consumption taxes. The positive economic performance of the Duchy from the mid-sixteenth century was producing a socialization of wealth which broadened the tax base, swelling the income of revenues and allowing further raises in local levies; new increases of the tariffs on wine and meat were settled and their increments were immediately transformed into securities. Budget deficits then kept around 200,000–300,000 lire (see Tables 2.1 and 2.2), except for the years 1590–1 when Milan, as well as many Mediterranean centres, suffered the repercussions of the conjuncture of adverse economic cycles, higher mortality rates and famine.[32]

In the last decade of the century, the financial straits of the Crown (which in 1596 declared a payment moratorium) grew, and the *Hacienda* was not able to provide the Milanese treasury with the vast amount of money needed; therefore military expenses weighed heavily on the municipal budget; during this period, with the exception of some few thousand lire spent settling the Naviglio Grande and the Adda river, almost the entire ordinary budget was committed to war costs, in 1596 it was more than 70 per cent.[33] Even when, in 1600, the *estimo del mercimonio* became effective and burdened the Milanese merchants for 55,000 lire (after a tough negotiation, instead of the initially 77,940 foreseen) the budgetary conditions did not improve.[34]

Wartime needs augmented so that the Governor of the state was forced to ask for a new and heavier burden to be raised with an increase of the direct taxes. The *Vicario di Provvisione*, head of the economic administration of the city, replied that fiscal justice required that the fiscal burden be endured by the 'generalità del popolo' ('majority of the people') and that tariffs and excise taxes should be chosen so as to hit artisans and merchants, who were the people most advantaged by the continuous passing through of armies while those owning houses and lands were heavily damaged by the housing of military men. Behind this argument, he was defending the interest of the ruling class, which because of its property, was more hit by direct taxes and less by indirect ones. There was, indeed, a tendency by the city government to avoid insisting too much on direct taxes, as the very weak commitment to collect them and the very weak efforts to recover the significant arrears show.[35]

Table 2.2: Revenues from the main taxes imposed by the city of Milan (current value in lire).

Tax	1578	1586	1591	1592	1600	1605	1612	1619	1633	1658	1690	1703
Dazio della macina	280,000	244,803	236,875	283,000	292,000	310,438	308,000	344,559	213,000	216,000		
Dazio dei prestini	85,671							98,367				
Dazio della carne	42,000	36,974	47,674	47,674	62,600	67,500	67,500	45,505	84,500	98,000		
Dazio del vino	125,775	17,500	17,500	62,150	253,000	265,000	250,000	223,025	288,000	354,000		
Dazio del carbone								27,575	16,400	26,000		
Tre perticati	125,000				187,500	205,00	226,000	495,000	533,400	500,000	532,000	530,000
Dazio della polleria							20,000	24,725	19,400	23,000		
Estimo merci						55,00	55,000	55,000	55,000	55,000		
Estimo merci straor.								37,500	37,500	37,500		
Tassa sulle case					172,000	191,500	195,000	320,000		198,000		150,000

Sources: see Table 2.1; 1606: ASM, belgiojoso, cart, 238, fasc. II, ff. 80; 'Informatione de i Dacj, e carichi che dalla Camera sogliono riscuodersi in partico-lare nella Città di Milano, oltre quelli che sono comuni con tutto lo Stato', 24 October 1619, in BAM, Mss, L. 123 sussidio, f. 6r s.

IV.

The mixture of recurrent deficits and uninterrupted requests of extraordinary funding by the Royal Chamber pushed the town government to go vigorously into debt with the Banco di Sant'Ambrogio (established in 1593), after that even selling of future revenues of city taxes did not bring any resolution.[36] The state of indebtedness would diminish only during the first two decades of the following century, when tax revenues increased due to new surtaxes and to the favourable economic cycle, which would end drastically in 1619. From 1590 the burden on local finances for troops' lodgements had become very oppressive: municipal authorities had calculated that from that year to 1604, 12 million lire were spent for that purpose, while from 1605 to 1615 the sum was equal to 20 million.[37]

Resort to the Banco di Sant'Ambrogio began in 1597 when the head of state finance, the *Magistrato ordinario*, asked the city to advance six months of the payment of the *mensuale*; the town accepted on condition that it could take out a loan to avoid raising taxes in the very delicate moment of testing the new *estimo mercimoniale*. So in August of the same year, under request by the *Vicario di Provvisione*, a loan 231,000 lire was subscribed through a bill of exchange, followed the next year by another of 100,000 lire.[38]

The very effective support given by the city administration to the spread of the institutional aims of the Banco di Sant'Ambrogio (which was created to ease clearing among local merchants, but primarily to collect capital to invest at public demand) was bringing to the bank (modelled according to the Genoese Banco di San Giorgio), huge amount of funds, both as *luoghi* (short-term investments) and *multiplici* (long-term investments at compound interest).[39] The reliable profitability, associated with the easy tradability of its bonds, represented attractive elements for a large number of craftsmen, bureaucrats, merchants, bankers, nobles and single women, who saw the purchase of these instruments as safe, non-taxable income and also as possible collateral to obtain other credit. Coupled with state securities the *luoghi* and *multiplici* soon became the preferred point of reference of local investors: in his will of October 1619 the merchant-banker Alessandro Modrone, which left to his heirs more than 1.5 million lire in possessions and loans, prescribed that all his credit should be invested in *luoghi* at the Banco.[40] Then the design of the Milanese administration took shape, using those funds in order to face the financial needs of the capital.

From that moment on, the Banco began financing the city in two ways: on the one hand by drawing up bills of exchange – everybody agreed on their legitimacy being a very useful tool to solve problems of public finance – and on the other hand by acquiring fiscal revenues belonging to the municipality.

In 1600 the Milan budget recorded a deficit of 278,243 lire (also caused by interest payments for 390,984 lire) and past debts for 1,053,063 lire of which 702,406 were for bills of exchange.[41] Consequently a decision was made to increase indirect taxes and in particular those which offended less the interests of the prominent groups. The proposal made by the *Congregazione del Patrimonio* to raise the *perticato civile* which was affecting Milanese citizens for 225,000 lire was rejected; in 1612 and in 1614 taxes were raised to supply 444,250 lire but only 180,000 was coming from the land tax while the rest was coming from the augment of the excise tax on wine, on meat (75,000 lire), on coal (25,000), a new excise on rice (11,000) and on coaches (12,000).[42] This move was conducted from 1613 to 1619 when the economy was in expansion.

Alongside the fiscal levy, which had apparently reached the maximum limit – in a 1619 report it is said 'veramente hora mai non resta più luogo a nuova gravezza, né sopra stabili né sopra persone, né sopra merce alcuna' ('there is no more room for a new tax, neither on buildings nor on people or goods')[43] – city authorities since the beginning of seventeenth century had been leaning on the Banco di Sant'Ambrogio more and more frequently. During this time the Banco was collecting private funds from a rich society and distributing dividends to investors with a rate of return fluctuating from 4.23 per cent and 5.65 per cent very successfully.[44] The city debt by bills of exchange grew especially when there was a shortage of food and rising military expenses (famine in 1606 and the first war of Monferrato) and decelerated when new tariffs were introduced between 1615 and 1618 (see Figure 2.1).

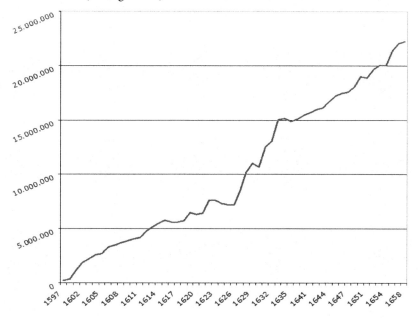

Figure 2.1: City debt by bills of exchange (current value in lire).

Sources: data elaborated from ASCM, materie, cartt. 395–6; Cova, *Il Banco di S. Ambrogio*, pp. 57, 69, 72.

Since 1627 the indebtedness of the capital with the Banco had stepped up quite rapidly (see Figure 2.1). Town budgets (yearly deficits were oscillating between 200,000 and 600,000 lire) worsened rather visibly because the lease of tax collection was producing less income and because tax collection itself was more difficult during this very hazardous time. Moreover expenses were climbing very fast because of the famine of 1628 which cost (trying to control the price of bread) the Milanese treasury 1,015,000 lire and the bubonic plague which cost directly 1.63 million lire and indirectly, through less revenues caused by demographic losses, an amount difficult to specify. Meanwhile the Royal Chamber raised its request because it was preparing the second war of Monferrato. On that occasion Milan had to pay in 800,000 lire for wages of Swiss and German mercenary troops and 400,000 for lodging.[45]

In 1638 interest on debt amounted to 1,595,026 lire, which was around 62 per cent of expenditures and 89 per cent of revenues: they were mostly produced, at the rate of 5.4 per cent, by the 15,192,748 lire that Milan owed to the Banco through bills of exchange.[46] In December of the following year, paying interest for funds borrowed through bills of exchange and for funds invested (6.5 million lire) by the Banco to buy back the *Regalie* (the municipal fiscal revenues sold in advance), a set of levies was chosen whose revenues had to be directly paid to the Ambrosian bank: part of the tariff on wine, on meat and on the *Macina* and parts of the *perticato civile*, the *tassa delle case* and the *estimo del mercimonio* were surrendered to the Banco for a total income of 812,173 lire. Nevertheless, since in 1641 the total amount of interest due to the Banco was 1,130,817 lire, a shortage of more than 350,000 lire occurred, but since in that year the current deficit of the City of Milan amounted to 614.708 lire there was no other choice other than turning again to bills of exchange.[47]

In the following decade however, as the most acute emergency was over, debt through bills of exchange expanded moderately (see Figure 2.1), even though it was more and more clear that the revenues dedicated to the Banco were not sufficient to vouch the entire sum allotted to the city. Between 1652 and 1658, more than 1.13 million lire of revenues due to the Banco was not paid because highly urgent municipal needs had to be met, while in 1655 military events with the Franco Piemontese army in front of Porta Romana (the southern entry to Milan) caused a sudden increase of defence expenditures (660,000 lire were used to reinforce the walls); in that situation the debt through bills of exchange kept on increasing. As the Banco was not able to pay satisfying dividends, its long-term funds were augmented to give interest of 7 per cent.

In 1658 out of total expenditure of 3,400,005 lire, interests payments to the Banco for its credit (bills of exchange, past interests, etc.) amounted to 2,080,009, while revenues were only 1,773,792 (mainly represented by direct taxes for 820,000 and indirect taxes for 726,700). It was a totally unbalanced situation with a deficit of 1,626,212 lire and with a debt service which was 63 per cent of the global expenditures.[48] This predicament was the result of expenditures coming from years of famine and of the spreading plague, but most of all it was the product of 45 years of military contributions which weighed heavily on the city budget: the *mensuale* for 430,540 lire, the *Tasso dei 14 reali* for 34,344 lire, the *Tasso della cavalleria* for 30,000 lire and the horse lodging for 80,000 lire. To meet these commitments the *Vicario di provvisione* asked permission to introduce permanently new tariffs (on drugs, on notebooks, on hides) and an extraordinary tax on houses and shops. The expansion of indirect taxes appeared as the only safe way to guarantee the estimated revenues since direct taxes were not paid regularly: in fact it was estimated that in 1658 an arrear of 3,400,000 lire regarding the *tre perticati* and *tasse della case* occurred, on which no interest was applied and no forced collection procedure was foreseen.[49] As a matter of fact, the *Magistrato ordinario* did not allow the tax increase requested, arguing that the raise in tariffs would hit the poorer classes out of proportion.

After continuing supports to the city were not compensated by a strengthening of endowments, in the first quarter of 1658 the Banco was not able to pay interests to its investors. An explored solution was to raise of the original endowment of 800,000 lire by 400,000 lire, but the plan was discarded since the town failed to find the money. It was decided then to concede to the Ambrosian institute the direct management of several taxes: tariffs on coal, meat, wine, poultry, olive oil, *Macina* and the ordinary tax on houses.

The outcome was a complete subordination of the general interest towards the interest of groups: the most important tax revenues were removed from the availability and control of the public sector; even the owners of the *luoghi* and *multiplici* issued by the Banco changed their nature shifting from a shareholder relationship including the risk of investment to a debtor-creditor relationship. With these adjustments and with the reduction to 2 per cent for the interest rate paid to its creditors, the Banco substantially improved its position.

In 1662 the Banco's governors were able to introduce more favourable pacts with the tax farmers. Starting with the Austrian Dynastic War and the French arrival in Milan – between 1700 and 1706 – the city still received 3,870,000 lire from the Banco in exchange for the administration of new fiscal sources, with revenues around 160,000 lire: the tariff on calfskin, on the production of white bread, part of the house tax and part of the tax on wine. On the eve of the entrance of Eugenio of Savoia into Milan, the Banco di Sant'Ambrogio was directly managing, besides the taxes on houses, the excise on bread, on brandy and the most important tariffs; the city had only the *tre perticati*, what remained of the *estimo del mercimonio* and some minor duties.[50]

V.

During the Spanish dominion the urban fiscal system mirrored the dynamics of the state fiscal system and acted mainly as a mechanism to face the needs of the centre. In the soaring economic phase of the second half of the sixteenth century, central requests were met by increasing indirect taxes, while, towards the end of the century, they were faced with debt. From the third decade of the seventeenth century the debt had increased quickly and led to a gradual privatization of the fiscal lever; as a result it was managed by the Banco di Sant'Ambrogio and by private purchasers of the urban revenues. As in the case of state securities, tax collectors directly paid those who bought in advance the rights to cash the levy income. This broke the weak relationship existing between the taxpayers and the municipal authority who decided on fiscal issues. As the tax collectors' profit derived from the difference with paid fees, the contractors' margins of embezzlement rose at the very moment they traded with private subjects, whom they paid less or with delay; frequently they did not pay the whole contracted amount of tax-farming to the city coffers complaining about a lesser taxes income. Such a situation deepened the difference between the real tax burden – which the Milanese citizens bore – and what the city, the Banco or the private investors, actually received. In addition, the municipal system (likewise the central system) progressively increased the complexity of the tax system because levies and their surcharges had risen. New taxes were introduced without eliminating the old ones. The system became gradually more stratified: commonly the same goods, such as wine for example, were hit with taxes imposed by the state and by the city.

Furthermore, in both contexts there were large groups of laity and clergymen and women, who were exempt from paying; citizenship was not yet associated with the obligation to pay tax and the fiscal duty strictly depended upon the kind of subject. All the different types of tax exemptions did not only worsen the redistribution of fiscal load among the taxpayers, but they also reinforced many abuses. In 1556 according to tax collectors, laity and clergy who were free from taxes, profited from their privileges introducing goods in the city, not for their own consumption but for selling. One third of wheat which entered the city of Milan was tax free, yet that figure did not match the number of the privileged people exempt from taxes. Between 1572 and 1587 the number of tax-free churchmen and women was fixed in 1,300, nonetheless the fiscal relationship between the city authorities and the ecclesiastical bodies continued to be object of negotiation.[51]

The urban fiscal system became stratified, entangled, largely dominated by bargaining and discretion; it was not at all transparent. The real fiscal load, which was levied on every single Milanese citizen remained undetermined and it was hard to distinguish the share coming from the city and the one imposed by the state. The system started to move towards a sort of equilibrium and progressiveness when, in 1543, the general *estimo*, which traced the path towards equity among subjects and among the different bodies of the state, was introduced. But obviously it did not reduce much of the gap; the prevailing view of the proper equality between goods and individuals in bearing the quota charged to Milan tended always to justify the minor load on individuals: the officers of the fiscal administration indeed sustained the idea that even goods contributed indirectly to the burden imposed on individuals as noblemen drank much more wine than workers.[52] In some way this remark mirrored the natural order of the local society. And such a society had to be ruled following the principles of 'distributive' justice (locally widespread by numerous treatises such as Leonardio Lessio's *De iustitia et iure*, printed by Giovanni Bidelli in Milan in 1618). Distributive justice aimed at distributing proportionally costs and benefits, respecting the status and the social differences of individuals. Hence not everybody had to pay in the same way or had to bear the same sacrifice.

From a fiscal perspective Milanese society could be depicted as a pyramid. The big landowners, the great merchants, the upper aristocrats, the major bankers and the *hombres de negocios* – who had already achieved a title of nobility and who were often tantamount to the members of the *patriziato* (the patriciate, namely the aristocracy who ruled the city) – were at the top. All these people were able to manage the entire fiscal system to their advantage, following a strategy of reciprocity which tied them to the Crown and to the political powers; many of them were lenders of the state and of the city and had been entrusted with the collection of taxes and the management of public funds. The central part of the pyramid included a thick group of small landowners, merchants, craftsmen and bankers who, thanks to their social position and their activities, were able, at least, partially to counteract the burden of taxation (also by their organization, like guilds). The bottom of the pyramid embraced a multitude of very small estate owners and wage earners, who were often overburdened in proportion to their assets. Furthermore within each class there were many divisions and controversies, but such a situation reflected reality quite faithfully.

The powerful ruling class, who firmly held the most important political positions in the state and with whom Madrid aimed at governing the Lombardy dominion, tenaciously defended the economic interests of its group. It had accepted the *estimo generale* imposed by the Spanish and the end of its jurisdiction on the *contado*, but, at the same time, found the way to largely preserve its precious privileges. On the one hand the freedom of collecting the city tax share established by the state, allowed it to lighten the burden upon landowners and merchants by shifting the taxation from direct to indirect taxes; on the other hand the scanty attention in collecting direct taxes (which remained often unpaid or were just partially paid), further diminished the pressure on the well-off classes; similarly, the large tax allowance for urban dealers and the presence of some tax-free products benefited the wealthiest consumers of the town.

The city administration soon became fully aware of the shortcomings of such a system and of all the difficulties in facing the rise of expenses. At the beginning of the seventeenth century, contemporary with the reforming endeavour which seemed to encompass public finance in the Spanish dominions, a special committee was organized to suggest solutions in order to balance the revenues with the city expenditures; in 1606 the councillor Gerolamo Caimi signed the proposal to create two municipal coffers, the former to collect the taxes necessary to pay the state charge, the latter to cash the revenues addressed to pay debt interests;[53] but in 1638, when the committee recommended the immediate abolition of all the exemptions as the only means to avoid the failure of the capital, a possible solution was still far from being found.[54]

Likewise the local environment was concerned with the enormous city debt and with the exhausted urban revenues. In the manner of the *arbitrios*, several suggestions were devised to restore urban indebtedness. In the first decades of the seventeenth century, one such proposal came from Gerolamo Zerbi (brother of Giovanni Antonio, the founder of the Banco di Sant'Ambrogio) which aimed at redeeming the alienated incomes by lowering the interest rate the holders would accept in exchange for a donation in moneys and an assurance of the restitution of the principal.[55] The plan presented in the middle of the century by the nobleman Carlo della Somaglia followed an identical scheme, but it was imbued with the persuasion that in the changed economic climate after the 1620s it was impossible to keep on drying up the local resources, by means of indirect taxes.

In his proposal the Milanese aristocrat wrote:

> as the State wealth stems from the private one, and the common from the particular, if the first diminishes the second decreases as well ... If people become impoverished because of taxation, they cannot trade, nor work, and hardly sustain themselves. Therefore they cannot give what they do not possess ... It is like a landowner who possesses many fruit trees in his lands. If he collects most of the fruit, he impoverishes his trees that are rich in fruit. The more he collects, the more he impoverishes the trees, and the latter will have only their leaves.[56]

Between 1657 and 1679 the accountant Francesco Bigatti suggested that indirect taxes on consumer goods should be unified, but, even if rational and far-seeing, his proposal was not accepted.[57] The local government decided to rely on the debt with the Banco di Sant'Ambrogio and progressively lose the management of all urban revenues. The penchant for debt financing was the result of two intertwining interests: the interest of city authorities, which aimed at obtaining immediate incomes, and the interest of buyers who sought the purchase in advance of fiscal revenues as a form of investment that was quite profitable, due to the stability of the Milanese lira and to the exemption from every kind of tax burden during the seventeenth century (at least for the natives).

Therefore, the fiscal system realized the progressive shift of wealth from taxpayers to revenues holders who had bought in advance fiscal incomes and hence received interest. The latter often occupied the top of the social pyramid, but they also represented merchants and entrepreneurs who used these proceeds as collateral to obtain credit which was applied to productive sectors.

VI.

Returning to debt financing, the Milanese fiscal system ended up interacting positively with the real economy of the whole region; the sales of urban revenues did not subtract funds from financing industry or trade, but they supplied incomes that could be used as a guarantee to borrow fixed capitals for the manufacturing of metals in Valsassina or for silk throwing in the countryside.[58]

While there is no doubt about the steep growth of taxation in Milan and in the whole Duchy – induced by the entry into the Empire orbit – it is no longer credible to ascribe the worsening of the regional economy to Spanish fiscal demands, as some scholars previously asserted.[59] The fiscal history of the city and of the entire state needs further in-depth analysis along this direction, but we have already some compelling evidence; it has been estimated that, for the land earnings in the Milanese *contado*, the tax rate was not superior to 8.83 per cent, on average, far below the 50 per cent rate that the country gentlemen complained to bear. The main excise duties (such as *dazio della carne, del vino*, and *della macina*) were fixed, not *ad valorem* and the increases and *addizioni* were not so great compared to the rise of prices of goods. Despite all the complaints made by contemporaries, the fiscal pressure was not so intolerable on the whole; in the second half of the sixteenth century the relevant demographic and economic expansion of the state, with the ensuing inflation that almost doubled the prices of consumer goods, reduced almost in half the real terms of the charge.[60]

In 1575 in order to proportion the yield of taxation to the depreciation of the Milanese currency (between 1555 and 1601 the silver content of the local lira diminished from 5.88 grams to 5.48 grams), urban authorities decided to increase by '4 quattrini per lira' (⅙₀) the value of the money used to pay taxes: an adjustment that favoured the taxpayers very much, especially the contractors, who often succeeded in being paid with revalued money and in paying with depreciated money.[61] When the *estimo mercimoniale* was accomplished, the Milanese merchants made an agreement with the Camera to pay only 10,000 scudi that, compared with the amount of trade of more than 29 million lire and a profit of 10 per cent, does not reach the rate of 2 per cent.[62]

Data on the seventeenth century are not very reliable, but there is sound evidence that, in the capital, consumer goods prices, as well as the real wages in the building and textile fields, were stable, if not decreasing slightly;[63] and this permits us to reject the thesis that the Spanish tax burden raised the urban real wages, provoking the loss of competitiveness of the local economy.

The traditional interpretative paradigm that looks at the Milanese fiscal system under the Austrias dominion only as a hindrance to the modernization and economic development is now showing its limits; according to the model of Smithian Growth, the more balanced equilibrium between the town and its countryside was a decisive element for development, as well as the policy of deficit spending permitted by debt financing having a multiplier effect according to the Keynesian perspective. Moreover, the fiscal system settled during the Spanish period can be considered as an organizational structure which bred the evolution of modern entrepreneurial behaviour and praxis. The tax-farmer entrepreneurs and the buyers of urban revenues became the protagonists of a cultural accumulation process that led to capitalistic modernization: they embodied a risk-oriented behaviour, evaluating an investment strategy based more on modern economic rationality than on distributive justice.[64] In 1582 the collection of main urban taxes, such as *dazio della macina* and *dazio del vino* of Milan, was managed by firms with a lot of employers and with a complex accounting structure; the owners were big names such as Cesare Negrolo, Tommaso D'Adda, Rinaldo Tettoni, the Littas, the Melzis, Pelegro Doria; they were the most important entrepreneurs of the state (in silk, long-distance trade), who later on would start other business in more innovative fields. In the first decades of the seventeenth century the tax-farming of *dazio del vino* was managed by Marcantonio Stampa and then by the Omodeis, who were by far the main entrepreneurs of the Milanese economic scene.[65] In the eighteenth century famous tax farmers of the Austrian period, such as Antonio Greppi, Giacomo Mellerio and the Giovannellis, were the leading representatives of the Milanese entrepreneurial world, as well.

3 THE URBAN TAX SYSTEM IN THE KINGDOM OF NAPLES (SEVENTEENTH TO EIGHTEENTH CENTURIES)

Alessandra Bulgarelli Lukacs

Summary

The aim of this paper is to point out the factors which determined the profile of the tax system developed by the Neapolitan cities during the seventeenth and eighteenth centuries, emphasizing the social and economic mechanisms which determined its evolution and the historical dynamics that it generated. It is well known that the tax system is not a purely technical mechanism, and that the ways to collect private resources to fund public objectives meet political criteria. The institution in charge of tax-levying (either the Royal Treasury or the local municipality) works as a redistribution mechanism, which, in general, is to the advantage of the lobbies.

The Kingdom of Naples – the biggest Italian state of the time – represents an interesting case study for a number of reasons. The Italian peninsula was one of the most populated and densely urbanized European areas. North-central Italy, along with southern Spain, Flanders, Île-de-France and the south of England, held the highest urbanization rates of the modern age. From the middle sixteenth century onwards, the growth rate of the urban population in southern Italy and the islands was relatively high. This growth was particularly important in the capital of the Kingdom, Naples, which in this period was at the top of the hierarchy of Italian and European towns.[1] From the fiscal point of view, since the Middle Ages the Neapolitan cities provided the Royal Treasury with its most important source of income (the so-called hearth tax or *funzioni fiscali*), which simultaneously was the most commonly demanded security by the creditors of the Crown.

The documentary source used in this paper is a government survey on the financial situation of the communities of the kingdom which includes their balance sheets for the years 1627–8. This survey has enabled us to analyse the structure of the revenues of a sample of fourteen towns, each one with at least

5,000 inhabitants or 1,000 hearths.[2] The analysis has to be horizontal; not dealing with the evolution of the incomes of one town in the different years, but
with the structure of the income of the fourteen towns of our sample in 1627–8.
The common reference year and methodology for data collection allowed us a
comparative perspective. In the following pages we have paid attention to some
relevant aspects:

1. the role of the towns in the Kingdom finance;
2. the autonomy of towns in local tax choices;
3. the urban tax system;
4. the fiscal burden which fell on urban populations;
5. the crisis of the local finance;
6. the influence of the local elites in the fiscal and financial policies adopted
   by the cities of the kingdom.

Between Documentary Vacuum and Historiography Vacuum

The study of the fiscal system set up by the Neapolitan cities during the early
modern period has to face some important obstacles. At first sight, this might
seem surprising, the kingdom of Naples being one of the most heavily urbanized
areas of the period. Its capital, Naples, was one of the biggest European cities and
there was also a dense net of ancient cities scattered all over the kingdom

However, two factors make any approach to the study of the fiscal and financial systems of the Neapolitan urban centres difficult. The first is the lack of
documentary sources. The original balance sheets of the provincial capitals of
the kingdom during the sixteenth to eighteenth centuries have disappeared and
all that it is left is a handful of sparse data on the expenditure, the revenues and
the deficit of some centres, contained mostly in informal documents (memo-
ries, reports, petitions). The *Archivio municipale* of Naples was largely destroyed,
together with the documents of the *Deputazione della pecunia* and the *Deputazione del disimpegno*.[3] The destruction of the municipal archives of the other
provincial towns, by negligence or a deliberate decision of local administrators,
compounds the problem and helps to explain the lack of research in the field of
urban finance for the early modern age.

The second problem that any reconstruction of urban finance has to face,
is the 'weak' urban identity of southern Italian towns. It is well known that,
unlike other areas of the country, this part of Italy did not go through the era
of the 'city-state'. This did not hamper the development of a flourishing urban
life in the kingdom, but helps to explain its peculiar course, heavily affected by
the early presence of the Crown and the relevance of the feudal system. These
factors contributed to limit the role of the Neapolitan towns except its capital,
Naples. The weak identity of countryside towns represented, from the territorial

side, a limit to the process of development and articulation of the urban system, which failed to define either a hierarchy among cities or a network of rural or urban settlement among entities of different relevance.[4] With reference to the Kingdom, it is more correct to speak of territorial segmentation, of a multispatial social system, as Medeiros has pointed out for southern Europe, and as Salvemini has employed for southern Italy with reference to the Puglia area.[5] The countryside towns had a limited capacity of spatial aggregation in a territory divided into local systems, where short-distance relationships, or conversely the international scenarios that trade relationships were able to outline, prevailed. This explains the lack of studies on the fiscal and financial life in southern Italian cities. In the late 1980s, referring to southern Italian urban reality, the definition was an 'unprecedented research scenario'.[6] Since then, historians, who have also produced contributions for the early modern age from single cases, have headed towards an overall view of southern Italian cities, of their functions and their relationships between the capital city and minor centres.[7]

The Countryside Towns and Their Relationship with the Royal Treasury.

This paper offers a contribution to this reconstruction through the study of the tax systems set up in a representative sample of Neapolitan cities. It is now possible to analyse this issue, after long research that led to the discovery of some copies compiled during the early eighteenth century of the balance sheets of nearly 300 communities and fourteen towns of the Kingdom for the years 1627 and 1628. The towns of our sample have been selected among those centres with at least 5,000 inhabitants (more than 1,000 hearths), which is the dimensional parameter commonly used by urban historiography. The cities included in the sample are: L'Aquila in the province of Abruzzo Ultra; Chieti and Lanciano in Abruzzo Citra; Caserta in Terra di Lavoro; Altamura, Gravina, Mola and Modugno in Terra di Bari; Taranto and Manduria/Casalnuovo in Terra d'Otranto; Melfi in Basilicata; Cosenza and Bisignano in Calabria Citra and Stilo in Calabria Ultra.[8] Scattered in the different provinces of the Kingdom, these towns show different economic traits: mountain or internal hill towns (L'Aquila, Melfi, Cosenza); coastal towns (Taranto); trade towns with famous fairs (Lanciano); administrative centres, either provincial capitals (L'Aquila, Chieti, Cosenza) or heavily fortified military towns (L'Aquila); single-cell towns (Altamura, Gravina) and towns ruling over a number of small subordinated centres (Cosenza, L'Aquila e Stilo); silk towns (Cosenza e Bisignano); wool towns (L'Aquila); and agricultural towns oriented to the production of wheat (Gravina e Altamura) and olive oil (Mola, Modugno). This diversity enables us a better understanding of how the regional and local economies shaped the evolution of their tax systems. From the institutional point of view, a further distinction can be made between Royal towns (Chieti, Lanciano, L'Aquila, Cosenza, Stilo, Taranto) and feudal towns (Altamura, Gravina, Modugno, Mola, Bisignano, Caserta, Melfi, Manduria/ Casalnuovo). A comparative methodology has been chosen, which, multiplying the points of view, allows understanding the specificity of the various urban situations.

Before analysing the specific features of the urban tax system, one must remember the role that towns, like all the local communities in the Kingdom, performed within the Neapolitan finances. Since the Angevin age (thirteenth to fourteenth centuries), the King had succeeded in establishing an ordinary tax framework based upon the regular collection of taxes. During this same period, taxation provided half of the overall revenues of the Royal Treasury, being its most important source of income. This could be considered as proof of the existence of a trend towards the emergence of the modern state in southern Italy during the Middle Ages.[9] Although scholars seem nowadays to be more careful with the use of the term 'state' for the Ancien Régime, categories such as *domain state – tax state*, identified by Schumpeter remain valid to understand the specificity of the Kingdom of Naples.[10] The *domain state*, based on the assumption that the prince had to 'live off his own means', governing the territory, relying on his crown lands, enforcing monopolies and royal patent rights and collecting duties and taxes, seems to fade in the Kingdom of Naples in the thirteenth and fourteenth centuries. The introduction of a permanent tax on hearths, to be paid in silver coins, took place in the following centuries. In fact, it is with the tributary reform carried out by the Aragonese dynasty in the middle of the fifteenth century, along with the development of the financial administration and the advances in bookkeeping techniques, that the tax-state was born in the Kingdom of Naples and that the King obtained the recognition of his right to tax people on a regular basis. This trend continued until the eighteenth century and during this time the structure of the revenues of the Crown remained basically the same, being taxes (and particularly the *funzioni fiscali* levied on *hearths*) the most important source of income. It was not a completely static structure, rather it was flexible enough as to adjust itself to the course of the economic fluctuations: the economic expansion of the sixteenth century led to the introduction of many indirect taxes, even in small and medium-size centres which traditionally had rested on the *cadastro/apprezzo*, whereas during the crisis of the following century the contraction of revenues coming from the taxes introduced in the previous phase led back to the *cadastro/apprezzo*.

During this long period there was no direct relationship between the Royal Treasury and taxpayer. The reason was the shortcomings of the Royal administration, something particularly relevant because an efficient administrative system would have been even more necessary in a regime based on direct taxation, as Gabriel Ardant pointed out referring to France and its *taille*.[11]

The administrative shortcomings of the Crown compelled the local communities of the kingdom to fulfil important functions in the fiscal field. The communities assessed the wealth of each household; apportioned the burden of taxation required by the Sovereign and allocated to each household its contribution quotas. They also collected the *funzioni fiscali* and submitted the value of the collections of this tax (in silver coin) to the royal ministers scattered in the provincial capitals. The link between Sovereign and *universitates* (the municipalities), then, was close because the latter had to collect the most important source of revenue of the former (*funzioni fiscali* or hearths tax) which, as has been mentioned before, was the security most demanded by the Crown's creditors. Consequently, the communities had to pay their quotas of the hearth tax dismissed directly to the creditors and not to the Royal Treasury. This meant a direct relationship to these people who acted without control over the methods of collecting the sums due. In the case of the seigneurial towns, the local communities also had to pay the obligations due to the feudatory.

The payments due to the Crown and feudatories increased the expenditures of the Neapolitan communities and reduced the relative importance of those expenses funding the local needs. In the case of the towns of our sample, the expenditure for local destination accounted for 12 per cent of the total expenditure, and to this should be added the payment of the interest of the local debt, which accounted for another 30 per cent.

Tax Revenues According to the Law

Considering the tasks that local communities performed on behalf of the Royal Treasury, the Royal Law paid specific attention to local finance. Through the regular payment of the taxes (*funzioni fiscali*) by the communities, the Crown obtained a basic part of its revenues, and the creditors were guaranteed with the service of the public debt, safeguarding the credibility of the Sovereign. The regular working of the local administrative engine was regulated with measures which, apart from limiting the worst abuses of the local oligarchies ruling the communities, settled the method to follow in the apportioning of the tax burden. At the local level, the cadastre had to be used, favouring it to any other formula, as it was perceived as the best way of ensuring that taxes (*funzioni fiscali*) were paid on the basis of each citizen's wealth. This system fitted perfectly with the government tax system, and it represented the second step in the distribution of the tax burden, which was distributed in two separate phases: 1) from the Royal Treasury to local communities, through the single indicator given by the demographic variable; 2) from communities to the taxpayer, through a number of indicators of the taxable basis. In the passage from the centre to the local communities there was no shift in the tax, which remained within the category of direct taxes.

The objective at the local level was to adjust the payment of taxes to the fiscal capability of households, identified through an algebraic sum which took into account several income sources, including the working activity of the taxpayers. The tax paid by each household included the head-tax (*testatico*), the tax on real estate, and the tax on animals. It is worth stressing here that during the early modern period there was not a clear orientation to tax the *res*; that is, to tax the land for its intrinsic value or the real estate in general.[12] The subjective character which pervaded the whole system was evident, and it was strengthened by the fact that some social groups were tax-exempt.

The fiscal burden was borne by the population, which was not able to save its assets from the payment of taxes. The *funzioni fiscali*, collected on the basis of the number of hearths in each community, was the main revenue for the Royal Treasury. An unequal distribution of the burden and the regressive trend of tax imposition to the detriment of the defenceless and less wealthy classes were the main features of the tax system in southern Italy.

The laws regulating the cadastre had general value, although local communities kept a certain autonomy, in line with the tradition and the usages prevailing in each single centre. The government kept its right to pass any act on whatever withdrawal the local parliament might have decided. In practical terms, however, the royal authorities took their decisions case by case and showed the flexibility necessary to make government initiatives successful in a political environment where the relationships between the Crown and subjects were defined in contractual terms.

In spite of the limitations of its administration, the government always retained some control on the fiscal and financial life of the communities of the kingdom. The Crown collected detailed information about the communities' fiscal and financial state (number of hearths, tax framework, debts), and monitored closely their fiscal and financial life, especially in times of deficit. This was usually done through the dispatch of officers (*commissari*) to single communities and through general surveys of the global fiscal and financial situation of the communities of the kingdom, as in 1627 and 1628.

The Tax System in the Urban Practice

At the local level, the fiscal history of the communities of the kingdom during the early modern period was characterized by the trend, promoted by the local elites, towards the use of indirect taxes and duties, which replaced the cadastre.

A tax system based on indirect taxation allowed the local elites, who owned a significant real state, to avoid the payment of direct taxes. As consumers of the agricultural commodities produced in their own properties, they also avoided the payment of duties levied on essential goods (olive oil, bread, wine, meat, flour). Yet a minimum development of trade and commerce was required to ensure the profitability of a fiscal system based on indirect taxes. In periods of crisis and stagnation, the fall in revenues coming from indirect taxes suggested a return to the cadastre, whereas the expansion in the 1500s induced an adoption of indirect taxation, even in small-medium centres, which had usually rested on the revenues coming from the cadastre.[13] Generally, it can be said that the higher the population, the wider the use of duties and taxes. The government left the communities free to arrange the collection of taxes, giving the royal assent to the introduction and renewal of their duties and taxes. The government imposed the cadastre in case of deficit or arrears in the payment of the taxes due to the Royal Treasury and the interests of the creditors.

Table 3.1: Revenues in the balance sheets of the cities of the Kingdom of Naples 1627–8.

CITIES	fiscal hearths	fiscal revenues (in percentage)				not fiscal (in percentage)			TOTAL
		t. inter cives	tithes	duties	total	demesne	jurisd. rights	total	values in ducats
Province of Abruzzo Citra									
Chieti	2195	0	0	92	92	0	8	8	8252
Lanciano	1878	0	0	89	89	5	7	11	9769
Province of Abruzzo Ultra									
L'Aquila	2077	60	0	36	96	4	0	4	15034
Province of Terra di Bari									
Altamura	2686	19	1	79	99	0	1	1	23820
Gravina	2734	6	13	75	95	5	0	5	22564
Modugno	1406	1	0	94	94	1	5	6	18093
Mola	1044	23	0	76	100	0	0	0	11790
Province of Terra d'Otranto									
Manduria/Casalnuovo	1009	15	21	60	95	0	4	5	11220
Taranto	3000	30	8	58	96	1	3	4	21315
Province of Basilicata									
Melfi	2180	0	0	94	94	5	0	6	15858
Province of Calabria Citra									
Bisignano	1237	0	0	100	100	0	0	0	5500
Cosenza	2389	30	0	70	100	0	0	0	13151
Province of Calabria Ultra									
Stilo e casali	1593	56	0	32	88	0	12	12	2721
Provincia di Terra di Lavoro									
Caserta	1379	5	0	92	97	3	0	3	7696
totals and averages	26808	17	4	75	96	2	2	4	186783

Sources: Archivio di Stato di Napoli, *Camera della Sommaria, Attuari Diversi*, ffs. 201 (Chieti), 202 (Lanciano), 187 (Modugno e Mola), 187/II (Altamura), 188/II (Gravina), 375 (Stilo e casali), *Processi Antichi, Pandetta Rossa*, ffs. 152 (Manduria/Casalnuovo), 170 (Melfi), *Pandetta II*, fs. 64 (Bisignano). N.F. Faraglia, *Il Comune nell'Italia meridionale (1100–1806)* (Napoli: Tipografia della Regia Università, 1883), pp. 357–61, 368–71, 385–92, 393–97 (L'Aquila, Caserta, Cosenza, Taranto).

As it may be seen in Table 3.1, taxes provided the greatest part of the total revenue (96 per cent) of the cities of our sample. The municipal properties, even being present, did not always supply an income: they were registered in eight towns only, where they accounted for a 2 per cent average of the total revenue. Apart from taxes and municipal properties, there were other sources of income, such as the rights coming from the exercise of minor jurisdictions, like mint, weights, measures, etc. that accounted for 2 per cent of the total revenue. As for the tax incomes, indirect taxation was preferred in place of the cadastre (*tassa inter cives*) in the Neapolitan towns. It was a tax behaviour opposite to that observed in a sample of 287 local communities analysed for the same years 1627–8: the *inter cives tax* was present in 95 per cent of the cases surveyed, and among the 276 communities that recorded its collection, ninety (32.6 per cent) obtained 100 per cent of their revenues from it.[14] On the contrary, in the fourteen towns of our sample the *inter cives* supplied around a paltry 17 per cent of their total revenues, and it is interesting to remark here that this tax was absent in three centres (Chieti, Lanciano, e Melfi). Sometimes this tax was levied only on those non-residents who owned assets in the towns, being therefore compelled to pay the so-called tax of *bonatenenza* (Caserta). In other cases, the tax was levied on the animals owned (the *gabella del mobile* at Altamura and Gravina and the *duty on cattle* at Modugno in Terra di Bari), excluding the taxes on 'the head' and on the real estate, which were registered at L'Aquila (in Abruzzo Ultra), Bisignano, Cosenza and Stilo, (in Calabria Citra), Mola (in Terra di Bari), Manduria/Casalnuovo and Taranto (in Terra d'Otranto). It can be assumed that when this tax provided a significant percentage of the total urban revenues, this reflected the relative underdevelopment of trade and commerce, which hampered the adoption of indirect taxation.

The local communities had also to pay the tithe, together with the other quotas of taxation on the production, which were frequently levied on some provinces such as Puglia and Basilicata and so were present in Altamura and Gravina (Terra di Bari), Manduria/Casalnuovo and Taranto, (Terra d'Otranto). The importance of these quotas was scarce and they represented a mere 4 per cent of the total revenues of the analysed sample, which rose to 10 per cent in Altamura, Gravina, Manduria/Casalnuovo and Taranto.

Indirect taxation was by far more important, under the form of duties, taxes and sole-rights. All the towns of the sample levied them and these taxes represented 75 per cent of their total revenue and 78 per cent of their tax revenues (see Figure 3.1).

All the solutions adopted reflected the structure of the local agricultural production. Indirect taxes were levied on saffron at L'Aquila, on silk at Cosenza, on olive oil at Modugno and Mola and on fish at Taranto. Even though they helped to reduce the burden of the tax on flour, those taxes were not able to replace its income.

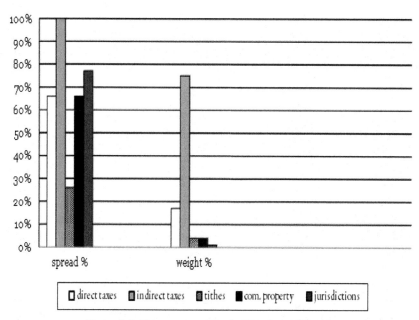

Figure 3.1: Urban revenues in the Kingdom of Naples
(sample of fourteen towns, 1627–8).

The tax on flour was ubiquitous and it accounted for 50 per cent of the tax revenue in the fourteen sampled towns and for 48 per cent of their total revenues. Apart from these taxes, the cities of our sample also collected sole rights on water and other taxes on the sales of bread, meat and other commodities.

Although the fiscal system set up by the Neapolitan cities should have provided enough revenues to fund urban spending, this was not the case and their balance sheets presented relevant current account deficits (up to 54 per cent of the revenues in Chieti and Stilo and up to 103 per cent at Bisignano) and huge arrears of three times (Lanciano and Cosenza), or even four (Bisignano) the size of their yearly revenue. At the beginning of the century the government tried twice to stabilize the difficult financial situation of the communities of the country (in 1613–16 and 1627–8), with expenditure cuts and a rise in tax revenues. The problems of local finance date back to previous decades, linked to the worsening of the economic climate, which started with the agricultural crisis of the 1580s, which, in its turn, was included in the economic conjuncture of the international market.

Being a part of the Spanish Empire was not meaningless for the financial stability of the cities of the Kingdom either. Although the *topos* of Spain's plundering tax system towards its domains seems outdated after the research carried out during the last decades, it is important to underline some analogies between the Kingdom of Naples and Spain in the field of urban finance. The studies on Castile have shown an urban decline from the late 1500s and the early 1600s. Among the various causes which have been invoked to explain this decay we may find the heavier tax pressure; the losses in the jurisdictional control traditionally exerted by the Castilian towns over their rural districts which became independent and the sales of quotas of the taxes traditionally collected by the Royal Treasury, such as the *alcabalas*.[15] These measures were due to the financial needs of the Spanish monarchy.

The crisis of urban finance became evident in cities such as Valladolid, whose revenues fell around 50 per cent after 1606, as Adriano Gutiérrez highlights in his study.[16] The introduction of the *millones*, which became the most important Royal tax during most of the seventeenth century, in 1590 had long lasting consequences, and not only for the structure of the royal tax system.[17] The relationship between the Castilian towns and the monarchy changed, and the former became subordinated to the latter in the fiscal and financial field. Simultaneously, from 1590 onwards the *arbitrios* became relevant among the tax revenues of the Castilian cities. Most of them resorted to the wide use of *sisas* levied upon the consumption of basic commodities such as meat, wine and olive oil.[18]

Similarly, a decline in the countryside towns of the Kingdom of Naples can be traced during the two centuries of Spanish domination. This decline shows, from an institutional level, the lack of jurisdictional functions, and from an economic level, the inability of the Neapolitan centres to attract and coordinate the surrounding territories. This poses the issues of 'peripheralization' and 'provincialization' of the towns compared to the growth of Naples which, was the main exception to the crisis suffered by the cities of the Kingdom.[19]

It is possible to measure through demographic data the extent of the urban decline and to compare it with the general demographic contraction recorded in the Kingdom. Towns were the territorial units with a higher percentage of population losses: 43 per cent in the urban centres with a population higher than 2,000 hearths, compared to an average of 37 per cent in the rest of settlements.[20] This is a pattern in which, along with a general demographic contraction, there was an internal redistribution of the population through internal migration which favoured the smaller centres and the capital city, Naples. It was a process of ruralization of the Kingdom, where the decline of urban centres confirms the relevant role of Naples as the capital city.[21]

The causes of the urban decline in the kingdom of Naples were manifold and the choices adopted to fund the financial needs of the Spanish Empire seem to have played a relevant role in the whole process. The tools used by the government were the same as those employed in Spain.[22] There was a growth in the number of taxes collected caused by the expansion of the public debt and the decrease in the yields of the taxes already existent. At the same time, the government resorted to the wide use of extraordinary finance, with the request of donations and the frequent town sales. The latter were particularly important. In some cases the sales were made without the willingness of the towns,

which became involved in expensive financial operations to keep their autonomy. In other cases, the towns suffered the progressive loss of control over the
small centres of their rural hinterland, either due to the small centres' desire for
independence from the town or to the sales of such small centres by the Royal
Treasury to fund its needs. The higher pressure on the territory in the first decades of the seventeenth century produced budget deficits and huge arrears in
the payment of taxes, while at the same time it emphasized the central role the
local communities and towns played in the field of public finance. This led the
Count of Lemos, viceroy from 1610 to 1616, to state that the local communities were 'the main wealth of the Patrimony'. In other words, the towns were the
main item in the kingdom's general balance sheet. This awareness, along with the
situation of local financial ruin, caused the government to adopt specific actions
early in the 1600s to balance the accounts.[23]

Now, I focus on town finance, in order to highlight two main aspects:
a) The measure of the tax burden on the urban taxpayer.
b) The role of the municipal oligarchies.

The Measure of the Tax Burden on the Urban Taxpayer

From the available data, it is possible to estimate the fiscal burden which fell on
the urban taxpayer. The local dimension is the only one which can show the different taxes paid by the inhabitants of the communities to the Royal Treasury,
the feudal lord, the Church and the municipality. An analysis based on the taxes
paid to the Crown, would only deal with a part, however important, of the taxes
effectively paid by the local communities of the kingdom, so it is through a study
of the balance sheets of these centres that we may take into account all the taxes
collected in them by the Central government, the feudal lord, the Church and
the municipality, measuring the exact value of the tax burden of each one.

Some indicative averages can be drawn from the analysis of the relationship
between tax revenue and the number of hearths, especially in the early years of
the seventeenth century, when the demographic data generated some controversy. The decline of the population led the towns, as well as other centres, to
ask for a reduction in the number of hearths listed in the general census of 1595
and to indicate the real number of hearths in their balance sheets. It is easy to
understand that neither the number of hearths listed in the 1595 census (*numer-
azione dei fuochi*) – which dated back to 30 years before, during the demographic
expansion – nor the figures listed in the cities' balance sheets were reliable. Obviously, depending on whether the number of hearths is that listed in 1595 or that
coming from the declarations of the towns, the results are different. In the first
case, the average size of the fiscal burden paid by each household is around 7
ducats per capita, while in the second it rises to 11 ducats. These figures have to
be related to the yearly income of the average household, which I have estimated

at 60–80 ducats per year elsewhere;[24] that means a tax burden between 8.7–13.7 per cent of the yearly average income of the Neapolitans. These are values which match those proposed for Spain, where during the same period the fiscal burden amounted to 9–11 per cent of the national wealth.[25] Compared with today's standards, this level of taxation may appear light and even contradictory with the trend towards the growing tax burden and aids which many towns and local communities were obliged to bear early in the seventeenth century.

However, a tax burden of about 10–15 per cent of the contributory capacity of the Neapolitan hearths can be considered important in an agricultural economy, with low productivity of land and work, poor infrastructures and reduced monetary circulation; all these factors affect the relationship between supply and demand. The difficulty in the circulation of goods made trade a peculiarity of urban and coastal centres, whereas large areas in the countryside lived on at a mere subsistence level. These data are compatible with those obtained from some 300 communities in the 1620s and from a sample of 981 localities in the early 1700s. The documents of that time show that the same municipalities reported that a burden of 12–13 ducats (that is 15–20 per cent of the income) would make inhabitants leave the area.[26]

The Role of Municipal Oligarchies

The exodus from provinces and small towns into the capital city could be due to the push exerted by the central government policy and its financial needs and to the pull of the capital city, Naples. It would also be important to consider the decisions in the fiscal and financial field made by the local oligarchies. These groups resorted to regressive measures, such as the taxes on primary consumption that penalized the low and middle sorts of the local communities which suffered the effects of the worsening economic climate of the period. This hypothesis, which has been largely accepted, should be supported by a study on the relationships between taxes on consumption and price and wage levels. In the Kingdom of Naples this comparison is precluded by the state of the current research. There are some studies on prices, in particular the price of wheat, and wages, but the main problem is that for the 1600s these analyses refer to a handful of years and single centres. This has made it impossible to estimate the overall trends of price and wage levels in southern Italy in the long run, as Paolo Malanima did for northern and central Italy.[27]

At the present moment, some hypotheses on the choices made by local administrators can be presented. The opposition to the use of the cadastre and the *inter cives* tax in many centres involved the refusal to a better apportioning of a fiscal burden which had grown as a result of the continuous government requests and the expenditures that many communities had to face, either to preserve or to acquire their independence. These oligarchies behaved in the same way towards the localities included within the urban jurisdiction, which were subject to an apportioning of the fiscal burden decided by the town. This originated many abuses, being prominent among them the evasion of the *bonateneza* (a tax due by non-residents). The cities' inhabitants owned the major part of estates in the countryside, but they usually evaded their payment. The *bonatenenza* question caused serious tensions between those in the city and countryside which continued during decades and centuries without a real solution. In the Kingdom of Naples, as elsewhere, the interests of urban ruling orders were oriented not only towards the control of the local fiscal systems, but also to the control of all the municipal resources through the usurping of municipality properties (mainly lands), the leasing of the municipality revenues and the supply of food during shortage periods.[28]

Continuities and Changes in the Urban Tax System

The urban tax system that arises from the balance sheets of the 1620s remained the same throughout the century, affected by the economic and demographic decline and the crisis of the countryside towns in particular. If the data of the 300 communities in 1627–8 are compared to those of the 1720s, the persistence of a system based on the direct taxation in most centres of the Kingdom can be observed.[29] The cities, where taxation rested on duties on primary goods, were the most important exception.

The existence of relevant continuities should not hide the presence of some changes in municipal finance. Here it is useful to recall the intertwined relationship between debt and tax systems, as a substantial part of the urban revenues were directed to pay the service of the debt, either contracted by the Sovereign or the local municipalities. The analysis highlights two relevant aspects: a) the birth of a secondary market for the bonds issued by the towns at a local level; b) the role performed by the owners of the bonds issued by the Crown to promote actions to balance the accounts of local finance, being particularly relevant among them the birth of the general cadastre of the Kingdom in the 1730s and 1740s.

The Local Indebtedness and the Birth of the Secondary Market

The debt of the towns of the Kingdom of Naples included both the public debt issued by the Royal Treasury and the debt issued by the local communities. The payment of the interests of the former was made through the taxes paid by communities according to the number of *hearths*. There are plenty of studies on the debt issued by the Neapolitan Treasury during the early modern period, while our knowledge on the debt of the local communities is more limited. Communities resorted to debt to fund ordinary and extraordinary expenditures (requests from the Royal Treasury, lodgements of troops, food supplies). Local debt rarely funded the purchases of real state or productive investment in public works and other services for the cities of the Kingdom, and more frequently it allowed them to face urgent cash needs. The debt had the advantage of deferring the costs of funding such expenditures to the following years. The temptation to finance extraordinary expenditure with the debt, then, was irresistible.

The local communities of the kingdom of Naples were heavily indebted. The survey carried out on 298 local communities in the Kingdom in 1627–8, including the fourteen towns of our sample, shows that 218 (73.1 per cent) resorted to debt to fund their expenditures. The payment of the interests of such debt accounted for almost 23 per cent of their expenditures, with a total of 171,081 ducats, and to this it should be added that the funds devoted by these same centres to pay their interests to the creditors (*fiscalarij*) of the Sovereign, accounted for another 24 per cent. In the analysis of the fourteen towns of our sample we find some differences: the payment of the interest owed to the creditors of the Royal Treasury drew 17 per cent of their expenditure, whereas the payment of the interest of the local debt drew another 30 per cent. Nevertheless, either by looking at the survey of 1627–8 with includes nearly 300 localities or looking at our fourteen town sample, almost half of expenditures (46–47 per cent) was devoted to the service of the public and local debt. Like the Crown, the provincial towns of our sample offered to their creditors their yearly revenues, demesne assets or tax items, to guarantee the payment of the interests of their debt, stimulating the progressive interference of such creditors in the fiscal and financial life of the communities. In some cases the urban revenues were not enough to cover the payment of the interest of the local debt, forcing the local councils to allow their creditors the control over the guarantees originally pledged to such end.

I am not going to dwell here on a study of the investors in urban debt, or on an analysis of the trend thanks to which most of the bonds issued by the Neapolitan towns became concentrated in the hands of a few individuals.[30] I would rather point out that the wide circulation of such bonds caused the development of a secondary market. It is possible to identify the moment of its birth in the agricultural crisis of the late 1500s in the Italian countryside, when the local communities became heavily indebted.

The credit demand was met by private and ecclesiastical investors, attracted by the interest rates of 9–10 per cent or even more offered by local communities. In the following years, two factors contributed to the emergence of the secondary market: the problems of many local communities to keep the regular payment of the interest of their debt forced investors to sell off their bonds, whereas other centres tried to find less expensive financial resources. Together, both factors caused the widespread circulation of substantial amounts of urban bonds. The secondary market which arose from here expanded in the following years due to the rise of transactions and the speed of the circulation of urban bonds, which attracted even smaller investors. However, the development of the secondary market was slowed down by the monetary policy followed during the 1620s, when a deflationary downturn, linked to the revaluation of the ducat, entailed the shrinking of the money in circulation, the reduction in the interest rates and the contraction of the money supply.

Smaller investors decided to sell their bonds, but the feudatories and the clergy, with a stronger position and the capacity to obtain the necessary information to operate in the territory, remained in the business. In their relationship with such creditors the municipalities were confined to a difficult position. In order to obtain loans and delays in the payment of their arrears, many communities allocated quotas of their tax revenues to the investors, exempting them (in case they were residents or owners of real state within the boundaries of the urban jurisdiction), totally or partially, from the payment of taxes. As can easily be inferred, this introduced a disturbing factor in the management of the local tax system and had at least two negative consequences: first, the total or partial exemption granted to their creditors tended to reduce the revenues from the *inter cives tax* and, second, it broadened the already large tax-exempt group. The municipalities passed through progressive steps of destabilization of their economic and financial structure. This way, the delicate balance between revenues and expenditures was threatened, forcing the local administration to a perennial deficit. In practical terms, when the community turned to the capital of a private or a local ecclesiastical body, with the commitment of the annual interest, a relationship of dependence of the community on the creditors was set up and this led to transfer of control over local finance to the creditors.

The Role Performed by the Creditors of the Royal Treasury in the Reorganization of Local Finance

The developments at local level mirrored those prevailing at the centre. In drawing the financial resources necessary to fund its policy, the Crown had involved the social and economic elite of the Kingdom. This group invested a big part of its capital in the public debt issued by the Crown and became heavily interested in the management of the Neapolitan finances through contracts, and purchases of public offices and rents. The tight links between the Crown and the local oligarchies lasted for decades if not centuries and the latter (the big aristocratic families, the provincial nobility, the members of the royal administration, the Church and the urban elites) were always very keen on the safeguard of their rights.

The relevance acquired by public debt owners is usually considered by scholars as a cause of the conservatism which pervaded the evolution of the Neapolitan finances during the early modern period and as a reason for the falling investment in productive activities during the period. Furthermore, the study of the relation between public debt owners and local communities provides us with another clue for a better understanding of the effects of the expansion of the Crown's debt on the social and economic life of the communities of the kingdom.

The recent reconstruction of the history of the *cadastre onciario*, one of the main fiscal reforms of Charles of Bourbon, allows us to analyse the crucial role performed by the owners of quotas of the tax on *hearths* as supporters of the Crown's intervention in the local finance[31]. During the first decades of the eighteenth century many communities had accumulated important arrears in the payment of the hearth tax which endangered the regular payment of the interests of the owners of public debt. Like the buyers of the bonds issued by the cities of the kingdom (*istrumentarii*) had done before, the owners of public debt (*fiscalarij*) became heavily involved in the financial life of the local communities of the country and obtained from the central government all kind of coercive measures to ensure their objectives. Sometimes, especially in the first decades of the 1700s, while warning the government on the insolvency of local municipalities, the *fiscalarij* also presented their proposals for the reform of local finances, in order to safeguard their interests. Their intimate knowledge of the communities' economic, social and demographic conditions, and their physical presence in them allowed the creditors to ask for interventions for a better apportioning of the fiscal burden and to fight tax evasion.

The direct observation of the local reality enabled the *fiscalarij* to detect the existence of an emerging social group which had avoided the effects of the growing fiscal burden until then, the *mas poderosi*. The *mas poderosi* were those who had taken advantage from by the expansive economic climate after the plague of 1656–7. Thanks to the connivance of the local municipal administrators, they had evaded their fiscal obligations and their growing wealth was virtually tax exempt. This awakened the suspicions of the owners of public debt bonds, who were willing to tax the wealth of this group in order to ensure the regular payment of the interests of their bonds.

The tool that best helped to reach this aim was the cadastre, especially in the provincial towns, which had not used it for more than a century as a result of the preference given to all forms of indirect taxation, such as duties and taxes. The delicate financial state of these centres had caused the growing interventionism of the Austrian and later Bourbon governments. The cadastre, through a new and global estimate of the wealth of the Neapolitan towns, would increase their fiscal revenues, ending tax evasion and fiscal deficits, and this would help the local communities to pay the interests of their debt (both the local and the public debt issued by the Crown). The trust in the possibilities of the cadastre was such that some creditors paid for the expenses brought by its creation, carried out under the direction of the royal officers. The interest on the cadastre was also widespread in royal circles and among the feudatories and other sectors, as it can be seen in the literature of the time. It was the pressure coming from all these social orders which gave rise to the awareness of the need of a reform of the cadastral system through the whole Kingdom.

The *cadastre onciario*, compiled in the 1740s was the result of an ambitious operation of fiscal reform driven by the pressure exerted by some influential groups. The *cadastre* embodied the principle of the uniformity of the tax system across the Kingdom, whose range reached even the real estate owned the clergy after the Concordat, ending with a long tradition of privileges and immunities. In many aspects the *cadastre* was oriented towards the past: unlike the geometric and detailed cadastral surveys carried out during the same time in Lombardy and Piedmont, the 1740 Neapolitan *cadastre* was characterized by the absence of maps and surveys and the whole project rested on personal instead of real taxation. Although this *cadastre* embodied the first step towards the curtailment of the tax immunities traditionally enjoyed by the privileged groups, it was far from representing a radical departure from the political traditions of the *Ancien Régime*. The nobility kept its immunity and, more importantly, the compilation of the new *cadastre* was carried out by the local communities themselves and not by any government department. Nevertheless, the 1740 *cadastre* embodied a clear contrast of interests between the creditors of the Crown and the local oligarchies of well-off and *mas poderosi*. Whereas the former ranked among the promoters of the cadastral regulation, the latter, the first targets to be hit by *cadastre*, brought up a strong resistance which the Crown could not disregard. Therefore, the Crown entrusted them tasks of control and management of resources, the guarantee of the social peace and the implementation of administrative reforms.

4 PUBLIC INSTITUTIONS, LOCAL POLITICS AND URBAN TAXATION IN SEVENTEENTH-CENTURY ARAGON[1]

José Antonio Mateos Royo

The tax systems of early modern Europe have attracted increasing interest in recent decades in view of their evident importance to economic history, and yet the research effort has been uneven. The clear priority of European historians has been the study of state taxes, an area that has benefited from the relative accessibility of historical sources held in national archives, which have yielded valuable information given the growing fiscal powers of the modern state. Local taxation has been largely ignored, however.

In view of the difficulties inherent in the study of local taxation in the early modern period, European historiography has tended to concentrate on the major cities as the principal centres of economic activity and tax revenues. However, this focus causes some problems. The general absence of agrarian towns in studies has made it difficult to establish nationwide comparisons that would provide a coherent overview of local taxation, the development of the tax system and its economic and social consequences. The purpose of this paper is, precisely, to study the fiscal systems set up by the local communities of a region whose urban structure was characterized by the preponderance of agrarian towns: the Kingdom of Aragon.

It is well known that any reform of urban taxes and finances attempted during the Ancien Régime was conditioned not only by the economic capacity of each town or city, but also by political and social consensus (or conflict) and that, given the authorities' limited control, social responses to tax pressure could have major consequences for municipal economies. Because of that, this paper advocates a wider analysis capable of integrating political, economic and social issues to throw light on local taxation in early modern Europe. The Kingdom of Aragon belonged to the Spanish territories of the Crown of Aragon, a federation of realms that had coalesced in the late medieval period and included Aragon, Catalonia, Valencia, the Balearic Islands and different Italian provinces. These territories maintained their own differentiated laws and institutions under the

Hapsburg monarchy until their abrogation by the new Bourbon dynasty in 1707 and 1714 in its efforts to build a more centralized state. As we shall see, the preservation of this legal and institutional framework affected the development of the local tax system in Aragon in the seventeenth century.

Municipal Administration and Revenues in Seventeenth-Century Aragon

In general terms, the towns of medieval and early modern Aragon owed their urban character not so much to their demographic importance as to their political, economic and cultural functions, contributing to the cohesion of the territory. Meanwhile, the already low urban population of Aragon came under considerable stress as a result of the demographic decline that set in during the seventeenth century.[2] A census of the kingdom performed between 1646 and 1650 counted 70,729 taxpaying households, of which 11,510 were in towns and cities, 24,959 in villages with more than 100 hearths (tax units), and 34,260 in settlements that had fewer than 100 tax units.[3] According to this general census, just 16.27 per cent of the Aragonese population lived in towns, most of which were medium-sized and small royal boroughs. Only Saragossa had more than 5,000 households and could be considered a real city as the capital of the kingdom. Next in importance were Calatayud and Huesca, each with some 1,000 hearths. Seven more towns (Barbastro, Tarazona, Borja, Daroca, Teruel, Caspe and Alcañiz) had between 500 and 800 households and a further twenty-five between 200 and 500. The rest of the population lived in some 1,500 villages with less than 200 hearths, which meant they had under 1,000 inhabitants.[4]

Municipal government in the Aragonese towns and cities had acquired some degree of complexity by the seventeenth century. In contrast to the simple systems inherited from the late Middle Ages, in which the administration revolved around a single, central treasury known as the *Procuraduría, Mayordomía* or *Bolsería*, the period of prosperity the towns had enjoyed in the sixteenth century saw the emergence of new offices that were subsidiary to the central treasury. These were mainly linked to the food supply and were created under a new social consensus regarding the functioning of the public market. The emblematic institution was the *Cámara de Trigo* or communal granary, which provided grain not only in the main towns and cities, but also in many villages and small towns, even in cereal-growing areas. More or less temporary boards of one kind or another were also set up to manage public works, such as the creation of infrastructure to supply drinking water. Meanwhile, the *Diputación*, which acted as a standing committee of the Aragonese parliament and protected its rights, provided financial support for these projects out of the revenue raised from customs duties. This public intervention favoured the consolidation of these boards between the mid-sixteenth and the early seventeenth century. While these secondary institutions generated their own administrative organization, their management depended ultimately on the central treasury. Hence, it is to the *Procuraduría* that we must look to discover the council's main sources of funding in all cases.

The revenues of the central treasury comprised the principal municipal assets or *bienes de propios*, consisting of rights and properties controlled by the council, which were keys to the management of the municipality's affairs. Such revenues varied widely depending on local geographical and climatic conditions, and on the historical development of the town.[5] Logically, the payments (known as *cequiajes* or *alfardas*) made by farmers or irrigation communities for the right to use water channels under municipal control were more substantial in irrigated than in largely unirrigated areas. Numerous councils in the Ebro valley, which controlled large tracts of land, parlayed the lease of pasture into a lucrative business. Towns such as Albarracín that exerted considerable political control over neighbouring villages used their power to shift a part of the tax burden onto their rural hinterland. As the cases of Saragossa and Huesca show, however, the feudal dues received consisted of fixed amounts, which became ever less significant for the municipal treasury, especially as new sources of income expanded during the seventeenth century.

Despite these variations, monopolies and charges levied on retail sales of certain goods made up the core of municipal finances in the seventeenth century. Thus, the main revenues were generated on monopolies and charges levied on retail sales of basic necessities (meat, pork belly, fish, bread, wine and oil), although the municipal authorities also introduced new taxes on some raw materials and luxury goods in this century. Data for the towns of Saragossa, Huesca, Daroca and Albarracín indicate that such monopolies and duties brought in between 65 per cent and 80 per cent of municipal revenues in the early decades of the seventeenth century. These rates trended upward in the second quarter of the century, as the fiscal pressure exerted by the monarchy increased.[6] With the exception of Saragossa, where taxation on basic foodstuffs was moderated after the middle of the century, monopolies and charges on foodstuffs peaked at between 80 per cent and 90 per cent of revenues in the closing decades of the seventeenth century. Daroca is the only case where primary sources have allowed the estimation of *sisas*, or temporary in-kind taxes levied on basic foodstuffs. These taxes were usually collected by specific administrations to pay royal services, to defray the cost of public services or to cancel municipal debts. Between 1628 and 1672, *sisas* accounted for 59.87 per cent of all tax revenues raised in Daroca. As the necessary data to estimate the amount of *sisas* is generally unavailable, however, the importance of duties as a whole to municipal revenues is understated in the other towns studied.

The significance of *sisas* as an extraordinary source of income for the municipal treasury stems from the development under the reign of Ferdinand the Catholic (1479–1516) of a stable procedure for the collection of royal subsidies, which lasted until the middle of the seventeenth century.[7] This system depended on municipal taxation, which provided around 78 per cent of services in the sixteenth century, payable by each town and village council based on the number of hearths it contained according to the censuses of 1495 and 1646, and its rights (or lack of them) as an urban centre.[8] The approval of every royal service at the parliament of Aragon or *Cortes* in the sixteenth century allowed town and village councils to apply *sisas* or taxes on basic foodstuffs, especially grain and meat. After collecting these imposts on behalf of the royal treasury for three years, the *municipios de realengo* or royal boroughs were permitted to levy further taxes for three more years to the benefit of the municipal treasury. In seigniorial or ecclesiastical boroughs, however, these additional taxes belonged to the feudal lord. Though every social group had to pay royal taxes or *sisas reales*, the clergy and the nobility were exempt from the additional taxes levied by the council as 'privileged estates'. However, the parliament always allowed councils to choose the specific taxes they would apply to pay the royal service. The towns and cities usually applied *sisas* to pay royal subsidies or boost municipal revenues, but rural settlements, where the communal tradition had deep roots, mostly preferred different forms of direct taxation.

The application of extraordinary taxes by town councils without prior approval from the *Cortes* was forbidden by the act of the Aragonese parliament *De prohibitione sisarum*, passed at Saragossa in 1398.[9] This law sought to preserve the fiscal capacity of citizens and commoners to pay royal subsidies by preventing the municipal elites from making any sharp rise in local taxes. This medieval law was conceived for a territory where the *Cortes* met regularly, and the king needed the subsidies voted because the royal purse was sempiternally empty. However, the parliament was convened less often under the reign of Philip II (1558–98), and as a consequence the royal boroughs had less opportunity to impose *sisas* for their own use. As a partial solution, the municipal authorities could petition the king for licences to impose taxes for specific purposes in the public interest, such as the development of public works. These levies were usually applied to all social groups. The importance of this law became clear when various royal and seigniorial boroughs sought to establish such taxes by stealth to contain their growing indebtedness in the latter decades of the sixteenth century.[10] However, these measures met with opposition from the feudal lords in territories under lay or ecclesiastical control, who considered themselves entitled to the proceeds from the *sisa*. Meanwhile, the impact of the taxes on basic foodstuffs prompted frequent formal complaints to institutions like the *Diputación* on the grounds of illegality where the necessary licences to circumvent local tax laws were not forthcoming. Eventually, the longer intervals between Aragonese parliaments in the seventeenth century (1626, 1645–6, 1677–8, 1684–6) forced the municipalities to negotiate the application of extraordinary taxes with the monarchy in order to reduce their indebtedness in exchange for the concession of particular services and donations.

The remaining municipal revenue sources aside from monopolies and tax charges were of minor significance. The existence of customs duties controlled by the *Diputación*, and royal tolls levied at the borders of the kingdom probably meant that monopolies and levies on other goods, and road and bridge tolls rarely yielded much income. The direct collection of cash from citizens (*repartos* or *compartimentos*) was usually a last resort, although it became more frequent in the seventeenth century. The fields, houses and other properties owned by the council generated only minor revenues, as they were usually let in perpetuity for a modest lease. The revenues generated on buildings used for the transformation of farm produce, such as flour and oil mills, ovens and bakeries were again moderate, as the municipalities were interested above all in ensuring the public supply of basic foodstuffs. Finally, the collection of fines and legal fees brought in minimal sums, as they were assigned either wholly or partially to the complainant, certain council officials or the person appointed to act as the local magistrate. Except for the transfers made to its subsidiary agencies and the provision of credit to the lessees of the main monopolies on basic foodstuffs, the central treasury would rarely lend cash to private parties or institutions in consideration of an annual interest payment. As municipal officials would regularly collect these sources of revenue, councils were not usually owed significant sums, and it was only where *compartimentos* were applied frequently, as in Daroca, that debts were significant enough to warrant the appointment of municipal debt collectors.

Tax Reform in Aragonese Towns and Cities in the Seventeenth Century

In contrast to their economic prosperity in the sixteenth century, town councils experienced a serious financial decline in the seventeenth.[11] Already unable to raise sufficient revenues to tackle the growth in their expenditure in the second half of the sixteenth century, the municipalities' situation worsened in the following century until even the perpetual recourse to contract credit became insufficient. At the same time, wealthy citizens and the lesser nobility had begun to transfer ownership of municipal loans to the clergy through sales or donations, while some town councils sought arrangements with their creditors at the end of the sixteenth century to defer payments or reduce the interest charges on their debts. This strategy became increasingly common in Aragon in the early seventeenth century and was precipitated in 1610 by the expulsion of the *Moriscos*, former Muslims who had been forced to adopt Christianity in 1526. Ordered by King Philip III, the expulsion edicts affected some 14,000 families in Aragon, or 18.85 per cent of the population, and some 127 towns and villages, which recovered only very slowly over the course of the seventeenth century.[12] Faced with the financial decline of the municipalities, the Aragonese parliament legislated in 1626 and again in 1646 to lower the rate of interest charged on their loans to 5 per cent and then 4.54 per cent. Arrangements between town councils and their creditors were subject to ratification by the king in the seventeenth century through the Council of Aragon, an administrative and judicial institution that helped the monarchy to govern the Spanish realms of the Crown of Aragon from the court. As town councils slid inexorably into bankruptcy, periodic reviews of these agreements gradually handed the management of the municipal treasuries over to the *conservadores*, administrators appointed by creditors, who guaranteed in exchange to respect the councils' political and judicial administration. These arrangements aimed to ensure the cancellation of loans or the continuation of interest payments, and they did not entail any reorganization of municipal treasuries in Aragon. Rather, they encouraged constant litigation between councils and the boards of creditors, dominated by the clergy, over the management of communal assets and rights, and the regulation of markets.

Faced with rising indebtedness, the municipal authorities were forced to seek new sources of revenue to stave off bankruptcy. The process was especially difficult for two reasons. First, municipal revenues in Aragon had not kept pace with economic growth in the sixteenth century. This stagnation was a consequence both of the legal obstacles in the way of new taxes and preservation of the medieval model of municipal administration, as well as the voluntary reduction by town councils of their revenues from charges and monopolies on retail sales of basic foodstuffs in order to support domestic demand and expand local public markets. This meant that the municipal authorities were obliged to raise taxation sharply in a period of economic decline, provoking stiff opposition from townspeople, who had grown accustomed to a light tax burden. Meanwhile, neither the *Cortes* nor any other public institution in Aragon took action to remove the legal obstacles that prevented councils from increasing their revenues. As a result, each municipality decided the fiscal measures it wished to adopt and then negotiated implementation with the monarchy, creditors and citizens, a process that further delayed fiscal reforms especially in the early decades of the seventeenth century, which only swelled municipal debt still further. Finally, town councils began to impose taxes on basic foodstuffs by stealth to boost their revenues, but such measures could not prevent their eventual bankruptcy.

The Initial Solution: Creation of New Taxes

As a first reaction to contain their indebtedness, many town councils introduced *arbitrios* or new taxes at the beginning of the seventeenth century.[13] If these measures were initially considered merely a temporary solution, many such taxes became permanent municipal revenue sources over the course of the century. *Arbitrios* usually consisted of monopolies over manufactured products like ice, tobacco, playing cards, distilled spirits, soap, iron and coal. In some cases, these were justified in terms of luxury or the harmful nature of the products concerned, but in most they affected goods the population consumed in large amounts on a daily basis. In any event, the opportunity to impose *arbitrios* arose from the absence of state monopolies in Aragon and they did not face serious opposition either from the 'privileged estates' (nobility and clergy) or the humblest social groups. These taxes emerged in the major towns and cities in the early 1600s. However, as these major towns had more scope to increase their income from taxes on basic foodstuffs, the importance of *arbitrios* gradually declined. In 1651–2, they accounted for 26.58 per cent of the revenues obtained from municipal monopolies in Daroca, but just 18.16 per cent in Saragossa and 16.86 per cent in Huesca.[14] By the mid-seventeenth century, *arbitrios* had become permanent only in more modest towns and villages, where they generated very moderate revenues. They failed to take hold at all in small villages, where there was scant demand for many of the products taxed.

Financial weakness also obliged the municipalities to raise direct cash contributions from the townsfolk more frequently than in the sixteenth century. Known as *repartos*, these levies were applied either to all inhabitants or to specific social groups (merchants, artisans and farmers) in order to defray the costs of royal subsidies or certain municipal services, such as the employment of watchmen to guard farm property, and urban planning and construction. The practice of revenue sharing among residents to pay for a local resident doctor also spread in Aragon from the second quarter of the seventeenth century onwards. At times, this practice faced serious opposition from the 'privileged estates'.[15] The reason was not just the continuity of this annual contribution, but also the view that it was a plebeian tax that ought not to be applied to the clergy or nobles. In fact, the 'privileged estates' only agreed to pay this tax in many towns and villages after protracted negotiations with the municipal authorities, which sometimes even granted the right to participate in the choice of the doctor from among a list of candidates.

Among these new sources of revenue, many town and village councils also created specific taxes earmarked for the reduction of the municipal debt. These contributions were frequently adopted in the last three decades of the sixteenth century, especially in towns under seigniorial or ecclesiastical lordship.[16] In these cases, the councils' financial problems became muddled with the difficulties of the Aragonese high nobility, whose disproportionate spending dragged them gently down into bankruptcy in the second half of the sixteenth century. The difficult financial situation of the councils under seigniorial lordship worsened dramatically in 1610, when they were hit by the expulsion of the *Moriscos* and their revenues from taxes on basic foodstuffs was sharply reduced. Increasingly overwhelmed by the burden of debt built up as a result of loans arranged at the beginning of the seventeenth century, elites, citizens and commoners found themselves obliged to negotiate the adoption of fresh charges (always temporary in principle) to cancel borrowings or meet annual interest payments. This process intensified as the deferrals and partial forgiveness of debts, or temporary reductions in interest payments, arranged with creditors often entailed new taxes in cash or in kind earmarked for the repayment of debts and cancellation of loans. The renegotiation of municipal debt became common in the smaller royal boroughs at the beginning of the seventeenth century, and by the second half of the century the practice spread throughout Aragon to reach the main towns and cities, which had not been much affected by the expulsion of the *Moriscos* and had greater economic resources than other municipalities.

Direct taxation was always an option. One solution imposed by the scarcity of gold and silver coinage was the annual in-kind payment of a part of the main crops produced, a practice that became common in many rural towns and villages. This occurred in numerous seigniorial and ecclesiastical boroughs from the late sixteenth century onwards, after the lords had assigned their creditors rights to levy taxes on their vassals. In districts such as the Matarraña valley and Lower Aragon, the assignment by the ecclesiastical overlords of *primicias*, which consisted of rights over the first crops harvested, allowed the municipalities to raise taxes of this kind beginning in the latter decades of the sixteenth century. The revenues generated were applied to cancel permanent loans in the following century. The tax imposed by the municipal authorities of Caspe in 1615 represented one fifteenth of the cereals harvested and the wool, wine and oil produced, plus other charges levied on the output of artisans and on silk and saffron.[17] In the seigniorial boroughs that had been affected by the expulsion of the *Moriscos*, the charters granted by the overlords to new colonists settling in the vicinity frequently included obligations related to the municipal and seigniorial debt alongside the lord's rights over his new vassals.[18] Not a few of the lay nobility thus found themselves obliged to assume the prior debt of the *Morisco* municipality in consideration of fixed cash sums payable by the new inhabitants in order to ensure the resettlement of deserted towns and villages on their lands.

Another form of direct taxation that was common in the smaller municipalities was the introduction of contributions to pay interest or cancel loans.[19] After collecting the eleventh part of grain, wine and oil produced by taxpayers between 1611 and 1617 to discharge debts, the town council of Barbastro resolved in 1618 to impose a tax equal to 0.4 per cent of the estimated means of every hearth, widows included, for a further ten years. As the legality of this new contribution was open to doubt, the municipality applied for permission from the *Real Audiencia*, the supreme court of justice in Aragon created in the late medieval period. Meanwhile, the village of Molinos belonging to the military order of Calatrava applied in 1644 to tax its inhabitants for twelve years to pay interest after reaching an arrangement with creditors to lower the interest rate on its loans. Where a royal commissioner mediated in such affairs, final terms would be ratified by King Philip IV in Madrid after consultation with the Council of Aragon. Many such agreements between municipalities and creditors were in fact confirmed by the King through the Council of Aragon from 1640 onwards, as the institution increasingly assumed the powers to approve tax reforms in Aragon.

The problem in the way of direct taxation was to distribute the burden fairly among the social groups affected. Thus, tithes on harvests affected landlords and their tenants while leaving rentier groups and the members of the liberal professions (doctors and lawyers) untouched. Conflicting interests also complicated the determination of the tax base. In both cases, the nobility and clergy forcefully contended that they must be legally exempt from such plebeian taxes, a stance that only reduced the number of wealthy taxpayers and increased the burden on other social groups. If some members of the petty nobility agreed to pay taxes as a necessary condition of council office and the continuation of their influence over the municipality, initial negotiations always lowered their contribution. The opposition of wealthy citizens to these initiatives centred on more indirect taxation. These difficulties not only led to tensions and delay but broke the social cohesion of the community and incited tax evasion. The speed with which the council of Barbastro abandoned its efforts to collect the eleventh part of all grain, wine and oil produced by the *vecinos* in order to repay loans in the first half of the seventeenth century clearly reveals how such conflicts limited the returns from and continuity of direct taxation.[20]

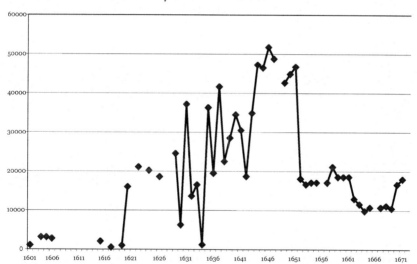

**Figure 4.1: Evolution of *sisas* received by the
municipal treasury of Daroca (1601–72), in *sueldos*.**

Sources: Mateos, *Auge*, pp. 467–8.
Note: The *sueldo* was a unit of account used in Aragon in the sixteenth and seventeenth centuries. After the Castilian system of weight and purity was adopted for all issues of silver coinage in 1519 and 1528, one *sueldo* was equal to half a *real*, the main silver coin minted in sixteenth and seventeenth century Aragon.

The second option was indirect taxation in the form of *sisas* or taxes on consumption of basic foods such as grain, meat and wine. Easier to collect, these charges were linked by tradition to the payment of royal services and to raise funds for public works. Among other towns that had suffered the ravages of the bubonic plague between 1648 and 1654, Jaca, Huesca, Saragossa and Borja introduced local charges applicable to all social strata for several years to recoup the costs of dealing with the epidemic.[21] In Huesca, the council obtained approval for the continuation of these taxes in 1680–7 and 1692–1700 in order to improve the town's water supply.[22] In contrast to the sixteenth century, however, it had become difficult to obtain the cooperation of the 'privileged estates' and the council was forced to make concessions. These problems only reveal the difficulty of maintaining social consensus around the financing of public goods in a period of economic decline, when previous expectations of prosperity are dashed.

Extraordinary taxes or *sisas* were slowly imposed by different town councils (e.g. Calatayud and Daroca) at the beginning of the seventeenth century in order to cancel loans.[23] As the example of Daroca (Figure 4.1) shows, however, a sharp increase in royal taxation after the parliaments of 1626 and 1646 diverted the receipts from *sisas* to pay subsidies to the monarchy between 1628 and 1652. The continuity of these extraordinary taxes to reduce municipal debts was tightly constrained by the need to seek temporary sanction from the King or the Pope. This institutional obstacle was enshrined in the medieval law *De prohibitione sisarum*, approved by parliament in 1398, which required municipalities to obtain a licence to impose the tax from the monarchy in consideration of specific services and donations.[24] Nevertheless, *sisas* were applied in Daroca throughout the seventeenth century and were also adopted by Jaca and Saragossa to reduce their debts in the second half of the century, showing that this form of taxation took root in the larger towns and cities where their indirect character aroused the interest of the municipal oligarchy, despite opposition from the nobility and clergy, who made their support conditional on papal licences granting them exemption as 'privileged estates', especially in the case of the clergy. As the purpose of the taxes was not considered a common benefit by these social groups, any possible concession the councils could offer would be fruitless. Exemption, however, increased the already heavy tax burden on the humblest social groups and bred resistance. These conflicting interests are reflected in the arrangements made by certain towns to hand over control of municipal revenue sources to creditors in the late seventeenth and early eighteenth centuries. The deals made by the municipal elites entailed the constant adoption of annual *sisas* to cancel loans.[25] In contrast, representatives of farmers and craftsmen opposed any prolongation of these indirect taxes after the expiration of licences and defended their replacement by direct taxes.

The Eventual Solution: Rising Taxation of Basic Foodstuffs

Faced with the difficulty of consolidating extraordinary taxes as permanent revenues, town and city councils found themselves obliged to find ways of raising significant, recurring revenues as their indebtedness increased during the seventeenth century without having to negotiate with higher institutions, creditors or other social groups. As a temporary solution, at least in principle, to the need to increase municipal revenues, further charges and monopolies were created on the sale of foodstuffs beginning in the late sixteenth century. This process was accelerated as the councils were forced to become more involved in the management of these revenue sources. Rising taxation and inflation obliged many town councils to switch from leasing the main food monopolies to running them in the late sixteenth and early seventeenth centuries, as private lessees became increasingly wary of the risk of losses caused by price increases. This practice gathered strength between 1620 and 1650 until the return to monopoly leasing in the second half of the seventeenth century due to falling prices for agricultural products.[26] Direct administration by the council oligarchy of monopolies and charges on basic foodstuffs not only facilitated the collection of royal taxes between 1628 and 1652 but also allowed taxes to be raised without the need to petition the monarchy or resort to negotiation with the 'privileged estates' and the townspeople. In all, the higher tax burden applied to basic foods in the period 1628–52 continued to some extent in the second half of the century after royal taxation was reduced. Meanwhile, the lessees of the main food supply monopolies and the managers of communal granaries, butchers' shops and oil boards developed stronger links to the ruling elite in order to maximize their returns, and municipal supervision of local management, formerly carried out by parish representatives, farmers and craftsmen, was restricted.

Aside from dearth years (1605–6, 1614–15, 1630–1, 1651–2), which obliged towns to increase wheat supplies and renounce any profit, the tax burden on foodstuffs allowed towns to siphon cash from the local granary, oil board and butchers' shops to the central treasury and slow the growth of their deficits.[27] The process was especially quick in the capital, Saragossa, where the city council seized on the strategy to preserve its political and economic dominance in Aragon (see Figure 4.2). While these transfers did not save town councils from bankruptcy, they did force them to abandon the sixteenth century policy of supporting local demand for foodstuffs. The stocks sold by granaries, oil boards and butchers' shops declined, especially as demand fell in the second half of the seventeenth century due to demographic and economic decline.[28] This process was slower in Saragossa, where demand was in any case greater, but it was abrupt in many smaller towns and villages. Smaller sales from the granaries were accompanied by loans and sales of wheat on credit to solvent residents for return or repayment after the harvest in order to ensure supplies for the population in dearth years, provide seed stock and replenish the granaries' stocks. Some oil boards also made loans of this kind in the second half of the seventeenth century, for example in the Matarraña valley, given the need to maintain a certain safety stock to ease possible shortages.

Many municipal elites imposed this form of taxation not only because it was indirect and easy to collect, but also because it suited their personal interests in the marketing of agricultural products. Thus, the tax pressure was especially acute on bread and meat, because the demand for these basic commodities was inelastic and they were in any case associated with the collection of royal taxes. However, the burden intensified from the mid-seventeenth century on as the municipal elites found incentives to export meat and grain to other territories such as Catalonia, which made internal consumption less significant to their economic interests. This process is clearly visible in municipal accounting.[29] The revenue generated from the butchers' shops of Daroca between 1651 and 1670 grew 513.40 per cent compared to the period 1550–70, and in an extreme case, this income rose in Saragossa by 1215.84 per cent between 1651 and 1695 compared to the amount brought in between 1550 and 1594 (see Figure 4.2). The Castilian army was billeted in Fraga during the Catalan war of secession (1640–52), which allowed the council to reduce its debt by almost 40 per cent between 1644 and 1648, as a result of the heavy taxes imposed on the principal foodstuffs, especially on wheat and meat. In Barbastro, the conflict saw troops quartered and the resettlement of refugees from the eastern part of Aragon, which again increased the income generated from the butchers' shops between 1641 and 1650.

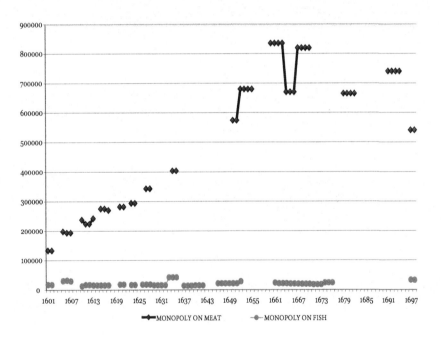

Figure 4.2: **Evolution of municipal revenues linked to monopolies on the sale of fish and meat in Saragossa (1601–98), in *sueldos*.**

Sources: Mateos, 'La política municipal', pp. 327, 337, notes 22, 83.

The counterpoint to this process was the taxation of agricultural products where the interest of the municipal elites was focused on local markets. Taxes on oil and wine were lighter and more intermittent than on grain and meat during the seventeenth century and were in fact cut to the point where they sometimes generated less revenue than in the preceding century.[30] The intention was either to stimulate supply or facilitate sales of local wine or oil in the market and limit competition from outside products in loss-making districts and those where products were of poor quality. Duties on wine in Daroca from 1651 to 1672 produced only 37 per cent of the income generated between 1550 and 1570. With the occasional exception of royal taxation, specific duties on wine were not applied in Huesca or Saragossa throughout the seventeenth century. The aim of this fiscal restraint was to sidestep residents' attempts to fix taxes in proportion to the harvest and to assure consumption of surpluses to the benefit of the local elite. In Saragossa oil was an insignificant component of revenues from local surcharges, and no sales monopoly was created until 1669. Even then taxation remained very light until the end of the seventeenth century. Meanwhile, regulation of the fish supply was influenced by religious considerations because fish was essential to the population in the periods of fasting prescribed by the Catholic Church. As a consequence, increases in the fixed taxes on fish in monopolies and other charges stayed moderate: 77.58 per cent in Daroca and only 31.12 per cent in Saragossa over the same periods studied as in the case of meat.

Economic and Social Results of Urban Fiscal Reform

Municipal taxation of basic foodstuffs increased in the seventeenth century, especially in towns and cities, because demand for these products was inelastic and taxes were easy to collect and well aligned with the commercial interests of the municipal oligarchies. This tax pressure eventually led to a split between the elites and the ordinary townspeople, especially those belonging to the humblest groups.[31] Taxpayers were poorly represented in municipal government, less protected from its actions, and more exposed to what was a regressive tax system. They therefore felt it was legitimate to defraud the council and trade outside the public market. Meanwhile, the 'privileged estates' also accused councils of creating new taxes on foodstuffs without their consent and demanded exemption. Their resistance was especially vigorous in those towns and cities where the taxes concerned raised significant revenues. The reaction of the clergy was especially important given the economic power, social influence and privileged position of the Church. As a consequence, places of worship and convents became hotbeds of cheating and fraud. The legal battle begun by the cathedral chapter of Saragossa in the middle of the seventeenth century against heavy fiscal pressure on the part of the municipality eventually ended in victory when it was licensed by king Philip V in 1722–4 to install its own butchers' shops for the consumption of the city's clergy. The existence of private ovens in towns and cities since the Middle Ages, and the donation or sale of ovens and bakeries to nobles, citizens and ecclesiastical institutions by King Philip IV (1621–65) also fostered cheating and affected municipal control over the bread market in the seventeenth century, above all in Saragossa. Tax evasion by residents also affected municipal regulation of the market and the tax burden in rural towns, which were more closely concerned with the agrarian economy, sometimes even forcing the authorities to cut taxes on basic foodstuffs, although unregulated activity was not systematic enough to supply local markets efficiently.

Confronted with their diminished ability to supply and control the market, the town councils handed over the initiative in this matter to individuals under their supervision,[32] for example allowing bakers and the owners of ovens greater leeway to buy wheat in the market, either from dealers working in the surrounding areas, or from merchants and carriers. In the last quarter of the seventeenth century, the Saragossa city council permitted its citizens to sell wheat from their homes and barns at a somewhat lower price than in the public grain market. From the middle of the century onwards, the declining activity of the communal granaries increased the interest of municipalities like Fraga, Barbastro, Daroca and Albarracín in regulating or taxing brokerage charged on private transactions in the grain market. Without repealing their monopolies, the councils also allowed merchants and townspeople to sell fresh or dried fish and relaxed controls over the meat supply, especially in livestock areas. The greater scope granted to private initiative and the declining purchasing power of the population made the agricultural markets in Aragon more competitive and in time more fluid and efficient. These developments could not, however, prevent the worst effects of the most serious shortages on the urban population, or the deterioration of the public food supply system.

These reforms generated other adverse economic outcomes, as the evolution of industrial and craft production clearly shows. In the context of declining domestic demand for manufactured goods, the rising prices of essential goods drove up the cost of Aragonese industrial output from the middle of the seventeenth century onwards. Already characterized by poor workmanship, quality decreased still further as master craftsmen restricted access to their guilds in order to benefit their sons and slow the influx of cheaper, better-made French manufactured goods.[33] The councils, led by Saragossa, were aware of this reality and supported the protectionist legislation voted by the *Cortes* in 1626, 1645–6 and 1677–8. These laws, which involved a temporary ban on the import of foreign textiles and raised customs duties, were ineffective and were finally repealed in 1684–6.[34] Despite their general support for industry, many town councils lowered some of the entry barriers raised by the guilds and allowed outside craftsmen to work in order to improve the local supply. This process was easier in many smaller towns where the guilds' grip on the markets was looser and they were less well organized. In fixing the prices of manufactured goods to moderate the upward pressure from the guilds, the councils considered not only the cost of raw materials but also the market price of grain, in order to ensure a living for artisans.[35] Nevertheless, all the efforts of the municipal authorities and guilds could not prevent a tide of higher quality and lower cost French manufactures from dominating a market in which demand was shrinking and the purchasing power of the population was falling.

In the main towns and cities like Saragossa, the rising cost of food pushed agricultural labourers and the artisans of the building trades to seek higher wages, particularly between 1625 and 1675. The growing labour shortage added force to their demands, which the councils could only partially contain by taxing wages and limiting the mobility of labourers and tradesmen.[36] Higher costs in turn affected new construction by private parties and public institutions, with the exception of religious buildings erected as the Catholic Church grew in power. Despite the fall in domestic demand, the rising exports of farm products (wheat, meat and oil) to Catalonia and Valencia provided some incentive for expansion in agriculture, especially in the second half of the seventeenth century.[37] Thus, a wide sector of the lesser nobility and the wealthier citizens acquired land from indebted individuals and councils, a process facilitated by their involvement in municipal government.[38] The Church also increased its estates, purchasing land and receiving donations from private individuals.[39] Though farmers endeavoured to align output with changes in demand and began to specialize to some degree,[40] there is no evidence of any real effort to improve farm productivity of the lands, as had occurred in Aragon in the sixteenth century.[41] Lumbered with enormous debts and lacking the means of production in the countryside, many landowners, merchants and moneylenders preferred to extract surpluses from the peasantry as an easier way to make a profit.[42]

Falling consumption and rising production costs caused by taxation discouraged agricultural and industrial investment by the wealthy in favour of the rents that could be generated from land, real property and loan principal. The evolution of the Aragonese mercantile bourgeoisie in the second half of the seventeenth century is a clear example of this process. Despite a partial recovery after the turn-of-the-century decline, the merchant class was not strong enough to prevent the active presence of French merchants in the kingdom and therefore became ever more focused on less commercial and more conservative activities.[43] This economic and social strategy is exemplified by the acquisition of lands from indebted nobles, the purchase and lease of property to individuals and the issue of loans to the Spanish monarchy, all activities that gained ground among the mercantile bourgeoisie in this period. Finally, the decay of economic activities depressed towns and cities as centres of trade, production and services, making them more markedly agrarian, although their modest size softened the impact of demographic losses in the seventeenth century.

Conclusions

The reform of municipal taxation in the kingdom of Aragon met with serious problems in the seventeenth century. First, these reforms took place during a period of decline, when new taxes increased the burden for a smaller, poorer population. Second, taxpaying citizens had grown accustomed to relatively low levels of taxation in the sixteenth century. Third, the kingdom's laws and institutional framework greatly complicated the introduction of new taxes on basic foodstuffs. Unfortunately, the virtual prohibition of new taxes affected the main sources of municipal revenues in the seventeenth century, such as monopolies and charges on the sales of basic goods. However, no public institution in Aragon could provide general legal avenues to circumvent local laws and reform the municipal tax system. As a result, every town council had to find its own solution, usually resorting to negotiation with higher institutions, creditors and the different social groups making up the residents of towns and cities. This situation led to delays in the adoption of fiscal reforms and often prevented a lasting increase in urban taxation in the early decades of the seventeenth century, prompting the expansion of municipal debt.

The negotiation of specific taxes to cancel municipal loans reveals the differing interests of urban social groups in the matter of tax reforms. Direct taxation, which was more usual in small towns and villages, encountered frequent problems related to the distribution of the burden among taxpaying citizens, which reduced both the yield from and the continuity of these taxes. Meanwhile, the introduction of charges on basic foodstuffs, an alternative that was commonly adopted in the larger towns and cities, was supported by wealthy citizens because such indirect taxes were easier to collect and were better suited to the interests of parties involved in the trade in farm products. In both cases, the 'privileged estates' of the nobility and clergy refused to pay 'plebeian' taxes of this kind, holding themselves to be exempt. As other new revenue sources were insufficient, town councils were forced to increase their revenues from monopolies on basic foodstuffs, especially wheat and meat. If some town councils moderated fiscal pressure, this decision often resulted in an increase in their indebtedness and sometimes even precipitated bankruptcy. Both the commoners and the 'privileged estates' protested against this obsolete and regressive tax system, demanding that local laws be upheld in the face of any abrupt hike in municipal taxation without licence or negotiation. Logically, residents increasingly resorted to cheating. This had adverse effects for public control of the market, and it could sometimes even limit municipal taxation. As their power to intervene waned, the councils had gradually ceded the initiative in the market to private parties under their supervision. As a result, the regional market became more fluid and efficient, but this could not prevent the worst economic and social effects of the deterioration in the public food supply system on the population.

This increased fiscal pressure on basic foodstuffs had wide-ranging consequences. Combined with economic and demographic decline, it discouraged consumption, lowered living standards and cut the purchasing power and ability to save of a large part of the population. This process was stronger in urban centres and intensified in the second half of the seventeenth century. Especially in the main towns, the higher price of food and the shortage of labour encouraged wage demands among agricultural labourers and in the building trades to the detriment of investment in these activities. In the context of declining domestic demand for manufactured goods, the rising prices of essential goods raised production costs in industry and the crafts while reducing the competitiveness of Aragonese products in the market because foreign manufactured goods were both cheaper and better made. The contraction in demand and higher production costs caused by municipal taxation discouraged agricultural and industrial investment and provided an incentive for rent-seeking among wealthy citizens. All of these developments clearly depressed towns and cities as centres of trade, production and services, making them more markedly agrarian.

5 TAXATION AND DEBT IN THE EARLY MODERN CASTILIAN CITIES: THE CASE OF SEVENTEENTH-CENTURY MADRID

José Ignacio Andrés Ucendo and Ramón Lanza García[1]

The evolution of the fiscal and financial systems set up by European towns during the early modern period was led by the interplay between local traditions and the process of state formation. Being key points for the accumulation of capital and wealth through trade and manufacture, the European states of the early modern period tended to increase the resources drawn from their towns by means of finance and taxation. The cities saw this development from an ambiguous perspective: on the one hand, the urban oligarchies looked with suspicion on the repercussions of state interference in their activities, but, on the other, they welcomed the protection for the expansion of trade and manufacture that central government might offer. It may be argued, then, that the exact consequences of the advance in the process of state formation on European urban centres depended on which one of these two effects prevailed. In the best case, the state set up an institutional framework that contributed to the enforcement of property rights, the lowering of transaction costs and the solving of market failures, whereas in the worst instances the rising power of the state posed agency and commitment problems that curtailed the prospects for political and economic advance of their cities.[2]

These possibilities have attracted the interest of the researchers and the aim of this essay is to examine how the Castilian state influenced the development of the fiscal and financial systems of the cities of the country during the seventeenth century through an analysis of the case of its capital, Madrid. Seventeenth century Castile is usually considered as one example which shows how the rising fiscal and financial needs of the state suffocated the prospects for urban and economic advance as a result of the close fiscal and financial links between the Castilian cities and the Crown.[3] Such links were particularly visible in Madrid, which became an appendix, in financial and fiscal terms, of the Royal Treasury during the central decades of the century. Between 1629 and 1679 Madrid granted 19 million ducats to the Crown in many gifts (*donativos*), especially from

1653 to 1679. As it will be seen in part I, these *donativos* caused the expansion of the city debt and its tax revenues. The greater part of the growing revenues collected by Madrid was devoted to the interest on the debt originated by the gifts of 1629–79, so that the city incomes actually funded the needs of the Royal Treasury rather than those of Madrid and this exerted a lasting influence on the later economic and social history of the Castilian capital, analysed in part II, below. After paying their interest to the owners of the city debt, Madrid was left with little room for the supply of public services to its inhabitants. This situation was worsened by the regressive features of the fiscal system of the Castilian capital. The taxes collected in Madrid by the Crown and the town council were levied upon the consumption of basic foodstuffs (especially meat and wine) and they exerted a strong influence on prices and wage levels. During the last third of the century taxation raised Madrid's price levels around 15–25 per cent, reducing the real wages earned by a building worker in the same measure, which may be considered another proof of the regressive trends of the Castilian Royal and municipal taxation of the time. Other features, such as the payment of *refacciones* and the generous tax exemptions granted to foreign ambassadors, caused the regressive features already prevailing in the fiscal and financial system of the capital to become even worse.

Madrid was the most relevant exception to the crisis and stagnation of Castilian towns during the seventeenth century. This raises the question of knowing to what extent the situation described in parts I and II, below, was representative of the rest of the towns of the country, and part III addresses this issue. There are sound reasons to suggest that the case of Madrid should have been fairly representative. The Castilian cities reached the first decades of the eighteenth century suffering the effects of heavy indebtedness caused by their close links with the Royal Treasury, and this was aggravated by a regressive fiscal system which rested on indirect taxation, although it is also worth stressing that such trends appear to have been especially important in the Castilian capital.[4]

The fact that the Madrid case can be considered representative of the other Castilian cities is particularly relevant for the purposes of this paper. Parts I and II suggest that the fiscal and financial system developed by the city authorities in the capital was oriented towards the payment of the interest of the municipal debt. To achieve this objective, the town council introduced many indirect taxes whose burden fell on the shoulders of the lower and middle sorts of the city population. This set in motion a redistributive process that benefited the narrow circle of the owners of the annuities issued by the town. It is admitted that states have to face agency and commitment problems.[5] Agency problems arise when the power of the state is directed towards the satisfaction of its own interests rather than those of its citizens, something which may eventually lead to the emergence of serious commitment problems if citizens decide to follow opportunistic behaviours as an answer. It seems clear that most Madrileños and Castilians did not reap the benefits they were entitled to in return for the sums they paid to the Royal Treasury and the town, in what resembles a typical form of agency problem. This situation was aggravated by the highly regressive character of a fiscal system which rested on indirect taxation and created a good climate for the massive development of tax evasion and all kind of opportunistic behaviours. These difficulties were a serious obstacle in the path towards the development of a notion of citizenship in Madrid and other Castilian cities which might have solved the coordination and commitment problems which hampered the political and economic development of the country. When we remember that this was mainly due to the way the fiscal and financial system set up by the city evolved as a consequence of the granting of *donativos* to the Crown, then it does not seem too risky to argue that the close subordination of Madrid to the Crown in the fiscal and financial arena should have been an important reason of such failure.

I.

The course of Madrid's fiscal and financial history during the seventeenth and eighteenth centuries was heavily determined by the ties between the council and the Crown. In 1629 Madrid granted to the Royal Treasury a gift of 60,000 ducats, and this opened a new phase in the fiscal and financial history of the city which lasted until 1679.[6] During the half-century between 1629 and 1679 Madrid provided the Crown with around 19 million Castilian ducats in a group of different *donativos*, being particularly important those of the years 1653–79, when the capital granted 17 million Castilian ducats to the Crown in nearly 90 donatives.[7]

The *donativos* of this period caused the simultaneous expansion of Madrid's debt. To raise the sums offered in each *donativo* the city issued annuities (*efectos de villa*). In order to provide its capital with a safe source of revenue to pay their interests to the owners of the annuities (*efectistas*), the Crown enabled the town council to create new municipal taxes, but this measure proved itself incomplete, and the next step was that from 1653 a substantial part of the royal taxes to be collected in the city and its fiscal district were also transferred by the Crown to its capital.[8]

During the early modern period Madrileños paid taxes to both the Crown and the town council. As in the rest of the country, the taxes collected by the Royal Treasury in Madrid were indirect. The most important were the *alcabala*, the four *cientos* and the *millones*, plus the tobacco monopoly. The *alcabala* (first collected in 1342) and the four *cientos* (introduced between 1639 and 1667) were sales taxes levied on a broad range of products, with the remarkable exception of bread. The *alcabala* amounted to 10 per cent of the price of all the products sold in Castile and the four *cientos* to 4 per cent, so taken together the fiscal burden levied by the Crown for both taxes should have amounted to 14 per cent of the price of all commodities, although in practical terms this percentage was considerable less, hovering around 5–7 per cent. The *millones* tax was created at the end of the sixteenth century and its collection, which lasted (as that of the *alcabalas* and *cientos*) until the liberal reforms of the first half of the nineteenth century, was consolidated in 1601. The *millones* soon became the most important royal tax. Unlike the *alcabala* and *cientos*, its main burden fell on vinegar, olive oil and, especially, meat and wine, and its arrival marked the beginning of a trend thanks to which the taxes on meat and wine soon achieved a central place in the sources of fiscal revenues of the Royal Treasury.[9]

Madrileños also paid taxes to their town council to fund the ordinary expenditures of the city. As it was the norm in most cities of the country, the taxes levied in Madrid by the town council were indirect and their burden basically fell on products also taxed by the *alcabala*, *cientos* and *millones* such as fish, olive oil, soap, wax, coal and especially meat and wine. In 1580 Madrid created a group of taxes on wine, mutton, pork, lamb and soap (the *Sisas Ordinarias*). Trying to obtain revenues to face the growing expenditures caused by the permanent settlement of the court in 1606, Madrid introduced new taxes during the first third of the century which raised the fiscal revenues of the city treasury from little more than 25 million maravedis (mrs) in 1606 to 113 million in 1631.[10]

Although the introduction of taxes (called *sisas* by the city clerks) did not cease during the third and fourth decades of the century, the city revenues remained stable until 1653 at around the levels of 1631.[11] In November 1653, Madrid granted the Crown the first *donativo* of the period 1653–79 and this paved the way for the sudden rise of the city incomes during the third quarter of the century.

To provide Madrid with enough income to pay the interest on the debts owed to the buyers of the city annuities, the Crown allowed its capital to create new municipal taxes and, as this proved not enough, from 1653 the Crown also began to transfer to Madrid a substantial part of the *servicios de millones* collected in the capital and its fiscal district, so that after 1679 the city Treasury controlled slightly more than 80 per cent of the sums collected in the capital and its fiscal district. This marked the birth of the *Sisas Reales*. The transfer of most part of the *servicios de millones* to the capital and the introduction of new municipal taxes were the main reasons for the sudden rise of the city revenues after 1653, whose extent may be appreciated in Table 5.1.

Table 5.1: Average yearly value of the fiscal revenues of Madrid, 1621–1700 (in million of maravedis).

	(1)	(2)	(3)	(4)
1621–5	114		*114*	8
1626–30	118		*118*	10
1631–5	110.5		*110.5*	8.5
1636–40	95		*95*	13
1641–5	99		*99*	10
1646–50	116		*116*	17.5
1651–5	137	6	*143*	32
1556–60	165	65	*230*	104.5
1661–5	210	108.5	*318.5*	192
1666–70	257	182	*439*	313.5
1671–5	279	194	*473*	345
1676–80	322	238	*560*	407
1681–5	233	225	*458*	348
1686–90	193	190	*383*	285
1691–95	188	192	*380*	284
1696–00	187	192	*379*	281

(1): average yearly value of the taxes levied by the City Treasury. (2): average yearly value of the *Sisas Reales* transferred by the Crown to Madrid. (3): average yearly value of the fiscal revenues of Madrid, (1) + (2). (4): average yearly value of the revenues of Madrid devoted to pay the interest on the municipal debt. Source: J. I. Andrés, 'Fiscalidad real y fiscalidad municipal', appendix 1 and 2.

Table 5.1 shows that the revenues of Madrid increased fivefold, from a yearly average of 114 million mrs in 1621–5 to a peak of 560 million mrs in 1676–80, well above price levels which during the same period rose to a comparatively modest 229 index.[12] Although after the measures of fiscal relief of the beginning of the eighties the yearly average value of the revenues of the town fell to around 380 million mrs and stabilized around such levels until 1700, nonetheless they were still well above the levels attained in the first decades of the century.

A substantial part of the rise in the fiscal revenues of the Castilian capital during the central decades of the century was due to the transfer to Madrid of those *servicios de millones* previously collected by the Crown (*Sisas Reales*) whose average yearly value soared from 6 million mrs in 1651–5 to 238 million mrs in 1676–80. From the very moment they were transferred to the city in return for the granting of *donativos* to the Crown, the *millones* disappeared from the Crown records and became listed, as *Sisas Reales*, in the tax records of the capital. A good idea of importance of the *Sisas Reales* for the city treasury may be gauged from the fact that during the last two decades of the century these taxes amounted to around 50 per cent of the fiscal revenues of Madrid.

The introduction during the middle years of the century of new taxes to pay their interest to the *efectistas* was the other cause of the rise in the revenues of the Castilian capital. The average yearly value of the taxes collected by the city (excluding the *Sisas Reales*) rose from around 100 million mrs in 1621–55 to 322 million mrs in 1676–80, falling to slightly less than 200 million mrs during the last decades of the century, when they provided the city treasury with the other 50 per cent of its fiscal incomes.[13]

The rise of Madrid revenues had long-lasting consequences. At the end of the seventeenth century Madrid was the town with the most important fiscal revenues of Castile, and it managed to keep this position during the eighteenth century.[14] However, such growth had been prompted by the need of funding, although indirectly, the royal expenditures, so the city treasury was closely subordinated to the convenience of the Crown. Both the taxes created by the local authorities during the middle decades of the century and the *Sisas Reales* shared the common destiny of paying the Royal needs rather than those of the town, as may be seen in column 4 of Table 5.1, which shows that during the last third of the century Madrid invested nearly 75 per cent of its fiscal revenues in the payment of the interest of the *efectos*.

The upsurge of Madrid's revenues drove the simultaneous rise of the global fiscal burden which fell on the shoulders of the city inhabitants. As should be expected, the close subordination of the city treasury to the Crown was the main force behind the upsurge (see Table 5.2).

Table 5.2: Fiscal burden in Madrid, measured in the number of daily wages of a building worker.

	(1)	(2)	(3)	(4)	(5)
1629	8.5	0.5	6	6.5	9
1654	17.2	2.2	5.7	7.9	19.5
1683	11	16.7	5,6	22.3	27.7
1695	9.7	14.4	4.8	19.2	24.1

(1): number of daily wages of a Madrid's building worker needed to pay the Royal taxes. (2): daily wages needed to pay those municipal taxes used to fund Royal expenditure. (3): daily wages needed to pay those municipal taxes funding the ordinary expenditures of the city. (4): daily wages needed to pay all municipal taxes (2)+(3). (5): daily wages needed to pay both the Royal taxes and the municipal taxes which funded the Crown expenditure (1)+(2).

Table 5.2 shows that, measured in the number of daily wages that a Madrilenian building worker had to use to pay his taxes to the town council, the burden of municipal taxation more than trebled, from 6.57 days in 1629 to nearly 20 days in 1695. This increase was brought by the growing importance of those taxes levied by the town council to pay the interests of the *efectos*. As can be seen in column 2, the daily wages that a Madrilenian building worker should have had to devote to such an end rose from 0.5 days in 1629 to 14.4 in 1695 (after peaking in 16.7 in 1683). If we add the daily wages needed to pay the royal taxes of column 1, Table 5.2 shows that during the second half of the seventeenth century the fiscal burden of taxes used to fund the Crown needs, either directly (*millones, alcabalas* and *cientos*) or indirectly (*Sisas Reales* and most of the municipal taxes), hovered around twenty to twenty-eight daily wages of a building worker, whereas during the same period the daily wages that the same worker should have had to devote to the pay the taxes which funded the ordinary expenditures of Madrid remained stable around four to six days.[15]

Tables 5.1 and 5.2 show that, measured in nominal terms and in the number of daily wages, during the last decades of the century the value of the taxes controlled by the town council was two times that of the taxes levied by the Crown in Madrid. It could be argued, then, that in the years around 1700 Madrid had become a well-endowed capital from a fiscal point of view, but this should not hide the fact that most part of the city revenues were used to pay the interest on the municipal debt, which experienced a sudden upsurge between 1653 and 1679 as a result of the granting of gifts (*donativos*) to the Crown. Perhaps better than anything else, the *donativos* reflect the subordination of Madrid to the Royal Treasury in the financial arena and in part II we will turn to some of the consequences of such subordination.

II.

To raise the sums granted to the Royal Treasury in each *donativo* Madrid expanded its municipal debt, issuing *efectos de villa*. Although from a legal point of view the *efectos* were financial assets like the *censos consignativos* and Madrid had the right to pay back the principals, the sudden expansion of the city debt soon made it impossible to achieve this objective. In 1665 Madrid's debt was nearly eight times the yearly value of its fiscal revenues and at the end of the century this number had risen to twenty. Not surprisingly then, the idea of redeeming the principals of the city debt was soon relegated to a secondary place by the more attainable objective of paying regularly the interests of the *efectos*, which became in practical terms annuities whose existence lasted until the last years of the nineteenth century.

The interest rate of the *efectos* was high by the Castilian standards during most of the seventeenth century. The purchases of public debt bonds issued by the Royal Treasury (*juros*) had been one of the favourite investments of the Castilian oligarchies during the sixteenth century, but the appeal of this financial asset began to vanish after 1608 and 1621, when the interest rate of the Castilian *juros* was reduced to 5 per cent. This was not the only attack against the profitability of the Castilian public debt bonds, because from 1625 and, especially, 1634–5, the Crown turned to a policy of continuous cuts in the sums annually paid to its *juris-tas* which amounted to a new reduction of the interest rate of the *juros* well below the 5 per cent settled in 1608 and 1621.[16] If we also consider that during this same period the Castilian economy went through a deep crisis which disheartened investment in agriculture, manufacture and trade, then it is easy to understand that the owners of the substantial wealth accumulated in the country faced the problem of finding safe havens for their investments, and Madrid took good note of this. Until 1670 the interest rate of the annuities issued by the Castilian capital (10 per cent) was twice that of the Castilian public debt bonds, settled at 5 per cent since 1621. It should also be added that, unlike the *juros*, the *efectos de villa* did not suffer any discount in the interest rates up until 1670, something which helps to understand the warm welcome these assets enjoyed among investors.[17]

After the *donativos* of 1653–69 the city debt soared from 2 million ducats to 10 million, so that in the latter year Madrid had to divert 82 per cent of its fiscal revenues to pay the interest of the *efectos*. This drove the town council to cut the interest rates of its annuities to 8 per cent in 1670. The new interest rate was nonetheless still higher than that of the *juros*, and the demand of *efectos* remained popular. Between 1670 and 1679 the city debt continued to expand, from 10.5 million ducats in the first year to nearly 19 million in the latter. From 1675 to 1679 the payment of the interests drew nearly 90 per cent of the municipal revenues. The situation was untenable in the long run, and prompted new cuts in the interest rates of the *efectos*, reduced to 5 per cent in 1680 and 4 per cent in 1684. Thanks to such cuts, the burden of the interest on the municipal debt experienced a relief, falling to a still high 70–5 per cent of the municipal expenditure during the last years of the century, although it was not until after 1703, when the interest of the city annuities was reduced to 3 per cent, that the payment of the interests of the *efectos* hovered around 60 per cent of the city incomes.[18]

Obviously, the burden of city debt was extremely high, particularly during the second half of the seventeenth century. Driven by the low value cooper coin manipulations, price levels in Madrid rose from an index 100 in 1653 to 174.5 in 1679, before falling to 111 in 1700, after the deflationary measures of 1680. During the same period the principals invested in the city debt rose well above price levels, from 2 million ducats in 1653 to 19 million in 1679, so their value measured in real terms grew from and index 100 in 1653 to 544 in 1679. As the town council had decided not to redeem the principals lent by the owners of the *efectos*, its debt stabilized at around 19 million ducats after 1679 and the value of this sum, in real terms, experienced a substantial rise after the fall in price levels brought by the deflationary measures implemented in 1680. The burden of the Madrid's debt also rose in 'per capita' terms. The city population peaked at 130,000 inhabitants in 1631, and then experienced a moderate fall until the final years of the century, when it regained the levels previously attained in 1631.[19] As a result, if in 1629 each Madrileño had to divert 0.45 Castilian ducats to the payment of the interests of the municipal debt, in 1700 this sum had become 5.7 ducats; nearly 8 per cent of the yearly income of an average Madrilenian building worker.

It is worth stressing that the indebtedness of the Castilian capital at the end of the century seems to have been high as compared to other European towns. Measured in 'per capita' terms, the value of the debt of the city of Amsterdam in 1680 was 405 silver grams and the yearly interests amounted to another 20.4 silver grams, whereas in that same year the value of Madrid's debt was 2,786 silver grams and the interest amounted to nearly 140 grams.[20]

The payment of the interest conditioned the municipal expenditure of Madrid during the second half of the seventeenth century and the eighteenth. As has been emphasized above, most of the city revenues paid the interests of the *efectos*, which curtailed the potential of the town council to supply public services to its inhabitants.

Given the nearly exclusive involvement of the royal government in foreign policy issues, local councils had a relevant role as providers of public services in early modern Castile and a basic part of the communication and transport infrastructure of the country was funded by them. Table 5.3 shows that, after paying the interests of its debt, Madrid was left with too little to fund its public services. In 1685 only a paltry 10 per cent of the city expenditures was used to such ends, mainly in the keeping of urban infrastructure and the funding of the city hospitals. Although Table 5.3 shows that this percentage experienced a moderate rise during the first years of the eighteenth century, it seems too low when compared with that invested by the local authorities of other cities, such as those of Zwolle in 1709 and Amsterdam in 1756, whose expenditures in the town hall, education, urban property and infrastructure amounted to 49 per cent and 67 per cent respectively of the total municipal expenditure, something made possible, among other things, because the interest on the debt of both cities required a moderate, especially by the Castilian standards, part of the urban expenditures (25 per cent and 2 per cent respectively).[21]

Table 5.3: Municipal expenditure in Madrid, 1685–1733 (in percentages).

	1685 (%)	1706 (%)	1721 (%)	1733 (%)
Interests	71	72	69	62.6
Religious 'refacción'	4	3.2	8	8
Crown 'refacción'	1			
Ambassadors	6.3	5.1		
Wages	1	1.2	4	10
Public services	10	12.6	18.4	16.5
Festivities	3.8	1.2	0.6	1
Miscellaneous	2.9	4.7		1.9

Sources: AVM, Secr. 3–268–18 and P. Madoz, *Diccionario geográfico-histórico-estadístico de España y de sus posesiones de Ultramar* (1848), (Agualarga: Madrid, 1999), pp. 479–84.

As has already been explained in part I, to pay the interests of the *efectos* Madrid turned to a group of indirect taxes levied on commodities also taxed by the Royal Treasury, such as meat and, above all, wine. During the last two decades of the century, the taxes levied on meat provided the city treasury with around 35 per cent of its fiscal revenues, whereas those levied on wine provided another 45 per cent. Taken together, then, between 1680 and 1700 around 80 per cent of the ordinary revenues of Madrid came from taxes on meat and wine, and the incidence of such kind of taxation on the prices of both commodities was high. During the same decades, municipal taxes amounted to 50 per cent and to 27–30 per cent of the retail price of a litre of wine and a kilogram of mutton respectively. To this it should be added that royal taxes were another 11 per cent and 8 per cent, so both types of taxes amounted to 61 per cent and 35–8 per cent of the retail price of wine and meat sold in Madrid at the end of the century. Our estimates suggest that Madrilenian consumers devoted around 33 per cent of their daily expenditure to the purchase of these commodities and to this it should be added that other foodstuffs such as olive oil and fish, whose burden in the daily expenditure of Madrileños hovered around 10 per cent, were also heavily taxed. Between 1681 and 1700 municipal taxes amounted to 20 per cent of the retail price of a kilogram of olive oil and to 6–10 per cent of the price of a kilogram of fish, whereas those taxes levied by the Crown on both commodities were another 6–9 per cent and 20–29 per cent respectively.[22]

Not every commodity was, however, as heavily taxed as fish, olive oil, meat or wine. During the last decades of the century the taxes levied on other products such as fruit, vinegar, eggs, textiles and coal were collected by the Royal Treasury and amounted to around 6 per cent of their retail price (although coal had been heavily taxed by the town council before 1680), and to this it should be added that bread, the most important product in the Castilian and European diet by far, was virtually tax exempt.

Although the tax exemption of bread and the relatively light tax burden which fell on other commodities dampened the incidence of taxation on Madrid price and wage levels, the heavy taxation on fish, olive oil, meat and wine had the opposite effect. During the last decades of the seventeenth century, taxes raised price levels in Madrid 15–25 per cent, reducing real wages by the same extent, and the main responsibility for this lay in those taxes collected by the town, which increased price levels around 16–17 per cent during the same period, reducing real wages in a similar measure.[23]

Latest research on the social profile of the buyers of urban annuities in Flemish and Dutch cities during the early modern period has shown that the ownership of these financial assets was widespread among a broad range of social groups. The investment in the municipal debt issued by those cities was seen as a way of providing many social categories with a sound source of income in times of infirmity and old age, which helped to ameliorate the worst redistributive effects of the indirect taxes collected in those same cities to pay the interest on the urban annuities.[24] Although this issue would deserve more research, the ownership of the *efectos de villa* in Madrid was confined to a narrow circle of members of the town council and their relatives, nobility, royal officers and religious institutions, whereas the numerically predominant middle and lower sorts of the Castilian capital did not invest in the purchases of annuities.[25] It may be stated therefore that the fiscal and financial system set up in seventeenth century Madrid was tainted by a wide redistributive effect, thanks to which the revenues obtained by the city council from the lower and middle sorts of the capital from a group of indirect taxes were transferred to the most privileged sectors of the city through the payment of the interests of the *efectos*.

The regressive features of Madrid's fiscal system were aggravated by other factors. As can be seen in Table 5.3 above, in 1685 around 10 per cent of the city expenditure was invested in the payment of the *refacciones* to the Church and court and the franchises to ambassadors. The taxes levied upon the commodities consumed in Madrid were collected by the tax farmers at the city gates the very moment such products were introduced into the city. The wine and meat destined for convents, the royal cellars and the embassies paid municipal taxes at their entrance in Madrid, but then the town council reimbursed these sums to the religious orders, ambassadors and the royal cellars. A good example of the importance of these sums may be gauged from the fact that, according to Table 5.3, the funds devoted by the town council to the payment of *refacciones* and franchises in 1685 were slightly more important than those invested in the supply of public services to the city inhabitants.

Apart from benefitting from the *refacciones* and franchises, religious orders and ambassadors, together with other groups such as the Royal Guards, also reaped the substantial profits of a massive tax evasion. Many convents, embassies and the Royal Guards introduced wine into Madrid without paying taxes and became centres of a flourishing market of illegal wine sales. The wine sold in convents, embassies and the illegal taverns of the guards was 5–10 per cent cheaper than that sold legally at the price settled by the Crown in the taverns of the members of the publicans' guild, which at the end of the century had lost an important part of the wine market of the capital. Our estimates suggest that at the beginning of the 1680s nearly 50 per cent of the wine sold in the capital had been introduced without paying taxes, to be illegally sold in convents, embassies and the guards' taverns. The losses suffered by the royal and municipal treasuries at the beginning of the 80s on account of the unpaid taxes amounted to slightly more than 260 million mrs, a sum which accrued the profits of all those involved in the illegal wine sales and which would have sufficed to pay 75 per cent of the interest on Madrid's debt in 1681, something which illustrates the importance of an activity that symbolizes the regressive trends prevailing in the fiscal system developed in the Castilian capital.[26]

III.

Parts I and II indicate that a substantial amount of the fiscal and financial resources of Madrid was put to the service of the Royal Treasury since the central decades of the seventeenth century. Between 1680 and 1700 around 75 per cent of the yearly value of the city taxes funded the Crown needs through the payment of the interests of the *efectos*. It can be stated, therefore, that as a consequence of the close financial links between Madrid and the Crown, an important part of the fiscal burden collected in the capital to fund the state expenditures during the last decades of the century was disguised under the municipal mantle, so it does not appear in the tax records of the Royal Treasury presently filed in the national archives of Simancas and Madrid. When we add the municipal taxes used to pay the interests of the *efectos* to those collected by the Crown in Madrid, then the exact amount of the fiscal burden which fell on the inhabitants of the city as a consequence of the need to fund the ambitious foreign policy followed by the Spanish Habsburgs in 1700 rises a further non-negligible 30–5 per cent, whereas in other cities such as the nearby Toledo and Jaén the fiscal burden increases another 10 and 26 per cent respectively on the same date.[27]

This poses the problem of analysing to what extent the fiscal and financial system set up by Madrid from the second half of the century may be considered representative of a situation developed in the rest of the Castilian cities at the time or, on the contrary, a particular case which should be accounted for because of the fact that Madrid was the main exception to the urban crisis prevailing in seventeenth-century Castile.[28] Although the answer to this question would require further research, there is enough evidence to suggest that at least the most important towns of the kingdom developed the same kind of financial links with the Crown as Madrid, granting the Royal Treasury substantial gifts which caused the expansion of their municipal debt and the simultaneous creation of a broad range of indirect taxes. The payment of the interest on the urban debt appears to have been the main expenditure of the Castilian cities during the seventeenth and eighteenth centuries, and this reduced their ability to supply public services in welfare, public works, health or education to the urban populations. At the same time, the indirect taxes collected by the Castilian cities had important effects on urban price and wage levels and their burden mainly fell on the consumers of the lower and middle sorts of the urban populations of the country. It seems fair, then, to state that this kind of taxation should be seen as a way of transferring revenues from taxpayers to the owners of the annuities issued by the cities and that it was presided by a highly regressive character which undermined tax morale and paved the way for the development of a massive fraud and tax evasion.

Apart from Madrid, other Castilian cities granted *donativos* to the Crown during the sixteenth and seventeenth centuries. To quote a few examples, between 1631 and 1677 Seville granted 2 million ducats to the Royal Treasury, whereas between 1601 and 1699 Málaga granted 1 million ducats and the ancient capital of the kingdom, Valladolid, another 0.5 million ducats between 1630 and 1670. The cases of Madrid, Seville, Málaga and Valladolid are the best known, but this should not hide that other cities such as Toledo, Jaén and Zamora also awarded *donativos* to the Royal Treasury, in what seems to have been a method widely followed by the rest of the Castilian cities, although it is difficult to know the real value of such *donativos* on account of the shortcomings of our documentary sources.[29]

The use of the urban *donativos* as a source of revenue for the beleaguered Royal Treasury, especially since the central decades of the century, should be seen in the context of the fiscal debate that developed in seventeenth century Castile. Trying to raise its fiscal revenues, the Crown had turned to the subsidies voted by the Castilian *Cortes* (the parliamentary assembly of the kingdom) since 1590. The importance of parliamentary taxation on Castile was on the rise during the first half of the century, although the Royal Treasury always looked with suspicion on this trend and tried to sideline the Assembly through direct negotiations with the cities which, on their turn, were not completely averse to this possibility. Like the Crown, the local oligarchies which ruled the Castilian towns feared the growing importance of the *Cortes* in the fiscal and financial arena and saw in the *donativos* a way of creating a direct link with the Crown which also offered other important advantages.[30]

To raise the sums offered in each *donativo* the Castilian cities set up the same method used by Madrid and expanded their debt, issuing annuities that yielded an interest well above that of the Castilian *juros*. Leaving aside the case of Madrid analysed in part II, the interest rate of the annuities issued by Seville was 10 per cent until 1674, when it was reduced to 8 per cent and to 5 cent in 1680, and the same happened in other cases.[31] Taking this into account it seems plain, then, that the desire of the urban oligarchies of finding sound investment opportunities for their wealth in times when the appeal of the Castilian public debt bonds plummeted and the economic crisis discouraged investment in agriculture, trade and manufacture should be considered as another factor which accounts for the wide use of the urban annuities as a way of raising the sums offered to the Crown in the *donativos*.

The expansion of the municipal debt heavily determined the structure of the urban expenditure of the Castilian cities, compelling them to use an important part of their revenues to pay the interest of the annuities. In 1596–1601 Seville devoted 72 per cent of its incomes to such end. This already high percentage rose to nearly 90 per cent in the case of Madrid in 1675–9, falling to 70–5 per cent at the end of the century, whereas between 1688 and 1705 Valladolid used 60 per cent of its ordinary revenues to pay the interests of the city debt. As the Castilian cities had to invest most of their revenues in the funding of their debt, their capacity to provide public services was seriously reduced.[32] To quote some examples, between 1688 and 1705 public works amounted to a meagre 2 per cent of the expenditure of Valladolid, and to this it should be added that recent research has emphasized that the amount invested by the Castilian towns in public works was always constrained by the burden of the urban debt.[33]

The creation of new indirect taxes, especially on meat and wine, seems to have been the favourite method of the Castilian cities to fund the growing municipal debt, and most of these taxes were levied on basic commodities such as olive oil, meat and wine, also heavily taxed by the Royal Treasury. As it has been mentioned earlier, at the end of the century municipal and royal taxes amounted up to 60 per cent of the retail price of a litre of wine, and around 30–5 per cent of that of a kilogram of mutton or olive oil in Madrid, whereas in 1657–61 royal and city taxes were 50 per cent of the retail price of a litre of wine and 33 per cent of a kilogram of olive oil in Valladolid in 1657–61 and 1668 respectively.[34] Although information about other Castilian towns is scarce, the cases of Madrid and Valladolid seem to have been far from exceptional. At the beginning of the eighteenth century the recently arrived Bourbon dynasty was deeply concerned about the incidence of municipal and royal indirect taxation on the prices of the main commodities in the cities of the kingdom and the new rulers saw in the sudden growth of the municipal debt during the central decades of the seventeenth century the main reason.[35] The effect of the proliferation of indirect taxes on price and wage levels should have been important. Although once again this issue would deserve further research, it is worth stressing here that during the last decades of the century indirect taxation raised price and wage levels in Madrid around 15–25 per cent, reducing real wages in the same measure, a proportion which seems to have been below what the Castilian economic commentators of the time (*arbitristas*) assumed, although it was nonetheless far from negligible.[36]

Taking all this into account, it seems possible to argue that the case of Madrid described in parts 1 and 2 of this paper was fairly representative and that the Castilian cities turned to the development of the same financial and fiscal methods set up by the capital in order to face the need of attending the growing demands of *donativos* made by the Crown during the seventeenth century. However, although the trend towards the consolidation of indirect taxation as a way of providing revenues to pay the interests of the municipal debt was present in nearly every Castilian town of the period, this trend was much more important in Madrid than in the other cities of the country, as may be gauged from that fact that in 1769 Madrid's was the most heavily indebted city of Castile by far and that the 19 million ducats borrowed by the city amounted to 60 per cent of the global value of the municipal debt in the whole country in that year. Remarkably, this difference between the relative levels of urban indebtedness in Madrid and the other Castilian cities was already visible at the end of the seventeenth century.[37] According to our data, in 1688 the value of Madrid and Valladolid debt in 'per capita' terms was 147.5 and 36.2 ducats respectively. To pay the interests of this debt, the average Madrilenian building worker had to divert 5.7 ducats (nearly 8 per cent of his yearly earnings), whereas his Valladolid colleague had to invest 1.56 ducats (3.4 per cent of his yearly earnings).

IV.

So far, the evidence considered suggests that the way the fiscal systems of Madrid and the Castilian cities evolved during the seventeenth century was heavily conditioned by their financial relations with the Royal Treasury. The granting of *donativos* by the Castilian towns to the Crown prompted the sudden expansion of the urban debt and drove the rise of indirect taxation in Madrid and the other cities of the country. The main burden of these taxes fell upon the lower and middle sorts of the urban populations, who suffered the effects of indirect taxation on price and wages levels and funded the payment of the interests of the annuities issued by the cities without obtaining public services proportionate to the sums paid to urban treasuries. If we also consider that the buyers of urban annuities were members of the urban oligarchies and privileged groups such as the clergy, which in some cases also reaped the advantages of the *refacciones* and that many of these same sectors even resorted to massive and illegal sales of wine and meat, then it is easy to understand that this fiscal system should have prompted the development of low levels of tax morale which led to massive tax evasion, whose existence has drawn the interest of historians and researchers since then.[38]

High levels of tax evasion have traditionally been one of the hallmarks of the Castilian and Spanish taxation and they embody the wide development of an opportunistic behaviour among broad sections of the society of the country. It might be argued that the roots of this problem lay in the developments described in the previous pages. The *donativos* helped the Crown to avoid the risks of an excessive dependence on parliamentary taxation, but this involved a heavy reliance on the local oligarchies of the cities of the kingdom which, in turn, set up fiscal systems tailored towards the fulfilment of their own objectives.

Latest research has emphasized the importance of the idea of citizenship, originating in the European city states during the Middle Ages as a way of solving the coordination and commitment problems faced by the state. It has been also emphasized that absolutist governments created a context opposed to the emergence of this notion, and the case of Madrid and Castile analysed in the previous pages is a case in point. The alliance between central government and the urban oligarchies whose main objective lay in the defence of their narrow local interests seems to have been one of the main reasons of the failure in the development of the idea of modern citizenship in early modern Castile. Both the Crown and the cities agreed in the marginalization of parliamentary taxation during the middle decades of the century, and this led to the development of close financial links between the Royal Treasury and the Castilian cities embodied in the *donativos*. In return for their support, the Crown allowed the Castilian cities to set up a markedly regressive fiscal and financial system whose main purpose was to pay the interests of the urban debt and whose burden fell on the shoulders of the lower and middle sorts of the urban population. Citizenship has been defined as the 'continuing series of transactions between persons and agents of a given state in which one has enforceable rights and obligations'.[39] Seen from a fiscal and financial point of view, in the years around 1700 an observer might have concluded that all the rights and profits derived from the fiscal system of the Castilian cities accrued to the narrow circle of the urban oligarchies through the payment of the interest on urban debt, whereas the obligations created by the same system had been transferred to the rest of the urban population by way of indirect taxation, high price levels, tax evasion and low supply of public services, and that this had created a climate which deserves to be considered as one of the main stumbling blocks in the path towards the emergence of the modern notion of citizenship in the country.

6 TAX COLLECTION IN SPAIN IN THE EIGHTEENTH CENTURY: THE CASE OF THE 'DÉCIMA'

Nadia Fernandez de Pinedo Echevarría

Introduction[1]

In the eighteenth century, the Castilian fiscal system was indirect. It was based on excises – such as the so-called *millones* paid on wine, vinegar, oil and meat – and on taxes that charged trades as *alcabalas*, *cientos* (both indirect taxes on purchases paid by the buyer), customs and monopolies. Moreover, there existed indirect taxes on specific products generally consumed by privileged groups with higher incomes who could afford for instance tobacco or certain colonial foodstuffs. Considering these characteristics, if we compare the Castilian fiscal system in the sixteenth and seventeenth century with that of the English, French or Dutch, two basic differences become apparent:

In England, France and Holland the fiscal system was a mixture of direct taxes – land tax, *taille réelle* or property taxes, and indirect taxes such as excises on salt, soap, oils and so on. Moreover, in the Dutch and English cases, privileged groups – nobility and clergy – were not, in general, tax exempt as they were in the French fiscal system, where nobility and clergy were exempt from direct taxes.

The financial revolution – to transform short-term national debt to long-term national debt – had been carried out in the sixteenth century in Castile, when for different reasons, national short-term debt (*asientos*) was turned into *juros* – or long-term debt. But the long-term debts issued were disproportionate and tended to devalue throughout the seventeenth century; thus the Spanish Crown was unable to obtain long-term voluntary loans from the 1730s. On the other hand, the Dutch Republic in the sixteenth century and England by the end of seventeenth and the beginning of eighteenth century were able to finance wars thanks to an efficient financial revolution.[2]

The Spanish Bourbon monarchy had been involved in numerous wars. In order to finance those wars, the Treasury had to increase state revenues, since neither ordinary nor extraordinary colonial income covered such expenses.

However, in order to finance these military expenses, the Crown could not issue long-term debt or increase consumption taxes due to the high tax burden and its influence on price levels and living standards.

Therefore, certain financial experts tried to increase collections through direct taxes. These were aimed at privileged groups obligated to pay direct taxes, and were attempted during two wars in particular, those of 1701–14 and 1739–42. In brief, during the War of Spanish Succession the so-called *donativo* tax was established in 1705 and during the War of Jenkins' Ear the so-called *décima* tax was settled in 1741.[3] In theory, the *décima* had to be collected as a direct tax of ten per cent of the liquid income of every subject of the Crown. But, as it was unclear who was to be taxed, a royal decree specified that the payment would be general, except for persons with special immunity such as clergy, but not nobility, and according to their assets. In fact, this extraordinary tax in times of war was collected by the system called *sistema de cupo* – a top-down quota system – that is to say, a fixed quota had to be distributed among Spanish peninsular provinces, and then this quota was apportioned among cities, towns or villages in proportion to the amount collected through the rest of the taxes on trade and consumption – *cientos, alcabalas, millones*. We were not able to ascertain the exact of amount of the *décima*. In some cases, the sum collected was pointed out in the source, for example in some provinces or villages such as the province of Granada or the city of Madrid. In these cases it has been possible to estimate the quantity, but not in other cases. However, the most important thing is not the precise amount of the tax but how it had been collected and all information related to the structure of spending and consumption it can offer.

Collected in different ways and at different times, the truth is that in some places the collection was based on direct taxes, although in others, perhaps due to the incapacity of the administration or the resistance of the privileged groups, the *décima* was also levied as an indirect tax. However, even collected in this manner, the example of Madrid and other places shows that the intention of the Crown was to tax certain groups with high incomes. It should be remembered that the case of Madrid is important due to its particular social structure, being the court and the administrative centre of the kingdom. The number of exempt groups – clergy, nobility, the royal family and so on – was higher than in any other place.

Spanish Public Finance at the Beginning of the Eighteenth Century

The Castilian tax system was based on indirect taxes – excises and taxes on trade: *millones, cientos, alcabalas*, customs and monopolies (salt, tobacco, etc.). The economic literature of the seventeenth century attributed to them the responsibility for the existing economic crisis – being the primary origin of high salaries, high prices of raw materials, as well as high production costs and low consumption.

During that century, indirect taxes were partly responsible for the price increase of basic or subsistence goods – although bread was exempted – as well as for the difficulties that Castilian tradesmen and artisans were experiencing. Moreover, indirect taxes were collected by middlemen who charged for their collection, so the King collected much less than what his subjects paid.

Wars were the best excuse to introduce changes in tax systems. Military expenses needed increasing state revenues and usually the subjects of his/her majesty were prone to pay more than they usually did to avoid war close to their homeland. These schemes were carried out in 1713 in Spain by the French native minister Juan Orry[4] and the Flemish native minister the Count of Bergeyck. The most obvious attempt to create a direct tax can be seen in 1705 with the so-called 'donation'.[5] For the *donativo* to be collected there had to be an account of assets that, according to Ofelia Rey Castelao,[6] was set up with the help of a type of *cadastre*, at least in the province of Tuy-Galicia. A second attempt to tax assets was carried out by the Marquis of Santa Cruz of Marcenado in 1732.[7] In brief, some financial experts were trying to increase collections through direct taxation.

The Bourbons were involved in numerous and not always successful foreign wars. As a result of the Utrecht Treaty of 1713, numerous territories were lost: Flanders and the Italian Possessions passed to Austria, Sicily to Savoy, and Gibraltar and Minorca were ceded to Britain – as they were occupied during the war. Furthermore, economic interests suffered as it was agreed to give the British a valuable monopoly slave-trading contract and the so-called *navio de permiso*.[8] The latter meant that the Spanish trade monopoly ceased in Hispanic America as the British were allowed to trade with the Spanish colonies through the yearly dispatch of a warship with a freight capacity of 500 tons. The British South Sea Company was also granted the monopoly of the supply of slave labour for a period of thirty years. This entitlement comprised 144,000 slaves: 4,800 per year and for a value of 33.5 pesos per head. This monopoly lasted until 1753.[9]

There were obviously attempts to recover the lost territories, such as the expeditions to Sardinia and Sicily between 1717 and 1720, and also to take control of the Atlantic commercial traffic through the establishment of the 'visitation right' on behalf of the coastguards in America thanks to the Treaty of Seville of 1729. This had a great relevance for the treasury as well as for the interests of the Castilians traders. One of the conflicts arising from the control of trade in Spanish America[10] ended in the little-known '*Guerra del Asiento*' or War of Jenkins' Ear.[11] This war, waged overseas and not in Europe, had two important consequences for the Crown. On the one hand, it consolidated or at least maintained the Spanish relative control in America. On the other, the Castilian treasury could attempt to establish an extraordinary direct tax in some places through a sort of cadastre, before the famous *Catastro de Ensenada*.[12]

With regards to the first consequence, it is worth mentioning that during the eighteenth century America was rife with privateers. The British had taken advantage of the *navío de permiso* to break the already fragile Spanish trading monopoly overseas. However, the Spanish made use of the visitation right to intercept and check the cargo of any ship suspected of smuggling, one of these captures giving rise to the name of the war of 1739 – the War of Jenkins' Ear.[13] The strain that this incident exerted – the British refusal to allow the visitation right to take place – along with Philip V's claim of £68,000 against the South Sea Company for the contract right of slaves, provoked the declaration of war on 23 October 1739. Although this conflict ended in 1741, the war cycle went on with the War of the Austrian Succession. This conflict finished with the Aachen (Aix-la-Chapelle) Treaty of 1748 where Philip V received Parma, Placentia and Guastalla in Italy.[14] After that, Spanish America recovered some stability, although Great Britain, through the Madrid Treaty of 1750, renounced the contract right of slaves and the *navio de permiso* in exchange for £100,000. Thus, Spain theoretically maintained, for the time being, the control of trade with its American territories.

Until 1739, conflicts had not brought about a modification of the tax system. Before that date expenses were not covered by ordinary or extraordinary income or by that coming from the Indies. In 1739, for instance, the Crown revenues – 20.9 million escudos – only funded 80 per cent of its global expenditure – 26.1 million.[15] It is quite clear that in times of war, due to naval and other military expenses the Crown would take on loans – short- and long-term – and issue extraordinary taxes.[16] Thus it was necessary to transfer funds and loans to the Royal Treasury from new contractors – *asentistas*. A new group of Spanish-native contractors grew stronger with the war of the Spanish Succession. The first Bourbon King – Philip – commonly issued short-term debt. He usually repaid these debts by empowering contractors to collect ordinary taxes. Nevertheless, the King also employed extraordinary measures. Some particular royal taxes were transferred to contractors in order to obtain long-term loans and debt payments. This occurred at least twice:[17]

In 1725, the tax named '*Renta de la población de Granada*' was transferred to Iturralde, who loaned the King 1 million pesos in exchange.

In 1727, the '*Tercios diezmos de Valencia*' was transferred to the Marquis of Santiago until the King paid back the loan of 1,103,700 pesos.

In 1737, Philip V admitted that the deficit's origins lay in the excessive expenses resulting from the wars within and outside Spain. Consequently, he ordered the creation of a committee to examine the state of the Royal Treasury and to propose measures to reduce the deficit. This committee, convened by the Marquis of Torrenueva, appraised the monarchy's expenses.[18] It revealed that 75 per cent of the expenditure was consumed by the army and navy as pointed out by Fernández de Pinedo Fernández.[19] It was also disclosed that the considerable tax incomes from the American colonies did not cover the expenses. When we compare the revenues obtained by the Monarchy from its Spanish and American colonies, the reduced importance of the latter as a source of tax incomes becomes evident. In the period 1731–5 the colonies contributed to the Spanish Monarchy with 12.05 per cent of total revenue – 27,298,432 reales – while in 1736–40 this percentage fell to 7.5 per cent – 16,171,011 reales. The bulk of the Monarchy's revenues, then, came from the peninsula.[20]

As the expenditure was not covered by the ordinary or American incomes, two measures were initiated: the Royal Decrees of 21 March and 22 December 1739 that suspended the payment of the short-term debt and created an extraordinary tax respectively.

The Décima[21]

In 1740 a new Royal Order issued on 22 December introduced a direct tax[22] of 10 per cent of the liquid income of every subject of the Crown to finance the war against England.[23] As it was unclear who was to be taxed, on 29 April 1741 a new decree was promulgated. It insisted that the payment be general, except for those individuals with especial immunity – clergy – and according to their assets, but its distribution varied. By means of this tax the Crown intended to collect a fixed quota that was distributed among the Spanish peninsular provinces, and within each province among the cities, towns and villages, in proportion to the amount collected through the rest of the taxes on trade and consumption – excises as *alcabalas*, *cientos* and *millones*.

However, there was not a single rule and particularities were frequent. Every place – village, town, city – paid the amount required but in different ways and with different timing and, therefore, their analysis must have taken these circumstances into account. The social structure of the town council was the key element in determining how the *décima* was going to be collected. As a result, in some places, the collection was based on direct taxes; in others, instead, it was referenced to the volume of the excises on consumption. This last was, for instance, the case of Santander.[24] Instead, in the town of Molina de Aragón[25], the tax was levied on trade and traffic of goods. In Andújar[26], it was charged based on the '*Memoriales de los caudales de los vecinos*' – individual wealth memorials – and in Jerez de la Frontera[27] and Ubeda[28] a census on personal and real properties was elaborated by the municipality in order to distribute the payment. In both places, records say that the properties of nobility were expressly taxed – fourteen marquises and marquises and four counts, in total.[29]

Two Particular Cases: Granada and Madrid

For the district of Granada, the existing records cover the whole city of Granada and surrounding areas – *partidos*.[30] In total, the payment duty was 2,190,197 reales and the city had to contribute with 46 per cent of that sum.[31]

In the city, the assessment of the tax followed the system used to collect common indirect taxes on consumption – *alcabalas*, *cientos* and *millones*. Nevertheless, two additional clauses were added: an ambiguous one on 'houses, credits and land' assumed to be linked to city dwellers and, the second one, on owners not settled in the city.[32] Table 6.1 displays the tax collection in Granada by craft industries, foodstuffs and real properties.

Table 6.1: Assessment of the *décima* in the City of Granada.

	Amount collected (reales–maravedíes)	Percentage (%)
Foodstuffs consumption	501,809–12	45.42
Craft activities		
Pottery	8,573–15	0.78
Construction/ building	11,786–26	1.07
Hide /leather	58,781–05	5.32
Timber	7,018–33	0.64
Metallurgy	17,835–27	1.61
Textile	299,770–07	27.13
Diverse craft industries	40,372–09	3.65
Diverse goods	14,899–18	1.35
Real estate & credits	143,997–08	13.03
Total	*1,104,844–24*	*100*

Source: AGS, Tribunal Mayor de Cuentas, leg. 1863, 'Granada. Contribuzn. Extraordinª del 10 por 100 mandada exigir el año de 1741'.

The burden of the *décima* mainly fell on a group of foodstuffs, although in the case of olive oil it is difficult to ascertain the burden levied on the oil used for manufacture (textiles and soap) and for human consumption. The collection was distributed as follows. Olive oil, spices and haberdashery[33], seeds and vegetables, fresh and salted fish, wine and vinegar, charcoal and sweets contributed to 45 per cent of the total. Craft activities, principally textiles, and raw materials accounted for 40 per cent. Real property, including the profits from mortgages in the city, came to 13 per cent, the most part paid by non-residents, and the majority being members of the nobility.[34] While it is clear that the consumption of food and craft activities was responsible for paying the bulk of the burden it is also true that the King made the nobility pay a part of the quota as landlords. Although their contribution was small, this fact clearly shows that the Bourbon's administration had in mind the extension of taxation to privileged persons, free from direct taxes.

As seen above, primary sources occasionally give detailed descriptions of the characteristics of the process of collection. The distribution was, in some cases, determined by the income of the taxpayers. But even where the manner in which the collection was carried out is still unknown, there is clear evidence that the King tried to avoid using indirect taxes. And where there was not any official register or cadastre, the administration tried to enlist properties or incomes under taxation by sworn statements.[35] However, personal taxing was not widespread.

Sometimes, the King authorized the creation of new excises (*sisas*), but in some cases, such as in Madrid, it was collected through indirect taxes charged on a group of commodities with a relevant place in the consumption patterns of the most well-off groups of the capital.

Table 6.2: List of products taxed by the *décima* in Madrid according to the Royal Decree of 6 July 1741, in reales de vellón.

Products	Measure	Resident introducers	
Barley	fanega	51	(1)
Straw	two-mule cart	100	(2)
Straw	saca de marca	32	(3)
Straw	saca de marquilla	22	(4)
Straw	costal	6	(5)
Wine	arroba	45	(6)
Oil and soap	arroba	80	(7)
Bacon/lard (pork)	canal (animal without intestine)	272	(8)
Salted ham and chorizo	arroba	85	(8)
Cocoa, chocolate and paste	libra (pound)	51	(9)
Sugar	arroba	102	(10)
Sugar loaf & refined	arroba	204	(10)
Sweets	price	8 per 100	(11)
Textiles, furniture	price	8 per 100	(12)

Note:

1. Carrier should pay 51 maravedíes + 12 maravedíes for *alcabalas*.
2. Carrier 100 maravedíes + *alcabalas* and *cientos*, not quanitified.
3. Carrier 32 maravedíes + *alcabalas* and *cientos*.
4. Carrier 22 maravedíes + *alcabalas* and *cientos*.
5. Carrier 6 maravedíes + *alcabalas* and *cientos*.
6. '*quedando [el vecino] igual de esta forma con el traginero, extravagante o tabernero que lo trae para vender*'.
7. Resident paid 80 maravedíes '*de aumento...quedando tambien por este medio igual en los derechos con el que introduce estos generos para la venta, y puestos publicos*'.
8. *El trajinero y el obligado pagarían los mismos derechos que hasta aquí, pero no se indican.*
9. It clarifies that: '*solo paga el vecino un real de impuesto, [y] se le ha de cobrar medio real mas, quedando por esta regla igual en dros. con el que lo introduze de ventta*'.
10. '*quedando por este medio igual con la que se introduze para vender*'. f. R.: from outside the Kingdom.
11. Resident '*el mismo ocho por ciento que se cobra de lo que se introduze para ventta*'.
12. '*Se ha de cobrar por su introducción del vecino el mismo ocho por ciento que se exige de todos los que los introduzen para vender*'.

At first, the district of Madrid[36] had to contribute theoretically with 1,196,254 reales and 2 maravedíes.[37] Nevertheless, a new Royal Decree issued on 6 June 1741 recognized that, owing to the particularities of the city of Madrid, the general rule established in April of the same year that determined the amount of this extraordinary tax and the way it should be collected was not applicable there.[38] While the *alcabala* and the *cientos* were levied on any sale conducted in the market and paid by the buyer in Madrid, they did not tax products entering into the city for personal consumption. For that reason, all the inhabitants of Madrid with land properties close to the city or those goods bought in tax-free fairs did not pay any of those duties. Instead, the *décima* taxed several goods, those detailed in Table 6.2, that were introduced into the city through any of the existing five doors for personal consumption. However, it is worth noting that most products subject to tax were not basic ones like bread and that the majority – wine, sugar, barley, straw, sweets, textiles, porcelain – were goods whose consumption was principally demanded by middle- and upper-class social groups rather than the lower strata of society.

On 8 July 1741 a new official document was issued to clarify the Royal Decree of 6 July. It manifested the King's desire of reducing the fiscal burden which fell on the poorer sectors of the city. Definitely the King wanted prices of goods sold in the market stall to remain unchanged and, in this way, to avoid social unrest.[39]

The case of Madrid is worth analysing in depth due to its particular social structure: it was there where the court was placed, as well as the main administrative centre of the kingdom, with all the implications this had in terms of the collection of taxes and consumption structures. The percentage of the total population of those exempted from ordinary taxes (clergy, nobility, the royal family and so on) was clearly higher than in any other city of the country.

Regularly, most of the products listed in Table 6.2 escaped being taxed with *alcabalas* and *cientos* if they were declared for personal consumption and, in consequence, were not bought in the city markets by nobility and wealthy people. In this way, the middle and upper classes broke away from taxation. The rules for collecting the *décima* pointed out the differences between this new levy and the common taxation system – which did not disappear as a result.

Barley and straw were introduced mainly to feed horses and mules, as can be appreciated when the amount of the tax was refunded to foreign ambassadors.[40] Owners of horses or mules were taxed by the *décima* if they bought barley or straw outside the town or if they introduced these products coming from rent paid by their tenants, but they were not taxed by *alcabalas* and *cientos*. In the case of wine, soap, olive oil, sweets, colonials, textiles or furniture introduced for private consumption, however, taxing through the *décima* avoided raising the price of these products purchased in shops, taverns or markets inside the town. This forced a segment of the population to pay who usually did not pay. Before and after the décima, proprietors of vineyards or olive groves who introduced wine and olives for self-consumption did not pay *alcabalas* and *cientos*.

The *décima* shows the intention of taxing the upper and middle classes, free from *alcabalas* and *cientos*, at least if they introduced goods from their own harvests and incomes or bought in markets or fairs outside the town free of taxes.

But the *décima* also reflects the intention of taxing commodities consumed by the privileged groups, such as barley and straw, food particularly consumed by horses and mules that pulled carriages used in Madrid by nobility and the rich. Eighty-two per cent of the revenue collected in the city of Madrid came from the taxes generated by barley and straw.

What can be inferred from the records of the *décima* is that those studies of consumption of products such as wine, sugar and oil based on the amount collected through the common taxes underestimate consumption because they only consider the quantities bought and sold in the city markets, setting aside the products free of charges introduced into the city by their consumers. Consequently, the tax system favoured those neighbours with land properties close, or relatively close to the city. This type of taxation avoided, on the other hand, charging the price of the products sold in taverns, shops or markets that would have penalized those consumers dependent on salaries or incomes for their subsistence.

In Madrid, the *décima* was not imposed until 19 September 1743. Protests against the duration of this extraordinary tax arose and the King ordered its withdrawal except for barley and straw, which lasted until 17 December 1748. It is difficult to assume that complaints arose from common people and not from privileged groups, since they were hypothetically the most affected, taking into account the type of products charged by this new tax.

Table 6.3: The collection of the *décima* in Madrid in reales de vellón.

Year	Barley	Straw	Wine, oil, etc.	Spices, woollen cloth	Total
9 July 1741	225,806	62,991	63,412	74,065	426,275
1742	207,610	77,613	157,116	88,542	530,881
1743	234,223	79,004	101,029	53,762	468,018
1744	255,340				255,340
1745	287,328				287,328
1746	332,435				332,435
1747	335,998				335,998
17 December 1748	290,033				290,033
Total according to the source					2,926,248
Total	*2,388,382*	*321,557*	*216,370*		*2,926,308*
Percentage	*81.62*	*10.99*	*7.39*		*100.00*

Source: AGS, TMC, leg. 1863. Madrid, town centre.
Note: The rounding down of maravedíes do not introduce significant errors in the amount.

In Madrid the collection of the *décima* was assigned to the *Cinco Gremios Mayores* – the Big Five Guilds – of the city as they were those who advanced the King the amount estimated to be yielded in the city: 2,662,191 reales and 6 maravedíes that were deposited in the General Treasury of War on 12 December 1741. When the collection finished in 1748, the *Cinco Gremios Mayores* had collected a total sum of 2,975,389 reales and 30 maravedíes. To that sum they added 319,808 reales and 27 maravedíes as interest plus the cost of the account books used and the quantities paid back to the ambassadors of Naples, Venice, Denmark and Holland for the barley and straw they consumed. In total, it came to 3,100,305 reales and 1 maravedí with a difference of 124,130 reales 20 maravedíes between the amount collected and the one they should have obtained. The King did not object to giving them back this money.

Conclusions

Although the Spanish Bourbon monarchy did not change the Habsburgs' fiscal system, the *décima*, in the first half of the eighteenth century, is the second attempt known, in times of war, to distribute a more equitable fiscal burden. In this case, the Crown, with the pretext of the War of Jenkins' Ear, taxed certain privileged groups. We have to wait until the Cadastre of Ensenada, years later in 1749, to try to establish a direct tax system. The *décima* was only a temporary tax destined to disappear once the assigned quantity was fully collected.

Nevertheless, its importance exceeds the mere particularity as one of the first attempts ever made to impose a direct tax in Castile because it offers accurate information on the structure of expending and consumption in cities such as Madrid since it gives a detailed account of the products introduced into the capital, who introduced and who consumed them. Indeed, the *décima* levied several goods. Some of them are commonly labelled by the economic literature as 'normal goods', goods such as olive oil that would have an income elasticity of demand between 0 and 1. Others, instead, are characterized as 'luxuries' – certain spices or textiles and sweets and in large cities barley – as their demand elasticity is commonly greater than one.[41] There would be another problematic classification – 'semi-luxury goods', a category that would match products such as sugar or cocoa since they might have been transformed from luxury to common goods during these years, particularly in urban environments. In short, this tax would not burden basic and popular consumption goods – such as bread – but others of a wider scope – wines, olive oil and pork fat, or those consumed by the rich – barley.

7 FINANCES, THE STATE AND THE CITIES IN FRANCE IN THE EIGHTEENTH CENTURY

Guy Saupin

The French cities, in spite of their charters of privilege, were neither city-states as in the Holy Roman Empire or the pillars of the political system as in the United Provinces, nor even administrative and regional centres, like in the decentralized monarchies such as England or Hapsburg Spain. Two great phases characterize the evolution of French towns during the early modern period. Until the personal reign of Louis XIV, the municipalities preserved great freedom to manoeuvre, since they were subjected only to control a posteriori by the Chambers of Accounts. As the size of their debt put in danger their role for the state finances, Jean-Baptiste Colbert imposed a financial framework by combining the clearing of their debts by partial bankruptcy with a strict regulation of their ordinary expenditure and the submission of the extraordinary expenditure to the preliminary authorization by the intendants, who were direct representatives of the central government in the provinces. However, this policy, characteristic of the absolutist perspective of the royal state, made neither the budget deficits nor the recourse to debt disappear in the eighteenth century.

The municipalities, doubly defined as representative and royal institutions, were to render at the same time the services expected by the urban community to guarantee social peace and to fulfil the financial and military requirements of the state. Our study is centred on the analysis of the possible configurations between these contradictory requirements, but also on their consequences on urban development and, furthermore, on the contribution of the cities to the financial means of the royal state.

The Political Context: The Administrative Development of the French Monarchy

The Concretization of an Absolutist Ideology

Following the definition of the term sovereignty by French lawyers during the preceding two centuries, the French monarchy adhered constantly to the absolutist model until the revolution of 1789. The latter was characterized by the progressive introduction of a relatively powerful state machinery in European terms for the early modern period. Venal offices were established on great scale, more typically in the domain of justice than in the financial sector, because of the involvement of tax farmers.[1] The fiscal explosion resulting from the participation of France in the Thirty Years' War led to a major structural change, with the implantation of intendants under the ministry of Cardinal Richelieu. After being suppressed in order to end with the Fronde (1648–53), the intendants were re-established by Cardinal Mazarin with the triple function to control the provincial councils in questions of jurisdiction, police and finance. The financial functions of the intendants exceeded however by far the others in the priorities of the King. Louis XIV promoted the role of these officials, by installing them at the site of each generality, by charging them with the control of the municipal finances in the edict of April 1683 and by allowing them to surround themselves with subdelegates and information agents through the decrees of the councils obtained by the royal commissioner, who were chosen among local lawyers.[2] Conceived originally as deputies of the governor and charged with the task of increasing the revenues obtained from the royal taxes, the intendants enjoyed a great autonomy, although they did not mark an end to the historical and honorific primacy of the military hierarchy in the control of provinces.

In the eighteenth century, the authority of an intendant in this field depended above all on the personality of the governor or the chief commander. If in most cases its role was predominant due to the distant control exerted by the major royal representative in the ordinary hierarchy, the importance of the intendant could always be limited by the presence of a dominant member of the aristocracy, like the duke of Aiguillon in Brittany, the duke-marshall of Richelieu in Guyenne or even more, the princes of Condé in Burgundy. The century of Enlightenment saw a widening in the functions of the intendants, from financial, mainly fiscal, questions to a broader range of economic and social issues (such as the development of trade and manufacture, the improvement of routes of communication, the regulation of the market of agrarian products, mainly of grain, the fight against diseases, social assistance and the repression of mendicancy as well as the provision of public works).[3]

Becoming aware of the increasingly outmoded character of its tax system, which, according to a common expression, led to a poor state in rich France, the royal power regularly sought to improve its collection methods in order to obtain revenues enough to fund its ambitions as a great European and world power. After resting on the traditional direct taxes, which prompted continuous internal revolts during half a century (1625–75), the French Monarchy turned to indirect taxes on tobacco, tin tableware and stamped paper. The expensive military commitments of the last decades of the reign of Louis XIV forced the state to return to direct taxation, which was politically very destabilizing as it involved the questioning of the privileges of the traditional society of orders, through the implementation of capitation. In front of the strong opposition of the traditional elites, the pillars of the monarchical system, it was necessary to exempt the clergy and to apply a special tariff for the nobility. Originally temporary, the capitation became permanent in 1701. A similar process was repeated with the tenth in 1710, a tax created to fund military expenditures, which was abolished in 1717, then reintroduced from 1733 to 1737, and finally restored from 1741 to 1749, and with the twentieth, introduced in 1749, and increased by a second then a third in 1756 and 1759.[4] The charge of inversion of the social order by a crawling tax egalitarianism nourished all the debates and thwarted the attempts of financial reforms until the final crisis of the monarchy in 1789.[5]

The Failure of the Financial Reform during the Eighteenth Century

The capitation was collected from 1695 to 1697 following a rate system according to which the kingdom's population was divided in twenty-two classes, although in 1701 it was decided to collect the new tax through the methods traditionally used in the collection of the head tax and its supplements.[6] The innovation was tolerated only with the acceptance of the exemption of the clergy (which nonetheless accepted a light increase of its voluntary gift) and an advantageous special taxation for the royal nobility and officers. The levying of the tenth on the immovable goods, offices and incomes of industry and trade, as an extraordinary contribution of wars of 1710–17, 1733–7 and finally of 1741–9, had to face the same resistance and was regulated in the same manner for the clergy and by subscription for the countries of the provincial states and many cities. Forced to obey, the nobility however benefited from the absence of reliable instruments of measurement of its incomes from land, mainly in the area of personal taxation, and something very similar happened in 1749 when the permanent twentieth replaced the temporary tenth, with its two supplements which were created in the context of the Seven Years' War in 1756 and 1759.[7]

From the year 1760, the governmental reforms experienced a major development under strong Physiocratic influence.[8] Resuming ideas already suggested since the beginning of the century, this current of thinking developed under the double effect of the publication of major texts by François Quesnay and Vincent of Gournay and the rise of new channels of sociability and public opinion in the discussion of politics. The decade witnessed a remarkable convergence in the reform projects, from the compilation of a land register based on the experience of the *terriers* of southern France[9] or the internal and external liberalization of the grain trade to the redefinition of the functioning of the local financial administration, the core of which was the reformation of the municipalities established and defended against strong resistance by the general inspector, Clément Charles François de Laverdy, in 1764 and 1765, until his disgrace in 1768.

This questioning of the old principles of economic and social government, closely related to the paternal figure of the absolute king, awakened strong opposition in many circles, which reacted to defend their threatened privileges, nourishing the parliamentary denouncements of the ministerial despotism. The two decades between 1760 and 1770 were marked by a strong instability of the governmental line marked out by the expulsion of the Jesuits in 1764, the speech of Scourging at the Parliament of Paris in 1766, the coup d'etat of Maupeou in 1770 against the parliamentary claims, the abandonment of this authoritarian reaction at the arrival of Louis XVI in 1774 and the rise of the reformer Turgot. The financial policy followed by Necker and the failure of the tax reform proposed by Calonne contributed to the worsening of the financial crisis which was going to finish with the absolute monarchy, unable to impose a reform of its tax system upon the elites of the kingdom or to or to get there through negotiation.

The political impotence of absolutism which led to its final crisis cannot be understood without the contradictions which blocked the reformist projects. The social tensions fuelled by the emergence of economic liberalism were fully exploited by a parliamentary opposition who saw them as the best guarantee for its role as privileged intermediary, interpreter of the new values disseminated by the philosophy of Enlightenment and promoter of the participation of the nation in the exercise of political power to their own advantage. Tax reform was swallowed up in the failure of the monarchical power to choose between – and to impose upon the social elites of the kingdom – the path of enlightened despotism, a solution that was its preference, and that of the parliamentary monarchy illustrated by the British model, the most foreign to French tradition.

Royal Taxation and Cities

The Royal Management of Privileged Communities

Under this growing monarchical pressure, the evolution of the imperial ambitions of the French monarchy and the political and military context of imposing them are of utmost importance to follow the irregular chronological trends and to distinguish two main types of town in the kingdom. The military logic, which played an almost sanctified role within the kingdom during the seventeenth and eighteenth centuries distinguished two distinct types of city: the greater part of them, those of the interior, being liable for lodging troops on passage for relatively short stays, increasingly organized through the system of stations, and the minority of border or frontier towns fully integrated into the defensive system, especially after the national fortification policy led by Vauban in the service of Louis XIV.

The monarchy transferred a substantial part of the costs brought by the building of new walls, citadels and barracks to its cities. This weighed heavily on the municipal accounts and shaped the configuration of the urban space. In addition, military garrisons promoted the advance of local markets by a sometimes spectacular increase in the number of inhabitants. Many craftsmen as well as small and large merchants migrated to the towns, which also stimulated the growth of agriculture and proto-industry. Whereas military constraints limited the expansion of the small frontier centres, the development of navy bases and arsenals promoted the rise of many coastal centres which form the best examples of urban growth in France during the final years of the early modern period. Some of these towns reached the rank of middle-size centres with around 20,000 inhabitants, having started very often from being little more than small fishing villages.[10] Under the direction of the naval administration, these centres contributed to support the manufacturing development in France, from a better planning of stock management in space and time to a better balance between resources of the kingdom and necessary imports from abroad.

Among the fifteen cities with the highest incomes listed in the inquiry of the general control of 1766, it is possible to find the biggest French cities, which dominated the urban hierarchy of the country during the early modern period, but more especially in the eighteenth century. On the top of the list there were Paris (4.5 million livres), Lyons (2.5 million), Marseilles (1.4 million) and Lille (1.1 million), followed by Bordeaux (505,000), Rouen (361,000), Toulouse (315,000) and Nantes (214,000).[11]

The outlyers, referring to the divergence between municipal taxation and demographic rank, belong almost all to the category of the frontier towns, continental as well as maritime, except for Aix-en-Provence (312,000 livres): Valenciennes (526,000), Dunkirk (496,000), Toulon (277,000), Douai (252,000), Metz (246,000) and Amiens (232,000). The same phenomenon is visible in the lower category of cities whose income is located in the region of 100,000–200,000 livres, involving eight quoted cities out of fifteen. Among the border towns are counted, in the order of their incomes: Besançon, Saint-Omer, Bourg, Arras, Grasse, La Rochelle, Bayonne, Cambrai. The cities of the interior were: Rheims, Arles, Orléans, Tarascon, Montpellier, Troyes and Rennes.

Measured in 'per capita terms', the monarchical pressure on municipal finances affected the urban populations in a different way.[12] The average value was correlated with population size, although not directly. The general average being 5.5 livres, a clear difference separated the small towns of less than 10,000 inhabitants – definitely more protected with 2.6 livres per capita – from the medium-size cities between 10,000 and 50,0000 inhabitants with 5 livres per capita.

However, the main burden of the royal requirements fell on the biggest towns of the country, where the average amounted to 9.7 livres per capita. However, this average should not hide the strong disparities inside each category. Hence, for the large cities, the rates went from very low levels (1 livre in Poitiers, 1.5 in Nîmes, 2.5 in Caen, 2.8 in Orléans, 5 in Nantes) to the 18 livres of Lyons and Marseilles. Reims, with an increase of 6 to 7 livres from 1771 to 1786, was in an advantageous intermediate situation by comparison with the cities of the north such as Valenciennes (7 livres in 1786), Lille (8.2 livres in 1785) and Douai (9.8 livres in 1785). The example of Reims also recalls that this average rate refers to very unequal social realities inside the urban space because the breakdown by *connétablies* (administrative districts of the military administration of the constable) passes from a variation of 2 livres 2 sols to 11 livres 16 sols in 1771 as opposed to a variation of 2 livres 14 sols to 16 livres 8 sols in 1786.

Such variations cannot be explained as a result of the differences between frontier and interior towns, because the policy of using some centres as sources of loans also played a role. In addition, they reflect variations in the local approach of the urban financial policies, the level of the accepted load being strongly related to the manner of financing it, in the balance between ordinary resources, exceptional taxation and loans. More generally, a tradition of weak taxation, often related to location in a privileged province, could override an ambition of supported municipal action.

The Ordinary Resources of the Cities

Municipal finances rested on two great types of resources of different importance. The patrimonial incomes came from the renting of properties of the community and also from financial assets owned by the municipality. The so-called octroi corresponded to the taxation levied on the circulation of commodities, at the entry and the exit of the city, and on urban consumption. The octroi taxed a considerable number of products, but everywhere the essential share of the revenues came from beverages, of which wine was the most heavily taxed, followed by beer and cider (in the northern and Breton cities respectively).

In the inquiry of 1766 above mentioned, the patrimonial revenues accounted for on average 14 per cent of the total, the octroi being the most important source of income by far. There were however strong regional inequalities. The receipts from real estate were relatively important in Provence, but also in the generalities of Bordeaux, Riom, of Franche-Comté, of Metz, of Amiens and the Châlons-on-Marne where more than one city out of three obtained at least 30 per cent of its receipts in that way. On the contrary, this type of resource remained marginal in the west and the centre of France, as some southern districts such as the generalities of Montpellier and Perpignan.[13]

Angers was the great exception, with the levying of the *cloison*, an old ducal tax introduced in the fourteenth century intended to fund the 'repairs and maintenance of the walls, bridges and gates' of the capital city and transferred to Angers by Louis XI during the creation of the Court of Aldermen in February 1475. Its two characteristics made it one of the major resources of the municipality in the eighteenth century. Not only did it tax a great number of foodstuffs, but it was paid by the whole province. In the eighteenth century, 90 per cent of its yield came from the three offices of Ingrandes, Rochefort and Les Ponts-de-Cé, that is to say from the commercial traffic on the Loire stimulated by the Atlantic trade. The last tariff was published on 2 January 1657 under the authority of the intendant. The growth of the revenues obtained from this tax from 1720 was remarkable, passing from 13,000–15,000 livres of the beginning of the century to almost 45,000 livres in 1780. Together with the incomes from a group of smaller rents, at the end of the Ancien Régime the *cloison* ensured almost 50,000 livres annually to the municipality of Angers, in comparison with the 26,000 livres collected on average from the octrois during the second half of the eighteenth century.[14] On the contrary, 11 per cent of the cities listed in the inquiry of 1766 did not have any octroi. They were generally small centres, most of them (66 per cent) with less than 1,000 livres of annual income.

In most cases urban revenues depended on the evolution of consumption levels and trade flows taxed through the levying of octrois, although it should be remarked here that the octroi reflects the commercial trends of any given centre in a somewhat distorted way as this kind of tax was mainly collected on beverages. To this it should be added that the urban elites benefited from the exemption of their personal consumption of the products from their land and buildings, so at the end the octrois were mainly paid by all those who purchased their wine, cider and beer in the urban taverns. Considering that the demographic evolution of the early modern cities was primarily related to its migratory balance, the strongest signs of urban growth of the eighteenth century thus indicate the most attractive urban centres, among which the principal harbour cities and the manufacturing centres clearly stood out. In Nantes, the octroi which produced 188,000 livres in 1753 falls back to 73,700 livres in 1761 to reach 300,000 livres in 1789.[15] If the provincial administrative structuring of the royal state exerted a real influence on the French urban hierarchy in the 16th and 17th centuries, this factor was progressively sidelined by the rise of the economy of exchange and consumption during the century of the Enlightenment. Within this total logic, particular local operations like the large urban fortifications in the frontier towns or the embellishments of towns of both kinds came to add particular fluctuations which did not fail to have an impact on the resources of the octroi.

One should not try to establish too close a relation between the octroi and the evolution of the urban economy and trade, even after taking into account the previous remarks. To some extent, this was also due to the fact that the levying of this kind of tax was conditioned by political considerations. On the one hand, municipal oligarchies oscillated between their desire to obtain more revenues for more ambitious community action and the convenience of maintaining a moderate level of taxation to protect themselves against possible urban protests. On the other hand, central authorities did not feel such preoccupations and were mainly concerned with the ability of local communities to pay their taxes. The unequal concessions of the octroi were thus in relation, in compensatory form, with the level of the financial requirements. In addition, the adjudication of the lease of the octroi introduced a complex game between financial backers and takers, mainly based on an estimate of the near future starting from the indicators provided by an immediate past, which could lead to an excessive pessimism or an optimism contradicted by the facts, which weighed directly on the negotiation of the lease. The adjudications of the Nantes octrois were thus under-evaluated during the second part of the reign of Louis XIV, before a vigorous correction under its successor;[16] the municipality of Reims was victim of an excess of confidence in the years 1770, plunging the city into a financial crisis.[17]

Municipal Policies Facing a Double Demand: Community and Royal Authority

The municipalities were at the at the same time responsible for the organization of the collective life of a major community of people and intermediaries between the royal power and the inhabitants of the kingdom, so they became increasingly integrated into the complex system of provincial administration of the monarchy. They were always in a position to arbitrate between the priorities of both systems which were rarely complementary. The obligation to respond in the first place to the royal demands, whether in the form of financial transfers or in the form of the construction of facilities for the military defence of the kingdom, was a political constraint that could not be questioned. They tried to negotiate in order to reduce the amount of these requirements as much as possible with unequal results, according to the place and the moment. As for their responsibilities towards the community, the ordinary functions of *échevinages* (offices of aldermen) and consulates consisted generally in public order, and sometimes also including public works, which was the other great function of local communities. Proposing a global overview of the nature of the municipal policy through the study of the structure of urban spending is problematic due to the lack of studies at our disposal. According to the authors, the groupings by categories change, which complicates the comparison.

There is no exact correspondence between the municipal activity, its transla-
tion in the accounts and the impact on urban development and the quality of
the life of the inhabitants. By their regulatory activity, the urban authorities had
the means to influence, with varying effectiveness, both the mindset and the life-
style of urban inhabitants, which were both difficult to transform, as well as the
labour market, social peace and the quality of life. By obtaining privileges favouring economic activity or by the introduction of new institutions, the *échevinages*
and the consulates were in a position to support the global development of their
city. The imposing registers of their deliberations filed in the local archives show
the time and the energy that they devoted to this activity. The study of the urban
accounts provides a glimpse of the extent of such effort, and this poses the problem of how to analyse the municipal policies through the study of the structure
of urban spending.

It seems to us that to achieve this objective we must take into account the
political culture of the city fathers of early modern times, in order to delineate the correspondence of their ideals and their financial choices, which were in
permanent tension between the needs of the royal state and those of the inhabitants. In a framework of municipal ethics, which were widely fashioned by the
Tridentine culture, it would be also important to measure the financial weight of
those measures whose aim was to improve the conditions of life for the population as this was the basis of the moral contract by which the municipal oligarchy
had its domination accepted by the body of the community, a fundamental
mental agreement the importance of which is revealed at the occasion of urban
riots, which function as crises of restoration to proper municipal conduct, from
which the community envisaged a separation. This approach calls therefore to
distinguish between the properly institutional functioning of the city and those
initiatives directed immediately towards the well-being of the inhabitants, even
if the two are intimately linked in municipal ethics.

While avoiding any grotesque exaggeration, it is convenient to make a distinction between the two first centuries when the municipal policy consisted
in finding resources to fund the huge deficits caused by a dramatic external economic and political climate which was not mastered (cyclic returns of epidemics
and agricultural crises) and the eighteenth century, when better prevention
against economic and sanitary risks, facilitated from the years around 1720 by an
expanding economy, allowed the opening of some perspectives on a longer term.
The great difficulty came from the increasing tax requirements of the state which
strained these margins lately offered, to a stronger or lesser degree. The majority
of provincial cities, however, could now raise the question of a restoration of their
material space, an ambition which had remained out of their range before.

On the basis of these principles, a comparative synthesis is not easy to carry
out because of the lack of homogeneity of the methodologies already applied,
which results from the lack of interest and the absence of a true historiographic
debate on municipal finances in France. Therefore, several questions arise. As to

the measurement of the tax rate, is it necessary to distinguish between the taxes related to the general policy of taxation, including all the expedients imagined by the central government, and in particular the occasional creation of municipal offices openly conceived for their repurchase by the body of cities, and those related to the financing of the military equipment of the border? If the consideration of the fundamental difference between the two types of cities invites us to answer in the affirmative, an objection can be raised that this would then mask the extent of the constraint coming from the central state. Moreover, it is not a question of a pure external transfer since the operation and construction costs for the army and the King's navy fall under the economic and social materiality of any city which constituted one of its bases of development. Even if the price to be paid seems to be to the disadvantage of the taxpayers, there was nevertheless a direct effect for the city in return.

In addition, does one need to globalize all the administrative expenditures or rather distinguish between those really related to the institutional organization and those justified by an immediate improvement of the living conditions of the inhabitants in their food, their health, their instruction, the simple reduction of the misery of those least provided for in the defence of the privileges of the most favoured in order to better determine and qualify the social dimension of the pursued financial policy? It is certainly not easy to separate these two aspects because institutions were always justified by the ethics of their time as well as by their service to these higher collective interests. This prospect could nevertheless add to the debate on the nature of municipal power, which is currently oversimplified to the self-promotional social mechanics of the most ambitious urban families. Finally, the only two points which are essential in the studies carried out are the need to measure the weight of the urban debt and the extent of the investments in the urban embellishment.

Table 7.1: Internal urban expenditures at Reims (1765–89).

Operation costs			
Community	%	*External relations*	%
Salaries of officials	14.4	Gifts	10.8
Salaries of lower officials	19	Annual meal	1.4
Police	3.6	Housing of guests	4.2
Process costs	2.8	Travel and deputations	7.1
Office costs	3.9	Equipment for militias	4.5
Accounting costs	9.7	Public ceremonies	5.4
Printing costs	2.5	Concerts	10.6
Maintainance of public buildings			
Streets and sidewalks	31.8	Street lights	16.1
Construction and repairs	22.7	Promenades	5.2
Military barracks	6.6	College, schools for mathematics and design	3.2
Public fountains	4.9	Salaries of teachers	9.4

Source: X. Hourblin, *Les finances de Reims à la fin de l'Ancien Régime, 1765–1789* (Paris: CHEFF, 2008), pp. 254, 269.

The expenditure of Reims is set out as an example in Table 7.1. Looking at the operation costs in the table, the remuneration of municipal officers represents one-third of all expenses. The two columns proposed seek to distinguish between the administrative costs and political investments dedicated on the one hand to the identity of the urban community and on the other to the maintenance of good relationships to the royal power or the royal administration. The only really problematic heading is the last 'Concerts', considering that it might be preferable to attach the expenses for concerts to the first column, those directed towards the community, in this case in the support of an animated cultural life, a traditional ostentatious sign of the urban dynamism in the second half of the eighteenth century, together with the construction of theatres and representative public architecture. The same remark relates to the last two posts related to schools and the salaries of teachers, which are also related to the quality of the cultural life at Reims. Considering public works, the importance of the streets and maintenance of the various municipal buildings are a good testimony of the priorities of the municipal officials.

In the case of Reims, one should however not consider only these data to measure the impact of the material transformation of the city. The large-scale operation of town planning related to the construction of the famous *Place Royale,* which was extended by the laying-out of four new streets (between 1757 and 1772) is not integrated in this table because it was registered separately by respect of the logic that it involved single instance expenses. A special account was created to ensure the financing of this imposing urban building site by means of loans and a royal contribution. It is thus advisable to add these extraordinary accounts to have an exact idea of the dominating weight of the policy of embellishment in the municipal finances, generally oscillating around 40 per cent of expenditure, and with a peak of 45 per cent in 1771.[18]

The accounting of various expenditures appears very disparate. It mixes allowances paid to the clergy to compensate it for the octroi as a consequence of the fusion of 1636 which allowed the administrative unification of the city, on the one hand, and the elimination of canonic houses during the construction of the Grande Place at the other hand. The first post would fit better among operational costs and the second would indicate the weight of town planning. This masks also more significant interventions like the financing of grain provisioning, the charitable workshops set up after the economic crisis of 1770–1 or the subsidies going to parishes that were victims of calamities such as fires. Even increased by the cultural expenditures mentioned before, it has to be recognized that these instances do not weigh heavily in the use of the resources.

To place the example of Reims in the French context, a comparison with Angers,[19] Nantes[20] and three cities of the north of France[21] can help to lighten up some perspectives of our investigation.

Table 7.2: **Breakdown of the expenditure in some large towns of France during the eighteenth century (in percentages).**

	Nantes 1711–12	Angers 1720	Angers 1780	Reims 1770	Reims 1784	Douai 1750–84	Lille 1740–80	Valenciennes 1730–89
Annuities	20.80	2.50	11.40	28.30	42.30	8.88	20.35	16.58
Royal taxes	26.20	22.30	21.10	4.60	1.00	42.17	43.51	55.79
Operating costs	36.17	48.20	41.20	17.90	13.10	40.82	33.28	26.67
Public works	16.83	18.30	17.10	42.60	41.40			
Diverse		8.70	9.20	6.60	2.20	8.11	2.81	0.96

At Angers operational costs represented an important part of the budget. Also costs related to the defence of its rights and privileges hold a significant place. That did not affect investments in urban embellishment because expenses related to the urban debt remained moderate in spite of an increase since 1740. The profile of Nantes at the beginning of the century is quite similar, with the only difference being the degree of urban debt. Whereas Angers could finance without borrowing too much thanks to its patrimonial incomes, and in particular the *cloison*, Nantes applied a systematic strategy of loans in order to maintain the octrois on the lowest possible level. Although being cities of the interior, the military charge of housing soldiers proved to be significant. The share of public works was still comparable in both cases in 1720, although it would not be so later on. Whereas the aldermen of Angers refused to use their patrimonial surpluses to finance large investments, Nantes stood out for its policy of embellishment, initially in the 1720s, but mainly in second half of the eighteenth century.

A comparison with three cities of the northern border of the kingdom immediately emphasizes their differences. The weight of the military charges is felt on an unknown level in the cities of the Loire valley or the Champagne. The reduced share devoted to operational costs and embellishment is the logical consequence of this mobilization of urban finances in the north in the service of the military interests of the state. Only Douai could benefit from its low degree of indebtedness to pursue a real urban policy. This conclusion, however, needs to be moderated because military expenditure cannot be considered as completely external to the city, without any impact on the urban development and the level of prosperity of its inhabitants. By taking up the distinction between external and internal expenditure, the examples of Angers and Reims can be used to mark a distinction.

In the Anjou capital, external charges, which were very low in the last third of the seventeenth century, increased and finally stabilized around a third of all expenditure. In Reims, they oscillated around 37 per cent in years leading up to 1770, to rise in the ensuing decade, until reaching 47.5 per cent in 1782 and 1783. Even then, the comparison is skewed as this increase is not so much external, since the increasing costs related to the debt are explained by the decline of the octroi, which the city overestimated in their long-term projection at the time and subscribed for high loans for the construction of the Grande Place, an eminently urban investment.

The Balance of the Municipal Accounts and Levels of Debt

The Municipal Accounts between Positive Balance and Deficit

In order to consider the problems of a countable balance correctly, one should distinguish two historical phases separated by the edict from April 1683, remembering the period of checking the debts on the initiative of Colbert after 1665 was transitory. Before that, there was no prior control of the municipal finances, the Chamber of Accounts restricting itself to checking the conformity of the operations with the urban ordinances. Then, an obligatory distinction was created between ordinary expenditures, a list of which was carefully drawn up, and extraordinary, the authorization of which was subjected to the evaluation of a 'general assembly' of the community and the approval of the intendant. The lack of a regular revision of ordinary expenditures led to a considerable inflation of the extraordinary ones, thus reinforcing the control of the royal administration. Logically, with such a framing, the municipal treasuries should never have had to amass such enormous deficits which had justified the intervention of Colbert in the first place. Nevertheless, the distinction was of no use.

Is this inefficiency due to the administrative limits of the control of the intendant who was often unable to correctly read the countable assessments presented by the cities, eager to mask the real state of their finances to preserve their margins of autonomy? Many testimonies of royal commissioners ask for this interpretation, such as that of Lefebvre de Caumartin who qualifies the accounts of Lille as a 'labyrinth' in 1776, or the distant follow-up of Rouillé d'Orfeil who only really began to understand the treasury of Reims in 1779. The intendants of Tours always ran up against the refusal of the aldermen of Angers to subject their ordinary expenditure to their control under the pretext that they were financed by their patrimony, especially the profitable toll of the *cloison*. When they were obliged to present statements of expenses on occasions, the latter were clearly under-stated. For a declared annual average of 23,368 livres for the period 1766–76 for the *cloison*, Jacques Maillard could reconstitute entries of at least 43,000 livres. The intendant confessed to the controller general Laverdy in 1766 that: 'the public moneys are dissipated and are employed at will by these officers, in a clandestine way ... it has been impossible in all times to me and my predecessors to acquire the exact knowledge of the use of the common incomes'.[22]

This strategy of opacity, as real as it was, cannot explain, however, the return of many cities to chronic indebtedness. It has to be stressed that the balance of the budget for the needs of the community never constituted the ideal nor the logic of the central government which rather regarded the deficit caused by the requirements of the state as a form of compensation for the privileges of the cities over the countryside. Persuaded that the cities had the means to fulfil the demands by taking recourse to their intrinsic wealth, the central government was hardly sensitive to the risk of discouraging the financial market of the public revenues and thus putting in danger an essential financial tool by an excessive debt rate. This policy, closely related to the management of privileges in general, made municipal financial policy a ceaseless adjustment of the resources to the expenditure which was imposed or considered to be essential and not the reverse.

The most common solution was to use short-term loans while waiting for an economic recovery to restore the finances in order to be able to refund creditors. The latter were generally constituted by the municipal treasurer or private individuals and institutions like religious and hospital establishments which thus employed their funds consisting of the charitable legacies of generous donators. When the royal levy required a strong increase or the deficit settled durably, the simplest solution was to request supplements of the octroi. There was however some restraint against this policy because of the hostility of the mass of the consumers and of the fear of the commercial circuits of a decrease in demand, which formed a powerful mental barrier against this type of adjustment. However, among unpleasant remedies, it was certainly not the worst. It was finally preferable to the more radical solution of direct taxation, even if the latter was always presented like an extraordinary remedy in order to overcome a particular crisis. Even so, a distinction had to be made if the load was to include a large part of the population, by excluding only the poor, or, if it concerned in priority the 'well-off', always in the name of the moral and political contract ruling the government of the city. It is striking to note that most of the time the various solutions were used one after the other as if the introduction of variety into taxation was to soften the psychological effects on the population and thus to facilitate its acceptance. Let us not forget either that this diversification also was due to the obligation to mobilize all the means available in consequence of a spectacular rise of financial needs, especially when a blaze of state taxation occurred in a bad economic period.

According to the inquiry of 1766, there is no correlation between the demographic scale and the surplus or deficit of the urban budget. The only thing we can observe is a larger difficulty to achieve a balance in the category of the medium-sized cities. The town of Chartres was the exception, however: it managed an average income of 43,750 livres between 1727 and 1788, and was visibly not affected by this weakness.[23] It appears more significant to confront the financial balance with the hierarchy of the urban incomes rather than with the demographic size. Out of the 907 cities of the inquiry, 214 had a deficit higher than 20 per cent of their receipts and, within this group in difficulty, 172 had to do with incomes lower than 5,000 livres per year. More serious still, two-thirds had a deficit higher than 50 per cent of their receipts.[24] The geographical distribution of deficits clearly reveals that the great majority of the cities of southern France, that is, south of a line connecting Bordeaux with Lyon, had a deficit of more than 50 per cent of their incomes. Thus the cities of Languedoc appear very weakened, perhaps because of voluntary undertaxation in a province where the attachment to franchises found a concretization in the administrative power of its states. In the northern part of the country, the deficit generally remained below that level, except in Alsace, Franche-Comté, along the northern border and in Upper Normandy. On the whole we can observe especially the capacity of the large cities to recover quickly from situations of crisis, since the inquiry was carried out only three years after the end of the Seven Years' War when deficits were general and deep. Among the eleven cities with incomes higher than 10,000 livres and with a deficit higher than one year of receipts, one counts nine cities of Languedoc, in declining order according to the degree of their deficit: Saint-Jean-de-Luz, Limoux, Uzès, Béziers, Narbonne, Castres, Puy-en-Velay, Pézenas, Agde, Carcassonne and Nîmes.

The loss of control of the financial balance was not only related to a lack of prudence in expenditure, but also to the fluctuations of the incomes of the octroi, affected by economic cycles of growth and contraction. When both factors added up, this could turn a town rather quickly from a virtuous circle to a negative spiral as the disastrous accounts of Reims in the second half of the eighteenth century illustrate. Urged by the classical ambitions of the intendance to start a large building project and carried away in an excessive euphoria by the very good results of the octroi brought about by the temporary migration of many workers for the construction of the Place Royale, the municipality resorted largely to credit without sufficiently measuring the signs of reversal. When the economic crisis of 1770–1 added up to the end of the works, the loss of incomes plunged the municipal finances into a chronic deficit, which justified the intervention of the intendant Rouillé d'Orfeil and the central government who imposed a strict regulation of the expenditure in the ordinance of 24 December 1780.[25] The limitation to 67,750 livres, representing a reduction of 17,490 livres, was considered to be excessive by the city council which managed to soften the remedy in 1783 by prolonging the time-limit of financial stabilization. The limit of expenditure was raised to 70,850 livres. The tradition of privileged treatment of the city where the kings were crowned and the reformist political context of the 1780s explain this possibility of negotiation.

The Impact of the Debt

In municipal finances, the recourse to loans had three great significations, two intrinsically related to the community, and one as a direct consequence of the requirements of the state. For what concerns urban management specifically, two political contexts weighing on the choices of the municipal oligarchies are to be distinguished. Either it was more a practice of adjustment of the incomes to rising expenditure imposed by a bad economic situation, a form of flexibility in the financial regulation hit by the misfortunes of the time, in the form of constraints the city had undergone. Or it corresponded to heavy investments made necessary by a voluntarist policy of modernization of the city. Also if the first formula covers the whole of the early modern period, it characterizes rather the first two centuries while the second rather refers to the century of Enlightenment. In all times, the loan was a simple way to respond to the extraordinary rise of the tax pressure of the monarchy, be it in the form of voluntary gifts, of special taxations, the repurchase of privileges threatened of suppression, the partial transfer of the octroi or the creation of municipal offices subjected to venality.

In Reims, the loans contracted between 1692 and 1775 thus exceeded the amount of two million livres: 15.1 per cent for the repurchase of offices, 9.8 per cent for public fountains and 75.2 per cent for the construction of the Place Royale.[26] This recourse to credit is neither exceptional, nor disproportionate. A comparison of two cities of the same demographic rank provides an illuminating illustration. The aldermen of Angers borrowed approximately 1.8 million livres between 1722 and 1789. This is beyond comparison with Valenciennes where the debt came to 8.2 million livres in 1740 or with the 9 million livre debt of Marseilles in 1789.[27]

The social identity of the municipal creditors shows some common features while presenting strong variations according to the cities in a fluctuating balance between religious and charitable institutions and private individuals. In Reims, the first were clearly of secondary importance in comparison with the latter while in Valenciennes the balance is much less clear. In the cities of the north, the borrowed capital was provided for 58.4 per cent by private individuals, 22.7 per cent by hospitals and charitable institutions and 18.9 per cent by religious communities.[28] In the cities of the Champagne region, religious and charitable communities had only a reduced role in comparison with the local (36.7 per cent) but especially Parisian (46.5 per cent) urban elites. This domination of the annuity market by the capital becomes even more significant if one considers the average share by category: 13,927 livres for the Parisian annuity-holder, 7,394 livres for the institutions against only 3,795 livres for the local annuity-holder.[29] In both cases, the external individual lenders contributed more than the locals: without any doubt we can see the effects of urban unbalance when a mid-sized city was located near a larger one and especially near the capital.

The central government never pursued an overall and systematic policy on the question of municipal debt. It treated towns in an extremely varied manner and required a reduction of the debt only when concern started to be spread in the world of the shareholders. The comparison of the treatment of the cities of the north[30] and Reims gives a good testimony of this. Valenciennes thus managed to release itself from almost all of its record debt in one half-century at the price of drastic measurements imposed on the lenders. The creditors of perpetual annuities had to renounce from their arrears to obtain the payment of half their interests. The holders of life annuities received one-sixth of their arrears under the condition of giving up the remainder. Thanks to this bitter medicine, the debt servicing passed from 21.7 per cent of the expenditure in 1750 to 11.9 per cent in 1770–4 and even to 0.62 per cent in 1785–9. Thanks to its plan of recovery of 1767 implying partial bankruptcy and an amortization fund, Douai managed to be released from the major part of its debts which did not make up any more but 10 per cent of expenditure in 1783. On the contrary, Dunkirk which had avoided any loans until the middle of the eighteenth century, indebted itself heavily afterwards, with a debt passing of 8.9 per cent of expenditure in the 1760s to 17 per cent in the 1780s. As for Lille, the cumulated total of the perpetual annuities and life annuities passed from 5 million in 1770 to 7.66 million livres in 1788, in other words, from 20 to 28 per cent of expenditure.

In order to understand the diversity of situations and rationale behind the state of the municipal finances after the inquiry of 1766, the evolution of the account balance and the level of the debt has to be confronted, while keeping in mind the indicators mentioned before: the relative importance of patrimonial income and the octroi, the amount of receipts and the measurement of financial burden per capita and the estimate of the relative weight of state taxation by comparing the proportion of the voluntary gift of 1759 to the income of the octroi, which was the principal ordinary receipt for the majority of cities. The cities are divided into three categories: cities with deficits higher than 20 per cent, those with a moderate deficit, that is, lower than this figure, and cities having a budget surplus.

The cities with the largest deficits actually accumulated several kinds of misfortunes. Equipped with a low level of financing, as shown by the low average rates per capita, they had to pay a high gift to the King in proportion to their incomes from the octroi whose limits are underlined by the relative importance of the patrimonial incomes. Among the fifty-one cities with a deficit higher than 50 per cent, twelve had not contracted any loans. For the majority these were very small cities of less than 2,000 inhabitants. From the thirty-nine others having made the opposite choice, fifteen had more than 5,000 inhabitants. For the group with a deficit between 20 and 50 per cent, the situation proves more disparate. The very small cities remain significant since forty-one out of eighty-nine did not have 3,000 inhabitants. On the other extreme we find twelve of the sixty-six cities of more than 10,000 inhabitants distributed evenly over northern France (Alençon, Le Havre, Caen, Dieppe, Tours and Nevers) and the south

(Nîmes, Alès, Montpellier, Béziers, Carcassonne and Castres). Most of them took recourse to loans.[31]

The category of cities with moderate deficits reveals a paradoxical situation in the sense that their financial characteristics seem better than those of the cities in surplus: slightly higher incomes per capita, relatively moderate contributions to the King rather in proportion of the octroi and a slightly lower debt level. For half of the towns of less than 10,000 inhabitants, this light budgetary imbalance is explained by the absence of loans. On the contrary, when there was a debt, it exceeded the threshold of 10 per cent in half of the cases. Therefore, a combination between two different profiles takes shape: a careful management disturbed by the brutal rising of royal taxation and a more ambitious policy not being satisfied with ordinary resources.

The group of cities with a surplus also displays two opposite situations. It is dominated quantitatively by the cities which kept away from loans or which resorted to them only with great prudence. But it contains also a number of medium-sized and large cities massively involved in debt like Orléans (22 per cent), Angers (25 per cent), Arras and Beauvais (27 per cent), Lille (28 per cent), Marseilles (34 per cent), Montpellier (35 per cent), Paris (38 per cent), Reims (44 per cent), Nîmes (49 per cent) and indeed, without comparison, Lyons (68 per cent). In 1766, sixteen cities whose incomes exceeded 30,000 livres had a debt higher than 20 per cent of their receipts. Here, the recourse to loans could be explained by insufficient receipts in relation to the population, that is, voluntary undertaxation, or the undertaking of great works exceeding the possibilities of the city, as in Reims during the creation of the Place Royale in the middle of the eighteenth century, or a strict budgetary separation between the patrimonial incomes and the octroi as in Angers, which led to a combination of hoarding and a massive recourse to loans at the same time. However, there is definitely a more decisive explanation which brings us back to the strategy of the central government to collect financial means from the major cities whose financial market appeared sufficiently solid and active. The discrepancy between receipts and expenditures proves to be considerable, revealing the great differences in municipal tax pressure per capita or the shifts of ambition according to different location. In fact the cities which contracted more loans were not the ones in strong budgetary imbalance, but restored their accounts rather quickly.

Drawing up the assessment of all these remarks within the framework of the three main categories of the urban demographic hierarchy shows, once more, the diverging character of the financial standings of the municipalities. Small cities easily ended up in the most perilous situations with each important increase of the royal taxation for circumstances of war. The smallest accumulated strong deficits because of not being able to borrow; those which risked, often because they were better located in economic networks, encountered problems getting their money back.[32] The medium-sized cities generally enjoyed healthy and balanced finances, except for those of Languedoc, which had higher rates of debt. The requirements of the state were in better proportion with their potential, so that they managed better to digest these without too many blows. The large cities constituted a world of their own in the financial relation between the monarchical state and the city governments. Generally enjoying surplus balances, the levels of debt could go up very high. The royal power regarded them as its principal means of adjustment during times of crisis for the royal treasury, relying on the reserves of their forced taxations or the fast recovery of their receipts of the octroi thanks to economic revivals following periods of great military conflicts. Lyons, for example borrowed 8.4 million livres in 1758–9, mainly to contribute a gift of 6 million livres to the central government.[33]

Finally, there are four variables which seem to have conditioned the impact of municipal finances on urban development: the position of the town along the inland or maritime border, the degree of insertion in the rising exchange economy, which affected the kingdom through the great international, mainly colonial, trade, and finally the acceptance of the level of local taxation, based mainly on the octroi ensuring a more or less strong borrowing power. Above all, however, the selective treatment of the cities as financial markets by the royal state as part of its own financial system played a crucial role.

However, the most direct impact on municipal finances lay in the Crown's consideration of the municipalities as particularly operational financial intermediaries for raising capital from a group of creditors putting more trust in these institutions of their proximity whose rate of debt was definitely lower than that of the monarchical state, with an average rate of 25 per cent against 40 per cent according to the inquiry of 1766. By charging urban finances, the royal treasury forced the municipalities to borrow. This policy concentrated mainly on the large cities, and particularly four of them during the eighteenth century: Paris, Lyons, Marseilles and Lille.

8 THE MAKING OF THE URBAN FISCAL SYSTEM OF ANTWERP UNTIL 1800: EXCISES, ANNUITIES AND DEBT MANAGEMENT

Michael Limberger

Introduction

Among the factors that influenced the formation of different urban fiscal systems we can count different political traditions on a regional level that have to do with differences in the development of urban autonomy as well as processes of state formation. However, there were also differences between individual cities, according to their socio-economic profile, their political importance or their size, and particular political or economic constellations throughout their history. In the case of Antwerp, the fiscal system showed a considerable number of similarities with other cities of north-western Europe, and in particular within the southern Low Countries. Towns such as Brussels, Bruges, Ghent or Louvain, for example, were comparable to Antwerp in their tax system, which was in great part based on proceeds from indirect taxes on beer, wine and grain. All these cities also frequently made use of annuity sales in order to finance larger expenses, above all taxes to the central government.[1]

Antwerp differed from these cities, however, in one important respect. During the sixteenth century, it was one of the major commercial and financial centres of western Europe. Moreover, it played a crucial role in the financial policy of Charles V who relied heavily on the financial market of Antwerp and also on its public credit. The expenses that went hand in hand with Antwerp's exceptional position would determine its financial policy for the centuries to come. The urban financial organization of Antwerp was again fundamentally changed as a result of the French occupation in 1794. Thereafter, the communal institutions as well as the financial system were replaced by a centralized system according to the French model.[2] In order to get a good look at the evolution of the early modern situation, the period just before this moment is, therefore, a good starting point.

The Fiscal System at the End of the Old Regime

By the end of the eighteenth century the financial situation of Antwerp presented a complex structure. Instead of one general town account the city had
three different funds which each had their own accountability. First there was an
account called account of the domains (*kasse van domeinen*). Until 1579 it was
the original town account and it still had the basic function of providing income
for the ordinary household of the city administration. It contained a variety of
sources of revenue, consisting of rents, income from public rights, excises on a
variety of goods as well as life annuities; its expenses, on the other hand, were
mainly for the salaries of town officials, public works and general costs.

A second account was the account of reduction (*kasse van reductie*). This
second town account was introduced in 1575 on the occasion of a general reduction of the interest on the town's annuities, which became necessary as a result
of the city's enormous debt. It was allocated a considerable amount of income,
especially from the excises on beer. The goal of this fund was to pay the annuities
on the urban debt, which had reached astronomical proportions by that time.
Finally there was a third town account, the account of consumption (*consumptiekas*), which was established shortly thereafter in order to pay the annuities that
had to be sold to pay the fine that was imposed upon the city and the rebuilding
of the citadel after the reconquest of the city by Spanish troops under Alexander
Farnese in 1585. The name *consumptiekas* comes from the taxes on consumption
that were to provide the necessary funds. Besides these three principal accounts,
which characterized the financial system of Antwerp during more than two
centuries, there were two more funds of less importance: the account for the
maintenance of the court and the account of the new means (*nieuwe middelen*),
a number of taxes that were introduced in 1745–6. These different funds were
interconnected. Surplus and deficits were shifted from one to the other, and
many income entries were distributed according to specific keys among the three
accounts. This makes the analysis not only difficult for the historian, but also for
the control organisms of the central government, which was a side effect that was
maybe not unwanted after all.[3]

Taken together, the Antwerp city finances had four major sources of revenue: the domain (not to be confused with the *account of domains* one of the
three town accounts), that is income from real estate and seigniorial rights,
income resulting from the public authority of the city government, taxes and
finally loans. These major sources of income for the city were already established
in the thirteenth century: these were essentially excises on the major goods of
consumption, especially on wine and beer, earnings related to the public authority of the magistracy, such as the right of citizenship, income from the urban
patrimony, and yields from loans, in the form of the sale of life annuities. From

this point of view, the city did not distinguish itself fundamentally from other Brabantine and Flemish towns of the same period.[4]

Antwerp's urban domain consisted of some revenue from leases and rents on the urban patrimony. These were land rents on the urban terrain as well as leases on real estate and public buildings such as storehouses. The income from these came to 22,700 guilders in 1776–77, that is 4.7 per cent of the total income.

Table 8.1: Income according to the Antwerp Town Accounts, 1776–7 (in guilders).

	Kas van Domeinen	Reductiekas	Consump-tiekas	Maintenance of court	New means	Total	%
Beer excise	34186	89524	80461			204171	42.2%
Grain tax	1176	3529	8594	6176	26695	46170	9.6%
Sale of offices	35940					35940	7.4%
Wine excise		9964	11228		6699	27891	5.8%
Taxes on fuel	38		24467			24505	5.1%
Income from property	21309		115			21424	4.4%
Tolls and road taxes	10537		8414			18951	3.9%
Half excise on beer and wine	16845					16845	3.5%
Excise on brandy		5578	3718	3260		12556	2.6%
Excise on fish	7773		1710		3015	12498	2.6%
Excise on dairy and fat	2689		8852			11541	2.4%
Pontpenningen (transfer fees)	5248	2624	2624			10496	2.2%
Interest of active loans			9000			9000	1.9%
Public sales			6038			6038	1.2%
Increase 20th penny					5153	5153	1.1%
Tax on annuities and stamp tax		4354				4354	0.9%
Meat excise	3675					3675	0.8%
Issuerecht		3066				3066	0.6%
Citizens and guilds	2342					2342	0.5%
Tax on tobacco	2081					2081	0.4%
Tax on horses	88		1884			1972	0.4%
Rents	1298					1298	0.3%
Tax on torches			1038			1038	0.2%
Fines	333					333	0.1%
Salt tax	19					19	0.0%
Mead tax		18				18	0.0%
Total	145577	114303	172497	9436	41562	483375	
%	30%	24%	36%	2%	9%		

Source: Boumans, *Het Antwerpse stadsbestuur.*

Income from the public authority included rights based on jurisdiction and contributions deriving from commercial transactions or the use of the commercial infrastructure. In 1776–7 they came to 57,566 guilders or 11.91 per cent. Some of these proceeds were originally only partly in the hands of the city. The rest belonged to the prince or individual noblemen. The city made concerted efforts, however, to gain control over these rights, such as the scale, the toll on Scheldt etc. The city magistrates bought them for a high price in order to increase the fiscal basis of urban finances, but also to increase its autonomy in the field of economic policy.[5] Thus between 1522 and 1542, the city purchased successively parts of the urban weighing right including the so-called *riddertol* from the duke and several other owners, and in 1677 the '*lepelrecht*' a ducal right on grain, for which the town did not spend less than 300,000 guilders.[6] In the seventeenth century, 15 per cent of the annuities sold by the city government were spent on the purchase of tolls and seigniorial rights. Only the payment of taxes to the central government cost the city more (see Table 8.3). In the eighteenth century the sale of offices became a considerable source of public revenue. While at the beginning of the century yearly income was still only *c.* 8,700 guilders, the amount was to increase and reached a level of 36,000 guilders, or 7.4 per cent of the total proceeds.[7]

Indirect taxes on consumption constituted the great majority of the fiscal income of Antwerp. At the end of the Old Regime, there were no fewer than sixty different taxes on thirteen different goods, in the first place on beer, wine and grain. In the city accounts, these so-called great excises accounted for more than 60 per cent of total urban income.[8] The large proportion of indirect taxes and excises, especially on consumption, was a common feature in the southern Low Countries. It has been described as a characteristic of mercantile cities and industrial centres.[9] In order to yield high returns, essentially goods of mass consumption were taxed, such as grain, meat, wine and beer. Especially the beer excise, which was considered the major means of urban taxation, provided by far the greatest share. It was frequently increased in order to provide the necessary financial means. In the eighteenth century there were therefore more than thirty different taxes on beer, which had been introduced throughout the early modern period. Some of them taxed all kinds of beer, others only a particular type. Furthermore they could be limited to certain groups of the population. So in 1643, the beer excises were raised for individual citizens with a '*laatste poortershoogsel*' in order to pay life annuities on a loan of 15,000 guilders, and in 1650 beer for a half stuiver per pint sold to individuals (*poorters halfstuiversbieren*) was taxed at 6 stuivers per *ame* in 1650 in order to pay life annuities on a capital amount of 150,000 guilders.[10]

Grain was the second basic consumption good that was taxed. The different excises on grain provided 9.55 per cent of the total income in 1776–7. The original wheat excise was one of the city's oldest excises, whereas the so-called 'impost on wheat and rye' was originally a tax levied by the Estates of Brabant and was leased by the city for 10,000 guilders per year. Both excises were grouped under the common name of milling-excise. 5,000 guilders of the yield were divided among the different funds of the city; the rest went to the court of the governor. Furthermore, there was the '*lepelrecht*', originally a princely right of one spoon of grain per sack, which was later transformed into a tax of 1 per cent. This right was purchased by the city against a loan in the huge amount of 300,000 guilders in 1676.[11] Grain taxes were increased to a considerable degree in the eighteenth century. The *nieuwe middelen* of 1745–6 were for the largest part grain taxes.

The wine excise was the third of the great excises. It was one of the city's oldest excises and existed already in 1263. It had been the most important source of taxation in the Middle Ages, but by the fifteenth century, its share had decreased while that of beer was gradually rising. Like the beer excise, its original tariff was repeatedly increased throughout the sixteenth to the eighteenth century, mainly in the context of the building of fortifications in the sixteenth century, in 1647 and in the framework of the introduction of the *nieuwe middelen* in 1779.

Other excises were levied on fish, butter and cheese, meat, linen, horses, fuel, salt, tobacco, as well as on the use of torches during ceremonies, although the income from these sources was much lower than that from the excises on beer and wine. Besides these excises, whose origins date back to the Middle Ages, other excises were added to generate urban income later on. So, in 1541, the city first introduced an excise on brandy, in order to compensate for the decreasing incomes deriving from the wine excise. During the financial crisis of the city after 1585, the city reintroduced the excise on wood, coal and peat, which had been levied in the fourteenth century, but had been abolished later on. In the seventeenth century, the Broad Council tended increasingly towards taxes on luxury goods, such as horses (1645 and 1663), candles and torches used during burials and other ceremonies (1663) and tobacco (1667). Public sales on the Friday market were taxed from 1664 onward as well as sealed paper and the sale of annuities (1658).[12] In response to financial problems during the seventeenth century, new taxes on oil (1668), torches (1661), a penny on sold goods (1663), and on the taxation of furniture (1664), 0.25 per cent on import and export by ship (1666), a tenth penny on the lease value of real estate (1667) and on tobacco (1667) were introduced; they did not, however, succeed in re-establishing an equilibrium in the urban finances. Hence in 1680 the tax on horses was increased to 50 guilders, and goods that were sold in public were taxed at one stuiver per guilder. In the eighteenth century this development continued. Here, especially, the introduction of the so-called *nieuwe middelen* in 1745–6 was a major step. However, the income that these new excises created remained of secondary importance in comparison with the beer excise and its numerous augmentations.[13]

Direct taxes are almost absent in the town accounts. The only permanent direct tax was the *issuegeld*, a tax related to the medieval *tallia*, which was a general practice until the thirteenth century. This was a right to 5 per cent of the value on goods that were sold outside the city and therefore lost to the *tallia*. When the *tallia* disappeared during the later Middle Ages, the *issuegeld* remained. It was abolished by Joseph II for the whole of the southern Low Countries in 1784; however, its levy continued in Antwerp.[14] Direct taxes were, however, imposed occasionally in cases of exceptional circumstances, like wars or other crises. In the second half of the sixteenth century, direct taxes on wealth became a relatively frequent form of taxation also on the urban level.[15] Especially during the period of the Calvinist domination, between 1579 and 1585, a series of direct taxes was introduced.

A last source of urban revenue was loans, which were generally obtained by selling annuities, either in the form of life annuities or perpetual annuities. The sale of annuities was a common way to obtain the money necessary for extraordinary expenses of all kinds, such as taxes due to the central state, building works and so on. Large amounts of money were difficult to find within a short time via common taxation. Alternatives were extraordinary taxes, lotteries or forced loans, which were unpopular and hence only imposed in cases of absolute emergency. The sale of annuities, on the contrary, promised a quick and relatively unproblematic payment, especially in a commercial city such as Antwerp with an active market for public annuities. Annuities were, however, closely linked to the tax system. Tax incomes were assigned to pay back the annuities and, as the number of annuities increased, new taxes had to be introduced or existing ones raised. The sale of annuities helped to raise large amounts of money in the short run but spread the cost over a long period.[16] By doing so they put enormous pressure on the fiscal system and gradually aggravated the fiscal burden of the citizens. While the ordinary expenses of the city could be paid through moderate taxation, the ever-increasing debt payments made frequent additional taxes necessary.

In 1776–7 no annuities were sold, hence, this category is not visible in Table 8.1. The role of the sale of annuities has therefore to be analysed over a longer period. The effect can be seen, however, by analysing expenditures, which went in large part to the payment of annuities. Throughout the early modern period, annuities accounted for almost 60 per cent of public expenses (Table 8.2).

Table 8.2: Major categories of public expenses, Antwerp 1530–1830.

Category	1530–1545	1665–1680	1744–1745	1782–1783	1815–1830
Debt payments	58%	59%	57%	65%	15%
Wages & administration	13%	14%	19%	15%	11%
Public works	9%	7%	6%	16%	18%
Taxes	17%	11%	7%		0%
Poor relief		0,1%			22%
Schools		8%	0,9%		5%
Fiests		0,2%	7%	1%	1%
Central authorities					
Security		0,3%	0,3%		7%
Military		0,1%	0,9%		6%
Purchase of real estate	1%				
Material		3%			
Religion		0,1%	0,1%		2%
Others	2%	4%	2%	4%	2%

Source: M. Limberger, 'City Government and Public Services in Antwerp, 1500–1800', presented at the conference, 'Civil Society and Public Services in Early Modern Europe', Leiden, 30 November to 1 December 2007.

The link between the urban tax system and public debt in the form of annuities was a key element in the urban finances of Antwerp just as in many other European cities. The practice of selling annuities can be traced back to the thirteenth and fourteenth centuries, but especially from the sixteenth century onwards it affected the balance of Antwerp's finances profoundly. According to the town account of 1782, the city had a debt of more than 8 million guilders, but only incomes of *c*. 480,000 guilders. The long-term debt was therefore almost seventeen times as big as the yearly income of the city.

A survey of the urban debt made in 1819 lists loans dating back to as far as 1453 (Table 8.3 and Figure 8.1).[17] It shows the enormous impact of the building of fortifications in the 1540s on the financial situation of Antwerp throughout the early modern period.[18] A second important entry was the purchase of public rights, which provided extra proceeds for the city, but for a high price. Debt management was another important item, which caused the city considerable costs. Taxes to the central government accounted for 14 per cent of the public debt. Many of these debts had their origin in the sixteenth century. Besides the fortifications of the 1540s, these consisted also of loans to the prince, and the debts incurred for the building of the town hall and the citadel. In total they accounted for 46 per cent of the public debt. The seventeenth century had a share of 34 per cent, and the eighteenth century 19 per cent.

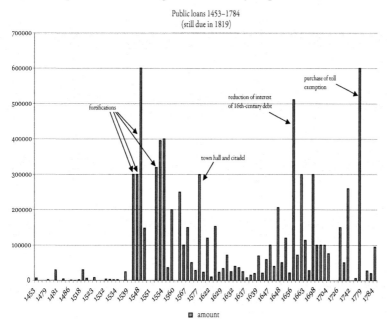

Figure 8.1: Public loans 1453–1784 (still due in 1819).

Table 8.3: Antwerp public loans 1453–1784 (still due in 1819).

Purpose	Amount	%
Fortifications (sixteenth century)	1,620,000	20%
Purchase of public rights	1,537,502	19%
Debt management	1,336,281	16%
Tax	1,122,901	14%
Loan to prince (sixteenth century)	3,98,000	5%
Famines	388,000	5%
Military	380,000	5%
Town hall and citadel (sixteenth century)	300,000	4%
Town hall (sixteenth century)	250,000	3%
Diverse	203,800	3%
Gifts to prince	152,800	2%
Lottery	148,000	2%
Paved roads	120,200	1%
Joyful entry	76,000	1%
Public assistance	72,000	1%
Dykes	36,193	0%
Grain	28,000	0%
Payment to prince	23,000	0%
Pesthouses	8,000	0%
Total	8,200,677	

Of this debt, 3.4 million (mostly to be paid out of the *reductiekas*), mainly contracted to pay taxes and loans to the prince, the fortifications of the city and similar expenses, dated from the sixteenth century. The rest were loans contracted in the seventeenth and eighteenth centuries. The *consumptiekas* was charged with a debt of more than 3.6 million mainly contracted during the period 1624–1739. The greatest part of this debt was related to taxes to the central government. In 1680, 43.69 per cent of the annuities payable from the *consumptiekas* was related to taxes to the central government. Purchases of tolls and seigniorial rights came second with 14.35 per cent. Debt management was another major reason for selling annuities: either for paying outstanding loans, to reduce the interest on former annuities or to pay them off. Only a relatively small percentage was lent for extraordinary expenses related to the urban infrastructure, poor relief and so on (see Table 8.4). Finally, the rest of the urban debt, 687,000 guilders, was charged on the account of the *nieuwe middelen*, created in 1745. The differences between the origins of the long-term public debt and the annuities sold between 1624 and 1679 deserve some explanation. First, the great weight of the fortifications and other building projects dates almost entirely from the sixteenth century and is, therefore, absent in the seventeenth-century annuity sales. They are felt only indirectly, through the costs related to debt management, mainly through interest reduction. There were other reasons related to the different nature of the two surveys. The survey from 1819 gives an overview of all kinds of long-term debts that still were outstanding at that time. For loans dating from the sixteenth or seventeenth century these were by definition almost exclusively perpetual annuities. Loans that were contracted on a shorter term or cancelled in the meanwhile are, therefore, not included. The list of the annuities of the *consumptiekas* contained all annuities of that fund during the period 1624–79, among which many life annuities which would become extinct with the death of their buyers (or, in some cases of their children).

Table 8.4: Reasons for annuity sales of the *consumptiekas* (1624–79).

Purpose	Capital (guilders)	%
Taxes	1,614,035	43.69
Purchase tolls and seigniorial rights	530,000	14.35
Debts	375,975	10.18
Military	241,546	6.54
Diverse	174,525	4.72
Deficit	170,018	4.60
Reduction of interest on annuities	165,728	4.49
Diking	138,000	3.74
Cancel annuities	66,200	1.79
Disease	58,000	1.57
Provisions	53,788	1.46
Entry of regent	36,000	0.97
Gifts to prince	27,800	0.75
Poor relief	25,000	0.68
Renovation brewery	18,052	0.49
Total	3,694,667	

Source: 't Hart and Limberger, *Staatsmacht en stedelijke autonomie*, p. 61.

Urban debt was also the major link between the urban tax system and central state taxation. The prince, first the duke of Brabant and later the Habsburg rulers or their governors, regularly asked for financial support from the estates in the form of taxes or directly from the city through loans. Antwerp, which was represented in the Brabant Estates, had considerable influence in tax negotiations. It could negotiate, to a limited extent, on the amount of taxes, but, more importantly, about the form of taxation. The big cities paid a quota of the total amount of the tax, which it could levy in different ways. The decision on how to levy a tax was part of the tax negotiations and could often take more time than the principal decision either to agree with the payment of the tax or not. The taxes thus imposed by the central state were negotiated in the Broad Council of Antwerp and became an inseparable part of the urban tax system properly speaking. They were, in fact, urban taxes serving to pay the city's quota, or the annuities it had to sell for the payment of its taxes.

The Historical Evolution of the Antwerp Tax System

The origins of Antwerp's tax system date back to the twelfth century. Antwerp had its own properties at that time, and it can be supposed that its patrimony was considerable already then, because the city guaranteed the obligations of the duke on several occasions. It is likely that the city had part of the proceeds from the tolls or from the rights levied on wine in the early thirteenth century. Documents from the thirteenth century speak also of the existence of local taxes on wine and on the use of the crane (1263).[19]

Generally, it can be supposed that towns had the right to levy taxes since their very origins. However, their fiscal autonomy was limited by the *regalia* of the prince and lordly rights. The interaction between towns and the prince was characterized by changing power relations so that, according to particular circumstances, the fiscal autonomy of the town increased or was, on the contrary, hampered by the prince. Town charters that were issued from the eleventh century onwards were a compromise between the claims of both parties. The situation they express was, however, far from static. It shifted frequently throughout history and differed fundamentally between different towns.[20]

The case of Antwerp shows this development clearly. In the thirteenth and fourteenth centuries, a period of strong political power of the Brabant cities, the city obtained additional sources of income through permission granted by the duke, through the payment of an amount of money, or, on several occasions, by purchase of ducal rights, such as in 1317, when the duke ceded his rights on the cloth-hall for 150 pounds. In 1360 the relations between Antwerp and its overlord became troubled, when the city was attached to the count of Flanders. The city not only had to pay a tax of 1500 Flemish pounds groat, it also had to pay a yearly amount in order to obtain the recognition of the right to levy excises. The permission had to be renewed every three years, and later on every twelve years. In the fifteenth century, the dukes of Burgundy transferred a considerable part of their rights in Antwerp to the city government in exchange for loans and subsidies. In 1453, Antwerp obtained permanent permission for levying excises. In exchange it had to pay 12,000 guilders[21] as well as a yearly sum of 700 guilders.[22] Generally the permission was only granted for limited periods. Philippe the Fair, and later Charles V, declared as a general principle throughout the Low Countries that urban taxes could only be levied with the permission of the prince. The latter also was to receive his share of the income.[23] The fiscal system therefore evolved on the one hand according to the power relationship between the prince and the city, but on the other hand it was the result of financial transfers, by which the city purchased its fiscal tools. After a period of strong princely influence, Antwerp obtained therefore a high degree of fiscal autonomy, which it was to maintain until 1585.

The sixteenth century was crucial for the financial development of Antwerp. Antwerp's golden age already began in the second half of the fifteenth century, when the trade in English cloth, German silver and copper and Portuguese imports from Africa gained increasing importance.[24] Archduke Maximilan of Austria, who had become the heir of the duchy through marriage with Mary of Burgundy, bestowed on the city a number of privileges which had major financial implications: the herring toll (1479), a right called the *innegeld* (1481), the staple for alum (1491) and the right to levy excises in the village of Wilrijk, in exchange for the payment of the village's share in the general tax (*bede*).[25] As compensation, the prince asked the city for financial support through loans and taxes. Charles V made use of the Antwerp money market for his imperial policy, and he relied on the town's credit in order to obtain long-term loans via the sales of annuities on the urban domain.[26] Between 1517 and 1530, Charles's debt to the city reached 500,000 guilders. This sum was reduced in the following decades and was brought down to 400,000 in 1537 and even 100,000 in 1555–6. At the same time the number of taxes (*beden*) also increased. In 1533 the city had to sell annuities in order to pay the quota for the *bede* of 1,200 guilders. In 1537, war against France forced Charles to levy another tax of 400,000 guilders. The city could not pay its quota from its ordinary earnings. The excises on wine and beer had to be increased and annuities to be sold. However, the amount could not be collected in time, and the city had to contract a short-term loan with local bankers. Shortly thereafter, a new tax came into existence and forced the city to offer new sales of annuities.[27]

Meanwhile, other circumstances contributed to further financial problems. In the 1540s and 1550s, the city built a new fortification, after the threat of an attack by troops from Guelders in 1542. Although these fortifications were built on the orders of the central government, they had to be financed exclusively by the city itself. During the first years, the funding took place by means of a special commission, the so-called fortification chamber, which hardly reported to the Broad Council. The traditional means of funding, excises on slaughtering animals, baking and the reintroduction of the excise on *kuit*, the cheapest type of beer, and the extensive sale of annuities proved far too insufficient. The city, therefore, had to take short-term loans totalling 2,265,235 guilders from the big German firms and local merchants to cope with the costs of the works.[28] To pay back these loans, the city sold even more annuities and thus increased the urban debt further still. Finally, the city was faced with a debt of almost 1 million guilders in 1547, which made necessary a complete revision of the urban income policy. Finally an agreement was reached with the personal intervention of Mary of Hungary: the excises for beer were increased, the 10 per cent tax on rents from real estate was maintained, the city would sell unnecessary urban property and sell 600,000 guilders' worth of perpetual annuities.[29]

The economic decline of the city, which began in the 1560s, also affected its financial position. A high urban debt could be sustainable as long as the economic climate was positive, and the earnings of the city were at least stable. The beginning of the religious troubles in 1566 was a turning point from this point of view. In view of the precarious situation, the city tried to reform its financial system profoundly. In 1575, the interest rate on the existing annuities had to be reduced. A new city account (*reductiekas*) was installed, to which the yields from the excises on wine, beer and grain were transferred, and which was intended to provide the necessary means for paying back the interest, but also to reduce the accumulated arrears. However, already in 1585, the city was confronted with another extraordinary expenditure, that is a fine of 400,000 guilders that had been imposed upon the city by Farnese and the rebuilding of the citadel. New consumption taxes had to be introduced, which would feed yet another fund, the *consumptiekas*. The latter should serve to re-establish the balance of the *reductiekas*.[30] However, all these reform plans were not successful. The public debt continued throughout the seventeenth and eighteenth centuries to be the major characteristic of Antwerp's public finances.

The Principles of Antwerp's Fiscal Policy

The decisions about the means for generating necessary funds were taken by the general council of the city, called the Broad Council (*Brede raad*). In order to maintain a certain balance in their accounts they continuously had to find new sources of income. Literally everything was taxed: movable and immovable property and possessions, goods and merchandise, revenues and work, nothing escaped taxation. Moreover, annuities had to be sold to provide the necessary means to pay the tax quota and extraordinary expenses. In practice, the city government proposed a list of possible taxes from which the members of the Broad Council could choose. In 1665, for example, for the payment of a subsidy of 50,000 guilders, the choice was to be made from the following: a head tax, a tax on housing rents, a household tax, a tax on smiths, a luxury tax on silk stockings and beaver hats, taxes on oil, sugar, tobacco, lard and on the surplus of the *consumptiekas*.[31]

Indirect taxes were generally the first choice. They had some obvious advantages, especially for the ruling elite represented in the Broad Council. First they were carried by the whole of the urban population, rich and poor alike. This principle was expressed as follows in the Broad Council: 'nobody is overtaxed, because everybody pays on the basis of his consumption' or 'this is to say that our ancestors considered the impost a just manner of taxation because everybody was taxed according to his position and consumption'.[32] As everyone was included in the tax, the burden was spread evenly and was relatively low for the individual inhabitant. Second, the collection happened on a daily basis, almost imperceptibly for the consumer, as a part of the purchase price, which made the collection easier than for direct taxes. Indirect taxes levied on the production or distribution of goods could be transferred to the consumer via the price. On the other hand, it was exactly the fact that the tax burden was carried by the whole of the population that the tax burden of the poor masses increased in relative terms. Especially the fact that excises were levied mainly on the basic goods of consumption meant that they affected a much greater part of the income of the poor than that of the wealthier population groups.[33] The wealthier classes, furthermore, had the possibility to recover part of their contributions through the purchase of annuities. The combination of excises and the sale of annuities as the basis of the urban fiscal policy led to a social transfer of funds from the mass of consumers of basic goods to the group of annuity buyers.[34]

In order to prevent excessive social injustice, the city government applied different tariffs. A distinction was made between heavy luxury beers and light beers, and between beer for home consumption and beer distributed in taverns. Luxury beer was subject to heavier taxation than the cheaper standard beer. Furthermore, it was frequently taxed with additional taxes throughout the sixteenth and seventeenth centuries, so that in the late seventeenth and eighteenth century, luxury beers were taxed at 104 shillings per *ame* in taverns and 66 shillings for individual citizens, and an extra 9 shillings for imported beer, while light beer was only taxed at 20 shillings per *ame*.[35] On the other hand, different tariffs for locally produced goods and imported goods could also be a mechanism for protecting the local business interests against competition from outside the city. The cheapest type of beer, the so-called *klein bier* was exempt from taxation altogether after 1525, and in 1539 also the *kuit*, another cheap type, was exempt due to public unrest and threats of riots. The excise was, however, reinstalled after 1542, in order to cover the costs of the new fortifications.[36] These different tariffs indicate that the city government tried to take into account the social differences within the city by taxing luxury products more heavily than products of basic consumption.

Similar considerations were taken in 1547, in relation to the introduction of a new excise on rye, the major bread grain, as well as on other grains, and an increase of the excises on beer and wine. The representatives of the citizens and the crafts in the Broad Council considered that these excises would harm the lower classes and asked for a solution 'without a great burden for the community and of great profit for the city'. The magistracy admitted that the excise on rye would be a heavy burden for the poor inhabitants and dropped it in its next proposal. This respect for a social repartition of the tax burden was one of the major claims made by the citizens and crafts in the Broad Council. The same argument for the just distribution of the tax burden was used, on the other hand, in 1666 to reject a tax on carriage horses – obviously a luxury tax – for the reparations of the fortifications. This tax was not acceptable to the city government because it was a taxation of individuals, which was not compatible with the public character of the fortifications.[37] The same principle was also used by the brewers guild in order to protest against the introduction of a tax of 6 stuivers per barrel of beer that they should pay.[38]

The sense of social justice had therefore a very variable meaning. It, furthermore, had also a pragmatic aspect. High taxes could easily lead to popular unrest and revolts, as had been the case in 1539 when *kuit* beer was exempt from taxation due to public unrest and threats of riots. Popular revolts related to taxation were a common phenomenon in early modern Europe although they were less frequent in the southern Low Countries than for example in France.[39]

Another consideration the Broad Council had to address was the yield of a tax. The latter had to be sufficient to pay the expenses for which they were introduced, or at least the annuities that were sold to generate the necessary amount. In 1537, the city planned to introduce a tax of 5 per cent on rents for houses and real estate. If this was insufficient, the rate could even be increased to 10 per cent. It seems however that the commission that was appointed to estimate the income from that taxation came to the conclusion that the income would be insufficient and hence the Broad Council chose for an increase of the excises on beer and wine.[40] In 1588, on the other hand, the tariffs of the wine excise had to be revised, because the former increases were so high that they had led to a decrease in consumption and hence also to a loss of tax income.[41]

Direct taxes were highly unpopular and levying them very difficult. A report from 1549 said that: 'collecting the tenth penny will cost much, and nobody wants to do it, because it gives little profit and creates great unrest among the common people, and it makes people unwilling to buy rents'.[42] This comment contains several points that were central to the fiscal logic of the Antwerp city council. The collection of a tenth penny was, in the first place, expensive and produced little profit. Furthermore, it created resistance among the population. Therefore, it was difficult to find a tax farmer who was willing to organize the taxation.

This attitude did change, however, albeit temporarily, during the last decades of the sixteenth century. In 1584, the magistracy in fact proposed a head tax (*hooftelijke quotisatie*) as being the most adequate means to help the city:

> especially because those with the lowest incomes shall be spared and supported, and that the money will be supplied by the most capable, without however upsetting or discouraging the rich and the merchants, and thus moving them to stop their commercial activity here and to leave the city ... They should be the ones who should help the common good with their means because of their quality and capability and help to carry the occurring burden.[43]

After 1585, when Alexander Farnese had recovered the city from the Protestant rebels, the city was again confronted with high financial charges. Even if the highest possible taxes were introduced, they could not produce enough income to pay the debt. Houses and real estate were already taxed at a hundredth and at a fifth penny, which was still to be collected, and as far as consumption was concerned, the magistrates were of the opinion that it could and should not be taxed even more heavily. Furthermore, the economic situation of the city was particularly bad in 1585. Hence they tried to find means that would be bearable for the poor community. The only remaining form of taxation was that of a forced loan, 'not only without personal damage, but even with considerable gain, so that nobody can be excused from supporting his hometown'.[44] The years around 1585 can certainly be described as a time of crisis, in which the fiscal logic described above was altered. The rhetoric of public responsibility and the policy of introducing forced loans and direct taxes have also been stressed as being typical for the northern Low Countries during the Dutch Revolt.[45]

The short comment against the introduction the tenth-penny tax from 1549 also contains an interesting reference to the attitude of annuity buyers, when it says that the introduction of the tenth penny would make people unwilling to buy annuities. It points out that they were less inclined to buy annuities mortgaged on an unpopular or otherwise conflictual kind of taxation. Excises on goods of mass consumption, such as beer excises, on the contrary, were considered reliable. In fact, it was generally on the latter that annuities were mortgaged.[46]

The credit of the city was an important issue for the city government. Considering the fact that the financial system of the city was heavily based on annuities, it was of crucial importance that the creditworthiness of the city remained intact. In 1680, the *rentmeester* complained that the account of the domain had arrears of 200,000 guilders and that he could not pay the annuities. The city had to find new sources of income quickly if it wanted to preserve its credit. The city government added that the arrears were causing damage to the rent owners of the city, who had agreed to a reduction in the interest they were to receive for several years under the explicit condition that they would be paid on time. Postponing the payments against all right and reason would cause great harm to the city's credit. 'It is impossible to have a multitude of reliable creditors of the city waiting and without being paid, among which there are many good citizens and inhabitants of this city'.[47] To maintain the credit of the city, the city government undertook major efforts and made several attempts to restructure urban finances. But also the central state was interested in the town's credit. On several occasions the central institutions intervened and organized audits of the urban accounts. In 1532, the commissioners who were to control the urban accounts commented that 'the excises of the city are not administered as well as they should be, and that they should produce more if they were well organized'.[48] In 1538, a thorough examination of the financial administration was undertaken which resulted in a number of changes involving accountability. These interventions, however, could not prevent the increase of the public debt, which was to take on extraordinary dimensions during the following decades.

Conclusions

The fiscal system of Antwerp had a number of general features that were comparable to those of many other European cities: A first element was the predominance
of indirect taxes, in the form of excises on drinks and consumables. Direct taxes,
on the contrary, were as good as absent and were only introduced on a temporary
basis in extraordinary circumstances. A second element was the heavy dependence on loans. Taxation was not sufficient to produce large amounts of money
in the short term. The history of Antwerp was characterized by frequent situations when such large amounts were necessary. These were often the demands
of the prince for taxes or loans. Other occasions for extraordinary expenses were
building projects, such as the building of the new fortifications in 1542, the new
town hall and others. These high amounts could best be raised by selling either
life annuities or perpetual annuities, which were to be paid back through the
income generated by urban taxes. Quite often the taxes were increased on these
occasions. Hence as a result of the policy of borrowing, an increasingly high proportion of the urban income was mortgaged for paying back the annuities on
these loans. The fact that annuities were mortgaged on the income from taxes
required that the latter produce a reliable, regular income over a long period.
This made excises on mass consumption the preferred type of urban tax. The
very fact that the tax system was so closely related to urban annuities made it, on
the other hand, very difficult to introduce fundamental changes in the system.[49]
Another feature was the close interconnectedness between urban and state taxation. Already from the Middle Ages on, the dukes of Brabant regularly relied on
the towns for financial support, either in the form of taxes or as loans. The city
had to provide these means from its ordinary income, or by finding new sources
of income. This meant that the urban finances were feeding the state finances.
Often the prince granted privileges to the city or ceded rights, which generated in
their turn income for the city. This apparent increase of fiscal means for the city
was, however, absorbed to a great extent by the fiscal needs of the central state.

The general tendencies we described here for Antwerp are to be found in
many other cities. The development of Antwerp's financial system was, however,
shaped in a distinctive way by its rise as a commercial centre from the fifteenth
century onwards and its period of economic prosperity during the sixteenth
century. This rise made Antwerp a centre of major economic importance for
more or less one century, which brought along special requirements for the city
government, such as investments in commercial infrastructure and defence. The
latter had to be financed through taxation and substantial loans. Loans were also
used to pay the contributions to the central state, which became particularly
onerous from the sixteenth century onwards. The financial needs of Charles V
during the first decades of the sixteenth century were notorious. The Golden

Age of Antwerp, thus, coincided with the rise of the Habsburg empire and, more generally, with the fiscal state, and Antwerp contributed strongly to its financial basis. The economic and demographic decline after 1585, however, left Antwerp with a huge debt burden, which was mortgaged essentially on the income from its excises. These were now levied on a much smaller and less prosperous population than before, which created a major problem for the financial policy of the city throughout the early modern period. The latter was in the first place characterized by the struggle for reducing the urban debt the city had accumulated during its Golden Age and its aftermath.

9 THE DUTCH FINANCIAL SYSTEM BETWEEN PUBLIC AND PRIVATE INTERESTS: URBAN DEBT (1500–1700)

Manon van der Heijden and Martijn van der Burg

In the sixteenth and seventeenth centuries the Dutch Republic became a striking example of a capital-intensive state, in which taxation relied heavily on the cooperation between rulers and capitalists.[1] The sale of urban and provincial annuities and the investment of citizens in such annuities and loans were a crucial part of this financial system for several reasons. First, taxation may have been the most import source of revenue for the Dutch Republic; a considerable part of the income of the state came from annuities and loans. The sale of annuities was an important source of income, particularly because loans were necessary for extraordinary expenses that could not be financed with regular tax money. Taxes and annuities were to a certain extent complementary. Second, the taxation system was often linked to the sale of annuities, and before the rise of a free capital market in the seventeenth century, coercion was a key factor in this. Sometimes additional taxes were imposed in the form of an annuity that would later be redeemed. Such *renten* were enforced contributions, quite similar to taxes. The legally forced nature of these loans makes it hard to discern between taxation and loans. Third, the financial success of the Dutch Republic between *c.* 1580 and 1650 was also made possible because taxes allowed for a funded debt. From 1547 onwards provincial annuities that were sold and managed by the cities created a debt that was backed by new permanent excises. In contrast to the former *renten*, the new provincial *renten* were fully redeemed by the provincial taxes, which guaranteed that the provinces would indeed annually pay the interest. This made investors more inclined to buy life annuities or redeemable annuities, which allowed the provinces to mobilize future revenues for present needs by successfully selling annuities on urban markets.[2] The new financial system of the Dutch Republic entailed a shift of power from the sovereign to the provinces, but also from the urban governments to the provincial administration.[3]

Although the major studies on Dutch financial history have focused on institutional developments, recently historians have begun to look at urban finances as an indicator of social-economic relations between citizens and governments.[4] The Flemish-Dutch research project on 'Citizens, money and urban governments 1400–1700', contributed to this kind of research by comparing the early modern finances of cities in the Low Countries.[5] The examinations within this project focused not so much on taxation policies – as most research on urban finances – but rather on a second important financial means of early modern cities: loans or annuities from citizens.[6]

This change of perspective in the work on urban finances in the Low Countries is inspired by the studies of Marc Boone on the urban finances of Ghent in the fourteenth and fifteenth centuries, which focused on the power balances between town, citizens, and the central government. Boone found that members of the local elite often would let their own interests prevail over the wider interests of the community by getting hold of profitable offices or by making advantageous arrangements for themselves and their friends and family.[7] Similar practices have been shown for the urban elites in eighteenth-century Holland, which often led to an unclear balance between private and public interests. One of the means that urban elites would have access to were profitable annuities. Members of the town councils could set aside the most profitable annuities for themselves, while the burden of the public debt was equally distributed among all citizens (through the urban excises).[8] Urban elites did not only profit from their central positions within the urban community, their social and political position entailed financial obligations towards the city as well.[9]

This article aims to examine the various motives of those who invested in urban public debt. Why did people lend their money to town councils, and for what reasons would they invest their money in annuities? Did they consider such investments as social obligations towards the rulers of the central government, as most of such loans and annuities were destined to the lord's military politics? Or did citizens indeed feel obliged to financially serve their city in times of hardship? Or where they perhaps coerced by urban governments, as William Bowsky and Anthony Molho have shown for the cases of medieval Florence and Siena?[10] Finally, did citizens consider their loans or investments as an interesting investment which could bring them profit, as suggested by the investigations of James Tracy on Holland or the studies of Rosenthal and Potter of Burgundy?[11] Such questions are related to the public nature of the urban annuity markets; citizens did not have equal access to bonds or annuities, especially where it concerned the less risky and more profitable ones.

Sources

Most late medieval and early modern cities in the Low Countries issued life annuities and redeemable annuities when they were in immediate need of funds or in case they received lesser revenues from the annual excises (the largest income of any city).[12] The annuities were meant as an extraordinary option in times of need, but in practice cities issued almost yearly life and redeemable bonds. The reasons why cities made structural use of such means are to be found in the constant pressure of the Burgundian and Habsburg rulers, such as Charles V and Philip II, who pressured rich merchant towns to collect money in order to fund their wars (against France especially). After the foundation of the Dutch Republic, cities would still collect funds, but now to finance the war of the new republic against the Habsburg rulers. The debts that followed the years after an issue were usually paid by issuing new annuities, though in the course of the early modern period there were also certain shifts in the destination of urban income from redeemable annuities. Instead of destining revenues from annuity issues to military purposes, towns would increasingly use such resources to fund public works such as the building of bridges, canals or harbours.[13]

In this article we examine the annuities of three cities of Holland and their investors in the northern part of the Netherlands during the sixteenth and seventeenth centuries: Dordrecht (1550–1700), Haarlem (1550–1650), and Rotterdam (1653–90). The study of Dordrecht and Haarlem concerned life annuities as well as redeemable annuities, while for Rotterdam we have data on life annuities only. Table 9.1 shows the number of persons that we have examined for all cities, based on various sources: urban accounts, lists of life annuities and redeemable annuities, ordinances of the Habsburg rulers and the province of Holland (States of Holland), and the resolutions of urban governments.[14] In addition, we undertook systematic prosopographical analysis for the investors of certain years, and in such cases we both identified investors as beneficiaries, and gathered information on the public offices they and their relatives were holding. Finally, we also examined taxation records and official lists of urban offices as well as various published and unpublished studies on the urban elite of the cities of Dordrecht, Haarlem, and Rotterdam, which provided ample information for explaining why people would invest their money in early modern annuities and if such motives changed over time.[15]

Table 9.1: The number of issues, annuity transactions and the people involved, in
Dordrecht 1550–1700, Haarlem 1550–1650, Rotterdam 1653–90 and a sample of
Zwolle 1550–9, 1570–9, 1600–4, 1621–5, 1646–50.

	Issues	Transactions	Individuals	Investors
Dordrecht	102	505	880	535
Haarlem	59	926	1286	1029
Rotterdam	11	599	966	367
Total	181	2117	3235	2025

Issue	Issue of urban annuities, redeemable annuities, life annuities or obligations (in which case an agent received 0, 5 per cent of the sum invested).
Transaction	Contract between town and investor on one of the above annuities
Individuals	The total number of persons involved: buyer, beneficiary, and representative
Investors	Person, in whose name the contract was signed, and who received an official document with conditions concerning the purchase.

Sources: Stadsarchief Dordrecht, rekeningen groot comptoir en reparatiën, 1550–1700;
Stadsarchief Haarlem, thesauriersrekeningen 1550–1650; Gemeentearchief Zwolle,
Jaarrekeningen, 1550–9, 1570–9, 1600–4, 1621–5, 1646–50; Gemeentelijke Archief-
dienst Rotterdam, OSA, inv.no. 3663, 1653–90.

Urban Policies to Attract Investors

The public nature of annuity markets depends on various factors: the supply of
capital of citizens who might invest in annuities, the attractiveness and security
of the investments and the access to the annuity market. In the early modern
period the latter factor largely depended on the policies of urban governments
to attract or to repel certain groups of investors and their ability to disclose and
circulate information about annuity issues.[16]

Under Habsburg rule, most cities in Holland sought after investors in the rich
merchant cities of the southern parts of the Netherlands, particularly in Flanders,
Brabant and Zeeland. Public officers were usually assigned to the task to find the
capital markets which would provide capital suppliers who would be the most
likely to invest in urban annuities. The lines between the representatives of the
city whose aim was to sell *renten* and possible investors who were willing to invest
in urban annuities were usually very short; public officers would contact suppliers
directly and offer them either redeemable or life annuities after which a contract
was signed. In the fifteenth and sixteenth centuries the cities of Holland would
attract investors from Flanders and Brabant especially as these cities formed the
financial centres of the Netherlands where rich investors were to be found.[17]

In the sixteenth century the province of Holland searched for investors in
the Flemish cities as well, arguing that there were more willing investors to be
found in one Flemish city than in the whole province of Holland.[18] During the
late Middle Ages there appeared to have been a large and diverse market for

urban (and provincial) annuities in the Flemish cities; a market which not only attracted suppliers of urban annuities from the cities from the south but from the cities of the north as well. The city of Dordrecht, one of the most important cities of Holland, looked for investors in Dordrecht's annuities especially in the Flemish cities of Antwerp, Bruges and Ghent.[19] In both the cities of Holland and Flanders the constant demands of the Habsburg rulers created a powerful incentive to search for investors who could deliver money in a very short time.[20] Cities that were much less attached to the Habsburg ruler, such as Zwolle in the northeast of the Netherlands, were much less inclined to look for capital outside their own town as they depended less on the central government's financial policies (the Habsburg ruler became the formal authority in the East as late as 1528).[21]

In the course of the fifteenth century there were some shifts in the policies of the cities of Holland to bring in investors. As one of the most important towns and the centre of the staple market in Holland, the city of Dordrecht had actively sought out foreigners who could invest huge sums of money in the public debt of Dordrecht. However, at the end of the fifteenth century as economic and financial decline set in, the cities of Holland stopped bringing in capital from outside Holland. Instead, the cities shifted their attention from rich foreign merchants to their own citizens, especially members of the urban elite.

There were clear reasons for such policies. The constant issuing of urban annuities (destined to the military operations of the Habsburg ruler) had caused huge financial problems for several cities in Holland, which led in some cases to urban bankruptcy. Though not all cities of Holland actually went bankrupt, most major cities such as Amsterdam, Dordrecht and Haarlem did face financial problems regarding their debts. As the cities were not able to redeem the yearly interest rates to annuity investors from the last decade of the fifteenth century, the arrears increased enormously in the years after. To secure their investments and to coerce cities to pay the outstanding debts to them, creditors would use the only means they had: citizens from those cities were imprisoned for debt. As a result, merchants whose trading activities took place in Flanders risked being held hostage, including their ship and crew, until the city had redeemed their arrears.

The policy of cities to bring in foreign investors did thus in the long run cause tremendous problems for the trading contacts between merchants from Holland and Flanders. Rich traders might invest huge sums, therefore providing the cities of Holland fast capital, but in times of financial difficulty such capital suppliers could also harm the commercial activities of citizens and consequently the city's trading position. For that reason the city of Dordrecht changed its policies regarding urban annuities. They now preferred their own citizens as investors and they made serious efforts to attract them. Firstly, they offered their own citizens extra profitable interest rates from which outside investors were excluded.

Secondly, they offered better guarantees of repayment to increase their credibility and to regain the belief of town inhabitants in their urban financial policies.[22]

Other cities would change their policies as well, though in some cases such
adjustments were established under pressure of the central governments which
took over control in case cities went bankrupt. After its bankruptcy in 1492,
the financial affairs of the city of Haarlem had become fully under control of
Habsburg officials who largely determined the urban financial policies from that
time onwards. Until well into the sixteenth century the town was not allowed
to issue new *renten*, or at least not on a public market and always on the terms
of the Habsburg rulers. In fact, sometimes citizens of Haarlem were pressured
to lend money to the city or to invest in unprofitable urban annuities.[23] Similar
shifts regarding the urban annuity policies were to be seen in several other cities of Holland. In the fifteenth century Rotterdam had sold its urban annuities
primarily to outside investors from Flanders and Dordrecht, however, during the
first decade less than half of the total number of investors resided in cities outside
Rotterdam.[24] In the course of the sixteenth and seventeenth centuries this trend
would set in even further, in fact between 1653 and 1690 by far the most buyers
of *renten* were town inhabitants, while only twenty-three investors came from
outside. Moreover, these investors resided in nearby cities which were ordered
by the Habsburg officials to not issue annuities, and which were most probably
in some way linked to the urban elite of Rotterdam.[25]

At the end of the fifteenth century the cities of Holland began to focus their
attention on local capital suppliers. From that moment on the town councils of
Haarlem and Dordrecht made efforts to attract their own citizens. The market
for annuities became less public and more restricted to buyers who were more
duty-bound to the city. In the course of the seventeenth century the tide would
turn for the cities of Holland and consequently their policies regarding the
annuity market changed. Between 1580 and 1620 it was no longer necessary
for Holland's towns to bring in foreign investors as economically prosperous circumstances encouraged a surfeit of capital suppliers from inside Holland.

Towards a Free Annuity Market

Citizens sometimes did not lend money to the city voluntarily, particularly at
times when the credibility of the city was at stake and towns did not succeed
in bringing in willing capital suppliers.[26] The means of cities to pressure citizens
to invest in urban annuities were twofold. Firstly, towns would order inhabitants to lend money or to buy unprofitable annuities with low interest rates or
with fewer guarantees. Secondly, towns sometimes instructed citizens to not buy
renten elsewhere in order to prevent rich inhabitants to invest their capital in
towns which offered better guarantees.[27]

Cities in the Low Countries used the instrument of pressure only during times of financial or political crisis. The boundary between a citizen's duty and coercion was often blurred. In several cities wealthy citizens – usually belonging to the governmental elite – were urged to invest their capital in urban annuities and in those cases the benefits were usually for both sides. In exchange for their willingness the investors received extra profitable annuities or the town offered them and their relatives lucrative business contracts.[28] Occasionally, citizens were directly coerced to lend or invest money, and such decisions were at all times initiated by the central government which ordered cities to pressure their citizens to buy *renten*.[29] At the beginning of the sixteenth century Haarlem pressured its citizens to invest capital in redeemable annuities, though the investors did receive extra guarantees. It was stipulated that the debtors would in any circumstances, even during times of financial crisis, receive their annual interest payments.[30] In 1567, the city of Haarlem urged urban elite families again to invest in *renten*, though this time the occasion concerned the building of public works. In this case citizens were not exactly coerced, like in the previous century, but clearly wealthy and influential inhabitants did feel obliged to bring in their share. Firstly, the project was aimed at improving the town's trading facilities, and would therefore benefit their businesses as well. Secondly, the willingness of the urban upper classes symbolized their own faith in the town's credibility, and that confidence was especially important because of Haarlem's lack of credibility from the end of the fifteenth century. The building of prestigious public works and the involvement of influential city dwellers demonstrated that the town was recovering from its financial crisis.[31]

In 1572 (the year of the Dutch Revolt against the Habsburg ruler) the citizens of Dordrecht also felt obliged to financially support the town by buying redeemable and life annuities. The issue concerned an agreement between Dordrecht and Philip II of the year prior to the Revolt. The city had to keep its promises to Philip II, but that was not easy as wealthy foreign investors stayed away because of the political turmoil and the consequent unstable financial circumstances. To fill this gap the urban elite brought their own capital; most of the investors were wealthy widows or in some way related to the governmental elite. The profits were two-sided: members of the town council encouraged their friends and relatives to bring in money by guaranteeing extra high interest rates up to 50 per cent.[32] More than a century later, the town council had to appeal to the citizen's duty to lend the city money once more, though this time the appeal was more direct as they formulated the amounts that each councillor was obliged to donate.[33] There is comparable evidence in eastern cities, such as Zwolle. In 1672, another year of political turmoil, the town council of Zwolle ordered each magistrate and the town secretary to contribute 500 guilders, while the members of the citizens' council (an advisory board of the town council) were to donate 200 guilders. Those who stated that they lacked the financial resources were threat-ened with a fine.[34] During the same year the citizens of Rotterdam (Holland) were pressured to buy annuities with lower interest rates as well.[35]

The data demonstrate that most cities would from time to time force their citizens to invest in urban public debt. Town councils would usually approach members from their own social and economic circles, because that was com-monly the easiest way to collect money. In such cases it was often difficult to distinguish between coercion, obligation, sense of duty, or private interest because the reasons to invest in urban annuities were often blurred and inter-mingled. Urban elites felt obliged to supply capital because it would improve the town's credibility, but this sense of duty was intermixed with their own private interests as town representative or merchants. The town's credibility had a clear bearing on the town council's policies regarding the public nature of the urban annuities. In times of political and financial crisis, town councils often saw no other way than to increase their resource by means of coercion or pressure.

Urban credibility thus varied noticeably from town to town and from time to time, however, in some respects there were significant differences between various types of towns. The high share of the urban upper classes in the investment of urban public debt was evident in all cities that were part of this examination, but it was clearly most evident in the cities of Zwolle and Dordrecht. There were two different reasons for this high share. As noticed, the role of the urban elite was usually smaller at times when towns were able to find an extended market for their annuities, which was often the case when towns could guarantee interest payments. In the seventeenth century the annuities of the town of Haarlem were secured because of the town's prosperous textile industry and increasing trading activities, so there were enough investors who were willing to bring in capital. The economic circumstances were different for Dordrecht and Zwolle. Dordrecht had been one of the most important and influential cities of Holland during the late middle Ages, but due to chang-ing political and geographical circumstances and increasing rivalry from nearby city Rotterdam, it lost its favourable position in the sixteenth century. Though the city remained an important regional centre which witnessed economic growth between 1580 and 1620, in the seventeenth century it became apparent that the cities of Haarlem and Rotterdam had surpassed the city of Dordrecht both economically and politically.[36] These differences were also reflected in the public that bought annuities: in both Haarlem and Rotterdam the majority of the investors in urban public debt came from various social and economic backgrounds, and not, like in Dordrecht, from the ranks of the urban elite.[37]

In the course of the sixteenth and seventeenth centuries the towns of Hol-land rarely pressured inhabitants to invest in urban public debt; clearly a more open and free market emerged after the foundation of the Dutch Republic.

There were several reasons for the changing public nature of urban annuity markets after 1580.[38] Firstly, the most important reason for compelling citizens to invest in urban annuities had been the financial policies of the Habsburg rulers. After the Dutch Revolt the cities of Holland were released from these constant demands. Secondly, and more importantly for the level of open annuity market, free annuity markets emerged only when towns were able to guarantee the payment of the interest rates, which would bring in capital from a broader variety of capital suppliers. During the financial crisis at the end of the fifteenth century most cities in Holland had failed their creditors, which harmed urban credibility in such a way that investors would seek for more safe investments elsewhere. Around the beginning of the seventeenth century the cities of Holland managed to regain their credibility when the economic growth set in, and from then on capital suppliers were again interested in the annuities of the cities of Dordrecht, Rotterdam and Haarlem. The are several indications for this: the interest rates were reduced, the diversity of investors increased, the interest payments were paid in time, and most cities managed to also reimburse the total sum of redeemable annuities after a few years.

At the end of the seventeenth century, several cities would fall into their old habits again. The immediate need for resources urged the city of Dordrecht to force loans upon their most wealthy citizens during the last years of the seventeenth century, while the town council of Rotterdam urged their citizens into life annuities with low interest rates. [39]

Civic Duty

The question arises then, as to what reasons the urban elites had for investing their money in urban annuities. Their share was higher in times of economic decline and political turmoil or when the funds were destined to large public projects which concerned city improvement, and in such cases probably public as well as private interests played a role in their investments. Various studies of early modern urban elites have also pointed to the additional financial profits which the urban elite could gain by investing in the urban public debt. The social-political upper echelon of citizens could profit from the most favourable life annuities with high interest rates, while the burden of the debt was divided among all the town inhabitants. Taxes that were designed to pay the yearly interest brought in the entire urban population. Furthermore, in times of arrears public officers could see to it that their interest and that of their families and friends were given preferential treatment.[40] Does the examination of the cities of Holland confirm such an assumption regarding the privileged position of higher social layers? Did urban elites indeed receive the most profitable life annuities?

It is likely that urban elites could profit more in cases where cities depended more strongly on the investments of insiders, as was often the case in Dordrecht after the fifteenth century. This seemed to have been in part true, since the most lucrative life annuities with high interest rates were often reserved for Dordrecht's upper classes. During the year of the Dutch Revolt the town council offered the urban elite life annuities for a yearly payment of 14.2 per cent interest. These annuities were extremely lucrative, not only for the high interest rate but also because the risk could be spread over more than two lives (up to ten people); a wonderful assurance for their children. However, despite this lucrative offer, the town did not manage to collect the adequate amount of money as promised to Philip II. And for that reason, the town council raised the interest rate for some citizens up to 50 per cent.[41] In periods of economic prosperity the political and economic elites of Dordrecht seemed to have profited as well. In 1604 – a period of economic prosperity for Dordrecht – life annuities were sold only to the town's highest office holders and some high-placed friends in other cities, while less favourable redeemable annuities were sold to a much wider public.[42]

However, the elites of Haarlem and Rotterdam did not receive such privileges because in these towns interest rates were adjusted to supply and demand on the public market. In Haarlem in the course of the sixteenth and seventeenth century the interest rates of redeemable annuities were reduced from 8.3 per cent to 4 or 5 per cent, while the life annuities were brought back from 14.2 to 10 per cent. Around the first years of the seventeenth century, the interest rates of Dordrecht were reduced as well, but that was only temporarily, because shortly thereafter the city had to raise its redeemable annuities to 6.25 per cent and its life annuities to 16.6 or 11.1 per cent again. Such measures were not necessary for Haarlem, because there seemed to have been more than enough capital suppliers who wanted to invest in Haarlem's annuities. In 1604 for example, the city issued three series of annuities each with different interest rates. However, the moment the town council noticed that there were many interested investors it decided to further reduce the interest rates of the same issues. As a consequence, some civil servants received less profitable annuities than people from outside the urban elites who had bought annuities from the same issue earlier that year.[43] In Rotterdam annuities were sold according the supply and demand on the market as well, as from 1672 the city offered variable life annuities by which the interest rates were related to the age of the bearer (or on the person they were destined to).[44]

Apparently, in Rotterdam as well as in Haarlem governmental elites and their social circles were not per se better off where it concerned urban annuities than the rest of the urban population. On the other hand, the stronger ties in Dordrecht between the private interests of urban elite and the public interest of the town did have some side effects for the elite as well. Their positions and relations might bring greater profits, but more often officeholders and their relatives felt obliged to invest in urban annuities even though it concerned annuities with lower interest rates compared to annuities of nearby cities such as Rotterdam or Haarlem.[45] Furthermore, because of the lack of Dordrecht's credibility, the purchasers of Dordrecht's annuities more often risked the chance that the interest rates were reduced even further in the years after the purchase. It was not uncommon for Dordrecht to conserve the interest rates of both life and redeemable annuities in times of economic decline, and exactly in those periods the town council would appeal to the civil obligation of wealthy citizens to invest in urban public debt. One might assume that town officials and their family member were treated differently during such conversion, though the interest rates of their annuities were as much reduced as the interest rates of others. So, at times the urban elite of Dordrecht did get more worth for their money than others, but more often they were the ones who were expected to invest money in less profitable and more risky annuities.

Reinforcing Networks

So, investing in the urban public debt was not always more advantageous for the urban elites compared to other investors such as outsiders or lower layers of urban society. However, the profits might have concerned not so much immediate financial advantages but other kinds of compensation. Boone's examinations of medieval Ghent have shown that the financial policies of town councils were strongly related to the interests of the urban elites. A considerable part of the town's income was destined to the expenditures on the clothing, travel and representation costs of higher civic officials. Furthermore, as Boone demonstrated, officeholders and their relatives were also important deliverers of goods, building contractors of public works and farmers of urban excises. In fifteenth-century Bruges, investors in the urban public debt assumed similar privileges in return, especially where it concerned the reinforcement of political and economic relations. Even more, investing in urban annuities seemed to have been one of the ways for wealthy foreigners to improve their political integration.[46]

Where there similar interminglements where it concerned the political and financial interests of the towns in Holland and the private interests of those investing in urban public debt? This seemed to have been the case in Dordrecht in the sixteenth century, for which we examined the years 1555 and 1572.[47] We explored in what ways and to what extent the investors in Dordrecht's annuities were rewarded for their contributions in the years after. The urban accounts of the city of Dordrecht show that the most rewarded investors in urban *renten* indeed concerned a small group of persons who were town officials themselves or in some ways related to town officials. It is evident from the urban expenses in the years of 1555 and 1572 that investments in urban public debt were often followed in the years after by various kinds of compensations that were arranged by the town council of Dordrecht. The urban elites seem to have been rewarded for performing their civil duty especially in a year of crisis, such as 1572, during which the town council had difficulties finding capital suppliers for annuities. Almost 70 per cent of those who had invested capital in the annuities of 1572 were in some way related to the town officials and their family members.[48] In the years after their donation almost half of these investors were given lucrative business agreements, were rewarded with interesting public offices and attractive travels trips, or they were invited to act as agents in business deals between the city and merchants. All of these activities and rewards reinforced the bond between investor and city, offering merchants and officeholders more opportunities to expand their political influence and trading activities.[49]

The group of people that belonged to these inner circles was small and limited to the most wealthy and influential factions of urban society. Furthermore, the interests were often blurred as both sides evidently gained by the investment in urban annuities. In times of need, the higher social and economic layers of urban society fulfilled their duty as loyal citizens by investing their money in sometimes less valuable annuities, but their loyalty was compensated in various ways. For them the investment in urban annuities was probably most of all one of the means to maintain and reinforce their political and financial networks within the urban community.

The Profits of Investing in Urban Public Debt

In the course of the sixteenth and seventeenth centuries the link between urban elites and municipal finances became much less strong because most towns managed to improve the public nature of the urban annuity markets. Instead of pressuring their own social circles to help the city out in times of economic hardship or political instability, town councils succeeded in finding sufficient capital suppliers on a free market. In other words, the selling and buying of urban bonds had become a (mostly) voluntary deed which took place on a public market on which various groups of investors could subscribe. In Rotterdam between 1653 and 1690 more than 60 per cent of the investors were not connected to the financial or governmental elite, and their share was even smaller if the invested amounts are taken into account: 76 per cent of the bonds of Rotterdam were bought by people outside the circles of magistrates and their relatives.[50] In Haarlem in 1604 more than 70 per cent of investors did not belong to the urban elite. Of course, the proportion of wealthy and powerful investors remained higher in Dordrecht, especially after the 1650s when financial difficulties rose again but during the years of economic prosperity (1580–1620) Dordrecht managed to also reduce the interest rate of its bond and henceforth to attract a wider public. For what other reason did the majority of financiers invest their money in urban bonds?

The urban accounts of the cities of Rotterdam, Dordrecht and Haarlem show that in each of these cities the annual interest was generally paid in time, though arrears did occur during long periods of crisis. The latter happened during the earlier mentioned financial crisis of the cities of Holland at the end of the fifteenth century.[51] During the years of the Dutch Revolt against Spain cities such as Dordrecht and Haarlem faced financial problems again, but now for not paying the interest to buyers of provincial bonds which had been placed and sold in the cities in the years before. The outstanding debts increased when the province of Holland did not succeed in redeeming the interest of these provincial bonds to the cities. In such cases towns had several options: they could decide on an extension of the interest payments which would cause higher debts in the years after, or they could convert the annuities to a lower interest rate.[52] During the years of crisis the cities of Dordrecht, Haarlem and Rotterdam chose for both options; they usually paid out to foreign investors first, while reducing the interest rates of a part of the annuities.[53] However, these were exceptional circumstances, because from the end of the sixteenth century onwards the cities of Holland managed to pay out the yearly interest for sold annuities without delay. Furthermore, more and more cities were obliged to account for such actions. In the crisis year of 1672 Rotterdam had sold bonds for an unusual low interest rate of 3.5 per cent, but in the years after the investors pressured the urban government to raise the interest, and so they did.[54] The restoration of urban (and provincial) credit and the recovery of the economy from the end of the sixteenth century would make the urban annuities much more secure, resulting in a much broader section of the public that could purchase urban bonds.

Redeemable Annuities

Early modern urban bonds concerned mostly redeemable annuities, though life annuities were the most popular because of the higher interest rates. In the course of the sixteenth and seventeenth centuries cities sold life annuities especially in times of political or economic crisis when they had to make extra efforts to attract investors. The expenditure on interest for urban bonds shows the large share of the redeemable annuities compared to life annuities. In Rotterdam more than 67 per cent of outstanding debts concerned redeemable annuities in 1653.[55] In Haarlem and Dordrecht on average 75 per cent of urban bonds were redeemable.

Only a small number of redeemable bonds were meant to buy a secure income for children or family members of the buyer. Those who did, usually destined the money to charity, to the orphanage especially.[56] Remarkably, only a very small number of investors consisted of public or religious institutions; in

Haarlem and Dordrecht 4–8 per cent only.[57] Their share was somewhat higher in Rotterdam; in the middle of the seventeenth century 10 to 25 per cent of the debt on bonds concerned bonds that were bought by religious charity institutions, though these bonds presumably concerned bonds prior to 1650 which were often not redeemed.[58]

Most redeemable urban annuities were sold to secure an income for the buyer himself or herself. The profits were usually not very high and the investments were in most cases rather small.[59] Apparently, the urban bonds were attractive also to people from the lower social layers of urban society, who could invest small amounts only. As appears from the Haarlem lists of buyers between 1550–1650 30 per cent of the investors in urban redeemable bonds consisted of women of which 65 per cent was unmarried.[60] The share of women was high in Rotterdam; half of the investors of life annuities consisted of women, a small number of whom were widows.[61] Though it is difficult to present more substantial figures, the professional backgrounds of the investors indicate as well that the capital suppliers mostly consisted of people with little capital. A considerable section of the investors consisted of simple artisans and labourers who had bought a redeemable annuity for 50 to 400 guilders, such as tailors, shoemakers, servants of brewers, maids, linen weavers and carpenters. We have no figures for Rotterdam, Haarlem and Dordrecht, but we do know from some recent examinations on Amsterdam that at the end of the sixteenth century around 21 per cent of the investors consisted of both artisans and industrial entrepreneurs (including brewers).[62] Clearly, the prosperous economic conditions during the golden age provided a number of artisans and labourers with the opportunity to set aside some money for urban bonds.[63]

Life Annuities as Insurance

Though not as much sold as redeemable annuities, life annuities remained the most popular urban bonds in the early modern period. The advantageous were several: the interest rates were higher than those of redeemable annuities and the risk could be distributed over a number of persons. The life annuities were extra profitable if cities did not calculate the age of the beneficiary. A life annuity was of course less favourable in case one of the beneficiaries passed away shortly after the transaction.[64] In the course of the seventeenth and eighteenth centuries cities began to also take into account the ages of the beneficiaries when determining the interest rate for life annuities. We have no indications that the cities of Haarlem and Dordrecht used such methods as well, but in Rotterdam the interest rates became indeed variable in 1672, a decision which was inspired by the publication of the first important work on variable life annuities of Johan de Witt, *Waerdye van lyf-rente naer proportie van los-renten* from 1671 (see Table 9.2).[65]

Table 9.2: Ages of beneficiaries and resulting interests rates on life annuities in Rotterdam, 1653–90.

Age:	1653–9	1672–3	1675	1689	1689–90
1–9	9.09	10	10	7	1.25
10–14	9.09	10	10	7	7.5
15–19	9.09	10	10	7	7.5
20–24	9.09	10.53	10	7	8
25–29	9.09	10.53	10	7	8
30–34	9.09	11.11	10.53	7	8.5
35–39	9.09	11.11	10.53	7	8.5
40–44	9.09	11.76	11.11	7	9
45–49	9.09	12.5	11.76	7	9
50–54	9.09	13.33	12.5	7	9.5
55–59	9.09	14.81	–	7	9.5
60–64	9.09	16.67	–	7	10
65–69	9.09	16.67	14.81	7	10
70–74	9.09	16.67	–	7	11
75–79	9.09	16.67	–	7	11
80–89	9.09	16.67	–	7	12

Dutch historians have suggested that the life annuities were not meant as a pension, but purely as a profitable investment of capital.[66] This might have been the case in cities where the age was calculated, because in those cases a higher age brought higher profits. This was indeed the case in Rotterdam, because the ages of the beneficiaries of life annuities rose after the implementation of age calculations in 1672. Consequently, here life annuities were more often meant as a retirement fund, destined to the one who bought the annuity.[67] However, where age was not taken into account, the investors were best off if the amount of the transaction was distributed over one or more younger persons. In Dordrecht the risk was indeed often distributed over more than one or two children, in which cases the investment served as an insurance income for children. Consequently, in these cases the interest was destined to persons other than the buyer. These differences become visible as one looks at the figures as well: in Rotterdam 38 per cent of the life annuities were put on the life of the owner, while in Dordrecht and Haarlem more than 80 per cent of the life annuities were destined to those others than the buyer.[68]

Those who did buy the life annuity as a pension were on average thirty years at the moment of the transaction, and they were often female and unmarried. In Haarlem and Dordrecht 63 per cent of the life annuities that were put on the life of the owner, consisted of unmarried women, while only 7 per cent were widows.[69] In Rotterdam as well, almost half of the life annuity purchasers were women, and seldom widowed. Apparently, the traditional image of wealthy widows as the most important buyers of urban life annuities had disappeared in the sixteenth and seventeenth centuries. Life annuities were especially bought by younger unmarried women who invested in an income assurance for later years. The second most important group of those putting the annuity on their own lives, were spouses who often jointly bought the annuity to put it on the life of the youngest of them.

However, most life annuities were not intended for one's personal purposes, because most investors used such them to arrange a yearly payment for others (81 per cent in Haarlem and Dordrecht; 57 per cent in Rotterdam). Life annuities were primarily bought by parents, guardians or close relatives who put the annuities on the lives of one or more children in order to secure them some steady income.[70] While common people usually distributed one life annuity over the lives of several children, wealthy citizens would buy a life annuity for each child they wanted to support. Most of these transactions were initiated by fathers (68 per cent) who destined the remittances to their children, though in such cases husbands most probably acted on behalf of the mother of children as well. Nevertheless, in Rotterdam fewer than 8 per cent of life annuities were bought by the mother.[71]

In conclusion, most buyers of life annuities intended the investment as a means to put some saving money aside for either themselves or their children. The suggestion that life annuities were bought primarily as a means of financial investment for those who would who were willing to taking some risks, is not confirmed by our findings.[72] On the contrary, most life annuities were destined to young children and family members, providing a small secured income which would make life a bit easier, especially in times of war, disease, or loss of income.[73]

Conclusions

In this article we examined the various motives of those investing in urban public debt of several towns in the province of Holland. Individual motives of investors were of great importance since the Dutch Republic relied heavily on cooperation between rulers and capitalists. In this conclusion we will first recapitulate and explain the development of the annuity market in sixteenth and seventeenth century Holland. Second, we will analyse the motives of investors to buy urban annuities.

There was a strong connection between the public nature of annuity markets and the credibility of cities. The attractiveness of urban annuities was closely connected to the trustworthiness of the towns in question. During the golden age urban finances improved and with it the public nature of urban annuity markets: between 1500 and 1700 the role of the free market grew particularly strong. Urban governments in Holland came to prefer the Venetian model, characterized by a great number of potential lenders, over the Florentine model, in which a narrow and closed circle furnished the necessary sums.[74] There were however regional variations. Dordrecht became less successful, due to political and geographical circumstances. In comparison to other towns, Dordrecht's magistracy had to pressure its elite more often.

For what reasons, then, did people invest their money in annuities, and why did they choose to lend their money to town councils? First, the urban elite profited greatly from the urban bonds, usually more than ordinary citizens. Quite often they would obtain higher interest rates. The elite was well informed and therefore the first to know of attractive life annuities. Also the investments reinforced the social, political and economic networks. However, the elite made up a small part of all investors. In all the towns we have investigated, the middle classes, and increasingly lower social layers, started to invest small sums, especially in redeemable annuities.

Three motivations made ordinary town dwellers buy annuities. First, urban annuities became less risky and more secure over time, making them more attractive. Second, from the late sixteenth century the potential number of buyers increased considerable. By the eighteenth century, urban annuities had become one of the most accessible ways for common male and female city dwellers to invest some money. Economic prosperity improved many citizens' financial situation, providing savings that enabled them to buy and profit from annuities. The increasing demand for urban annuities also improved the security of annuities: the broad base from which loans could be contracted allowed stable financial policies. Third, annuities were seen as an investment for oneself or for close relatives. Life annuities especially had to provide family members a small and secured income which would make life a bit easier in times of hardship, disability, sickness or old age.

10 THE URBAN FISCAL SYSTEM IN THE HABSBURG MONARCHY: THE CASE OF THE AUSTRIAN HEREDITARY LANDS IN THE SIXTEENTH TO EIGHTEENTH CENTURIES

Andrea Pühringer

Introduction

The early modern Habsburg monarchy was a complex structure of diverse and locally administered territories, and, likewise, the fiscal system varied considerably. Therefore, it is only possible to consider towns in a specific part of the monarchy in the following study. Because of the great variety of fiscal systems within the Habsburg Monarchy, only the hereditary lands[1] – the core lands – will be examined here. Towns in these territories had similar systems of administration and taxation, and they also stood in a similar position, directly between the princely ruler (*Landesfürst*) and the territorial estates. From the end of the fifteenth and the beginning of the sixteenth century, princely rulers regularly raised taxes of different kinds. During the early modern period not only the height but also the sorts of taxes increased. The main reason of this was not so much the growing court expenditures, but the increasing military costs. Military expenditure was a main contributory factor which influenced the fiscal system during the entire period, starting with the Ottoman wars in the sixteenth century, which lasted until the eighteenth century, the Thirty Years' War or the conflicts with France.[2] So warfare was also an important factor in state formation in the Habsburg Monarchy.

No imperial city or city-state existed in the hereditary lands, therefore there were only two types of towns: the territorial and the seigniorial (*grundherr-schaftliche*) towns. As the latter were part of the noble properties, they were also part of the seigniorial fiscal system and hence will not be considered in this paper.[3] The urban landscape[4] of the Monarchia Austriaca varied in its diverse territories. In 1500 we find thirty-five towns in Lower Austria, ten in Upper Austria, twenty-one in Styria, eleven in Carinthia, twelve in Carniola and ten in Tyrol, including Gorizia. Generally they were small centres, Vienna being the exception, with about 20,000 inhabitants in 1500 and 320,000 in 1700.[5] Some of these towns were princely and, due to this status, part of the estates.[6] The number of princely towns varied. In Austria above the Enns there were seven towns part of the estates, in Austria below the Enns about fourteen,[7] including Vienna,[8] and in Styria and Carniola each thirteen.[9] On the one hand, these towns had the advantage of being part of the territorial estates – the fourth estate – but on the other they had the inconvenience of being obliged to pay their tax quota to the princely ruler. Since the thirteenth und fourteenth centuries taxes became customary, and progressively, the Austrian territorial estates – including the towns curia – decided to pay their taxes in a certain rate per curia.[10] Since the beginning, the Austrian towns had the worst financial position with regards to the *upper estates* – the noblemen (*Herren*), prelates and knights[11] – and it became customary that the towns had to contribute the fourth and even (in the sixteenth century) the fifth part of the tax demanded by the princely ruler. However, this did not mean that all the towns had to pay the same rate; it depended on the respective regional rates of the estates, which were subdivided. Thus, taxation depended on the negotiating skills of the 'urban curia' within 'their' estates. When the number of towns in the curia decreased, the percentage rate did not change and the towns had to contribute the same rate. The first complaints relating to this fact date back to the early sixteenth century, when to speak of the '*mitleidenden*' *vicariously suffering* – towns and markets, that is, being assessed for taxes directly as part of the estates – became usual.[12]

But the towns were not only in opposition to the other estates over fiscal and financial issues, they were also opposed to the princely ruler, who tried to restrict their autonomy, and considered his towns as part of his domain (*Kammergut*). This caused a long-lasting dispute, which depended on urban financial capabilities and weakened the urban position by raising tax accounts and raising debts.[13]

Additionally, the political-religious fact of the counter-reformation had crucial socio-economic consequences for the towns. In the second half of the sixteenth century, almost all urban communities were converted to the new religion, especially the town councils; the urban elite and wealthier citizens became protestant. Apart from towns, many seigniorial lords and noble members of the estates – with the exception of the curia of the prelates – also became protestant.

As they all formed the political opposition to the princely ruler, who stuck to the old belief, religion became a highly contentious issue. As the ruling dynasty needed the subsidies of the estates, the Habsburgs negotiated the so called *concession to religion* in 1568, which allowed the members of the *upper two estates* and their subjects to practice protestant religion in their properties. The towns and markets were explicitly excluded from the concession of 1568, although they nonetheless ignored this fact, arguing as members of the estates and also contesting with their financial resources. Starting in Inner Austria, that is, Styria,

Carinthia, Carniola, the Windic March, Gorizia, Trieste and the coastal lands, the counter-reformation or, to avoid using this controversial term, the return to Catholicism was forced by the Habsburgs in the entire hereditary lands until the 1630s. The consequences were crucial. Those who refused to adopt Catholicism had to migrate, while many members of the estates were executed and their families lost their properties. A whole stratum of society, the high nobility, was replaced by a group of frequently foreign and ambitious newcomers. As for the towns, the consequences were similar. Until the 1630s – depending on the regional political conditions – the towns experienced several 'waves' of emigration.[14] The problem was not only the number but also the socio-economic status of emigrants as it was mainly the leading citizens in trade and commerce who left the towns. Often they used their business contacts to find a new residence abroad. This fact not only had consequences for the administration of the towns, which had lost many of their aldermen and members of municipal administration, along with their knowhow, but also for the outbalancing of their financial stability. As a consequence of the emigration of the urban elite, the cities lost not only the sums invested in trade and manufacture, but also the funds invested in loans and, above all, the possibility of using the private capital accumulated during the previous phase in times of distress to fund their spending. This development was worsened by the Thirty Years' War.

On the other hand, this development marked the end of the small margin of political self-government that the towns had held until that time. From now on, the princely ruler saw the cities definitely as part of his domain. Many of them had to leave the curia and if they remained, they were forced by the *upper estates* to reduce their debts. Even elections of the town councils took place under the control of a commission ordered by the princely ruler and often chaired by a prelate.

Socio-Economic Profile

Let us now briefly consider the economic profile of the towns, because this was the key factor determining the structure of its revenues. Any overview of the economic structure of the Austrian cities of the time must begin with its capital, Vienna, because, due to its size, it differed in many ways from the other towns, although its general political development was very similar. Vienna set standards and led by example: privileges were given and town administrations, as well as town rules, accorded to the Viennese model. Although Vienna was the largest town of the hereditary lands, it had low political and economic potential. It only managed to retain the status of an imperial city for a short period, as the princely ruler was too interested in remaining the urban overlord. The economic crisis of the mid-fifteenth century was intermingled with a decline of the political autonomy of the town, a process which reached its peak with the 1526 municipal law, which subordinated the city to the power of the princely ruler. Generally speaking, in early modern times, Vienna was an important town in comparison with the other cities in the hereditary lands, but, from an international perspective, its importance lay on being the residency of the Habsburg court and the imperial administration. Its economic structure differed from that of the other towns. With the exception of viticulture, a bourgeois occupation, agriculture was negligible, whereas intermediate trade and manufacturing industry of consumer and luxury goods dominated; likewise, handicraft was more differentiated than in the other cities.

In the fourteenth century the Viennese financial system was decentralized into several independent accounts: a tax account; a mayoral account, responsible for the debts of the town, a treasurer, administrating only dues and fees and the cadastre account. Until the fifteenth century, the treasurer was the centre of the whole system; the other accounts were subordinated to it. The respective employees submitted the revenues to the treasurer who registered the different types of burdens, wages and administration costs. At the end of the century, the position of the treasurer was split, so the second treasurer got his income from the first treasurer, but invoiced at cost independently. As in other towns the number of subordinated accounts increased, but unfortunately, it is impossible to delineate a complete picture of the whole municipal household.[15] Until the 1620s, the emigration of traders and skilled labourers caused Vienna a capital drain of about 300,000 fl.[16]

Most other Austrian towns produced only to a small extent for export and acted mainly as regional market centres, as their charters and town's medieval privileges show. Those privileges followed the Viennese model and regulated a broad range of economic matters like weekly markets and fairs, the rights of staple supporting intermediate trade, variable toll charges or monopolies of goods such as salt or tobacco. Beyond this, the towns also ran a variety of commercial facilities until the administrative reforms of the eighteenth century. Apart from providing infrastructure services like brick kilns, mills or similar, such facilities were also oriented towards the obtaining of revenues. In wine-producing regions, towns produced and traded their own wine whereas in metalworking regions they traded with metal products. In salt mining regions, towns were deeply involved in the salt trade and in nearly every case they brewed beer, bred fish and traded in grain and livestock. They also leased houses, mills and taverns and were involved in the real estate business.

As far as the connection between the regional urban economy and international trade is concerned, only a few links can be noticed. In the early sixteenth century, viticulture and mining industries reached their peak and their products were sold internationally. Mining was practised not only in Styria, where the best-known mining region was located, but also in Tyrol and Carinthia. Metalworking was situated in Carinthia, Styria and Austria above and below the Enns, followed by the saline towns in Styria and Austria above the Enns and the salt trade centres on the rivers Inn, Danube and Mur. Beyond this, the fairs of Bolzano, Linz, Villach, Judenburg, Krems and Vienna had super-regional relevance.[17] But with the crisis of the seventeenth century, which had begun at the end of the sixteenth century, only part of their former economic power remained and this affected the urban fiscal and financial systems. The period of the commercial facilities administered by municipalities finally came to an end through administrative reform in the eighteenth century.

The Urban Financial System[18]

This paper deals mainly with small towns, and with towns with hardly any self-rule or scope for political action in a comparatively lowly urbanized region.[19] The Austrian territorial towns had enjoyed a limited autonomy during the sixteenth and seventeenth centuries, which enabled them to control the administration of taxes collected on them, although not their amount.[20] This ended in the middle of the eighteenth century. At that time the traditional fiscal and financial system of these centres was replaced by the so-called *Steuerrektifikationen*, a centralized system, which separated the taxes due to the central government from those funding the financial system related to urban spending. But also, the territorial towns had previously only held a part of self-government in administrative concerns, as the town councils could never determine the height of taxes but merely their administration.[21]

Until the *Steuerrektifikation* each town – in spite of the small size – had a complex financial system, composed of a main account and some subordinate accounts with more or less independent means, which followed the Viennese pattern.[22] In some cases the main account, the *Kammeramt* or *Oberkammeramt* in bigger towns, administered only the surplus or deficits from the subordinate accounts, which sometimes paid their administrators and other salaries – for example in case of the accounts of hospitals, which often had domains and had to administer public trusts. When looking at the financial situation, the system was quite complex: the subordinate accounts were not only interconnected with the main account, which used this mechanism to solve problems of decreasing liquidity by transferring money from one account to the other, but also among themselves, without the main account being involved at all.

A complex system of loans and credits between the different accounts was therefore in operation. These accounts were introduced systematically from the Middle Ages. Ever-increasing revenues and expenditures were assigned to particular accounts, depending on their respective administrator. The increasing budget was mainly the result of privileges granted by the princely ruler, in exchange for public loans. They had to serve as credit guarantees as the credit demand of the ruler exhausted the financial capacity of the hereditary towns.

With the exception of the Viennese budget,[23] which was more diversified, the households of the other cities considered in this paper were very similar. Their incomes consisted of direct and indirect taxes, credits and loans, incomes from public rights, rents and incomes from commercial activities. Their expenses were mainly on taxes to be paid to the princely ruler or the territorial estates, salaries of town officials, public works, costs of the municipal administration as well as for commercial and war activities.

The size of the municipal budgets varied, but generally correlated to the size of inhabitants increasing from the sixteenth to the eighteenth century. The budgets of the larger towns ranged from 14,000–25,000 fl. (gulden) in the sixteenth to about 20,000–70,000 fl. in the eighteenth century, whereas those of the smaller towns increased from about 1,000–4,000 fl. in the sixteenth to 2,000–7,000 fl. in the eighteenth century. Interestingly, this increase of the household during the seventeenth century occurred in all towns, independently of their size, or the political and economic problems of the era.

The relative importance of the different types of revenue and expenditure[24] can be established in those towns with a budget of more or less than 10,000 fl. a year. So the major categories of revenues and expenses in towns with a more than 10,000 fl. budget were, on average, taxes and excises (30.8–35.9 per cent); credits, loans and funds (19.9–26.8 per cent); surpluses from or payments to subordinated accounts (9.1–9.6 per cent); trade and commerce (3.3–19.8 per cent); administration (2.4–16.5 per cent); military purposes (3.9–5.4 per cent);[25] expenditure on building and construction (1.6 per cent); and unspecified costs (6.5–8.5 per cent). In smaller towns with lower budget taxes and excises amounted for 27.4–33.6 per cent; credits, loans and funds for 6.2–7.8 per cent; subordinated accounts for 3.4–7.3 per cent; trade and commerce for 7.8–35.4 per cent; administration for 8.2–37.5 per cent; military purposes for 2.75–3.4 per cent; expenditure on building and construction for 6,3 per cent; while 4.3–8.7 per cent of the expenses were unspecified.

This sample[26] of sixteen towns of Austria above and below the Enns,[27] ranged by their budgetary size, demonstrates, on the one hand, the importance of the loans and funds, as well as of the subordinated accounts for the financial system of the larger towns. On the other hand, the importance of commercial activities for the smaller towns can also be seen. The high costs of administration were the result of not outsourcing to subordinated accounts.

Table 10.1: City-size and height of budgets (in mean values in fl.).

	Houses 1576–90	Houses* seventeenth/eight- eenth century	Budget sixteenth century	Budget seventeenth century	Budget eighteenth century
Steyr	702	748	–	47,500	66,500
Linz	252	445	16,500	42,000	78,200
Wels	453	552	17,200	18,300	27,400
Freistadt	239	238	13,200	14,600	25,600
Krems	400	435	25,200	18,000	36,200
Bruck/L.	212	306	15,000	14,500	12,000
Korneuburg	182	223	–	15,000	11,800
Baden	140	270	–	3,300	10,600
Hainburg	193	252	–	2,800	8,000
Laa/Th.	160	181	–	–	3,800
Tulln	189	214	–	1,800	5,000
Eggenburg	180	217	4,200	2,400	3,200
Waidhofen/Th.	138	174	–	2,800	3,000
Retz	94	135	1,400	1,200	2,900
Weitra	134	248	850	1,700	2,700
Drosendorf	68	93	–	1,200	1,900

* The numbers of the Lower Austrian towns (in Italics) refer to 1795.

Table 10.1 shows the relative small value of the budgets of the cities included in our list and their correlation to their demographic size.[28] It can also be seen that in most cases the value of the budgets grew significantly during the early modern period, but only a small number increased in terms of population.

The Taxes

Taxes were originally voluntary, exceptional and appropriate. But this changed during the Middle Ages when territorial towns obtained the right of taxation, which means that rather than the individual paying taxes to the lord of the town, the town as a corporation was liable. The council had to distribute the payable amount among the citizens through the levy of a property tax and collected it autonomously. The legal basis for this was the privilege of autonomous self-assessment of taxes, which was changed in the sixteenth century, because the funds effectively collected did not correspond to the real value of the property owned by the taxpayers. Ordinary taxes were collected regularly whereas extraordinary taxes were used when necessary to fund especial needs (mainly warfare). In these times regular grants, in terms of land and property taxes, house and poll taxes, by the *Landtag*, the meetings of estates and princely ruler, became usual.[29]

As any tax increase depended on the approval of the estates, the princely ruler felt compelled to demand extraordinary taxes. Since the end of the sixteenth century taxes rose due to the Ottoman Wars and this development continued until the end of the eighteenth. The so-called *turktax* was actually an imperial tax, which was distributed among the subjects.[30] In fact, it entailed as usual practice that the territorial rulers collected a higher tax rate than required, and used the surplus for their own expenses. On the other hand, since the estates had renewed the debts of the princely ruler in exchange for collecting his taxes, they also tried to pay less of their own debt than the towns and furthermore, pay them later. Moreover, they were still able to pressure the towns through military execution. Although the higher estates were without their political power until the 1620s, and were partly replaced by a loyal higher nobility, they nonetheless kept enough financial resources for supporting the princely ruler.[31]

The Ottoman Wars allowed the consolidation of the tax system. The Thirty Years' War increased the level of taxation in general. But problems of centralization and standardization of the fiscal system dated back to the sixteenth century[32] and became urgent after the conflict, because of the high indebtedness of the towns. In 1665 Count Ferdinand Maximilian von Sprinzenstein, commissary of the princely ruler, examined all territorial towns and markets in Austria below the Enns because they had arrears of taxes amounting to 167,635 fl. Sprinzenstein was told to reform the tax system. But Austria below the Enns was the region which suffered most during the Thirty Years' War, particularly at the beginning and the end of the conflict. From a total number of 3,457 houses in all towns and markets, only 916 were habitable, 718 were dilapidated and 1,823 ruined.[33] Tax arrears continued to rise during the second half of the seventeenth century and the first decades of the eighteenth and in 1748 they amounted to 815,990 fl., the major part of which were bad debts. Due to this critical economic situation an evaluation of the financial system of the towns in Austria below the Enns was ordered and realized by Count Anton von Gaisruck, who chaired a commission of the court. The result was an assessment of 50,973 fl., whereas until this moment the towns had paid a quota of 163,262 fl. The difference was to be paid by the other estates. This development is important, because it marked the beginning of the end of the tax appropriation power of the estates. Only in this moment the central government was able to enforce a consistent policy towards the centralization of taxation – and it was only the beginning of a process which led to the famous administrative reform of Joseph II, the 'Magistratsregulierung'. To calm the estates, they were offered a standardization of taxation, particularly regarding taxes for military purposes.[34] The *instructions of Gaisruck* entailed the separation of taxation from the municipal household, obliged the towns to sell or lease out their commercial activities, because they were not profitable, and restricted administration efforts. This entailed not only standardization and integration in the central state, but also the modernization and professionalization of the urban financial and fiscal system.

Table 10.2: Tax yield per year in mean values (fl.).

	Linz		Krems		Wels	
	Revenue	Expenditure	Revenue	Expenditure	Revenue	Expenditure
1570s	–	–	–	–	1,770	2,054
1580s	–	–	–	–	2,378	2,779
1590s	2,164	0	4,487	4,232	3,481	3,967
1600s	1,732	2,000	3,868	1,395	8,230	6,403
1610s	7,122	3,450	4,569	150	6,698	6,492
1620s	10,227	807	11,119	26,796	7,547	4,953
1630s	9,368	4,575	6,749	2,564	6,427	4,752
1640s	4,655	10,044	6,749	6,051	6,709	3,851
1650s	38,192	41,037	6,723	6,310	10,750	6,582
1660s	16,458	8,834	4,332	4,176	5,600	931
1670s	11,427	10,663	3,114	3,698	3,494	2,193
1680s	7,421	9,936	3,458	3,952	4,677	4,502
1690s	12,872	13,408	7,000	6,621	9,484	10,316
1700s	13,319	13,380	12,380	10,125	11,360	10,980
1710s	10,574	17,819	12,758	11,271	11,207	11,838
1720s	27,892	18,668	10,259	9,957	11,297	11,015
1730s	18,368	16,522	7,720	10,931	11,688	11,249
1740s	18,934	17,851	8,303	10,289	12,945	12,246

As seen in Table 10.2, the tax revenues of the three largest towns[35] of Austria above and below the Enns demonstrate not only the increasing amounts but also the difference between the sums on both sides of the balance, which rarely corresponds. In particular, the development of taxes in Wels demonstrates at first glance the collapse of the post-war period, but also the general increase of taxes to heights never reached before. Beyond that, the decreasing difference between income and expenditure shows the declining economic situation of the town.

Excises

In contrast to many other urban tax systems in Europe, excises played a less important role than direct taxes in the financial system of the Austrian towns.[36] In the following section I will separate excises (as consumption taxes) from municipal levies like customs and tolls, collected on imports and commodities in transit, and from other urban dues which had to be paid for security or other municipal matters.[37] In contrast to excises, tolls as taxes of consumption were a specific income of the towns, and the incomes were not transferred to the princely ruler. They were part of the urban privileges and served for infrastructural measures, often for building repairs.

The most important excises were levied on alcoholic beverages, on beer, wine, fruit wine and mead. Most of them were leased out by the towns to private individuals in return for an amount of money. The *Ungeld*, initiated about

1359 by Rudolf IV as a general beverage tax (*Tranksteuer*) on wine and beer, was the first excise of a princely ruler. The *Ungeld* originally was levied on each tenth *Achtering* (about 1.5 litres) of sold wine and beer was increased step by step over the years. The *Taz* or the *Zapfenmaß* (double of *Taz*) were excises of the estates and were also leased, and in later times they were bought by the towns.[38] In 1657 all estates obtained the right not only to lease but also to alienate the *Taz*.[39] During the 1660s and 1670s nearly all towns bought it, which had the advantage that the revenues coming from the *Taz* became controlled by the local councils. More harmful was, however, the fact that towns increased their debts by buying the *Taz*.

Furthermore, excises were also levied temporarily[40] on grain, meat and other goods, mainly food in case of need. Compared with the revenues of taxes, these amounts were lower. In spite of the incomes obtained from excises reached neither the height nor the progression of the direct taxes. On the contrary, the importance of excises decreased in many towns in the late seventeenth and the beginning of the eighteenth century. There is no really plausible explanation for this, but we have to assume that it was not caused by changes in consumption patterns. Only the instructions given to Gaisruck gave a hint. According to them, excises were collected carelessly, the rate was undercharged by a third and generally there was a lot of tax evasion.[41] On the general level of the entire Habsburg Monarchy, the share of excises amounted to approximately a third of taxation. A change from property taxation to indirect taxation failed, although it had been planned for the entire monarchy, due to the resistance of the estates.[42]

The rich documentary sources of Wels, a middle-sized town in Austria above the Enns, allow a detailed view of its household, because not only the main but also the subordinated accounts have been preserved. The development of the excises of Wels demonstrates not only the decreasing income obtained from them by the city, but also the decreasing expenditure, caused by the acquired *Taz*. However, the revenues coming from the *Ungeld* had to be transferred to the prince, particularly as the catchment area of Wels was larger than in other towns and reached to the hinterland. In this case, the lack of excises was explicable by changes in bookkeeping. The incomes from excises were included in another subordinated account.[43] Considering that the developments in other towns were very similar, the question of decline is not really applicable in this context.

Annuities, Funds and Loans

The internal credit systems of the towns were highly complex. Apart from annuities and funds, which were administrated in subordinate accounts, the main accounts were involved in a broad range of financial activities and even fulfilled banking functions, raising credits at the same time as granting them. But this fact meant often a debt conversion, and the reasons were either a creditors' recall of loans, as a consequence of which the towns had to look for another creditor, or the term ended, or new cheaper loans were raised for repaying older expensive loans.

At the beginning of the sixteenth century usually small, short-term loans were granted to citizens – sometimes without adding an interest rate. Later on most loans proved less often to be credit mortgages, interests or tax arrears, so credit policy and the credit system were closely interconnected to the tax system. Moreover, the major part of the funds invested in such activities came from the subordinate accounts, which in some periods fulfilled important financial functions. They administrated a broad variety of funds. So in some towns these funds played a crucial role in the credit policy of towns, because – as shown – they raised and granted loans by themselves, autonomously from the main account. These subordinated accounts varied from town to town but generally they administrated funds, often religious, annuities, orphans' social benefits, but also toll charges, infirmaries or hospitals. The subordinate accounts were also frequently endowed with a non-negligible patrimony. The properties of agricultural land and subjects, which provided not only the inhabitants with food, but the surplus, mostly of grain, was sold on the market and brought up additional capital to be invested in their financial activities. Simultaneously, many citizens lent sums to the main account which then served to provide means of subsistence to orphans and widows.

Austrian towns also granted more or less compulsory loans to the prince, many times without consideration of the economic situation. After the decline caused by the Thirty Years' War the funds invested in such activities increased, without however reaching the heights of the pre-war period. The bookkeeping was too complex to reconstruct the credit situation of each city in particular. The annual balance sheets showed only the actual capital transfer, but no general survey on incomes and debts.

The only exception is again Wels, where for about fifty years – from 1592 to 1638 – the balance listed the entire debts and receivables.[44] This list shows that, in thirty years, debts tripled – from about 50,000 to 150,000 fl. – while the revenues only doubled – from about 40,000 to 90,000 fl. But the receivables contained not only credits but also tax arrears. In 1629 Wels owed 13,326 fl. to the estates, with 9,000 fl. of tax revenues of 1627 and 1628 and 2,240 fl. of excise revenues of 1628. In 1648 and 1649 a military execution by the estates was only avoided by means of a private loan by two aldermen. In 1657 the town had debts of 224,858 fl. and revenues of 92,473 fl., thus a net debt of 132,385 fl. – without considering bad debts on both sides. In the 1680s military execution was not inevitable anymore. Finally, at the end of the century, the level of debt led to a new financial policy of the estates. Wels, like other towns of the period, obtained an annual grant to the budget until 1750. Another problem in this context was the entanglement of debts of taxation and of credit, a problem, which can be found also in the administration of the estates. It is almost impossible to separate the variety of posts, but most of this complexity is also caused by the system of bookkeeping.[45] The reform of the municipal administration of the central government made a clear distinction between annuities, loans and credits. As a result of the same reform, the towns became embedded in the hierarchic system of state administration and lost their financial margin.[46]

Conclusion

In spite of the variety of local situations the early modern period and the different socio-economic profile, some general statements on the development of the municipal household for the towns in the Habsburg hereditary lands can be made. Many of the smaller centres lost their status and functions, and even the larger centres lost their political importance during this period as a result of their economic decline. The best examples are those towns in Austria below the Enns founded for the protection and defence at the frontier with Bohemia during the late medieval period. The frontier lost its importance as well as the towns, which now left the estates in default of paying the tax rates or by being mortgaged by the princely ruler. The larger towns, on the contrary, had a better financial standing, but suffered as well from the general economic conditions, particularly export-oriented towns. However, all of them held at least their positions in the regional or super-regional urban network.

At a first glance, the taxes were the most important source of income in the municipal household, but they were not really relevant because they had to be transferred to the estates and/or to the princely ruler. However, they gained more importance in context with the credit system; particularly the larger towns with higher budgets, which raised loans to pay taxes and also vice versa. Yet the taxes increased during the whole period analysed, while the loans at first glance decreased, although this was the effect of accounting. All towns became indebted during the seventeenth century. During the Thirty Years' War taxes reached a high level which they never fell below; quite on the contrary, they continued to rise.

The development of excises on the other hand became less important in the second half of the seventeenth and finally in the eighteenth century. There is no simple or convincing explanation for this phenomenon but maybe some likely reasons. The excises were leased out, so maybe their incomes were registered in another way, perhaps as part of the complex credit system. For the central state, the usual tax-collecting methods had proved more effective and were more profitable than the excises.

The question of how fiscal systems evolved in the region can only be answered from the point of view of the central state. The territorial towns had no influence on the surrounding countryside because of the opposition between the princely ruler, the town's lord, and the noble estates, owning the countryside seigniories. The seigneurial towns however were part of these seigniories and therefore bound to pay their part of the taxes to the land lords. On the other hand these lords, as members of the estates, had assumed obligations to the princely ruler and were therefore also responsible for tax collection. They tried to reduce their debts or pay them later than the territorial towns and pressured the latter even by military execution.

Taking in consideration the whole financial system, the incomes and surpluses of rents, commercial activities and privileges seemed to be the backbone of the budgets. They financed the expenditure on administration and infrastructure. These activities in connection with the subordinated accounts enabled the towns to evade problems of liquidity on the one hand and getting credits on the other hand. But these possibilities ended when the central state demanded not only a rigid segregation of the tax account and the rest of the budget, but also terminated the municipal commercial activities. From the point of view of the central state, the only function of the municipal financial and fiscal system was to administrate, because it was embedded in a hierarchic structure of administration. It was convenient for the higher authority to supervise standardized, accessible, manageable administrative departments, which did not act independently, particularly regarding financial concerns.

11 TAXATION AND DEBT IN EARLY MODERN GERMAN CITIES

Bernd Fuhrmann

A survey of the fiscal system of the early modern German Cities has to be undertaken with an important restriction in mind: given the scarce literature on the subject, a comprehensive description of taxation and debt in the cities of the Holy Roman Empire is beyond the scope of this paper. It is not without good reason that in the volume on the 'The Rise of the Fiscal State in Europe, c. 1200–1815' a chapter treating the Empire in early modern times is missing.[1] Therefore, this essay is rather an account of a research agenda than an analysis of the municipal taxes and debts from the sixteenth to the eighteenth centuries in German cities. We can only present some general trends of urban tax and debt policies, since many developments followed different or even opposed courses as a result of the high number of princely states within the Empire, and the analysis of the individual cases is rendered still more complex by the fact that most cities did not have a single town account. For these reasons we present first and foremost examples of different municipal tax and debt policies in a sample of German cities of the time.

A fundamental distinction has to be made between imperial cities and territorial cities. In the imperial cities, taxes already had a long tradition, justified by the principle of joint obligation (*Mitleiden*) of all citizens and residents. By contrast, in the territorial cities the originally limited rights of the sovereigns to levy taxes were extended with new legitimizations, especially since the sixteenth century. That is why the first part of this chapter deals with the developments in the imperial cities, whereas in the second we will turn to the territorial towns, emphasizing how their fiscal and financial evolution was conditioned by the pressure exerted by the expanding modern state.

The imperial cities, whose number fell from eighty-eight in 1521 to only forty-seven around 1800, had the status of autonomous members of the Empire, just like secular or sacred territories. They could settle their own fiscal and financial policies, although given the diversity of developments prevailing in them comparisons are often problematic. Although the early modern period and especially the seventeenth and eighteenth centuries are no longer considered as a phase of decline by the German historiography of the last decades – in 1969 Erich Maschke and Jürgen Sydow still characterized these years as 'the two darkest centuries in the history of German cities' – the financial aspect has remained often marginal.[2] The late Middle Ages as well as the history of territorial states have been subject to more research than the financial history of German cities in the early modern period. In the last decades a few works about early modern communal households have been published, in clear contrast with countries such as England, Belgium, the Netherlands or Spain. The situation is better for Switzerland, too, but the Swiss Confederation left the Empire de facto at the end of the fifteenth century and therefore is not part of our research area.

Direct taxes often combined a poll tax and a property tax. The poll tax had to be paid by all heads of a household. The property tax was collected from a particular asset and in the sixteenth century in most cases the minimum accounted to 50 or 100 guilders. Additionally we can detect differences in the assessment: movable and immovable property was subject to different rates of assessment and the household effects and the grain supplies were exempt. The levying of poll taxes was justified with the above mentioned *Mitleiden*, the participation of all residents in urban expenditure, and it was characterized, at least in theory, by some principles already developed in the fifteenth century, such as universality or the desire of distributing the fiscal burden in a fair way among taxpayers, although in practical terms assets were generally charged by a linear tax rate, leaving the graduated ones as the exception.[3]

The collection of indirect taxes (*Ungeld, Akzise*) took place inconsistently. Basic foodstuffs like wine, beer, cereals, bread or salt, but rarely meat, were often taxed in order to achieve high proceeds. Indirect taxes, also levied on cloths and spices, drove rises in price levels.[4] In particular, the fiscal burden which fell on bread, the staple food in the late Middle Ages and in the early modern age, awakened strong criticism, although this did not change the preference for indirect taxation visible in many German cities.[5]

However, rising indirect taxes could lead to unrest. To quote an example, after the Nördlingen council had increased the taxes levied on beverages in 1505, it had to return to the old rates nine years later. After the tax rise of 1505, house wines were taxed with an *Ungeld* of 20–2 per cent, while the rate had been 11–16 per cent before. At the end of the fifteenth century the Strasbourg Council frankly stated that indirect taxes had to be paid only by those who contributed little or nothing to the collection of property taxes. With this argument, the overall contribution of the population to tax revenues stood in the centre again. Indirect taxes could cause substantial price increases. At the beginning of the sixteenth century the fiscal burden on house wine in Nuremberg, a product whose consumption was widespread among the inhabitants of the city, is calculated to have been 33 per cent, and in Strasbourg the surcharge by the *Mahlgeld*, a tax for milling, weighed on bread with 30 per cent.[6] In most cases, however, the rates levied upon foodstuffs and basic commodities were lower.

Imperial Cities

In Nuremberg, the first example of an imperial city, the council increased the revenues obtained from direct taxes since the last quarter of the fifteenth century, and the local council gave up their annual collection only exceptionally during the following centuries.[7] The incomes from indirect taxes also rose significantly, and by the middle of the sixteenth century they were more important than those coming from direct taxation. Wine and beer were heavily taxed during this period. Instead of borrowing, the Nuremberg council preferred taxes as the central instrument of financing the city household. In the first half of the sixteenth century, borrowing funded territorial acquisitions, the purchase of rights, the restructuring of debt with more favourable conditions for the city and Nuremberg's involvement in the War of Schmalkalden in 1546 and 1547. On average, taxes contributed to more than half of the city's revenues between 1490 and 1549; during the decade 1501–9 this percentage was slightly lower, falling to 49.6 per cent. From 1510 to 1549 the share of taxation increased to more than two thirds.[8] However, from 1552 until 1570 the debt rose dramatically, so that the Second Markgrave War posed serious difficulties to the city treasury. In 1570 the payment of the interest on its debt amounted to 67 per cent of Nuremberg's expenditure, whereas both direct and indirect taxes accounted for around 76 per cent of the city revenues, (excluding two debt redemptions by the bishops of Bamberg and Würzburg). Thanks to tax increases and the introduction of temporary taxes, the burden of Nuremberg's debt was reduced during the first decades of the seventeenth century, although it was on the rise again after the beginning of the Thirty Years' War.

In the eighteenth century direct taxes, often raised through increases of already existing taxes, became the most important source of income. The tax system massively favoured the estates of patricians in comparison with merchant goods, a system that did not change before the introduction of the base contract (*Grundvertrag*) in 1795. Besides drinks, indirect taxes were levied on an increasing number of commodities. From 1576 to 1617 and then from 1633 onwards an increase in the taxes levied on cereals was introduced to fund the protection of the city, in what deserves to be considered as a good example of the consolidation of originally extraordinary taxes. Since the end of the sixteenth century the inhabitants of the rural territory controlled by Nuremberg also had to pay direct and indirect taxes.[9]

Despite the difficult circumstances, the city council managed to reduce its debt until 1660, but the following wars and the Wars of the Spanish Succession made the debt explode again, and this time the city household could not recover from the expenses.[10] These ruinous developments can be seen as the price paid by Nuremberg for being an imperial city. The debt service persisted at a high, but relatively stable level, and it amounted to more than 50 per cent of the urban spending in most years. At the end of its time as an imperial city Nuremberg like other imperial cities was heavily indebted. By 1785 the treasurers did not get enough revenue to cover expenses.

By the time of its absorption into Bavaria in 1806, Nuremberg's debt amounted to just over 12.2 million guilders (about 8.1 million Reichstaler). The interest rates oscillated between three and five per cent, and only a paltry 10 per cent of such debt was owned by foreign lenders.[11] Nevertheless, loans were not a regular source of income in the eighteenth century and repayments were made only sporadically, with the exception of the years 1764 and 1765. Unfortunately, after the mid-sixteenth century detailed studies, which could offer further information on this aspect, are missing. In the eighteenth century the municipal household became more and more opaque,because of the proliferation of special case budgets and the lack of a main account. In the seventeenth and eighteenth centuries reforms were complicated by the stiffness of the administration, the accumulation of offices in a few hands and the so-called '*Anciennitätsprinzip*'. Furthermore the majority of patricians had withdrawn from trade.[12] Changes and upgrades took place below the highest political level. The mercantilistic economic policies followed by the neighbouring states reduced the economic power of Nuremberg, but despite of its often claimed decline and the changes in trade routes the city remained an important trading centre in the Empire. Its large territory and the access to the Upper Palatinate resources had a stabilizing effect. Like in the former centuries, the Nuremberg merchants were the main lenders to the city treasury during the eighteenth century.[13]

As in Nuremberg, in Augsburg the citizens were the major lenders to the town, and according to a 1606–7 list their share of the urban debt amounted to 38.4 per cent, followed by charitable institutions. On the revenue side, indirect taxes contributed to more than 60 per cent of the city revenues and direct taxes over a quarter. Overall, the city budget was largely in balance. Because of the high pressures brought by the Thirty Years' War the total value of Augsburg's debt raised to around 1.56 million guilders, as a result of the frequent loans and payments to the Emperor and the credit needs of the powerful neighbours, the dukes of Wittelsbach, which the city could not refuse (although, in contrast to the crown, the dukes at least paid back their debts). After the war the council increased the tax burden which fell on the inhabitants, which was pushed to a maximum. Nevertheless, thanks to its renewed economic heyday, Augsburg shouldered the growing fiscal and financial burdens of the wars of the seventeenth and early eighteenth and in the years around 1670 it was a desirable place for investments again.

From 1771 we can see – when looking through the general sources again – a sharp rise of Augsburg's debt, but only in 1789 rumours about the problematic financial situation reached the public of the city. Since the middle of the eighteenth century religious foundations were the most important financial creditors of the city. The cause of the rising debt lay in the survival of a financial and administrative system, almost unchangeable since the late Middle Ages, which allowed more or less uncontrolled borrowing, while the council and the patricians took no serious effort to reform it. In the eighteenth century indirect taxes remained the main source of income, followed by direct taxes, based on a self-assessment of taxpayers. Until 1806, just before Augsburg became a Bavarian city, its debt ran up to the relatively modest sum of 3.1 million guilders (more than 2 million Reichstaler). Measured in per capita terms the value of the city debt amounted to 109 guilders, well below Nuremberg, where such sum amounted to 485.[14]

In the smaller town of Ulm direct taxes yielded between 15.5 and 32.4 per cent of the city revenues in the eighteenth century, whereas indirect taxes on beer, mead, wine, spirits and vinegar, whose importance tended to fall, provided between 3.9 and 15.4 per cent. Taxes on cattle and flour provided less than 5 per cent, and the share of custom duties oscillated between 2.5 to 7.0 per cent. Bonds made up for 8.4–32.4 per cent of the city revenue and on the second half of the century their importance rose, so that in 1795–6 Ulm's debt was over 3.1 million guilders. The taxes collected on its rural territory were another important source of income for the Treasury of the Swabian city, although they were managed separately and used to fund military expenditures, providing between 6.1 and 24.9 per cent of revenue. From 1720 to 1775 urban spending was presided over by the payments of the principals and interests of the city debt, which required from 44 to 57.5 per cent of total expenditure.[15]

In Memmingen direct taxes of the residents and the rural subjects were the main source of fiscal revenue during the second half of the eighteenth century, when they provided an average 46 per cent of the city incomes, closely followed by indirect taxes and customs duties, which provided another 43 per cent. The rest of the city revenues came from a broad range of small items. On the other hand, until the 1740s Memmingen, like other cities, made efforts to reduce its debt, which grew from 500,000 guilders in the year 1740 to over 1.25 million guilders in 1802–3. Around 1800 the main creditors of the city were the citizens (nearly 75 per cent), followed by urban institutions (15 per cent). In 1708 the main lenders came from the Swiss Confederation, and before the Thirty Years' War most loans were raised from the citizens.[16]

The development of Hamburg, heavily influenced by the expansion of its trade during the early modern period, shows a clear contrast to that of Nuremberg. Whereas the fiscal and financial history of the Hanseatic city during the fifteenth century is well known, studies about Hamburg's household between the sixteenth–eighteenth centuries cover only a few years, supplemented by some average values. Between 1497 and 1521, direct taxes amounted to an average of 21.4 per cent of revenue, indirect taxes to 7.3 and extraordinary taxes to 4.2 per cent. In the period from 1522 to 1562 the figures were 13.7 per cent, 5.9 per cent and 14.1 per cent respectively.[17] Until the middle of the seventeenth century revenues from customs remained the main source of income. However, in the subsequent decades the share of consumption taxes increased, and in some years they could account for up to 40 per cent of the city revenue. On average, from 1563 to 1578 direct taxes contributed with 12 per cent of the income (of which 5 per cent based on extraordinary taxes), customs duties with 17 per cent, indirect taxes with 17 per cent, and loans with 32 per cent. For the period from 1579 to 1602 the figures are 15 per cent (9 per cent), 22 per cent, 14.5 per cent and 20.5 per cent; from 1603 to 1619, 16 per cent (3 per cent), 23 per cent, 17.5 per cent and 16.5 per cent. Finally from 1631 to 1650 the distribution was 19 per cent (11 per cent), 14 per cent, 28 per cent and 23 per cent. The main taxes collected by the Hanseatic city were levied on ground corn, beer, wine, brandy, meat, vinegar and animals for slaughter.[18] In face of a high level of debt (caused by the construction of a canal to Lübeck and the development of the city fortifications) in 1563 major administrative changes took place including the introduction of a central fund and the general booking of gross amounts (*Bruttoprinzip*). Nevertheless, researchers consider the Hamburg public debt an extremely safe investment, despite occasional problems in the payment of interests after the War of Schmalkalden. In the second half of the sixteenth century the importance of foreign lenders declined significantly.[19]

For the seventeenth and the eighteenth centuries, samples of the years 1626, 1659, 1686, 1716, 1746 and 1800 indicate substantial budgetary surpluses. With the exception of the first two years, direct and indirect taxes predominated among the incomes, and income from loans went together with large redemption payments. The share of direct taxes in total revenue fluctuated between 15.7 per cent (1716) and 32.5 per cent (1686); that of indirect taxes between 10.4 per cent (1800) and 31.9 per cent (1659). Together with customs revenue, the share of indirect taxes rose from 19.1 per cent (1775) to 48.0 per cent (1659). For bonds and lottery we can quote proportions between 1.5 per cent (1659) and 48 per cent (1716), but as in other cities, the totals fluctuated enormously. Interests, loan repayments and lotteries required from 8.8 per cent (1659) to 48.3 per cent (1716) of the Hamburg expenditure.[20] Unlike many other cities, Hamburg escaped the ravages of the Thirty Years' War, and despite of its strained relations with Denmark, the town benefited from the shift in world trade routes and became the most important port in the German Empire. The arrival of new mercantile groups such as the Merchant Adventurers and the giving up of some Hanseatic traditions had a positive effect also. The same is valid for the setting up of a clearing bank, the fixing of exchange or bills by written law (*Wechselrecht*) and the new commercial practices. Many construction projects in the public sector, including the new fortifications in the seventeenth century, indicate a strong financial position, and just like the following century the consequences of the cyclical fluctuations find their expression in the city household.

Another city that played a special role was Frankfurt am Main. Although Frankfurt gradually lost the importance it had enjoyed in the fifteenth century, it managed to keep a central role in supra-regional trade. Unfortunately, the account books were almost completely destroyed during the Second World War, so only some scarce data can be presented here. In the years 1580, 1593, 1607 and 1610 the share of direct taxes oscillated between 12.7 per cent and 24.5 per cent. Indirect taxes and other consumer charges (meal, customs, road toll, deposited wine), increased in the years 1515, 1525, 1540 and 1560, and contributed with 40 per cent of income in the first half of the sixteenth century, reaching their lowest point in 1580 (21.9 per cent) to rise to 37.6 per cent in 1593. Because of the costs of the Schmalkalden War and risky copper speculations, in 1575–6 the value of the urban debt was 1 million guilders, and this posed a serious threat of bankruptcy. Only in 1576, the town council decided to introduce a direct tax which was to be levied annually. However, citizens had to pay taxes for a maximum of 15,000 guilders of their property, in the interest of the upper class the rest was exempt. In the seventeenth century the rates of the indirect taxes (*Rentenamt, Fleischamt, Stadtwaage*) increased and in 1733 they provided 45.5 per cent of the revenue, 37.9 per cent in 1753 and 29.0 per cent in 1783. For the direct taxes the shares were 18.2 per cent, 16.5 per cent and 21.0 per cent. The interest payments due by the city treasury made up for 9.6 per cent of the expenditure in 1733. [21] After the Thirty Years' War trade met with difficulties, but at least since the last quarter of the seventeenth century one can find traces of an expansion, which lasted during the eighteenth century. This economic development had, of course, a positive effect on the city finances, but it is difficult to quantify. Many merchants moved to Frankfurt and enlarged the spectrum of trade and production, but not without frictions with the local population, accompanied by other social conflicts. [22]

The last example of imperial city finances in the eighteenth century to be presented in this paper is Cologne. In the seventeenth century Cologne increasingly lost its importance in international and supra-regional trade, although it remained one of the most important trading places in the Empire. Moreover, its hinterland, which stretched about 100 kilometres to the east, gradually emancipated from Cologne's economic domination and achieved more independence. Both developments led to a loss in the tax revenues of the city and hampered its recovery. Indirect taxes levied on the most important commercial and consumer goods (wine, beer, bread, salt, cattle and fish) and on the markets of Gürzenich and Altermarkt, remained the most important source of revenue by far in the eighteenth century, providing between 70–90 per cent of income. From 1784–5 the road toll completed the whole panoply. Those indirect taxes which provided low revenues were usually leased out. Just like in the previous centuries the council raised direct taxes only irregularly and particularly in times of crisis.

Borrowing took place regularly from the sixteenth to the eighteenth century, namely in the form of life annuities and redeemable rents. In the second half of the seventeenth century the city was able to reduce the interest rates on redeemable annuities to 3 or 4 per cent as it had already done in the fifteenth century, but again not in a systematic way. The last life annuity may have been sold in 1701. Above all, wars and payments to the Empire led to an increase of the debt, and in 1700 the arrears in the payment of interests amounted to eight or nine years. In this year nearly half of the expenditure of Cologne (48 per cent) funded the payment of the interests of the city debt. The growing difficulties in the payment of interest led to frequent confiscations of commodities belonging to citizens of Cologne abroad which damaged its trade. Even so, Cologne's trade recovered again in the eighteenth century, before suffering the adverse consequences of the mercantilist policies followed by the territorial states after the 1770s. Until 1734 the delays in the payments of interest could be reduced to two or three years, although after the Seven Years' War they rose again to six or eight. Two-thirds of the debt at the end of the century had been taken up in the sixteenth and seventeenth centuries, and repayments were made only sporadically. Like in Nuremberg, it was not until the last quarter of the eighteenth century that committees for the reorganization of the financial administration were formed.[23]

For the first time in the early modern period, after the abolition of the local council by the French in 1797 a comprehensive inventory of the debt was made which reveals that the main creditors of the city were parish churches, hospitals and monasteries. The debt amounted to 1.7 million Reichstaler, significantly less than in Nuremberg. Four years later the administration started a project of debt management in order to pay off the urban debt.

At the end of the eighteenth century the vast majority of south German imperial cities had to invest more than half of their revenues in the payment of interests and the redemption of their debt, although in the northern towns this development was different. The debts, which reached in some cases fabulous dimensions, were the result of several factors: High payments to the Empire and the Imperial Districts (*Reichskreise*), the shift in trade routes, progressively more oriented towards the Atlantic, and a broad range of administrative problems. In spite of the difficulties caused by the Thirty Years' War, at the end of the conflict the cities had managed a far-reaching financial consolidation. In order to achieve this consolidation interest payments had been adjusted, repayments were postponed or the cities organized a rescheduling of the debt. In contrast, many merchants had to write off huge sums, which they had lent to cities, states, princes or nobles.[24] Only in the eighteenth century and especially in the second half including the French Revolutionary Wars the debts were reduced to a barely manageable level. Nördlingen was able to reduce its debt in the second half of the eighteenth century, before the French Revolutionary Wars caused a new upsurge. An administrative reform together with the reduction of costs for the district levy and staff proved to be the most important pillars of the financial recovery of this city.[25]

The fiscal policies followed by the German imperial cities could by very different from case to case. Cologne and, to a lesser extent, Frankfurt and Hamburg obtained the bulk of their incomes from taxes on consumption and trade as well as duties, which in some cases cannot be clearly distinguished. Fluctuations in the incomes from the wine taxes may be explained by the fluctuations on the harvest, even though the tax was levied on tapped wine. On its turn, those cities endowed with important rural territories like Nuremberg or Schwäbisch Hall resorted to taxes levied upon the inhabitants of such districts mainly from the late sixteenth century. As already indicated, apart from the increasing indebtedness and the growing tax burdens, no single trend in the fiscal and financial evolution of the imperial cities can be found, but in contrast the developments show the presence of a broad range of peculiarities, depending on the economic structure of each case.

Territorial Cities

The second part of the paper focuses on territorial cities, whose evolution during this period was characterized by the progressive loss of their former autonomy, especially in northern and central Germany. Many cities kept a quasi-autonomous status until the end of the Middle Ages and managed to check the trend towards a growing interventionism by the local rulers in their fiscal and financial policies, but the Thirty Years' War and the following decades brought a drastic change.

In the course of the sixteenth century the use of direct taxes as an ordinary source of fiscal revenue was frequently acknowledged in theoretical discussions. In addition to the traditional extraordinary taxes, the early modern state managed to impose taxes without agreement of the states. Direct taxes were removed from their earmarked expenditure, and for example in Bavaria at the end of the seventeenth century the functionalistic ideas of cameralists on public revenue were so widespread that the necessity of taxation did not have to be justified anymore. Taxes could be imposed generally for the 'handling of major challenges'.[26] As for indirect taxes, its acceptance in theoretical writings and treatises was delayed until the seventeenth and the eighteenth centuries.[27] All this was accompanied at least since the sixteenth century by an intensive debate about the effects of taxation, and this interest was strengthened after 1789.[28] On the course of this debate different principles of taxation were proposed and applied.[29] At first – leaving aside the *Mitleiden* – the *common good* (or *common benefit*) provided the central legitimacy to the municipal councils to demand taxes, but this consideration plays a role as part of the good policy on the national level only after 1500, just as in the territorial states in early modern period.[30]

The building of palaces, together with the development of capital cities full of baroque splendour, urban improvements and the consolidation of permanent armies, led to a dramatic increase of the financial needs of the early modern territorial states. Richard Bonney stated that the expansion of the financial state posed the need of developing new sources of income, whether taxes or loans, the maximization of revenues being one of its main goals.[31] Numerous models of tax collection first developed in the cities, were later adopted by the territorial administrations which overtook the control of local governments because of their greater resources. However, the territories of the Holy Roman Empire until the end of the Old *Reich* could not be characterized as tax states since the tax state defined itself precisely through the widespread introduction of indirect taxes, a practise that was not spread countrywide.[32]

The princes controlled increasingly the tax system of the territorial towns in the early modern period, on the ground of their right to tax collection. Although state interventionism in the urban fiscal and debt policies had been a constant feature since the late Middle Ages, the pace of this process quickened after the Thirty Years' War and it was accompanied by additional tax claims and the direct collection of taxes among the inhabitants. Furthermore, not all the loans the cities granted to the rulers were voluntary. Once again, however, it is difficult to describe accurately the degree to which the early modern territorial states intervened in the urban households, and different developments can be identified, although we have to rely on a handful of relevant studies. Even in their centres of power the rulers and their administrations proceeded inconsistently, according to the different conceptions of 'economic policy' prevailing in the literature or among their advisors. Some authors such as Volker Press see this trend in an unfavourable light: 'We can almost say, that the emerging territorial power vacuumed up at the same time the financial strength and the autonomy of the cities'.[33] However, the reach of early modern states was limited, and could be extended only slowly. Moreover, the number of goods and merchandise charged with indirect taxes grew, and further taxes and levies raised the financial burden of the inhabitants. Many functionaries at court or in the administration were exempt from local taxes, and this led to growing tax deficits, especially in capital cities. On the other hand, however, many territorial cities benefited from the growth of early modern states, because the policy followed by them tended to promote the development of urban economies. Furthermore, as mentioned before, since the second half of the seventeenth century the mercantilistic or cameralistic policies increasingly restricted the sales potential of the imperial cities. However, the different cameralistic approaches do not form a closed system, and the cameralism, especially maintained in the Empire and in Austria, was an extension of mercantilism.[34] Only slowly did public finances develop into an independent discipline.[35] Functions at court and in the administration however developed to very desirable job opportunities for citizens. The city councils became increasingly an executive organ of state power with little room to manoeuvre on its own.

In Marburg, a middle-sized town, direct taxes constituted always more than half of the revenue until the first third of the sixteenth century, but then their relative importance tended to fall. Over the sixteenth century the absolute tax revenue remained stable, and in the first two decades of the seventeenth century their share fell below 20 per cent (always in ten-year averages). Indirect taxes were levied on beer and wine, but only one-third of the sums collected from them reached the city treasury, the Hessian landgraves won control of the rest. However, the council successfully established an additional permanent tax on wine, which had been granted by Landgraf Philipp in 1523 for a limited period to fund the construction of the town hall. From 1520–9 to 1610–19 indirect taxes contributed from 21.6 per cent to 30.6 per cent to the communal incomes. In this way until 1570–9 the Marburg household was financed in more than 50 per cent by taxes and borrowing played a secondary role, the loans to the rulers being especially limited.

Taxes paid to the country's sovereign, both regular and extraordinary, from the beginning of the records in 1451 to the mid-sixteenth century amounted to always more than one third of city expenditure. Novelly, after 1555 not all taxes paid by residents are listed in the city's books, instead being occasionally included in special accounts set up to fund special needs of the territorial state. This was codified finally by the Landgraf and the Estates in 1557 and thanks to this the rulers gained direct insights in the individual financial circumstances of the residents, although the compilation of such registers, in which all residents and their taxable assets were to be listed, proved to be a hard and strenuous task. The first tax paid regularly to the territorial ruler was a beverage tax on beer and wine first approved in 1553, which was higher in the cities than in the countryside. This tax also limited the further possibilities of municipal tax collection.[36]

As in Marburg, the relative importance of fixed, regular urban taxes in Munich tended to fall, but other charges had to be shouldered. A history of the Munich city household in the early modern period is missing unfortunately, so only broad trends can be presented here. Additionally, the Bavarian dukes participated in the duties, extraordinary taxes and indirect taxes levied by the town, which also lent important sums to them. During the second half of the sixteenth century the city had to borrow more than 200,000 guilders, just under 100,000 guilders of which between 1586 and 1600. As a partial payment of their debts the dukes transferred parts of its indirect taxes to the city. At the beginning of the seventeenth century tax revenues amounted to more than 70 per cent of the Bavarian state budget, primarily paid by the inhabitants of the cities and the markets. At this stage the dukes' financial management had overtaken that of the city in terms of technical sophistication. Two monopolies of the Bavarian dukes led to a capital loss of the urban merchants, a decline of trading assets, and as a result also the local tax revenue: in addition to the existing wheat beer monopoly, the lucrative salt trade, the most important commodity in the territory, was monopolized in 1587, but the salt monopoly at Burghausen had a stronger impact than the one at Munich.

Forced loans threatened the stability of Munich's finances in the eighteenth century. Like in other cities the volume of the household saw a marked rise and an important part of the taxes paid by the inhabitants of the Bavarian capital during the eighteenth century was used to fund the needs of the territorial state: if in 1731 still 27 per cent of house-owners and 20.2 per cent of the households paid taxes directly to the dukes, in 1762 these figures had risen to 37.8 per cent of homeowners and 33.8 per cent of the households, which led to a reduction of tax incomes of the city treasury. Duties and charges, tin money, fines and penalties remained the most important sources of income (1600–4: 29.0 per cent, 1700–4: 41.2 per cent, 1790–4: 27.5 per cent), followed by direct taxes (1600–4: 22.2 per cent, 1700–4: 23.3 per cent, 1790–4: 23.0 per cent). The incomes from indirect taxes show significant variations (1600–4: 17.5 per cent, 1700–4: 4.7 per cent, 1790–4: 14.7 per cent). Already in some years of the first half of the eighteenth the city's treasury was unable to service its debt, and so to achieve this, in 1749 a beer penny was introduced. If in 1700 the debt amounted to 87,000 guilders, in 1750 it had fallen to nearly 67,000 guilders to rise again to 281,000 guilders in 1790 and to 458,000 guilders in 1800. The abolition of the beer penny from 1777 to 1781 had serious consequences for the financial stability of the city, because in 1781 Munich had to stop all interest payments.[37]

In Freiburg in the Breisgau once again direct taxes and contributions proved an important source of revenue, and from 1651 to 1677 their share fluctuated on average between 16.9 per cent and 45.4 per cent, and mostly between 20 and 30 per cent. The same is true for indirect taxes, which ranged from 19.5 per cent to 36.0 per cent. Duties contributed to a further 4.4 per cent to 9.3 per cent. Higher borrowings are registered only for a few years, while redemptions and the payment of interests amounted up to 16.8 per cent to 52.7 per cent of urban spending between 1659 and 1671.[38]

In another residential centre, Koblenz, the lord of the city, the archbishop of Trier, controlled the fiscal policy followed by town council and decided to resort to direct taxation. The financial situation of the city was complicated by regulations according to which the nobility living within the city walls, the electoral officials and the clergy paid their taxes directly to the elector, so a large part of the real estate was not taxable by the council, something which involved a tax increase for the other inhabitants. At least since the year 1259 Koblenz could levy indirect taxes, but later the ruler of the territory claimed half of these revenues, described as his fiefs in 1362 by the archbishop. No later than the second half of the eighteenth century a strong debt of the city can be observed, especially since the crisis of the urban crafts in this century reached its peak.[39]

In 1696 the taxes on beer levied by Düsseldorf were transferred to the state, although the city preserved the control of the profitable wine tax. In the last three decades of the eighteenth century this tax accounted for an average of 17.5 per cent of revenue, whereas other trade and infrastructure charges and fees provided another 16.2 per cent. However, the main source of income were the mills, which provided about a third of the revenue. The city treasury only participated in the direct taxes through the collection of a surcharge on the tax levied by the Estates. The long-term debt in 1788, about 20,000 Reichstaler, partly came from the later Middle Ages. In 1803 this sum had risen to almost 120,000 Reichstaler, as a result of the unfavourable commercial activities of the council and the costs of the Revolutionary Wars. Wine taxes dominated the incomes of other cities, such as Jülich in the second half of the sixteenth and the first decade of the seventeenth century, when they provided more than 50 per cent and sometimes even 60 per cent (with the exceptions of 1561–2 and 1581) of the city revenues. Taxes on beer came up to 10 to 25 per cent and those taxes paid to the dukes amounted to more than 35 per cent until the 1580, later increasing by 25 to 35 per cent as a result of an increase of household sizes. In the duchy of Jülich, then Jülich-Kleve-Mark, of which Düsseldorf was a centre, indirect taxes on wine, beer and bread were raised occasionally since the fifteenth century, but when in 1700 the ruler decided to replace property taxes with these the project awakened strong resistance and had to be abandoned after one year. Two years later a second attempt followed, but the collection of these indirect taxes was finally stopped in 1705. Until 1715 Jülich, Düren and Düsseldorf remained exceptions. This case clearly shows the differences in state power in the territories of the Empire in the eighteenth century.[40]

In the case of St Johann and Saarbrücken the development of indirect taxation was irregular, and their share in the rather modest revenues of both cities oscillated between zero (1618–19) and 42.1 per cent (1596–7). After 1741 its share in the urban revenues exceeded the ten per cent threshold only one year. During the Thirty Years' War direct taxes in various forms became the most important source of income, and in some cases they amounted to more than 80 per cent of the revenues. Until the early 1620s the loan liabilities of both cities did not matter, they rather acted as lenders, and subsequently they acted only sporadically as a borrower. What proved to be more important, during and after the Thirty Years' War was the non-payment of repayments and interest by the debtors. In the eighteenth century Saarbrücken had to reschedule its loans more frequently than St Johann, but without increasing the debt significantly.[41]

The fiscal and financial policy followed by Würzburg since the fifteenth century was decided by the bishop and the cathedral chapter – the city had to give up their striving for autonomy after the defeat at the battle of Bergheim 1400 – but the council temporarily took advantage of tensions between both. The bishops introduced many taxes, as in 1410, for the extremely high amount of the twelfth penny, to repay their debts, although they allowed the city to participate in the incomes. More clearly than, for example, in Munich the financial policy of the diocese or rather the territory determined the evolution of the city's finances, and so rising taxes and duties, large sums of money for mercenaries or for the maintenance of the fortifications limited the financial autonomy of the town council. To aggravate the situation, wealthy merchants left the city since the beginning of the fifteenth century and massively again after the expulsion of the protestants in 1587, just to continue their business in less crowded conditions; this exodus had a significant impact on the tax revenue of Würzburg. Since the late seventeenth century the bishops by themselves could finally determine the tax claims, because no more provincial assemblies (Landtage) were convened, and the chapter was satisfied with being informed about the decisions. In 1676 bishop Philip of Dernbach ordered on one hand the increase of indirect tax rates, and on the other he increased the range of commodities taxed. From now on all market goods were taxable, and all houses of the inhabitants were inspected by employees of the episcopal administration, in order to estimate the private consumption and stocks of its inhabitants. From 1676 to 1699 the revenues coming from indirect taxes flowed completely into the bishop's office, before the city was awarded a third of the revenue.[42]

In Hanover, another seat of power, the direct tax revenues remained relatively constant in absolute terms, and their share of the city income amounted to 66.1 per cent in 1625, 22.6 per cent in 1650, 23.2 per cent in 1700, 19.2 per cent in 1750 and to 17.9 per cent in 1800. This relative decrease was due to the growth of the total revenue of the Saxon city, while the figure of 1625 is explained by an extremely low budget. More stable was the importance of indirect taxes, which provided 28.8 per cent of the city revenues in 1650, 24.9 per cent in 1700, 31.7 per cent in 1750 and 24 per cent in 1800. With the exception of 1800, tax revenues accounted for around half of the total incomes. On the expenditure side, debts (including forced loans) weighed heavily on the budget. In 1650 the city treasurers had to spend 66.2 per cent of expenditure for this purpose, in 1700 a high 77.3 per cent and in 1750 and 1800 only 39.1 and 20.8 per cent respectively. Unlike many other cities, in eighteenth-century Hannover borrowing played a lesser role than in the previous century, and the high budgetary surpluses at the end of the analysed period show a development running counter to the trend prevailing in the other cities so far considered. The main creditors of Hanover were citizens of the city, most of them from the upper class and those clearly ascribed to the politically influential group. Among the borrowers, on the other hand, appear a greater number of craftsmen.[43]

Berlin offers another interesting example of the strong involvement of local rulers (in this case the margrave of Brandenburg and then the kings of Prussia) in the fiscal and financial affairs of a German city. The twin cities of Berlin and Kölln (Cölln) had lost the freedom of the city after inner city conflicts in 1442. The interventions of the elector, chancellor and privy council in the issues of the city were already common in the sixteenth century. In 1643 all taxable houses had to be newly recorded by an instruction of the margrave of Brandenburg, in order to obtain a reliable basis for the financial administration. After the gradual introduction of indirect taxes (Akzisen) in all cities of Brandenburg since 1667, Berlin-Kölln still could dispose a portion of these revenues and even exert some influence in the choice of the methods of taxation, but the city had to resort to the levying of taxes on houses and apartments. The excise was definitively introduced in 1680 and its collection was controlled by state tax commissioners since 1681, so any urban influence on such taxes waned. The value of the indirect taxes collected in the city rose from 169,822 Reichstaler in 1705 to 318,026 Reichstaler forty-three years later, the state being the main beneficiary of the rise, although this should not hide the fact that even in 1765–6 incomes from the domains made up 30.7 per cent of the total revenues of Prussia, compared to 37.5 per cent from indirect and 31.8 per cent from direct taxes. Reforms of the financial administration in 1766 resulted in higher tax rates and as a result higher tax revenues, further increased by a tobacco sales monopoly, and since 1781 by a coffee monopoly. However, the financial autonomy of Prussian cities was severely curtailed. Surplus in municipal treasuries could be confiscated as the government wished. A specific feature were the so-called Prussian excise cities mainly in east Prussia and in Westphalia, which were endowed with a city status in the eighteenth century only in order to impose indirect taxes.[44]

Although the lack of a single account in many cities and the presence of special-case budgets pose serious difficulties for the study of the financial and fiscal history of the German territorial cities of the early modern period, the existing literature enables us to describe some broad trends which would deserve further research. The financial situation of most of the territorial cities had deteriorated probably since the second half of the seventeenth century and the territorial states enforced their sovereign rights of taxation to a growing degree, levying direct and indirect taxes upon the inhabitants of their cities. Thus, state interference in urban finances became common, as it may be seen in the cases of Würzburg and Berlin. Indebtedness seems to have been less important in the territorial towns than in the imperial cities, because loans often had to be approved by the rulers of the cities in the framework of budgetary control. In contrast, as far as taxes on real estate are concerned, a tendency to continue taxation of assets after its acquisition by personally exempt persons can be observed, in order not to reduce the number of taxable houses and other buildings. Especially during and after the thirty years' war territorial lords retained taxes and contributions, and perpetuated them after the war. Another element that can be observed is the decrease in the influence of the provincial assemblies, which had been able to negotiate with the secular and ecclesiastic rulers until then, and which could favour the cities.

NOTES

Andrés and Limberger, 'Introduction'

1. R. Bonney (ed.), *Economic Systems and State Finance* (Oxford: Oxford University Press, 1995); R. Bonney (ed.), *The Rise of the Fiscal State in Europe c.1200–1815* (Oxford: Oxford University Press, 1999); and S. Cavaciocchi (ed.), *La Fiscalità nell'economia europea, secc. XIII–XVIII* (Firenze: Olschki, 2008).
2. M. Boone, K. Davids and P. Janssens (eds), *Urban Public Debts: Urban Government and the Market for Annuities in Western Europe (14th–18th Centuries)* (Turnhout: Brepols, 2003), pp. 75–92, on p. 83. W. Fritschy, 'Indirect Taxes and Public Debt in the World of Islam', in Cavaciocchi (ed.), *La Fiscalità nell'economia europea, secc. XIII–XVIII*, pp. 51–73 on p. 52. J. Zuijderduijn, 'The Emergence of Provincial Debt in the County of Holland (Thirteenth–Sixteenth Centuries)', *European Review of Economic History*, 14 (2010), pp. 335–59 and O. Gelderblom and J. Joonker, 'Public Finance and Economic Growth: The Case of Holland in the Seventeenth Century', *Journal of Economic History*, 71:1 (2011), pp. 1–38.
3. J. Tracy, *A Financial Revolution in the Habsburg Netherlands: Renten and Rentiers in the County of Holland, 1515–1565* (Berkeley, CA: Berkeley University Press, 1985). M. 't Hart, *The Making of a Bourgeois State: War, Politics and Finance during the Dutch Revolt* (Manchester: Manchester University Press, 1993). R. Carande, *Carlos V y sus banqueros* (Barcelona: Crítica, 1991). W. M. Bowsky, *The Finance of the Commune of Siena, 1287–1355* (Oxford: Oxford University Press, 1970). A. Molho, *Florentine Public Finances in the Early Renaissance, 1400–1433* (Cambridge: Cambridge University Press, 1971). L. Pezzolo, *L'Oro dello Stato. Società, finanza e fisco nella Reppublica Veneta del secondo '500* (Venice: Il Cardo, 1991).
4. M. Prak and J. L. van Zanden, 'Tax Morale and Citizenship in the Dutch Republic', in O. Gelderblom (ed.), *The Political Economy of the Dutch Republic* (Bodmin: Ashgate, 2009), pp. 143–66, on p. 148. M. van der Heijden, E. van Nederveen Meerkerk, G. Vermeesch and M. van der Burg (eds), *Serving the Urban Community: The Rise of Public Facilities in the Low Countries* (Amsterdam: Aksant Academic Publishers, 2009). J. L. van Zanden and M. Prak, 'State Formation and Citizenship: The Dutch Republic between Medieval Commnunes and Modern Nation States', in J. L. van Zanden, *The Long Road to the Industrial Revolution: The European Economy in a Global Perspective, 1000–1800* (Leiden: Brill, 2009), pp. 205–32.
5. M. A. Arnould, 'L 'impôt dans l'histoire des peuples. Exposé introductive au colloque', in L'impôt dans le cadre de la ville et de l'etat. Colloque international, Spa 6–9 IX, 1964, *Pro Civitate, Collection Histoire, in 8°, nr 13* (1966), pp. 13–26, on p. 18.

6. W. Blockmans, 'Voracious States and Obstructing Cities: An Aspect of State Formation in Preindustrial Europe', *Theory and Society*, 18:5 (1989), pp. 733–56, on p. 735 and pp. 751–3 and C. Tilly, 'Cities and States in Europe, 1000–1800', *Theory and Society*, 18:5 (1989), pp. 563–84, on p. 565.

7. S. de Moncada, *Restauración de la Abundancia de España* (1619), ed. J. Vilar (Madrid: Instituto de Estudios Fiscales, 1974). G. de Uztáriz, *Teoría y práctica de comercio y de marina* (1724), ed. G. Franco (Madrid: Aguilar, 1968); C. M. Cipolla, 'The Economic Decline of Italy', in B. Pullan (ed.), *Crisis and Change in the Venetian Economy*. (London: Methuen, 1968), pp. 127–45.

8. A. Smith, *The Wealth of the Nations* (1776), ed. K. Sutherland (Oxford: Oxford University Press, 2008), pp. 315–16.

9. Cipolla, 'The Economic Decline', pp. 138–9. D. Sella, *Italy in the Seventeenth Century* (London: Longman, 1997), p. 37. E. Hamilton, 'The Decline of Spain', *Economic History Review*, 8 (1938), pp. 168–79. A. García Sanz, 'Repercusiones de la fiscalidad sobre la economía castellana en los siglos XVI y XVII', *Hacienda Pública Española*, I (1991), pp. 15–24. J. E. Gelabert, *La Bolsa del Rey* (Barcelona: Crítica, 1997), p. 350. A. Marcos Martín, '¿Fue la fiscalidad regia un factor de la crisis?', in G. Parker (ed.), *La crisis de la Monarquía de Felipe IV* (Barcelona: Crítica, 2006), pp. 186–8. C. Wilson, 'Taxation and the Decline of Empires: An Unfashionable Theme', *Bijdragen en Mededelingen van Historisch Genootschap*, 77 (1963), pp. 10–26. J. Israel, *The Dutch Republic: Its Rise, Greatness and Fall, 1477–1806* (Oxford: Oxford University Press, 1995), p. 630. J. de Vries and A. van der Woude, *The First Modern Economy: Success, Failure and Perseverance of the Dutch Economy, 1500–1815* (Cambridge: Cambridge University Press, 1997), pp. 103–5, 287, 336 and ch. 12.

10. D. McCloskey, 'A Mismeasurement of the Incidence of Taxation in Britain and France, 1715–1780', *Journal of European Economic History*, 7:1 (1978), pp. 209–10.

11. Wilson, 'Taxation and the Decline of Empires', p. 18. R. Rapp, *Industry and Economic Decline in Seventeenth-Century Venice* (Cambridge, MA: Harvard University Press, 1976), p. 140.

12. G. Sivori, 'Il tramonto dell'industria serica genovese', *Revista Historica Italiana*, 84 (1972), pp. 897–997, on pp. 921–5. P. Malanima, *La decadenza di un'economia cittadina. L'industria a Firenze nei secoli XVI–XVIII* (Bologne: Il Mulino, 1982), p. 171. G. Vigo, *Finanza pubblica e pressione fiscale nello Stato di Milano durante il secolo XVI* (Milan: Banca Commerciale Italiana, 1977), pp. 92–4.

13. M.'t Hart and M. van der Heijden, 'Het geld van de stad. Recent historiographische trenes in het onderzoek: naar stedelijke financiën in de Nederlanden', in *Tijdschrift voor Sociale en economische Geschiedenis*, 3:2 (2006, Special Issue: Het geld van de stad), pp. 3–35, on p. 24.

14. K. G. Persson, *An Economic History of Europe: Knowledge, Institutions and Growth, 600 to the Present* (Cambridge: Cambridge University Press, 2010), pp. 28–30.

15. M. Boone, K. Davids and P. Janssens, 'Urban Public Debts from the 14th to the 18th Century: A New Approach', in M. Boone, K. Davids and P. Janssens (eds), *Urban Public Debts: Urban Government and the Market for Annuities in Western Europe (14th–18th Centuries)*, pp. 3–11, on p. 5. W. Blockmans, 'Finances publiques et inégalité sociale dans les pays-bas aus XIVe–XVIe siècles', in J. P Genet and M. Le Mené (eds), *Genèse de l'état moderne: prélèvement et redistribution: Actes du colloque de Fontevraud* (Paris: CNRS, 1987), pp. 77–90.

16. B. Blondé and J. Hanus, 'Beyond Building Cratsmen. Economic Growth and Living Standards in the Sixteenth-Century Low-Countries: The Case of 's-Hertogenbosch (1500–1560)', *European Review of Economic History*, 14 (2009), pp. 179–207.

17. D. Keene, 'Towns, Fiscality and the State: England, 700–1500', paper presented at the World Economic History Congress, Utrecht, 2009, Session Q6: 'Urban Fiscal Systems and Economic Growth in Europe', <http://www.wehc2009.org> [accessed at 29 March 2011].

18. V. Harding, 'The Crown, The City and The Orphans: The City of London and Its Finances, 1400–1700', in M. Boone; K. Davids and P. Janssens (eds), *Urban Public Debts: Urban Government and the Market for Annuities in Western Europe (14th–18th centuries)* (Turnhout: Brepols, 2003), pp. 51–60, on p. 53.

19. M. Braddick, *The Nerves of State: Taxation and the Financing of the English State, 1588–1714* (Manchester: Manchester University Press, 1996), p. 49 and P. K. O'Brien and P. Hunt, 'The Rise of a Fiscal State in England, 1485–1815', *Historical Research*, 66 (1993), pp. 129–76, on p. 140.

20. I. Archer, 'The Burden of Taxation on Sixteenth-Century London', *Historical Journal*, 44:3 (2001), pp. 599–621 on p. 600. Braddick, 'The Nerves', pp. 180–8. O'Brien and Hunt, 'The Rise of a Fiscal State', pp. 135–6.

21. Archer, 'The Burden of Taxation', p. 618.

22. W. M. Ormrod, 'England in the Middle Ages', in Bonney (ed.), *The Rise of the Fiscal State in Europe*, pp. 19–56, on p. 36. Harding, 'The Crown, The City and The Orphans', pp. 53–4.

23. R. B. Outhwaite, 'The Trials of Foreign Borrowing: The English Crown and the Antwerp Money Market in the Mid-Sixteenth Century', *Economic History Review*, 19 (1966), pp. 289–305 and R. B. Outhwaite, 'Royal Borrowing in the Reign of Elizabeth I: The Aftermath of Antwerp', *English Historical Review*, 86 (1971), pp. 251–63.

24. J. I. Andrés Ucendo, 'Fiscalidad municipal en Castilla durante el siglo XVII: el caso de Madrid', *Investigaciones de Historia Económica*, 5 (2006), pp. 41–70, on pp. 66–7.

25. Archer, 'Taxation in Sixteenth-Century London', pp. 601–3.

26. Ibid., p. 611 and Harding, 'The Crown, The City and The Orphans', pp. 53–9.

27. Harding, 'The Crown, The City and The Orphans', pp. 57–60.

28. P. Slack, *The English Poor Law, 1531–1782* (Cambridge: Cambridge University Press, 1990).

1 Piola Caselli, 'From Private to Public Management'

1. Sources come from the Rome State Archive, *Archivio di Stato di Roma* (hereafter, ASR), Camerale II, *Dogane* and *Conti dell'Entrata e dell'Uscita*. Left Chamber's documentation dealing with contract rules and various related items is available only from 1621. The Chamber records, instructions, papal decrees concerning duties, customs and lawsuits against tax farmers are abundant from 1630 onwards. The bankers' bookkeeping is also available from 1630, starting with a brief summary of gross figures concerning the Rivaldi period. From 1640 to 1663 the accountancy drawn up from customs management is more and more complete. Unfortunately, the ledgers for the period from 1665 to 1689 have actually gone missing, except for the sole, very important ledger for the year 1685. Regular customs accounts start again from 1689 with the Leonardo Libri ledgers. However, from 1643 onwards, another series of small accountancy books help with some additional information. These books are entitled *conti giurati* (officially sworn

figures), and were drawn up to obtain a formal approval and release from the treasurer on the yearly prices paid by the custom officers to the Chamber. Yet the books are not abstracts or copies of the ordinary customs account books, as they were conceived only for the Chamber administration needs. The *conti giurati* do not therefore mention customs management expenses, or allowances given to the town of Rome, nor is a single figure concerning the customs yield indicated. However, they carefully record the contract price owed to the Chamber, how much out of it had already been turned to the public debt service, with all refundable duty-free goods, which represent a cameral debt towards the customs management. The *conti giurati* series ended in 1689, when private bankers were excluded from customs business.

2. S. Malatesta, *Statuti delle gabelle di Roma* (Roma: Tipografia della Pace, 1885), p. 23.
3. I. Ait, 'La dogana di S. Eustachio nel XV secolo', in *Aspetti della vita economica e culturale a Roma nel Quattrocento* (Rome: Istituto di Studi Romani, 1981), pp. 81–147, on p. 85.
4. A. Esch, 'Mercanti tedeschi e merci a Roma nella seconda metà del Quattrocento', *Archivi e Cultura*, 37 (2004), pp. 47–56, on p. 48.
5. For a general outlook of the papal debt in the sixteenth century, see E. Stumpo, *Il capitale finanziario a Roma fra Cinque e Seicento. Contributo alla storia della fiscalità pontificia in età moderna (1570–1660)* (Milano: Cedam, 1985), pp. 219–64.
6. R. Masini, *Il debito pubblico pontificio a fine Seicento. I monti camerali* (Città di Castello: Edimont, 2005), pp. 19–20.
7. J. Delumeau, *Vita economica e sociale di Roma nel Cinquecento* (Firenze: Sansoni Editore, 1979), p. 219.
8. Cesare de Cupis, *Le vicende dell'agricoltura e della pastorizia nell'agro romano. L'annona di Roma giusta memorie, consuetudini e leggi desunte da documenti anche inediti. Sommario storico* (Roma: Tipografia nazionale di G. Bertero, 1911), p. 199.
9. F. Piola Caselli, 'Public Debt, State Revenue and Town Consumption in Rome (16th–18th Centuries)', in M. Boone, K. Davids and P. Jansenns (eds), *Urban Public Debt: Urban Government and the Market for Annuities in Western Europe (14th–18th Centuries)* (Turnhout: Brepols, 2003), pp. 93–105, on pp. 104–5.
10. C. M. Travaglini, 'The Roman Guilds System in the Early Eighteenth Century', in A. Guenzi, P. Massa and F. Piola Caselli (eds), *Guilds, Markets and Work Regulations in Italy, 16th–19th Centuries* (Aldershot: Ashgate, 1998), pp. 150–70, on pp. 166–9.
11. Figures of the Roman population in early sixteenth century are in A. Esch, 'Immagine di Roma tra realtà religiosa e dimensione politica nel Quattro e Cinquecento', in L. Fiorani and A. Prosperi (eds), *Storia d'Italia. Annali 16. Roma la città del Papa. Vita civile e religiosa dal giubileo di Bonifacio VIII al giubileo di papa Wojtyla* (Torino: Einaudi, 2000), pp. 5–29, on p. 21; P. Partner, *Renaissance Rome 1500–1559. A Portrait of a Society* (Berkeley, CA: University of California Press, 1976), p. 83.
12. H. Gross, *Rome in the Age of Enlightenment: The Post-Tridentine Syndrome and the Ancien Regime* (Cambridge: Cambridge University Press, 1990), p. 199.
13. M. Petrocchi, *Roma nel Seicento* (Cappelli: Bologne, 1970), p. 77.
14. L. Nussdorfer, *Civic Politics in the Rome of Urban VIII* (Princeton, NJ: Princeton University Press, 1992), p. 64.
15. F. Piola Caselli, 'Merci per dogana e consumi alimentari a Roma nel Seicento', in *La popolazione italiana nel Seicento* (Bologne: Clueb, 1999), pp. 387–409, on pp. 399–401.
16. References to several famous roman households are in C. A. Bertini, *La storia delle famiglie romane*, 2 vols (Rome: Collegio Araldico, 1914) and in J. Delumeau, *Vie économique et sociale de Rome dans la seconde moitié du XVIe siècle*, 2 vols (Paris: Boccard,

1957–9). The Leonardo Libris curial career is mentioned in L. Dal Pane, *Lo Stato pontificio e il movimento riformatore del Settecento* (Milano: Giuffré editore, 1959), p. 108.

17. M. Caravale and A. Caracciolo, 'Lo Stato pontificio da Martino V a Pio IX', in G. Galasso (ed.), *Storia d'Italia* (Torino: Utet, 1978), vol. 14, p. 389.

18. F. Guidi Bruscoli, *Benvenuto Olivieri, i 'mercatores' fiorentini e la Camera apostolica nella Roma di Paolo III Farnese (1534–1549)* (Firenze: Leo S. Olschki, 2000), p. 153.

19. K. J. Beloch, *Storia della popolazione italiana* (Firenze: Casa Editrice Le Lettere, 1994), pp. 190–2.

20. L. Palermo, 'L'economia', in A. Pinelli (ed.), *Storia di Roma dall'antichità ad oggi. Roma del Rinascimento* (Bari: Gius. Laterza & figli, 2001), pp. 49–91, on p. 57.

21. ASR, *Dogane*, 43, int. 5.

22. Contract of the first seventeenth decades are in ASR, *Dogane*, 42, int. 1–3. Later contracts come from ASR, Dogane, 43, int.1.3.5 and 44, int. 1.

23. ASR, *Dogane*, 42, int. 4, ff. 843r/v.

24. ASR, *Dogane*, 127, ff.1–7.

25. ASR, *Dogane*, 43, int. 5.

26. ASR, *Dogane*, 42, int. 4, ff. 425r–429r and 440rv; ff. 243 and 253r–263r.

27. ASR, *Dogane*, 127, int. 1–2.

28. ASR, *Dogane*, 42, int. 4, ff. 627 segg.

29. ASR, *Dogane*, 127, ff. 1r.–83r.

30. ASR, *Dogane*, 52–54.

31. ASR, *Dogane*, 53 int. 62.

32. ASR, *Dogane*, 43, int. 5.

33. ASR, *Dogane*, 127.

34. G. De Gennaro, *L'esperienza monetaria di Roma in età moderna (secc. XVI–XVIII). Tra stabilizzazione e inflazione* (Napoli: Edizioni Scientifiche Italiane, 1980), p. 31. Further information about papal coins are in L. Londei, , 'La monetazione pontificia e la zecca di Roma in età moderna (secc. XVI–XVIII)', *Studi Romani*, 38 (1990), pp. 303–18.

35. According figures already mentioned.

36. F. Piola Caselli, 'Public Debt in the Papal States: Financial Market and Government Strategies in the Long Run', in F. Piola Caselli (ed.), *Government Debts and Financial Markets in Europe* (London: Pickering & Chatto, 2008), pp. 105–19, on chart 8.2, p. 107.

37. P. Partner, 'The Papacy and the Papal States', in R. Bonney (ed.), *The Rise of the Fiscal State in Europe 1200–1815* (Oxford: Oxford University Press, 1999), pp. 359–80, on pp. 363 and 369.

38. Regular state yearly balance sheets are kept in ASR, Camerale II, *Conti dell'entrata e dell'uscita della Reveranda Camera Apostolca*. The 1619 balance sheet has been published by W. Reinhard, *Papstfinanz und Nepotismus unter Paul V. (1605–1621), Studien und Quellen zur Struktur und zu quantitativen Aspekten des päpstliche Herrschaftssystems*, 2 vols (Stuttgart: Anton Hiersemann, 1974). The series is quite complete at least from 1653 onward, when the whole Chamber accountancy was entrusted to the chief bookkeeper Nunziato Baldocci. The 1657 balance sheet has been published in G. V. Parigino, *Il bilancio pontificio del 1657* (Napoli: Edizione Scientifiche Italiane, 1999).

39. Beloch, *Storia della popolazione italiana*, p. 192; E. Sonnino and R. Traina, 'La peste del 1656–57 a Roma: organizzazione sanitaria e mortalità', in *La demografia storica delle città italiane* (Bologne: S.I.D.E.S., 1982), pp. 433–52, on pp. 442 and 445.

40. Delumeau, *Vie économique et sociale de Rome*, pp. 689–750.

41. V. Reinhardt, 'Annona and Bread Supply in Rome', in P. van Kessel and E. Schulte (eds), *Rome * Amsterdam: Two Growing Cities in Seventeenth Century Europe* (Amsterdam: Amsterdam University Press, 1997), pp. 209–20, on pp. 215–17.

42. D. Strangio, *Crisi alimentari e politica annonaria a Roma nel Settecento* (Rome: Istituto Nazionale di Studi Romani 1999), table 7, p. 83.

43. ASR, *Dogane*, 42 int. 2, f. 302.

44. Petrocchi, *Roma nel Seicento*, p. 51.

45. Ibid., p. 76.

46. ASR, *Dogane*, 43 int. 6.

47. Sources as in Tables 1.2–4.

48. D. Strangio, 'Debito pubblico e sistema fiscale a Roma e nello Stato pontificio tra '600 e '700', in S. Cavaciocchi (ed.), *Fiscal Systems in the European Economy from the 13th to the 18th Centuries: atti della 'Trentanovesima settimana di studi'* (Firenze: Firenze University Press, 2008), vol. 1, pp. 499–508, on p. 505.

49. 1 *rubbio* = 294 kg.

50. ASR, *Dogane*, 53 int. 1.

51. R. Ago, *Carriere e clientele nella Roma barocca* (Bari: Laterza, 1990), p. 75.

52. F. Colzi, *Il debito pubblico del Campidoglio. Finanza comunale e circolazione dei titoli a Roma fra Cinque e Seicento* (Napoli: Edizioni Scientifiche Italiane, 1999), p. 122.

53. A short history of the wine taxation system is in ASR, *Dogane*, 253, int. 3.

54. ASR, *Dogane*, 111, int. 3.

55. D. Busolini, 'Il porto di Ripa Grande a Roma durante la prima metà del XVII secolo', *Studi Romani*, 42 (1994), pp. 249–73, on p. 256.

56. ASR, *Dogane*, 43, int. 5.

57. ASR, *Dogane*, 42, int, 4, ff. 425r–429r and 440r.v.

58. ASR, *Dogane*, 54.

59. E. Lo Sardo, *Le gabelle e le dogane dei papi in età moderna. Inventario della serie Dogane della Miscellanea per materie* (Roma: Archivio di Stato di Roma, 1994), p. 84 n.1.

60. ASR, *Dogane*, 127, f. 172.

61. ASR, *Dogane*, 129, int. 1–3.

2 Bognetti and De Luca, 'From Taxation to Indebtedness'

1. Albeit this essay is the outcome of a shared thinking, parts I, II and III are by Giuseppe Bognetti while parts IV, V and VI are by Giuseppe De Luca.

2. We owe the achievement, through the nineteenth century, of the vision of the overall decay of the State of the Milan during the Spanish epoch to Carlo Cattaneo and Alessandro Manzoni; the former emphasized the economic and moral deterioration of Lombardy in the seventeenth century to emphasize how remarkable the outcomes were in the progress of its time; the latter in the unrivalled success of his masterpiece, *The Betrothed*, which heightened the depressing reality under the seventeenth century foreign rulers in order to metaphorically blame the foreign government of the Austrians. See G. Signorotto, 'Aperture e pregiudizi nella storiografia italiana del XIX secolo. Interpretazioni della Lombardia "spagnola"', *Archivio Storico Lombardo*, CXXVI (2000), pp. 513–60, on pp. 526–37.

3. G. Vigo, 'Alle origini dello stato moderno: fiscalità e classi sociali nella Lombardia di Filippo II', in *Studi in memoria di Mario Abrate* (Turin: Università di Torino, 1986), vol. 2, pp. 765–75; C. Capra, 'The Italian States in the Early Modern Period', in R. Bonney

(ed.), *The Rise of the Fiscal State in Europe, c. 1200–1815* (Oxford: Oxford University Press, 1999), pp. 417–42, on pp. 418, 422–3; G. Chittolini, 'Notes sur la politique fiscale de Charles Quint dans le Duché de Milan: Le nuovo catasto et les rapports entre ville et campagne', in W. Blockmans, P. Mout and E. H. Nicolette (eds), *The World of Emperor Charles V* (Amsterdam: Royal Netherlands Academy of Arts and Sciences, 2004), pp. 143–60.

4. See G. Vigo, *Finanza pubblica e pressione fiscale nello Stato di Milano durante il secolo XVI* (Milan: Banca Commerciale Italiana, 1979); G. De Luca, 'Government Debt and Financial Markets: Exploring Pro-Cycle Effects in Northern Italy during the Sixteenth and the Seventeenth Centuries', in F. Piola Caselli (ed.), *Government Debts and Financial Markets in Europe* (London: Pickering & Chatto, 2008), pp. 45–66.

5. See the case of the community of Vimercate in 'memoriale del Magistrato', 18 May 1602, Archivio di Stato, Milan (hereafter ASM), Finanze reddituari, cart. 293 (fasc. Carcassola). For the issue of tax shifting in the Kingdom of Naples see G. Sabatini, *Proprietà e proprietari a L'Aquila e nel contado. Le rilevazioni catastali in età spagnola* (Naples: Edizioni Scientifiche Italiane, 1995), pp. 289.

6. 'Elenco alfabetico dei Dazi e delle Gabelle dello Stato di Milano con alcune memorie storiche sui medesimi composto verso il 1680' ('Alphabetical list of Duties and Tariffs of the State of Milan with some historical comments on the same issue, composed around 1680'), Biblioteca Ambrosiana, Milan (hereafter BAM), Mss, C. 17 sussidio; G. Vigo, *Fisco e società nella Lombardia del Cinquecento* (Bologne: Il Mulino, 1979), pp. 26–32.

7. S. Pugliese, *Condizioni economiche e finanziarie della Lombardia nella prima metà del secolo XVIII* (Turin: Fratelli Bocca, 1924), pp. 179–81.

8. G. Muto, 'The Spanish System: Centre and Periphery', in Bonney (ed.), *Economic Systems and State Finance* (Oxford: Oxford University Press, 1995), pp. 238–9.

9. M. Ostoni, *Il tesoro del re. Uomini e istituzioni della finanza pubblica milanese fra Cinquecento e Seicento* (Napoli: Istituto Italiano per gli Studi Filosofici, 2010).

10. K. J. Beloch, *Bevölkerungsgeschichte Italiens* (Leipzig, De Gruyter & Co: 1961), vol. 3, p. 242; S. D'Amico, 'Crisis and Transformation: Economic Reorganization and Social Structures in Milan, 1570–1610', *Social History*, 25 (2000), pp, 1–21, on p. 6.

11. Vigo, *Finanza pubblica e pressione fiscale*, p. 19.

12. Lire (1 lira equals 20 soldi, and 1 soldo equals 240 denari) and scudi were used as currency unit of account; this type of scudo corresponded to 110 soldi.

13. Chittolini, 'Notes sur la politique fiscale de Charles Quint', pp. 148ff.

14. Quoted in Vigo, *Fisco e società nella Lombardia del Cinquecento*, p. 31.

15. Capra, 'The Italian States in the Early Modern Period', pp. 418–25.

16. The *pertica* was the unit of area and equalled 0.06 hectare.

17. Tabacchi, S., 'Il controllo sulle finanze delle comunità negli antichi Stati italiani', *Storia Amministrazione Costituzione*, 4 (1996), pp. 96–8.

18. See Vigo, *Fisco e società nella Lombardia del Cinquecento*, pp. 35–119, 162–4.

19. G. De Luca, 'Mercanti imprenditori, élite artigiane e organizzazioni produttive: la definizione del sistema corporativo milanese (1568–1627)', in A. Guenzi, P. Massa, A. Moioli (eds), *Corporazioni e gruppi professionali nell'Italia moderna* (Milan: Franco Angeli, 1999), pp. 79–116.

20. Vigo, *Fisco e società nella Lombardia del Cinquecento*, pp. 265–8.

21. 'Elenco alfabetico dei Dazi e delle Gabelle dello Stato di Milano', ff. 31 s; Vigo, *Finanza pubblica e pressione fiscale*, pp. 57–8.

22. The reductions allowed to the other towns and communities were in average of 20 per cent, while the quota of Milan was lowered from 27,960 scudi to 10,000 and that of

its *contado* from 3,027 to 1,665; see the distribution of the *mercimoniale* tax according to the apportionment of 1594 and 1599, in Archivio Storico Civico, Milan (hereafter ASCM), materie, cart. 262; 'Discorso et Bilancio sopra la suddivisione della quota del Mensuale', undated, in ASCM, materie, cart. 613.

23. Shares of *estimo fondiario* 1561 and 1564 in ASCM, materie, cart. 198.

24. 'Sommario della controversia che pende fra la Città et Ducato', undated, in ASCM, materie, cart 264; P. Neri, *Relazione dello stato in cui si trova l'opera del censimento universale del Ducato di Milano nel mese di maggio dell'anno 1750* (Milan: G. R. Malatesta, 1750), p. 16.

25. But within the two following years, it had already arisen respectively to 10 and 12 soldi, 'Elenco alfabetico dei Dazi e delle Gabelle dello Stato di Milano', f. 32; M. C. Giannini, 'Conflitti e compromessi. Il problema dell'esenzione fiscale del clero nella Città di Milano nella seconda metà del Cinquecento', *Trimestre*, 40 (2007), 1–4, p. 129. A *brenta* was equivalent to 0.75 hectolitre.

26. Conversely the correspondent burden on the *contado* was of 412,500 lire, '1556. Carichi straordinari imposti alla città di Milano et al suo contado', in ASCM, belgiojoso, cart. 238, fasc. II, f. 2.

27. 'Notta delle gravezze straordinarie toccanti alla M.ca Città di Milano', undated, ASCM, materie, cart. 202.

28. A *moggio* corresponded to 1.46 hectolitre.

29. 'Elenco alfabetico dei Dazi e delle Gabelle dello Stato di Milano', ff. 32–3; 'Informatione de i Dacj, e carichi che dalla Camera sogliono riscuodersi in particolare nella Città di Milano, oltre quelli che sono comuni con tutto lo Stato, 24 ottobre 1619', in BAM, Mass, L. 123 sussidio, f. 6r.

30. See A. Salomoni (ed.), *Memorie storico-diplomatiche degli Ambasciatori, Incaricati d'affari, Corrispondenti, e Delegati, che la città di Milano inviò a diversi suoi principi dal 1500 al 1796* (Milan: Tipografia Pulini al Bocchetto, 1806), on pp. 118–82.

31. Vigo, *Finanza pubblica e pressione fiscale*, pp. 20–1. On the plague, that killed approximately 15 per cent of the inhabitants of the town, see D'Amico, 'Crisis and Transformation', p. 6.

32. G. De Luca, *Commercio del denaro e crescita economica a Milano tra Cinquecento e Seicento* (Milan: Il Polifilo, 1996), pp. 120–2.

33. Pugliese, *Condizioni economiche e finanziarie della Lombardia*, pp. 431–2.

34. Vigo, *Fisco e società nella Lombardia del Cinquecento*, pp. 324–5.

35. See the legation of Antonio Pirovano to Filippo III, 1615, in Salomoni (ed.), *Memorie storico-diplomatiche degli Ambasciatori*, p. 281.

36. Up to now, we don't have continuous information about the alienation of city taxes in advance; see for example '1596, 20 settembre. Editto della città di Milano per vendere ... in ragione del 7 per cento il prodotto di una Tassa e mezza sopra case' and '1596, 16 ottobre. Editto della città di Milano per vendere ... in ragione del 7 per cento il prodotto di una parpagliola per ogni brenta di vino', in ASCM, belgiojoso, cart. 238, fasc. II, ff. 54–6. We can also glean it from the fluctuating revenues of some levies, as the case of the wine tax, see Table 2.

37. Ibid.

38. A. Cova, *Il Banco di S. Ambrogio nell'economia milanese dei secoli XVII e XVIII* (Milan: Giuffrè, 1972), pp. 33–4.

39. Ibid., pp. 23–32.

40. Will of 3 October 1619 in Archivio Visconti di Modrone, Università Cattolica del Sacro Cuore, Milan, I, cart. 195.
41. Pugliese, *Condizioni economiche e finanziarie della Lombardia*, p. 432.
42. 'Breve relazione de i Dacj e delle imposte che si riscuotono in nome della Città di Milano per pagare i carichi Camerali e per sodisfar agli Esenti, a Reddituari, al Banco di Sant Ambrosio e altri suoi debiti correnti, 24 ottobre 1619', in BAM, Mass, L. 123 sussidio, f. 7v. s.
43. Ibid.
44. Cova, *Il Banco di S. Ambrogio*, p. 54.
45. Report of Pozzobonelli, 1637 in ACSM, dicasteri, cart. 149.
46. Budget of the city of Milan in ASM, belgiojoso, cart, 238, fasc. II, ff. 157–8.
47. Cova, *Il Banco di S. Ambrogio*, pp. 68–70.
48. Ibid., pp. 71–7.
49. Ibid., pp. 68–70.
50. Ibid., pp. 85–100.
51. Giannini, 'Conflitti e compromessi', pp. 132–43.
52. 'Discorso del Dottor Gio Batta Visconte, sopra il ripartire giustamente carichi e debiti tra il reale e il personale della città di Milano', 2 June 1602, and 'Informatione del dottor Alessandro Rovida', undated but before 1605, in ASM, belgiojoso, cart. 238, fasc. II, ff. 56–64, 86–98.
53. '1606. Adì 30 Genaro. Discorso et considerazioni fatte dalla Gionta', in ASM, belgiojoso, cart. 238, fasc. II, f. 80.
54. '1638. La città di Milano che nelle difficoltà de rimedi riconosce la gravezza del male', in ASM, belgiojoso, cart, 238, fasc. II, ff. 157–8.
55. 'Facilissimo modo col quale la Città di Milano potrebbe redimere', undated but probably 1602–6 in ASM, belgiojoso, cart, 238, fasc. II, ff. 72–8.
56. 'nascendo la Ricchezza pubblica dalla privata e la Commune dalla particolare, quanto questa si diminuisce tanto quella resta scemata … Il perché mentre gli popoli talmente s'impoveriscono con le gravezze che non ponno né trafficare né lavorare né appena sostentarsi come ponno dare alla Camera ciò che non hanno … In quella guisa appunto avverrebbe ad un signore che si pregiasse di havere nelli suoi poderi grande quantità di alberi carichi de frutti. Certo è che quanto più ne coglie tanto più impoverisce le piante e cogliendoli tutti alle piante rimarranno le sole frondi', 'Nuova inventione certissima, e facilissima per liberare la città di Milano e le provincie dello Stato da loro debiti senza cagionare alcuna Gravezza, del sig. Carlo della Somaglia, patricio milanese, in Milano per Filippo Ghidolfi, Milano', undated but 1648, in Biblioteca Nazionale Braidense, Milan, 14. 16 C. 11/6.
57. S. Agnoletto, *Lo Stato di Milano al principio del Settecento. Finanza pubblica, sistema fiscale e interessi locali* (Milan: FrancoAngeli, 2000), pp. 287–90.
58. De Luca, *Commercio del denaro*, pp. 110–15.
59. Vigo, *Finanza pubblica e pressione fiscale*, pp. 72–107; D. Sella, *Crisis and Continuity: The Economy of Spanish Lombardy in the Seventeenth Century* (Cambridge, MA: Harvard University Press, 1979), pp. 113–43.
60. Vigo, *Finanza pubblica e pressione fiscale*, pp. 80–4.
61. 'Elenco alfabetico dei Dazi e delle Gabelle dello Stato di Milano', f. 3. See for the silver content of the lira G. Felloni, 'Finanze statali, emissioni monetarie ed alterazioni della moneta di conto in Italia nei secoli XVI–XVIII', *Atti della società ligure di storia patria*, 38:1 (1998), p. 485.

62. Vigo, *Finanza pubblica e pressione fiscale*, pp. 88–100.
63. S. Sella, *Salari e lavoro nell'edilizia lombarda durante il secolo XVII* (Pavia, Editrice Succ. Fusi, 1968); G. Vigo, 'Real Wages of the Working Class in Italy Building Workers' Wages (14th to 18th Century)', *Journal of European Economic History*, 3:2 (1974), pp. 379–99; L. Parziale, L., *Nutrire la città. Produzione e commercio a Milano tra Cinque e Seicento* (Milan: FrancoAngeli, 2009).
64. S. Agnoletto, 'The Spanish Heavy Tax-Regime: A Constraint on Capitalistic Modernization or a Matrix for Innovation? An Aspect of Accumulation in the "State of Milan" at the End of the Spanish Domination (1706)', in G. De Luca and G. Sabatini (eds), *In The Shadow of an Empire: How Spanish Colonialism Affected Economic Development in Europe and the World, 16th-18th Centuries* (Milan: FrancoAngeli), forthcoming.
65. De Luca, *Commercio del denaro*, pp. 40–4.

3 Bulgarelli, 'The Urban Tax System in the Kingdom of Naples'

1. P. Malanima, 'Italian Cities 1300–1800: A Quantitative Approach', *Rivista di Storia Economica*, 16:2 (1998), pp. 91–126, on pp. 104–10; for a general overview, P. Bairoch, *Da Jericho a Mexico. Villes et economie dans l'histoire* (Paris: Gallimard, 1985).
2. A. Bulgarelli Lukacs, *La finanza locale sotto controllo. Il regno di Napoli di primo Seicento* (Venice: Marsilio, 2012).
3. B. Capasso, *Catalogo ragionato dei libri, registri e scritture esistenti nella sezione antica e prima serie dell'Archivio municipale di Napoli (1387–1806)*, I (Naples: Giannini, 1876); G. Coniglio, *Il viceregno di Napoli nel secolo XVII. Nuove notizie sulla vita commerciale e finanziaria tratte dagli archivi napoletani* (Naples: Edizioni di Storia e Letteratura, 1955), p. 234, R. Mantelli, *Burocrazia e finanze pubbliche nel Regno di Napoli* (Naples: Lucio Pironti, 1981), pp. 254–7.
4. B. Salvemini, 'Sui presupposti materiali dell'identità locale in antico regime: le città della Puglia centrale fra XVI e XVIII secolo', in A. Musi (ed.), *Le città nel Mezzogiorno nell'età moderna* (Naples: Guida, 2000), pp. 13–24; Id, *Il territorio sghembo. Forme e dinamiche degli spazi umani in età moderna* (Bari: Edipuglia 2006).
5. F. Medeiros, 'Espaces ruraux et dynamiques sociales en Europe du Sud', *Annales ESC*, 5 (1988), pp. 1081–107.
6. G. Barone, 'Mezzogiorno ed egemonie urbane', *Meridiana*, 5 (1989), pp. 13–47.
7. A. Musi (ed.), *Le città nel Mezzogiorno*.
8. The references are in Table 3.1.
9. J.-P. Genet, 'L'état moderne: un modèle opératoire?', in J. P. Genet (ed.), *L'état moderne: genèse. Bilans et perspectives* (Paris: CNRS, 1990), pp. 261–81.
10. K. Kruger, 'Public Finance and Modernization: The Change from Domain State to Tax State, in Hesse in the Sixteenth and Seventeenth Centuries – a Case Study', in P. C. Witt (ed.), *Wealth and Taxation in Central Europe* (New York, 1987). R. Bonney and W. M. Ormrod, 'Introduction, Crises, Revolutions and Self-Sustained Growth: Towards a Conceptual Model of Change in Fiscal History', in W. M. Ormrod, M. Bonney and R. Bonney (eds), *Crises, Revolutions and Self-Sustained Growth* (Stanford, CA: Shaun Tyas, 1999), pp. 1–21.
11. G. Ardant, *Histoire de l'impôt* (Paris: Fayard, 1971), pp. 335–8.
12. A. Bulgarelli Lukacs, *L'imposta diretta nel regno di Napoli* (Milan: FrancoAngeli, 1993).

13. G. Galasso, *Economia e società nella Calabria del Cinquecento* (Milan: Feltrinelli, 1975), pp. 353–61; F. Caracciolo, *Sud, debiti e gabelle. Gravami, potere e società nel Mezzogiorno in età moderna* (Naples: Edizioni Scientifiche Italiane, 1983), pp. 153–67, 183–222.

14. Bulgarelli Lukacs, *La finanza locale sotto tutela*, table 14.

15. J. E. Gelabert González, 'Urbanization and De-Urbanization in Castile', *The Castilian Crisis of Seventeenth-Century* (Cambridge: Cambridge University Press, 1994), pp. 182–205; idem, 'Cities, Towns and Small-Towns in Castile', *Small Towns in Early Modern Europe* (Cambridge: Cambridge University Press) 1995, pp. 271–94.

16. Gutiérrez Alonso, 'Ciudades y Monarquía. Las finanzas de los municipios castellanos en los siglos XVI y XVII', in L. Ribot Garcia y L. De Rosa (dir.), *Ciudad y mundo urbano en la epoca moderna* (Madrid: Actas, 1997), pp. 187–211.

17. J. Ignacio Andrés Ucendo, *La fiscalidad en Castilla en el siglo XVII. Los servicios de millones, 1601–1700* (Bilbao: Universidad del País Vasco, 1999).

18. Gutiérrez Alonso, 'Ciudades y Monarquìa', pp. 199–205.

19. G. Galasso, 'Puglia: tra provincializzazione e modernità, in Civiltà e culture di Puglia', vol. IV in C. D. Fonseca (ed.), *La Puglia tra barocco e rococò* (Milan: Electa, 1982), pp. 373–86; R. P. Corritore, 'Il processo di "ruralizzazione" in Italia nei secoli XVII e XVIII', *Rivista di Storia Economica*, 2 (1993), pp. 353–86.

20. A. Bulgarelli Lukacs, 'La popolazione del regno di Napoli nel primo Seicento (1595–1648). Analisi differenziale degli effetti distributivi della crisi e ipotesi di quantificazione delle perdite demografiche', *Popolazione e Storia*, 1 (2009), pp. 77–113.

21. Bulgarelli Lukacs, 'La popolazione del regno di Napoli', pp. 95–9; on the migration phenomena as a first sign of unbalance in resources availability, P. Malanima, *La fine del primato. Crisi e riconversione nell'Italia del Seicento* (Milan: Bruno Mondadori, 1998), p. 121.

22. A. Marcos Martín, 'Deuda pública, fiscalidad y arbitrios en la Corona de Castilla durante los siglos XVI y XVII', in C. Sanz and B. J. García (eds), *Banca, crédito y capital. La monarquía Hispánica y los antiguos Países Bajos (1505–1700)* (Madrid: Fundación Carlos de Amberes, 2006), pp. 345–75.

23. Bulgarelli Lukacs, *La finanza locale sotto tutela*.

24. A. Bulgarelli Lukacs, 'Misurare l'imponibile. Le scelte dello Stato tra gruppi di pressione e ceti emergenti (Regno di Napoli, secolo XVIII)', in R. De Lorenzo, *Storia e misura. Indicatori sociali ed economici nel Mezzogiorno d'Italia* (Milano: FrancoAngeli, 2007), pp. 39–74.

25. A. Domínguez Ortiz, *Políca y Hacienda de Felipe IV* (Madrid: Editorial de Derecho Financiero, 1960), pp. 182–3; I. A. A. Thompson, 'Taxation, Military Spending and Domestic Economy in Castile in the Later Sixteenth Century', in *War and Society in Habsburg Spain: Selected Essays* (Aldershot: Ashgate, 1992), p. 4, cap. II; M. Sebastián Marín and F. J. Vela Santamaría, 'Hacienda Real y presión fiscal en Castilla a comienzos del reinado de Felipe IV', in J. I. Fortea Pérez e C. M. Cremades Griñán (eds), *Politica y Hacienda en el Antiguo Régimen* (Murcia: Universidad de Murcia, 1993), pp. 556–8. In posizione prudente nell'accettare tali valutazioni, A. Marcos Martín, '¿Fue la fiscalidad regia un factor de crisis en la Castilla del siglo XVII?', in G. Parker (ed.), *La crisis de la monarquía de Felipe IV* (Barcelona: Crítica, 2006), pp. 173–253, on pp. 175–6.

26. Bulgarelli Lukacs, 'Misurare l'imponibile', pp. 41–5 and idem, 'The Fiscal System in the Kingdom of Naples: Tools for Comparison with the European Reality (13th–18th Centuries)', in S. Cavaciocchi (ed.), *La fiscalità nell'economia europea. secc. XIII–XVIII*

– *Fiscal Systems in the European Economy from the 13th to the 18th Centuries* (Florence: Olschki, 2008), pp. 241–57, on p. 252.

27. P. Malanima, *L'economia italiana. Dalla crescita medievale alla crescita contemporanea* (Bologna: Il Mulino, 2002), pp. 385–426; the eighteenth century is richer in studies, which we recall: R. Romano, *Prezzi, salari e servizi a Napoli nel secolo XVIII. 1734–1806* (Milan: Banca Commerciale Italiana, 1965) and P. Macry, *Mercato e società nel Regno di Napoli. Commercio del grano e politica economica nel Settecento* (Napoli: Guida, 1974).

28. For the Spanish case, A. Marcos Martín, 'Oligarquías urbanas y gobiernos ciudadanos en la España del siglo XVI', in E. Belenguer Cebrià (ed.), *Felipe II y el Mediterraneo*, II, *Los grupos sociales* (Madrid: Sociedad Estatal para la Conmemoración de los Centenarios de Felipe II y Carlos V, 1999), pp. 265–93; B. Yun Casalilla, 'Mal avenidos, pero juntos. Corona y oligarquías urbanas en Castilla en el siglo XVI', in *Vivir el siglo de oro. Poder, cultura e historia en la época moderna: estudios en homenaje al profesor Ángel Rodríguez Sánchez* (Salamanca: Universidad de Salamanca, 2003), pp. 61–75.

29. Bulgarelli Lukacs, *L'imposta diretta*, pp. 205–9.

30. A. Bulgarelli Lukacs, 'Il debito pubblico in ambito municipale. Stato, comunità e creditori nel Regno di Napoli tra Seicento e Settecento', in G. De Luca and A. Moioli (eds), *Debito pubblico e mercati finanziari. Secoli XIII–XX* (Milan: FrancoAngeli, 2007), pp. 327–46.

31. A. Bulgarelli Lukacs, *Alla ricerca del contribuente. Fisco, catasto, gruppi di potere, ceti emergenti nel Regno di Napoli del XVIII secolo* (Naples: Edizioni Scientifiche Italiane, 2004).

4 Mateos, 'Public Institutions, Local Politics and Urban Taxation in Seventeenth-Century Aragon'

1. This study forms part of research projects HAR2008–05425, entitled 'Fiscality, Property Rights and Institutional Change in Spain during the Seventeenth Century' and HAR2008–1074, entitled 'Economy and Politics in the Building of the Modern Spanish State, 1650–1808'. Both projects were financed by the Spanish Ministry of Science and Innovation.

2. J. A. Salas, 'La evolución demográfica aragonesa en los siglos XVI y XVII', in J. Nadal (ed.), *La evolución demográfica bajo los Austrias* (Alicante: Instituto Juan Gil Albert, 1992), pp. 169–79.

3. D. J. Dormer, *Discursos histórico-políticos* (Saragossa: l'Astral, 1989), pp. 129–31.

4. Library of the Royal Academy of History, Nasarre Collection, Manuscript 11–1–1, ff. 547r–562v. Historians and demographers estimate between four and five inhabitants on average for each 'hearth' or taxpaying household in the censuses performed in the Spain of the medieval and early modern periods.

5. J. A. Salas, 'Las haciendas concejiles aragonesas en los siglos XVI y XVII. De la euforia a la quiebra', in *Poder político e instituciones en la España Moderna* (Alicante: Instituto Juan Gil Albert, 1992), pp. 11–66.

6. J. Inglada, *Estudio de la estructura socio-económica de Huesca y su comarca en el siglo XVII* (graduate dissertation, Saragossa University, 1987); J. A. Mateos, *Auge y decadencia de un municipio aragonés: el concejo de Daroca en los siglos XVI y XVII* (Daroca: Institución Fernando el Católico, 1997) and 'La hacienda municipal de Albarracín en el siglo XVII: crisis, endeudamiento y negociación', *Teruel*, 88–9:2 (2000–2), pp. 171–212; Municipal Archive of Saragossa, accounting records (748–782).

7. In 1677–8 the Aragonese Parliament removed direct municipal contributions and raised the customs duties charged at the kingdom's borders to pay royal subsidies, as many town councils were financially exhausted. Faced with adverse effects on trade and industrial production, however, the Parliament of 1684–6 again lowered duties and instead introduced new monopolies on tobacco and salt. See G. Redondo, 'Las relaciones comerciales Aragón-Francia en la Edad Moderna: datos para su estudio en el siglo XVII', *Estudios*, 85–6 (1985), pp. 141–9.

8. J. A. Mateos, 'Propios, arbitrios y comunales: la hacienda municipal en el reino de Aragón durante los siglos XVI y XVII', *Revista de Historia Económica*, 21:1 (2003), pp. 55–6.

9. B. de Monsoriu, *Summa de todos los fueros y observancias del reyno de Aragon y determinaciones de micer Miguel del Molino* (Saragossa: Colegio de abogados, 1982), ff. 156r–157r.

10. Mateos, 'Propios', pp. 56–7.

11. Ibid., pp. 68–72.

12. Salas, 'La evolución', p. 171.

13. Inglada, *Estudio*, pp. 246–8; Mateos, *Auge*, pp. 130–3 and 'La hacienda', p. 208.

14. Inglada, *Estudio*, p. 291; Mateos, *Auge*, pp. 460–4; Municipal Archive of Saragossa, accounting records (769).

15. F. Otero, *La vila de Fraga al segle XVII* (Calaceite: Institut d'Estudis del Baix Cinca, 1994), vol. 1, pp. 113–4; Mateos, *Auge*, pp. 151–3, 470.

16. A. Abadia, *La enajenación de las rentas señoriales en el reino de Aragón* (Saragossa: Institución Fernando el Católico, 1998), pp. 56–8, 195–8, 249–56, 282–3, 294.

17. G. Colás, *La bailía de Caspe en los siglos XVI y XVII* (Saragossa: Institución Fernando el Católico, 1979), pp. 209–13.

18. A. Atienza, G. Colás, E. Serrano, *El señorío de Aragón (1610–1640). Cartas de población* (Saragossa: Institución Fernando el Católico, 1998).

19. Salas, 'Las haciendas', pp. 31, 49–50; Mateos 'Propios', pp. 58–9.

20. Ibid.

21. J. Maiso, *La peste aragonesa de 1648 a 1654* (Saragossa: University, 1982), pp. 176–80.

22. J. A. Mateos, 'The Making of a New Landscape: Town Councils and Water in the Kingdom of Aragon during the Sixteenth Century', *Rural History*, 9:2 (1998), p. 136.

23. Mateos, 'Propios', p. 59.

24. See note 9, above.

25. Mateos, *Auge*, pp. 141–4; J. Olivo, 'La evolución de la hacienda municipal de Calatayud durante el siglo XVII', *Jerónimo Zurita*, 76–7 (2002), pp. 231–2.

26. J. A. Mateos, 'La política municipal de abastos en Aragón durante los siglos XVI y XVII: fiscalidad y mercado preindustrial', *Revista de Historia de la Economía y de la Empresa*, 4 (2010), pp. 336–7.

27. Ibid., p. 335.

28. Ibid., pp. 336, 340–1.

29. Ibid., p. 337.

30. Ibid.

31. Ibid., p. 338.

32. Ibid., p. 339. As examples of these developments in Aragonese local markets, see Otero, *La Vila*, vol. 1, p. 148; Mateos, *Auge*, pp. 321–2, 337.

33. G. Redondo, *Las corporaciones de artesanos de Zaragoza en el siglo XVII* (Saragossa: Institución Fernando el Católico, 1982); J. A. Mateos, 'Municipal Politics and Corporate Protectionism: Town Councils and Guilds in the Kingdom of Aragon during the Sixteenth and Seventeenth Centuries', in B. Blondé, E. Vanhaute and M. Galand (eds),

Labour and Labour Markets between Town and Countryside (Middle Ages-Nineteenth Century) (Turnhout: Brepols, 2001), pp. 189–95.

34.	For a detailed analysis of this legislation, see Redondo, 'Las relaciones', pp. 127–49.

35.	See note 33, above.

36.	A. Peiró, *Jornaleros y mancebos. Identidad, organización y conflicto en los trabajadores del Antiguo Régimen* (Barcelona: Crítica, 2002), pp. 72–8.

37.	J. A. Mateos, 'Control público, hacienda municipal y mercado agrario en Aragón durante los siglos XVI y XVII', *Hispania*, 66:223 (2006), pp. 560–7.

38.	Mateos, 'Propios', pp. 60–1.

39.	This process increased the Church's economic power as demand for grain and land rose in Aragon towards the middle of the eighteenth century. See A. Atienza, *Propiedad y señorío en Aragón* (Saragossa: Institución Fernando el Católico, 1993).

40.	See note 37, above.

41.	Mateos, 'The Making'.

42.	J. I. Gómez Zorraquino, *Zaragoza y el capital comercial: la burguesía mercantil en el Aragón de la segunda mitad del siglo XVII* (Saragossa: City Council, 1987), pp. 86–8.

43.	Gómez Zorraquino, *Zaragoza*.

5 Andrés and Lanza, 'Taxation and Debt in the Early Modern Castilian Cities'

1.	This paper has been funded by the research projects of the Spanish Science Ministry 'Niveles de vida y desigualdad. Aproximación social y regional en la España preindustrial', HAR2008–04978 and 'Fisco, Mercado y fiscalidad. Derechos de propiedad y cambio institucional en la España del siglo XVII', HAR2008–05425.

2.	C. Tilly, 'Cities and States in Europe', *Theory and Society*, 18 (1989), pp. 563–84, on p. 570.

3.	F. Ruiz Martín, 'Procedimientos crediticios para la recaudación de los tributos fiscales en las ciudades castellanas durante los siglos XVI y XVII. El caso de Valladolid', in A. de Otazu (ed.), *Dinero y Crédito* (Madrid, 1978), pp. 37–47.

4.	C. García García, *La crisis de las Haciendas Locales. De la reforma administrativa a la reforma fiscal, 1743–1835* (Valladolid: Junta de Castilla y León, 1996), pp. 109–49.

5.	M. Prak and J. L. van Zanden, 'State Formation and Citizenship: The Dutch Republic between Medieval Communes and Modern Nation States', in J. L. van Zanden, *The Long Road to the Industrial Revolution: The European Economy in a Global Perspective, 1000–1800* (Leiden-Boston: Brill, 2009), pp. 205–32, on pp. 207–13.

6.	Archivo de la Villa de Madrid, Secretaría (hereafter AVM, SECR), 2–247–8.

7.	C. de la Hoz, 'El sistema fiscal de Madrid en el Antiguo Régimen: las sisas', *Anales del Instituto de Estudios Madrileños*, 25 (1988), pp. 371–86, on pp. 371–2 and 380. J. I. Andrés Ucendo, 'Government Policies and the Development of the Financial Markets: The Case of Madrid in the Seventeenth Century', in F. Piola Caselli (ed.), *Government Debts and Financial Markets in Europe* (London: Pickering & Chatto, 2008), pp. 67–80, on p. 71–2.

8.	C. de la Hoz, 'El sistema fiscal', pp. 380–1 and J. I. Andrés, 'Government Policies', p. 66–8.

9.	J. I. Andrés, 'Castile's Tax System in the Seventeenth Century', *Journal of European Economic History*, 30:3 (2001), pp. 597–616 and J. I. Andrés, 'Fiscalidad real y fiscalidad municipal en Castilla durante el siglo XVII: el caso de Madrid', *Investigaciones de Historia Económica*, 5 (2006), pp. 41–70.

10.	Andrés, 'Fiscalidad Real y fiscalidad municipal', pp. 66–8.

11. Ibid.

12. For price levels in seventeenth-century Madrid, J. I. Andrés and R. Lanza, 'Municipal Taxes, Prices and Real Wages in XVIIth Century Castile: The Case of Madrid', paper presented at the World Economic History Congress, Utrecht, 2009, Session Q6: 'Urban Fiscal Systems and Economic Growth in Europe', <http://www.wehc-2009.org> [accessed 29 March 2011].

13. Andrés, 'Fiscalidad real y fiscalidad municipal', pp. 66–8.

14. C. de la Hoz, 'Las reformas de la Hacienda Madrileña en la época de Carlos III', in Equipo Madrid (ed.), *Carlos III, Madrid y la Ilustración. Contradicciones de un proyecto reformista* (Madrid: Alianza, 1988), pp. 77–101, on pp. 82–3.

15. For the burden of taxation in daily wages in Holland and France, M. Prak and J. L. van Zanden, 'Tax Morale and Citizenship in the Dutch Republic', in O. Gelderblom (ed.), *The Political Economy of the Dutch Republic* (Bodmin: Ashgate, 2009), pp. 143–66, on p. 148.

16. M. Artola, *La Hacienda del Antiguo Régimen* (Madrid: Alianza, 1982), pp. 154–5.

17. Andrés, 'Government Debts', pp. 73–4.

18. Ibid., pp. 76–8.

19. M. Carbajo, *La población de la villa de Madrid desde finales del siglo XVI hasta mediados del siglo XIX* (Madrid: Alianza, 1987), pp. 227–8.

20. For the data on Amsterdam's indebtedness in 1680, W. Fritschy, 'Three Centuries of Urban and Provincial Public Debt: Amsterdam and Holland', in M. Boone; K. Davids and P. Janssens (eds), *Urban Public Debts. Urban Government and the Market for Annuities in Western Europe (14th–18th Centuries)* (Turnhout: Brepols, 2003), pp. 75–92, on p. 83.

21. F. J. Vela, 'Las obras públicas en la Castilla del siglo XVII: un gravamen oneroso y descon-ocido', *Studia Historica. Historia Moderna*, 32 (2010), pp. 125–77, on p. 173.

22. J. I. Andrés and R. Lanza, 'Municipal Taxes'.

23. Ibid.

24. See the articles included in Boone, et al. (eds), *Urban Public Debts*.

25. J. M. López García (ed.), *El impacto de la Corte en Castilla. Madrid y su territorio en la Época Moderna* (Madrid: Alianza, 1998), pp. 313–16.

26. J. I. Andrés, '¿Quién pagó los tributos en la Castilla del siglo XVII? El impacto de los tributos sobre el vino en Madrid', *Studia Historica. Historia Moderna*, 32 (2010), pp. 229–57.

27. Andrés, 'Fiscalidad real y fiscalidad municipal', pp. 65–8. On the cases of Toledo and Jaén, Archivo Histórico Nacional (hereafter AHN), Consejos, legajo 12639, 1–2; Archivo General de Simancas (hereafter AGS), Contadurías Generales, legajo 1057 and 1297; Dirección General del Tesoro, Inventario 4, legajos 308 and 328.

28. On the Castilian urban crisis, D. Ringrose, *Madrid y la economía española* (Madrid: Alianza, 1985).

29. On the cases of Seville and Málaga, J. I. Martínez Ruiz, 'Crédito público y deudas munic-ipales en España (siglos XV–XVIII)', in A. M. Bernal (ed.), *Dinero Moneda y Crédito en la Monarquía Hispánica* (Madrid: Marcial Pons, 2000), pp. 863–77, on p. 868. For Valladolid, A. Gutiérrez Alonso, *Estudio sobre la decadencia de Castilla. La ciudad de Valladolid en el siglo XVII* (Valladolid: Universidad, 1989), p. 368. As for the cases of Toledo, Jaén and Zamora, AHN, Consejos, leg. 12639 1–2.

30. J. I. Fortea Pérez, *Las Cortes de Castilla y León bajo los Austrias. Una interpretación histórica* (Valladolid: Junta de Castilla y León, 2008). See also, Martínez Ruiz, 'Crédito público y deudas municipales', p. 867.

31. Martínez Ruiz, 'Crédito publico y deudas municipales', p. 869. This should not hide the existence of some exceptions. Probably the one of the most important is that of Vallado-lid. During the seventeenth century the average interest rate of the annuities issued by this city was the same, and even less, as that of the *juros*. Gutiérrez Alonso, *Estudio sobre la decadencia de Castilla*, p. 383.

32. Martínez Ruiz, 'Crédito público y deudas municipales', p. 871. Andrés, 'Government Debts', p. 73 and Gutiérrez Alonso, *Estudio sobre la decadencia de Castilla*, p. 387.

33. Vela Santamaría, 'Las obras públicas en la Castilla del siglo XVII', p. 173.

34. Andrés and Lanza, 'Municipal Taxes' and Gutiérrez Alonso, *Ensayo sobre la decadencia de Castilla*, p. 160.

35. Biblioteca Nacional (hereafter BN), Mss, 6749, pp. 34–184 and A. Marcos Martín, '¿Fue la fiscalidad regia un factor de crisis?', in G. Parker (ed.), *La crisis de la Monarquía de Felipe IV* (Barcelona: Crítica, 2006), pp. 173–253, on p. 213.

36. Andrés and Lanza, 'Municipal Taxes'.

37. García García, *La crisis de las haciendas locales. De la reforma administrativa a la reforma fiscal*, p. 110.

38. B. Cárceles de Gea, *Fraude y administración fiscal en Castilla. La Comisión de Millones (1632–1658): poder fiscal y privilegio jurídico-político* (Madrid: Banco de España, 1994) and B. Cárceles de Gea, *Reforma y fraude fiscal en el reinado de Carlos II. La Sala de Millones* (Madrid: Banco de España, 1995).

39. C. Tilly, 'Citizenship. Identity and Social History', *International Review of Social History*, 40 (1995), pp. 1–49, on p. 8.

6 Ferndández de Pinedo, 'Tax Collection in Spain in the Eighteenth Century'

1. This paper has been funded by the research project 'Fisco y mercado: fiscalidad, derechos de propiedad y cambio institucional en la España del siglo XVII', HAR2008-05425 /His, of the Spanish Education and Science Ministry. A previous version has been presented in Session Q6 'Urban Fiscal Systems and Economic Growth in Europe, 15th–18th Centu-ries' of the Fifteenth World Economic History Congress in Utrecht, in August 2009. I wish to thank Ernesto López Losa, Emiliano Fernández de Pinedo and Fernando Esteve for their comments and help with this paper.

2. See M. 't Hart, 'The Emergence and Consolidation of the "Tax State": II. The Sev-enteenth Century', in R. Bonney (ed.), *Economic Systems and State Finance* (Oxford: Clarendon Press and European Science Foundation, 1995), pp. 281–94; M. 't Hart, J. Jonker, and J. L. van Zanden, *A Financial History of the Netherlands* (Cambridge: Cambridge University Press, 1997); J. D. Tracy, *A Financial Revolution in the Habsburg Netherlands* (London, Berkeley and Los Angeles, CA: University of California Press, 1985) J. de Vries and A. van der Woude, *The First Modern Economy: Success, Failure, and Perseverence of the Dutch Economy, 1500–1815* (Cambridge: Cambridge Univer-sity Press, 1997); P. G. M. Dickson, *The Financial Revolution in England: A Study in the Development of Public Credit, 1688–1756* (London: MacMillan, 1967); L. Neal, *The Rise of Financial Capitalism: International Capital Markets in the Age of Reason* (Cam-bridge: Cambridge University Press, 1990).

3. The Spanish Succession War (1701–14) ended by the Treaty of Utrecht in 1713 and the Treaties of Rastatt and Baden in 1714. The War of Jenkins' Ear concluded in 1742 but after that the conflict continued as part of the War of Austria Succession.

4. Juan Orry (1652–1729) was a French economist and politician as well as Secretary of the Treasury of the Spanish King Philip.

5. 'mandaba que por vía de donativo se cobrase un real por cada fanega de tierra labrantía, dos de la que contenía huerta y árboles (viñas, olivos, moreras …), cinco por ciento de los alquileres de las casas, arrendamientos, dehesas, pastos y molinos, rentas y derechos, un real por cada cabeza de ganado mayor y ocho maravedíes por la de ganado menor'. R.O. 22 February 1705.

6. O. Rey Castelao, 'Mutaciones sociales en una sociedad inmutable: el Reino de Galicia en el reinado de FelipeV', in E. Serrano (ed.), *Felipe V y su tiempo. Congreso Internacional* (Saragossa: Editorial de la Institución Fernando el Católico, 2004), vol. 1, pp. 343–74.

7. The Marquis Santa Cruz of Marcenado, *Rapsodia económica política monárquica* (1732) (Oviedo: Universidad, 1984), pp. 173, 183, 187–8. Llombart has already remarked on the importance of this author in relation to the attempts to reform the Castilian Treasury Department in the eighteenth century as opposed to the project of *Única Constribución*. V. Llombart, 'A propósito de los intentos de reforma de la Hacienda castellana en el siglo XVIII: Campomanes frente al proyecto de la Única Contribución', *Hacienda Pública Española*, 38 (1976), pp. 125–7.

8. J. M. Zapatero, *La Guerra del Caribe en el siglo XVIII* (Madrid: Servicio Histórico y Museo del Ejército, 1990), map 88. L. Ribot García, 'Las reformas militares y navales en tiempos de Felipe V', in E. Maza Zorrilla and Mª de la C. Marcos del Olmo (coord.), *Estudios de Historia. Homenaje al profesor Jesús María Palomares* (Valladolid: Universidad de Valladolid, 2006), pp. 129–62, on p.153.

9. P. D. Curtin, *The Atlantic Slave Trade: A Census* (Madison, WI: University of Wisconsin Press, 1969), p. 131.

10. See D. Téllez Alarcia, 'La independencia de los EEUU en el marco de la "Guerra Colonial"', *Tiempos Modernos: Revista Electrónica de Historia Moderna*, vol 2 (2001); J. M. Zapatero, *La Guerra del Caribe en el siglo XVIII*; T. R. Reese, *Colonial Georgia: A Study in British Imperial Policy in the Eighteenth Century* (Athens, GA: University of Georgia Press, 1963) and also T. R. Reese, 'Georgia in Anglo-Spanish Diplomacy, 1736–1739', *William and Mary Quarterly*, 15:2 (1958), pp. 168–90.

11. See Biblioteca Nacional de España (hereafter BNE), VC/218119, *Cotejo de la conducta de SM con la del Rey Británico, en lo acaecido de la convención de 14 de enero de este año de 1739 como de lo obrado después hasta publicación de las represalias y declaración de guerra* (London, 1739); *Declaración hecha por el Rey Cristianísimo de Francia en la Haya, corte de Olanda, sobre la presente guerra de España e Inglaterra* (Paris, 22 August 1740) and S. Boyse, *An Historical Review of the Transactions of Europe from the Commencement of the War with Spain 1739 to the Insurrection in Scotland in 1745*, pp. 28–9.

12. A. Matilla Tascón, *La Única contribución y el Catastro de la Ensenada* (Madrid: Servicio de Estudios de la Inspección General del Ministerio de Hacienda, 1947).

13. J. M. Rodríguez, *Blas de Lezo. El vasco que salvó al Imperio Español* (Barcelona: Altera, 2008). In 1731, off the coast of Florida, the Spanish coastguard Juan León Fandiño had intercepted the British warship Rebecca under the command of Captain Robert Jenkins and confiscated its cargo, believing it to be smuggling. According to the British officer who stressed the customary Hispanic cruelty, Fandiño cut off his ear and uttered the infamous 'Go and tell your King that I will do the same if he dares to do the same'.

Jenkins must have kept his severed ear as seven years later he attended the House of Commons and showed it as he told his story. See Rodríguez, *Blas de Lezo. El vasco que salvó al Imperio Español* and C. Alonso Mendizábal, *Blas de Lezo 'El Malquerido'* (Burgos: Editorial Dossoles, 2008).

14. The 'Asiento contract' or 'Visitation Right', was renewed by this Treaty.
15. See also A. Rodríguez Villa, *Patiño y Campillo: reseña histórico-biográfica de estos dos ministros de Felipe V* (Madrid: Establecimiento tipográfico de los sucesores de Rivadeneyra, 1882), p. 18; M. Morineau, *Incroyables gazettes et fabuleux métaux (XVIe–XVIIIe siècles)* (Paris: Cambridge University Press et Maison des Sciences du Homme, 1985), p. 369; A. García Baquero, 'Las remesas de metales preciosos americanos en el siglo XVIII: una aritmética controvertida', *Hispania*, LVI/I (1996), pp. 192–233.
16. The main income of the Crown in Spain in 1739 came from *excises and taxes on trade* (26.28 per cent), *customs* (16.91 per cent) and *tobacco monopoly* (21.43 per cent) and the major expenses from the *infantry and calvary* (59.35 per cent) and the maintenance of *marine war* (11.49 per cent), followed by the expenditure on *King's and Queen's houses* (9.96 per cent). '*Estado actual de las cargas y obligaciones de la Corona y de los fondos del Real Herario en fin del año 39 y en todos sus ramos ...',* Mss 12.641, Madrid, Biblioteca Nacional de España, f. 5.
17. J. de Canga Argüelles, *Diccionario de Hacienda con aplicación a España* (1834), vol. 2 (Madrid: Instituto de Estudios Fiscales, 1968), pp. 127 and 522.
18. Fr. Cos-Gayón, *Historia de la administración pública de España* (1851) (Madrid: Instituto de Estudios Administrativos, 1987), pp. 120 and 124. Canga Argüelles, *Diccionario de Hacienda,* vol. 1, pp. 64–5.
19. E. Fdez de Pinedo, 'Coyuntura y política económicas', in M. Tuñón de Lara (dir.), *Historia de España, vol VII. Centralismo, Ilustración y Agonía del Antiguo Régimen (1715–1833)* (Barcelona: Editorial Labor, 1980), pp. 9–173, 85–7, and F. Comín, *Hacienda y economía en la España contemporánea (1800–1936)* (Madrid: Instituto de Estudios Fiscales, 1988), p. 167.
20. García Baquero, 'Las remesas de metales preciosos americanos en el siglo XVIII', p. 233. To transform pesos in reals de vellón we have used the information given by E. J. Hamilton in *War and Prices in Spain* (1947) (New York: Russell and Russell, reissued 1969), pp. 43, 46–8; J. Sardá, 'La política monetaria y las fluctuaciones de la economía española en el siglo XIX', in R. Ortega (ed.), *Escritos* (1948–80) (Madrid: Banco de España, 1987), pp. 65–283, on p. 72. Especially A. M. Bernal, *La financiación de la Carrera de Indias* (Seville-Madrid: Escuela de Estudios Hispanoamericanos, 1992), pp. 322 and 325 and his sensible warnings and J. García Lombardero 'Algunos problemas de la administración y cobranza de las rentas provinciales en la primera mitad del siglo XVIII', in A. de Otazu (ed.) *Dinero y Crédito (siglos XVI al XIX)* (Madrid: Editorial Moneda y Crédito, 1978), pp. 63–87, figures pp. 79–83.
21. Archivo General de Simancas (hereafter AGS), Tribunal Mayor de Cuentas, leg. 1862 and 1863 '*Contribución extraordinaria del 10 por 100 manda exigir el año de 1741'.*
22. *Copia de la instrucción dada, en consecuencia de lo que mandó S. M. por el Ilustrísimo Señor Don Joseph del Campillo, a todos los Superintendentes del Reyno, para la cobranza del Diez por Ciento,* BNE, Mss. 11.259 (39). Aranjuez, 31 May 1741. Theoretically, the *décima* could be paid in two parts: one at the end of August, and the other at the end of December 1741. On the *Décima,* see A. Domínguez Ortiz, *Sociedad y Estado en el siglo XVIII español* (Barcelona: Ariel, p.76) and M. Artola, *La Hacienda del Antiguo Régimen* (Madrid: Alianza, 1982), pp. 252–3.

23. The Royal Order of 22 December 1740 established 'que S. M. se había servido valerse del diez por ciento de la renta líquida que en 1741 tuviese cada uno de sus vasallos, descontados costes de administración, intereses de los censos y cargas de justicia'.
24. AGS, Tribunal Mayor de Cuentas, leg. 1862, Santander.
25. Ibid., leg. 1862, Molina de Aragón.
26. Ibid., leg. 1862, Andújar.
27. Ibid., leg. 1862, Xerez de la Frontera.
28. Ibid., leg. 1862, Úbeda.
29. The Marquise of Villanueva was the major contributor with 7,689 reales and 20 maravedi. However, the Marquis of Mirabel and the Marquis of Montecorto, only paid 33 reales and 30 reales and 30 maravedi respectively. On the whole, nobility has been charged with 10 per cent of the total. Only doctors were tax free.
30. AGS, Tribunal Mayor de Cuentas, leg. 1863, '*Granada. Contribuzn. Extraordin^a del 10 por 100 mandada exigir el año de 1741'. Cuenta original. Fenecida y sacadas las cargas. Lib° 2° de dicho valimiento'*.
31. Vega, Sierra & Cortijos & Caserías contributed with 337,258–13 reales; El Valle with 84,294–03 reales; Orxiua y Toruiscon with 53,109–28; Partido de las Alpujarras with 343,509–12; Partidos de Motril, Almuñecar & Salobreña with 214,289-09 and Partidos de Loxa & Alhama with 148,540–00. AGS, Tribunal Mayor de Cuentas, leg. 1863, '*Granada. Contribuzn. Extraordin^a del 10 por 100 mandada exigir el año de 1741'.*
32. 'casas, censos y heredades'.
33. It's not possible to sort out spices from haberdashery because both are included in the same section.
34. 19 Marquis, 6 Counts, 1 Viscount, 1 Admiral, 1 Duke, 1 *Mayorazgo*.
35. BNE. Mss. 11.281, ff. 403–4.
36. AGS, Tribunal Mayor de Cuentas, leg. 1863. '*Contribuzn. Extraordin^a del 10 por 100 mandada exigir el año de 1741 Madrid. A cargo de los cinco Gremios mayores. Cuenta original. Fenecida. Lib° 2° de dho valimiento'*.
37. AGS, Tribunal Mayor de Cuentas, leg. 1864, Provincia de Madrid.
38. For that reason, in Madrid, the big five guilds *(los Cinco Gremios Mayores)* of the city were assigned to collect the *décima* as they were probably the only institution with financial capacity to pay in advance the amount required.
39. It was established that the collection of the *décima* would start on the following Sunday morning, 9 July.
40. All the barley entered into the town as a consumption good paid 1.5 reales per *fanega*. But in the case of being introduced to be sold in the market, *alcabalas* and *cientos* were added – 12 maravedi per *fanega*. Tax on straw was similar.
41. Many of those types of goods are also labelled 'positional goods'. They give consumers position and prestige with respect to others. R. H. Frank 'Consumption externalities', in S. N. Durlauf and L. E. Blume (eds), *The New Palgrave Dictionary of Economics*, 2nd edn (Palgrave: MacMillan, 2008).

7 Saupin, 'Finances, the State and the Cities in France in the Eighteenth Century'

1. F. Bayard, *Le monde des financiers au XVIIe siècle* (Paris: Flammarion, 1988). D. Dessert, *Argent, pouvoir et société au Grand Siècle* (Paris: Fayard, 1984). Y. Durand, *Les fermiers généraux au XVIIIe siècle* (Paris: Maisonneuve et Larose, 1997). G. Chaussinand-Nogaret, *Les financiers de Languedoc au XVIIIe siècle* (Paris: SEVPEN, 1972).

2. M. Bordes, *L'administration provinciale et municipale en France au XVIIIe siècle* (Paris: SEDES, 1972), chs 9–14.
3. F.-X. Emmanuelli, *Un mythe de l'absolutisme bourbonien. L'intendance du milieu du XVIIe siècle à la fin du XVIIIe siècle (France, Espagne, Amérique)* (Aix-en-Provence: PUP, 1981).
4. J. Felix, *Economie et finances sous l'Ancien Régime. Guide du chercheur (1523–1789)* (Paris, 1994).
5. M. Touzery, *L'invention de l'impôt sur le revenu. La taille tarifée, 1715–1789* (Paris: Comité pour l'histoire économique et financière de la France, 1994).
6. A. Guery, 'Etat, classification sociale et compromis sous Louis XIV: la capitation de 1695 ', *Annales, ESC* (September–October 1986), pp. 1041–60.
7. Guery, 'Les finances de la monarchie', *Annales, ESC* (March–April 1978), pp. 216–39. M. Morineau, 'Budgets de l'Etat et gestion des finances royales en France au XVIIIe siècle', *Revue historique*, 264 (1980), pp. 289–336.
8. M. Bordes, *La réforme municipale du contrôleur général Laverdy et son application (1764–1771)*, Toulouse, Fac. Lettres,1968. J. Felix, *Finances et politique au siècle des Lumières. Le ministère L'Averdy (1763–1768)* (Paris: CHEFF, 1999).
9. M. Touzery, *Atlas de la généralité de Paris au XVIIIe siècle* (Paris: CHEFF, 1995). M. Touzery, (ed.), *De l'estime au cadastre en Europe. L'époque moderne* (Paris: CHEFF, 2007).
10. J. Meyer and J.-P. Poussou, *Etudes sur les villes françaises. Milieu du XVIIe siècle à la veille de la Révolution française* (Paris: SEDES, 1995), chs 9, 10, 14.
11. J. Felix, 'Les finances urbaines au lendemain de la guerre de Sept Ans', in F. Bayard (ed.), *Les finances en province sous l'Ancien Régime* (Paris: Comité pour l'histoire économique et financière de la France, 2000), pp. 179–228, on p. 192.
12. M. Morineau, 'Panorama de l'Ancien Régime fiscal en France', in Bayard (ed.), *Les finances*, pp. 305–38.
13. Ibid, p. 188.
14. J. Maillard, *Le pouvoir municipal à Angers de 1657 à 1789* (Angers: PU Angers, 1984), vol. 2, pp. 9–35.
15. G. Saupin, 'Les octrois de la ville de Nantes à la fin de l'Ancien Régime', in D. Le Page, (ed.), *Usages et images de l'argent dans l'Ouest atlantique aux Temps modernes*, Enquêtes et Documents, CRHIA, n°35, (Rennes: PU Rennes, 2007), pp. 211–29.
16. G. Saupin, 'Les octrois de Nantes de la création de la municipalité à 1732', in P. Haudrere, (ed.), *Pour une histoire sociale des villes* (Rennes: PU Rennes, 2006), pp. 43–57.
17. X. Hourblin, *Les finances de Reims à la fin de l'Ancien Régime, 1765–1789* (Paris: CHEFF, 2008), pp. 111–28.
18. Hourblin, *Les finances de Reims*, p. 188.
19. Maillard, *Le pouvoir municipal à Angers*, vol. 2, p. 28. J. Maillard, 'Les ressources de la ville d'Angers au XVIIIe siècle', in Bayard, (ed.), *Les finances*, pp. 169–177, on p. 175.
20. Calculated on the basis of the data provided by P. Gerard, *Ethique d'une action. Les budgets municipaux à Nantes (quatre comptes entre 1663 et 1712)* (unpublished thesis, University of Nantes, 1994).
21. P. Guignet, *Le pouvoir dans la ville au XVIIIe siècle. Pratiques politiques, notabilité et éthique sociale de part et d'autre de la frontière franco-belge* (Paris: Ed. EHESS, 1990), pp. 116–23, 183–240, on pp. 216–24.
22. Maillard, 'Les ressources', pp. 176–7.
23. B. Garnot, 'Les budgets de la ville de Chartres de 1727 à 1788', in *Enquêtes et Documents* (Paris: CHEFF, 1993), vol. 5, pp. 79–98.

24. Felix, 'Les finances', pp. 221–8.
25. Hourblin, *Les finances de Reims*, pp. 299–338.
26. Ibid., pp. 132–3.
27. M. Courdurie, *La Dette des Collectivités Publiques de Marseille au XVIIIe siècle. Du débat sur le prêt à intérêt au financement par l'emprunt* (Marseille: Institut Historique de Provence, 1974).
28. Guignet, *Le pouvoir*, pp. 206–11.
29. Hourblin, *Les finances de Reims*, p. 129–41.
30. P. Guignet, 'Logiques financières, contraintes étatiques externes et fluctuations conjoncturelles: l'inégale originalité du modèle financier des grandes villes de la France du nord au XVIIIe siècle', in Bayard, (ed.), *Les finances*, pp. 229–57.
31. Felix, 'Les finances', pp. 203–13.
32. C. Lamarre, *Petites villes et fait urbain en France au XVIIIe siècle. Le cas bourguignon* (Dijon, EUD, 1993).
33. F. Adla, 'L'endettement de la ville de Lyons au XVIIIe siècle', in *Etudes et Documents*, (Paris, CHEFF, 1997), vol. 9, pp. 195–229.

8 Limberger, 'The Making of the Urban Fiscal System of Antwerp until 1800'

1. For Louvain, see R. Van Uytven, *Stadsfinanciën en stadsekonomie te Leuven, van de XIIe tot het einde der XVIe eeuw* (Brussels, 1961), for Ghent, H. Van Werveke, *De Gentse stadsfinanciën in de Middeleeuwen* (Brussels, 1934); and M. Boone, *Geld en macht. De Gentse stadsfianciën en de Bourgondische staatsvorming (1384–1453) (Verhandelingen der Maatschappij voor Geschiedenis en Oudheidkunde te Gent, XV)* (Ghent, 1990). For a comparison of Antwerp with Louvain and Brussels, see K. Van Honacker, *Lokaal verzet en oproer in de 17de en 18de eeuw: collectieve acties tegen het centraal gezag in Brussel, Antwerpen en Leuven* (Heule, 1994) (Anciens pays et assemblées d'états/Standen en landen 98), pp. 235–364.
2. R. Boumans, *Het Antwerpse stadsbestuur voor en tijdens de Franse overheersing. Bijdrage tot de ontwikkelingsgeschiedenis van de stedelijke bestuursinstellingen in de Zuidelijke Nederlanden* (Ghent, 1965).
3. F. Blockmans, *De stadsfinanciën, in Antwerpen in de XVIIIe eeuw, Instellingen, economie, cultuur* (Antwerpen, 1952), pp. 46–63, 48.
4. The classic studies are: H. Van Werveke, *De Gentse stadsfinanciën in de middeleeuwen* (Brussels, 1934). R. Van Uytven, *Stadsfinanciën en stadseconomie te Leuven van de XIIe tot het einde der XVIe eeuw* (Brussels, 1961); C. Dickstein-Bernard, *La gestion financière d'une capitale à ses débuts: Bruxelles 1334–1467* (Brussels, 1977).
5. M. 't Hart and M. Limberger, 'Staatsmacht en stedelijke autonomie. Het geld van Antwerpen en Amsterdam (1500–1700)', in *Tijdschrift voor Economische en Sociale Geschiedenis*, 3 (2006) special issue: *Het geld van de stad*, pp. 36–72.
6. See T. Masure, *De stadfinanciën van Antwerpen 1531–1571. Een poging tot reconstructie*, 2 vols (unpublished thesis, Ghent, 1986), p. 206; N. De Vijlder, *De publieke rentenmarkt van Antwerpen, een sociaal-economische analyse 1630–1709* (unpublished thesis, Ghent, 2010); Antwerp, City Archives, R 1401 Account consuptiekas 1 February 1679–31 January 1680.
7. R. Boumans, 'Het verhandelen van stedelijke officiën te Antwerpen in de XVIIIe eeuw', *Bijdragen voor de geschiedenis der Nederlanden*, 3 (1948), pp. 42–68.

8. R. Boumans, *Het Antwerpse stadsbestuur voor en tijdens de Franse overheersing. Bijdrage tot de ontwikkelingsgeschiedenis van de stedelijke bestuursinstellingen in de Zuidelijke Nederlanden* (Ghent, 1965), p. 89. For a detailed study of the city accounts of 1530–42, see 't Hart and Limberger, 'Staatsmacht en stedelijke autonomie'.

9. J. C. Hocquet, 'City-State and Market Economy', in Richard Bonney (ed.), *Economic Systems and State Finance: The Origins of the Modern State in Europe. 13th to 18th Century* (New York: Oxford University Press, 1995), p. 85, see also F. Irsigler, 'Akzise', in R.-H. Bautier (ed.), *Lexikon des Mittelalters*, (München, 1997).

10. SAA, R 1387 Account consumptiekas 1665–6.

11. De Vijlder, *De publieke rentenmarkt*.

12. A. Kreglinger, *Notice historique sur les impôts communaux de la ville d'Anvers* (Brussels, 1845), pp. 92–110.

13. During the period 1665–80, the great excises (on beer, wine, brandy and grain) still yielded 68.6 per cent of the total income of the city, while the other excises only made up for 15.4 per cent. 't Hart and M. Limberger, 'Staatsmacht en stedelijke autonomie', table 3.

14. Boumans, *Antwerps stadsbestuur*, p. 67.

15. M. A. Arnould, 'L'impot sur le capital en Belgique au XVIe siècle', in *Le Hainaut économique*, 1 (1946), pp. 17–45, 24.

16. Boone, Davids and Janssens (eds), *Urban Public Debts*, p. 6.

17. Published in Kreglinger, *Notice historique*, pp. 173–180.

18. The classic study on this topic is H. Soly, *Urbanisme en kapitalisme te Antwerpen in de 16e eeuw. De stedebouwkundige en industriële ondernemingen van Gilbert van Schoonbeke* (Brussels, Gemeentekrediet van België, 1977).

19. Kreglinger, *Notice historique*, pp. 48–9.

20. See for example: W. Blockmans, 'The Impact of Cities on State Formation: Three Contrasting Terrtiories in the Low Countries, 1300–1500', in Blickle (ed.), *Resistance, Representation, and Community*, part V. *The Urban Belt and the Emerging Modern State*, pp. 256–71, for the duchy of Brabant: R. van Uytven, 'Vorst, adel en steden: een driehoeksverhouding in Brabant van de twaalfde tot de zestiende eeuw', in *Bijdragen tot de Geschiedenis*, 59 (1976), pp. 93–122.

21. The Carolus-guilder of 20 stuivers was equivalent to the pound artois, the most current money of account in the Low Countries after *c.* 1540. All amounts in other currencies are therefore calculated in (Carolus-)guilders throughout this paper.

22. Ghent, for example, was granted an octroy of thirty years in 1455; see Boone, *Geld en macht*, p. 54.

23. This principle was expressed in a edict by Philippe the Fair from 1495 and in the Joyful Entry of Charles V in 1515, cited in Kreglinger, *Notice historique*, p. 21.

24. H. Van der Wee, *The Growth of the Antwerp Market and the European Economy, 14th–16th Centuries*, 3 vols (The Hague, 1963).

25. Kreglinger, *Notice historique*, pp. 48–79.

26. Braudel, *Les emprunts de Charles-Quint*. For a more recent survey, see P. Stabel and J. Haemers, 'From Bruges to Antwerp: International Commercial Firms and Government's Credit in the Late 15th and Early 16th Century', in C. Sanz Ayan and B. J. Garcia Garcia (eds), *Banca, crédito y capital: la Monarquía Hispánica y los antiguos Países Bajos (1505–1700)* (Madrid: Fundación Carlos de Amberes, 2006).

27. Masure, *Stadsfinanciën*, pp. 279–80.

28. Among the creditors were Anton Fugger, the Welser firm, Wolf Puschinger, Ulrich Hainhofer, Anton Haug, the major German merchants active in Antwerp, as well as the

Antwerp residents Lazarus Tucher, Erasmus Schets and his sons; H. Soly, 'Fortificaties, belastingen en corruptie te Antwerpen in het midden der 16e eeuw', *Bijdragen tot de Geschiedenis*, 53 (1970), pp. 191–210, see also: D. J. Harreld, *High Germans in the Low Countries: German Merchants and Commerce in Golden Age-Antwerp* (Brill, Leiden en Boston, 2004).

29. See Soly, 'Fortificaties', pp. 204–5.
30. Boumans, *Antwerps stadsbestuur*, pp. 56–7 and 95–9.
31. SAA, Pk. 2071: Minutes of the Broad Council 1664–1666, 28 August 1665.
32. SAA, PK 2072: 1666–67, 11 March 1666, and 7 July 1666.
33. W. Buchholz, *Geschichte Der Öffentlichen Finanzen in Europa in Spätmittelalter Und Neuzeit. Darstellung, Analyse, Bibliographie* (Berlin: Akademie Verlag, 1996), p. 19.
34. Boone, Davids and Janssens (eds), *Urban Public Debts*.
35. Boumans, *Antwerps stadsbestuur*, pp. 70–1, The Antwerp ame contained 142,18 l.
36. Masure, *De stadfinanciën van Antwerpen*, p. 150.
37. Antwerp City Archives, PK 2072: 1666–67; Broad Council 22 and 24 May 1667.
38. Van Honacker, *Lokaal verzet*, p. 297.
39. Ibid., p. 235.
40. Masure, *De stadfinanciën van Antwerpen*, p. 219.
41. Antwerp City Archives, Brede Raadsboek 1588, f. 120, cited in Kreglinger, *Notice historique*, p. 81.
42. 'als vanden xen penning te ontfaene het sal vele costen, ende nyemant en willet doen alsoe luttel profyts inbrengende ende groot rumoer ondert gemeijne volck makende, ende om renten te coopen seer onwillig maken'. SAA , R 1756 f. 44r.
43. Antwerp State Archives, Archives of the Brede Raad nr. 7, Breeden raedboek van de meersche: 1584, f. 1v: 13 juli 1584.
44. State Archives Antwerp, Archives of the Antwerp Broad Council nr.8, ff. 35–41.
45. M. Van der Burg and M. 't Hart, 'Renteniers and the recovery of Amsterdam's Credit (1578–1605)' in Boone, Davids and Janssens (eds), *Urban Public Debts*, pp. 197–218. And W. Fritschy, 'Three Centuries of Urban and Provincial Debt: Amsterdam and Holland', in ibid., pp. 75–92.
46. L. Pezzolo, 'The Venetian Government Debt, 1350–1650', in Boone, Davids and Janssens (eds), *Urban Public Debts*, p. 70 also points out that fact.
47. Antwerp City Archives, Pk 2084: Brede Raad 1680, 8 and 26 november 1680.
48. 'dat de accysen van der stadt niet soo wel en werden geadministreert als wel behoorde, ende dat de selve wel bedient werdende nogelyck meer behoorden vuyt te brenten dan deselve nou waeren vuyt benghende' cited in Masure, *Stadsfinanciën*, p. 281.
49. We can actually speak of path dependency in this context; compare: 't Hart and M. Limberger, *Staatsmacht en stedelijke autonomie*, p. 66.

9 van der Heijden and van der Burg, 'The Dutch Financial System between Public and Private Interests'

1. C. Tilly, *Coercion, Capital and European States, A.D. 990–1990* (Oxford: Blackwell Publishing, 1992), p. 151; M. 't Hart, 'Tussen kapitaal en belastingmonopolie. Interne grenzen aan staatsvorming in Nederland, 1580–1850', in H. Flap and M. H.D. van Leeuwen (eds), *Op lange termijn. Verklaringen van trends in de geschiedenis van samenlevingen* (Hilversum: Verloren, 1994), pp. 133–6.

2. The 'revolution' also entailed the end of forces annuity sales., J. D. Tracy, *A Financial Revolution in the Habsburg Netherlands. Renten and Renteniers in the County of Holland, 1515–1565* (Berkeley, CA: University of California Press, 1985).

3. M. van der Heijden, 'State Formation and Urban Finances in Sixteenth and Seventeenth-Century Holland', *Journal of Urban History*, 32:3 (2006), pp. 429–50.

4. R. van Uytven, *Stadsfinanciën en stadsekonomie te Leuven van de XIIe tot het einde der XVIe eeuw* (Brussels: Paleis der Academiën,1961); J. W. Marsilje, *Het financiële beleid van Leiden in de laat-Beierse en Bourgondische periode, 1390–1477* (Hilversum: Verloren, 1985); for a social-economical approach see M. Boone, *Geld en macht. De Gentse stadsfinanciën en de Bourgondische staatsvorming (1384–1453)* (Gent, 1990); R. van Schaïk, *Belasting, bevolking en bezit in Gelre en Zutphen (1350–1550)* (Hilversum, Verloren, 1987).

5. This research project focused on fifteenth-century Bruges and sixteenth- and seventeenth-century Dordrecht, Haarlem and Zwolle. The papers of a 2001 conference in Ghent were published in M. Boone, K. Davids, P. Janssens (eds), *Urban Public Debts: Urban Goverment and the Market for Annuities in Western Europe (14th–18th Centuries)* (Turnhout: Brepols, 2003). The most recent synthesis in Dutch is M. van der Heijden, *Geldschieters van de stad. Financiële relaties tussen burgers, stad en overheden 1550–1650* (Amsterdam: Bert Bakker, 2006).

6. For a historiographical overview: M. van der Heijden, 'Stadsrekeningen, stedelijke financiën en historisch onderzoek', *NEHA. Bulletin voor de economische geschiedenis*, 14:2 (1999), pp. 129–66; M. van der Heijden and M. 't Hart, 'Recente historiografische trends in het onderzoek naar stedelijke financiën in de Nederlanden', *Tijdschrift voor Sociale en Economische Geschiedenis*, 3:3 (2006), pp. 3–35. For the comparative work: M. 't Hart and M. Limberger, 'Staatsmacht en stedelijke autonomie. Het geld van Antwerpen en Amsterdam (1500–1700)', *Tijdschrift voor Sociale en Economische Geschiedenis*, 3:3 (2006), pp. 36–72.

7. Boone, *Geld en macht*, p. 110.

8. M. Prak, *Gezeten burgers. De elite van een Hollandse stad, Leiden 1700–1748* (Hilversum 1985), pp. 117–20, 256.

9. J. D. Bangs, 'Holland's Civic Lijfrente Loans (XVth Century): Some Recurrent Problems', *Publications du Centre Européen d'études Burgondo-médianes*, 23 (1983), pp. 75–82; M. van der Burg and M. 't Hart, 'Renteniers and the Recovery of Amsterdam's Credit (1578–1605)', in Boone, Davids, and Janssens (eds), *Urban Public Debts*, pp. 197–218. Cf. M. van der Heijden et al. (eds), *Serving the Urban Community: The Rise of Public Facilities in the Low Countries* (Amsterdam: Aksant Academic Publishers); M. van der Heijden, 'Renteniers and the Public Debt of Dordrecht (1555–1572)', in Boone, Davids, and Janssens (eds), *Urban Public Debts*, pp. 183–96.

10. W. M. Bowsky, *The Finance of the Commune of Siena, 1287–1355* (Oxford: Oxford University Press, 1970), pp. 166–88; A. Molho, *Florentine Public Finances in the Early Renaissance, 1400–1433* (Cambridge: Cambridge University Press, 1971), pp. 60–112.

11. Tracy, *A Financial Revolution*; M. Potter and J.-L. Rosenthal, 'Politics and Public Finance in France: The Estates of Burgundy, 1660–1790', in: *Journal of Interdisciplinary History* 27:4 (1997), pp. 577–612.

12. For the southern Netherlands: Boone, *Geld en macht*; M. Boone, '"Plus dueil que joie". Renteverkopen door de stad Gent in de Bourgondische periode: tussen private belangen en stedelijke financiën', *Gemeentekrediet van België: driemaandelijks tijdschrift*, 45 (1991–2), pp. 3–25; M. Boone, *Immobiliënmarkt, fiscaliteit en sociale gelijkheid te Gent* (Kortrijk-Heule: UGA, 1983); J. Dambruyne, *Mensen en centen. Het 16de-eeuwse Gent*

in demografisch en economisch perspectief (Ghent: Maatschappij voor Geschiedenis en Oudheidkunde te Gent, 2001); For the northern Netherlands: M. 't Hart, 'Public Loans and Moneylenders in the Seventeenth Century Netherlands', *Economic and Social History in the Netherlands* (NEHA), 1 (Amsterdam 1989), pp. 119–39; Boone, Davids and Janssen (eds), *Urban Public Debts*; Martijn van der Burg, *Tot laste der Stadt Rotterdam. De verkoop van lijfrenten en de Rotterdamse renteniers (1653–1690)* (MA thesis, University of Amsterdam, 2002); van der Heijden, *Geldschieters van de stad.*

13. A clear distinction between redeemable annuities and bonds is hard to make. Theoretically, bonds (*obligaties* or *penningen op interest*) were short term loans, which in contrast to annuities were registered bonds. In practice however, the differences between bonds and annuities were less clear, being sold under the same conditions. See 't Hart, 'Public loans and moneylenders', pp. 136–37.

14. Gemeentearchief Dordrecht (GAD), rekeningen van het groot comptoir, de rekeningen van de reparatiën en de tolrekeningen (1550–1700); Stads Archief Haarlem (SAH), Thesauriersrekeningen (1550–1650); Gemeentearchief Zwolle (GAZ), Jaarrekeningen en maandrekeningen (the years 1550–9, 1570–9, 1600–4, 1621–5, 1646–50) en charters van losrenten; Gemeentelijke Archiefdienst Rotterdam (GAR), Oud Stadsarchief (OSA), aantekeningen uit de resoluties van vroedschap en burgemeesters inzake financiële aangelegenheden, inv. no. 3071; Thesaurier Extraordinaris 1653–73, inv. no. 3164–85; Blaffert van de lijfrenten verkocht door de stad Rotterdam 1653–90, inv. no. 3663.

15. Dordrecht 1555, 1572 and 1604; Haarlem 1567 and 1604; Zwolle 1573 and 1625; Rotterdam 1653–90.

16. For the accessibility and transparency of the Parisian credit market in the seventeenth century see P. T. Hoffman, G. Postel-Vinay and J.-L.Rosenthal, *Priceless Markets: The Political Economy of Credit in Paris, 1660–1726* (Chicago, IL: University of Chicago Press, 2000), pp. 11–30.

17. For Ghent: H. van Werveke *De Gentse stadsfinanciën in de Middeleeuwen* (Brussels, 1934), pp, 285–89; Boone, 'Renteverkopen door de stad Gent', pp. 3–25, in particular pp. 14–16; for Venlo: J. J. M. de Groot, *Venle/Venlo. HOeo een stadje begon* (Zutphen: Walburg Pers, 2003), p. 60; for the province of Holland: J.A.M.Y. Bos-Rops, *Graven op zoek naar geld: de inkomsen van de graven van Holland en Zeeland, 1389–1433* (Hilversum: Verloren, 1993), pp. 128–9, 170 and Tracy, *The Financial Revolution*, pp. 113–22; for Dordrecht: H. W. Dokkum and E. C. Dijkhof, *Oude Dordtse lijfrenten* (Amsterdam: Verloren, 1983), p. 76; for Brugge: L. Derijcke, 'The Public Annuity Market in Bruges at the End of the 15th Century', in Boone, Davids and Jansens, *Urban Public Debt*, pp.166–7; P. Stabel, *Dwarfs among Giants: The Flemish Urban Networks in the Late Middle Ages* (Leuven: Garant, 1997), pp. 264–6. According to the data provided by Derijcke, renteniers were also located in seaports like Nieuwpoort and Sluis, in regional centres like Bergues-Saint-Winocq and Veurne, and the riverside towns of Oudenaarde, Courtrai and Dendermonde.

18. Tracy, *The Financial Revolution*, pp. 110–11; Boone, 'Renteverkopen door de stad Gent', p. 15.

19. Dokkum and Dijkhof, 'Oude Dordtse lijfrenten', p. 76.

20. For the relations between urban annuities in the Low Countries and the Habsburg monarchy in 1550–72 see van der Heijden, *Geldschieters van de stad*, pp. 125–89.

21. See Reitsma, *Centrifugal and centripetal forces*, pp. 72–117.

22. Dokkum and Dijkhof, 'Oude Dordtse lijfrenten', pp. 76–7.

23. See van der Heijden, *Geldschieters van de stad*, pp. 63–143.

24. J. H. W. Unger and W. Besemer, *De oudste stadsrekeningen van Rotterdam* (Rotterdam: Gemeentelijke Archief Dienst, 1899), pp. 17, 471–2.

25. The seventeenth-century Dutch Republic offered good prospects for investing in urban and provincial public debt – in particular in the highly urbanized province of Holland. Therefore citizens had little need to seek alternative investments. Van der Burg, *Tot laste der Stadt Rotterdam*, pp. 72–3.

26. For coercion see Molho, *Florentine Public Finances*, p. 69.

27. J. H. Kernkamp, *Vijftiende-eeuwse rentebrieven van Noordnederlandse steden* (Groningen: Wolters, 1961), p. 7.

28. Van der Burg and 't Hart, 'Renteniers', pp. 210–13; Derijcke, 'The Public Annuity Market in Bruges', pp. 170–3; Van der Heijden, *Geldschieters van de stad*, pp. 125–89.

29. Kernkamp, *Vijftiende-eeuwse rentebrieven*, p. 7.

30. SAH, Thesauriersrekeningen 1576, f. 8 verso.

31. See: I. Prins, *Het faillissement*; E. L. M. Sewalt, *Atterminatie ende staet. De rol van het landsheerlijke gezag bij de ondercurarelestelling van de stad Haerlem in de late Middeleeuwen* (doctoral thesis, Rijksuniversiteit Leiden, 1994); van der Heijden, *Geldschieters van de stad*, pp. 63–143.

32. GAD, groot comptoir, inv. nos 2596, 1573, ff. 15–16; van der Heijden, 'Renteniers and the Public Debt', pp. 183–96.

33. GAD, rekeningen van het groot comptoir en de reparatiën, inv. nos 2695, 1694, f. 43 verso and f. 54; inv. no. 3052, 1695, f. 11 verso; inv. nos 2697, 1696, f. 52 verso; archief 3, resoluties van de Oudraad 10 mei 1694–5, inv. no. 62, ff. 48 recto–49 recto, 115 verso–116 recto.

34. J. C. Streng, *Stemme in staat: de bestuurlijke elite in de stadsrepubliek Zwolle 1579–1795* (Hilversum: Verloren, 1997), p. 204.

35. M. van der Burg, 'Burgers en bestuurders. Rotterdams stadsfinanciën in de tweede helft van de zeventiende eeuw', *Rotterdams Jaarboekje*, 11:1 (2003), p. 115.

36. Van der Heijden, *Geldschieters van de stad*, pp. 146–89.

37. In Rotterdam between 1653 and 1690 about 40 per cent of the annuity buyers belonged to the economical and administrative elite; in comparison Haarlem's administrative elite accounted for 29 per cent in 1604 and in Dordrecht the administrative elite made up 48 per cent in 1555 60 per cent and 48 per cent in 1604. Van der Burg, 'Burgers en bestuurders', p. 117; van der Heijden, *Geldschieters van de stad*, pp. 146–89.

38. However, during the political crises of 1748 and the late 1790s, when few citizens were eager to invest in public debt, forced loans made a short-lived comeback. M. C. 't Hart, *In Quest for Funds: Warfare and State Formation in the Netherlands, 1620–1650* (PhD thesis, Leiden University, 1989), pp. 119–20; M. 't Hart, 'The Merits of a Financial Revolution: Public Finance, 1550–1700', in M. 't Hart, J. Jonker and J. L. van Zanden (eds), *A Financial History of the Netherlands* (Cambridge: Cambridge University Press, 1997), p. 21.

39. Van der Burg, *Tot laste der Stadt Rotterdam*, pp. 49–51.

40. For Leiden see Prak, *Gezeten burgers*, pp. 117–20, 256.

41. For the loans of 1572: GAD, groot comptoir, inv. no. 2595, inv. no. 2596, ff. 15–16. A few years later the *thesaurier* was no longer able to pay interest. Between 1576 and 1593 annuity buyers received little money. In order to prevent citizens from being taken hostage, Dordrecht succesfully requested extention of payment from the Province of Holland. See: Van der Heijden, *Geldschieters van de stad*, pp.100–45.

42. GAD, rekeningen groot comptoir, inv. no. 2619 (1604), ff. 39–51.

43. SAH, thesauriersrekeningen 1604; Van der Heijden, *Geldschieters van de stad*, pp. 146–89.

44. Van der Burg, *Tot laste der Stadt Rotterdam*, p. 54.
45. GAD, rekeningen groot comptoir, inv. no. 2695 (1694) fol. 43; SAH, thesauriersrekeningen (1627–43).
46. Boone, *Geld en macht*, p. 110; Derijcke, 'Public Annuity Market in Bruges', pp. 170–1.
47. For the years 1555, 1572 and 1604 we have analysed the administrative backgrounds of the annuity buyers.
48. Van der Heijden, 'Renteniers and the Public Debt, pp. 183–96.
49. SAD, archief 3, reparatiën 1572, inv. no. 481, ff. 19–20, groot comptoir 1572, inv. no. 456, ff. 85 verso, 86 verso, 90, 132 verso; groot comptoir 1573, inv. no. 2586, f. 50; Matthys Balen, *Beschrijvinge der stad Dordrecht* (Dordrecht: Symon Onder de Linde, 1677), vol. 1, pp. 317–22; vol. 2, pp. 1062–3.
50. Van der Burg, 'Burgers en bestuurders', pp. 117.
51. Also see Kernkamp, *Vijftiende-eeuwse rentebrieven*, pp. 11–12.
52. Van der Heijden, *Geldschieters van de stad*, pp. 125–32.
53. SAH, Thesauriersrekeningen 1558–9, ff. 78 verso–79 verso, 84–90.
54. As a consequence the city had to sell life annuities to pay for the higher interest: Van der Burg, 'Burgers en bestuurders', p. 115.
55. GAR, OSA, inv. nos 3164–85.
56. GAD, Groot comptoir, inv. nos 2621, 1606, f. 37; For Bruges see Derijcke, 'Public Annuity Market of Bruges', p. 170.
57. Dokkum and Dijkhof, 'Oude Dordtse lijfrenten', pp. 57–62; Van Schaïk, 'The Sale of Annuities in Zutphen', p. 113; Dambruyne, *Mensen en centen*, pp. 109–80; Dambruyne, *Corporatieve middengroepen*, pp. 104–8; Boone, Dumon and Reusens, *Immobiliënmarkt*, pp. 204–10; H. Soly, *Urbanisme en kapitalisme te Antwerpen in de 16ᵉ eeuw: de stedebouwkundige en industriële ondernemingne van Gilbert van Schoonbeke* (Brussels: Gemeentekrediet van Belgie, 1977), p. 81.
58. Van der Heijden, *Geldschieters van de stad*, pp. 125–89; Van der Burg, *Tot laste der Stadt Rotterdam*, annexes.
59. GAD, rekeningen groot comptoir, inv. no. 2628 (1614), f. 52.
60. Van der Heijden, *Geldschieters van de stad*, pp. 125–89.
61. Van der Burg, 'Burgers en bestuurders', pp. 118–9.
62. Tracy, *Renten and renteniers*, pp. 169–70; Van der Burg and 't Hart, 'Renteniers', pp. 209.
63. Van der Heijden, *Geldschieters van de stad*, pp. 125–89.
64. De Blécourt en Fischer held the view that life expectancy partly determined the purchase price, Blok also argued that this was taken into account; yet Houtzager and Kernkamp argued this had not been the case. P. J. Blok, *Geschiedenis eener Hollandsche stad* (Den Haag: Martinus Nijhoff, 1910), vol. 1, p. 252; Dirk Houtzager, *Hollands los- en lijfrenteleningen voor 1672* (Schiedam: Roelants, 1961), p. 22, note 4; A. S. De Blécourt and H. F. W. D. Fischer, *Kort begrip van het Oud-Vaderlands Burgerlijk Recht* (Groningen: Wolters, 1959), pp. 130; Kernkamp, *Vijftiende-eeuwse rentebrieven*, p. 9; SAD, archief 3, inv. nos. 2452–3, 'Negotiatie van lijfrenten'; Johan de Witt, *Waerdye van lyf-rente naer proportie van los-renten* ('s-Gravenhage: Jacobus Scheltus, 1671); Ida H. Stamhuis, 'De ontwikkeling van de actuariële theorie tot de zeventiende- en achttiende eeuw', in Jacques van Gerwen en Marco van Leeuwen (eds), *Studies over zekerheidsarrangementen: risico's, risicobestrijding en verzekeringen in Nederland vanaf de Middeleeuwen* (Amsterdam: NEHA, 1009), pp. 158–74.
65. Van der Burg, *Tot laste der Stadt Rotterdam*, p. 54.

66. Stamhuis, 'Levensverzekeringen 1500–1800', in Gerwen and Van Leeuwen (eds), *Studies over zekerheidsarrangementen*, pp. 141–56, Houtzager, *Hollands los- en lijfrenteleningen*, p. 9.
67. Van der Burg, 'Burgers en bestuurders', p. 110.
68. Stamhuis, 'Levensverzekeringen', p. 144; Van der Burg, *Tot laste der Stadt Rotterdam*, pp. 56–60; Van der Heijden, *Geldschieters van de stad*, pp. 190–213.
69. Thera Wijsenbeek's research shows that the estates of widows did not contain relatively more life annuities, not did estates of deceased unmarried women. T. Wijsenbeek-Olthuis, *Achter de gevels van Delft: bezit en bestaan van rijk en arm in een periode van achteruitgang (1700–1800)* (Hilversum: Verloren, 1987), p. 126.
70. In total 4.3 per cent of Rotterdam's *lijfrenten* were bought by one or more guardians; 41.4 per cent by one or both parents. Other relatives, among them many grandmothers, bought 12 per cent of all life annuities.
71. An example from Haarlem: Adriaen Kertens van Thijn bought a life annuity of 1,100 guilders, which was put on the life of the two sons he had with Maria Muys van Holy. SAH, Thesauriersrekeningen 1626, f. 41 verso.
72. Stamhuis, 'Levensverzekeringen', pp. 148–9, 155.
73. For instance, 38 per cent the life annuities sold by Dordrecht in 1555 and 1572 had been put on the life of a minor.
74. Compare Luciano Pezzolo 'The Venetian government debt, 1350–1650', in Boone, Davids and Janssens (eds), *Urban Public Debt*, pp. 61–74 and Van der Burg and 't Hart, 'Renteniers', pp. 197–218.

10 Pühringer, 'The Urban Fiscal System in the Habsburg Monarchy'

1. The hereditary lands included the archduchies of Austria above the Enns and Austria below the Enns (in contrast to the terms of Lower and Upper Austria meaning a group of territories, i.e. Lower Austria meant Austria above and below the Enns, Upper Austria meant the county of Tyrol and Further Austria, the Habsburg possessions in south-western Germany), Styria, Carinthia, Tyrol, the duchy of Carniola and the county of Gorizia. The lands of the Bohemian Crown will not be considered because there are too many differences concerning taxation from the Austrian lands.
2. T. Winkelbauer, *Ständefreiheit und Fürstenmacht. Länder und Untertanen des Hauses Habsburg im konfessionellen Zeitalter* (Wien: Ueberreuter, 2003), vol. 1, p. 450, pp. 453–5; R. Bonney, 'Introduction. Economic Systems and State Finance', in R. Bonney (ed.), *Economic Systems and State Finance* (Oxford: Clarendon Press, 1995), p. 13; J. Bérenger, *Finances et absolutisme autrichien dans la seconde moitié du XVIIe siècle* (Paris: Champion, 1975), pp. 334–7; W. Schulze, *Reich und Türkengefahr* (München: Beck, 1978).
3. In 1677 hardly any taxation list existed for these towns, so one would also face the problem of lack of sources in analysing their exact tax rates. But on the other hand, they paid, for example, in 1709 only half of the tax rate paid by the territorial towns. F. Mensi, *Geschichte der direkten Steuern in Steiermark bis zum Regierungsantritt Maria Theresias* (Graz and Wien: Styria, 1921), vol. 3, p. 26; F. Baltzarek, 'Beiträge zur Geschichte des vierten Standes in Niederösterreich. Eine vergleichende Stadtgeschichtsuntersuchung mit besonderer Auswertung der Gaisruckschen Städteordnungen von 1745–1747', *Mitteilungen des Österreichischen Staatsarchivs*, 23 (1970), pp. 64–104, on p. 84.
4. For the term of 'urban landscape' and the importance of small towns for structural urbanization see generally H. T. Gräf, K. Keller (eds), *Städtelandschaft – Réseau urbain*

– *Urban network. Städte im regionalen Kontext in Spätmittelalter und früher Neuzeit* (Köln and Wien: Böhlau, 2004); H. Flachenecker, R. Kießling (eds), *Städtelandschaften in Altbayern, Franken und Schwaben. Studien zum Phänomen der Kleinstädte während des Spätmittelalters und der Frühen Neuzeit* (München: Beck, 1999); M. Escher, A. Haverkamp and F. G. Hirschmann (eds), *Städtelandschaft – Städtenetz – zentralörtliches Gefüge. Ansätze und Befunde zur Geschichte der Städte im hohen und späten Mittelalter* (Mainz: von Zabern, 2000). For the Austrian towns see A. Pühringer, 'Die landesfürstlichen Städte ob und unter der Enns. Funktionale Städtelandschaften?', in Gräf and Keller (eds), *Städtelandschaft*, pp. 135–54.

5. K. Klein, 'Die Bevölkerung in Österreich vom Beginn des 16. Jahrhunderts bis zur Mitte des 18. Jahrhunderts', in H. Helczmanovszki (ed.), *Beiträge zur Bevölkerungs- und Sozialgeschichte Österreichs* (Wien: Verlag für Geschichte und Politik, 1973), pp. 47–112; K. Klein, *Daten zur Siedlungsgeschichte der österreichischen Länder bis zum 16. Jahrhundert* (Wien: Verlag für Geschichte und Politik, 1980). For the developement of Vienna see A. Weigl, 'Residenz, Bastion und Konsumptionsstadt: Stadtwachstum und demographische Entwicklung einer werdenden Metropole', in A. Weigl (ed.), *Wien im Dreißigjährigen Krieg. Bevölkerung – Gesellschaft – Kultur – Konfession* (Wien and Köln: Böhlau, 2001), pp. 31–105.

6. The 'urban curia' of the Austrian Estates consisted not only of towns but also of territorial markets, which some of them had a higher financial potential as some of the towns. For example in Austria below the Enns the four 'viticulture-markets' in the south had a higher tax capacity than the small frontier towns in the north. But they got in debt in eighteenth century, when wine as beverage of mass consumption was ousted by beer and therefore felt in crisis. Assuming from the total number, for example in the Styrian curia the number of markets was higher than this of towns. From the total number of thirty-one, eighteen were markets. Austria above the Enns had only a small number of towns and no market in its urban curia at all. Mensi, *Geschichte*, p. 39; Baltzarek, 'Beiträge', p. 85.

7. The numbers changed in the early modern period, either some of them dropped out because they were not able to pay their tax rates or they were mortgaged by the princely ruler and lost their status in this way. In Austria below the Enns the 'urban curia' had the highest fluctuation compared with the other regions. Baltzarek, 'Beiträge', p. 73–4.

8. Vienna's position corresponded with the *half of the fourth estate* in Austria below the Enns, whereas the other towns and markets were called *the small towns and markets* or the *half fourth estate*. A. F. Přibram, 'Die niederösterreichischen Stände und die Krone in der Zeit Kaiser Leopolds I.', *Mitteilungen des Instituts für Österreichische Geschichtsforschung*, 14 (1893), pp. 589–652, on p. 598.

9. A. Pühringer, '"Mitleiden" ohne "Mitsprache"? Die landesfürstlichen Städte Österreichs als Vierter Stand', in G. Ammerer, W. D. Godsey, Jr, M. Scheutz, P. Urbanitsch and A. S. Weiß (eds), *Bündnispartner und Konkurrenten der Landesfürsten. Die Stände der Habsburgermonarchie* (Wien and München: Oldenbourg 2006), pp. 90–113, on pp. 93–5. The different status of the urban curias depended also on their internal cooperation. For example in Austria above the Enns and Carinthia the towns were organized in leagues, which strengthened their status within the Estates during the entire period. Ibid., p. 95; A. Hoffmann, 'Der oberösterreichische Städtebund im Mittelalter', *Jahrbuch des Oberösterreichischen Musealvereines*, 93 (1948), pp. 107–45, on pp. 111–14; H. Ebner, 'Zur Ideologie des mittelalterlichen Städtebürgertums aufgrund österreichischer Stadtrechte des späten Mittelalters', *Jahrbuch für Geschichte des Feudalismus*, 7 (1983), pp. 157–84,

on p. 167; H. Knittler, *Städte und Märkte. Herrschaftsstruktur und Ständebildung* (Wien: Verlag für Geschichte und Politik 1973), pp. 11–15.

10. Yet in the fourteenth and fifteenth century the so called *town tax* was bonded by the princely ruler. Mensi, *Geschichte*, p. 3.

11. Concerning the noble curia, regionally small differences are discernable, but they are not interesting in our context. Generally to the Estates of the Habsburg Monarchy and their involvement in the financial system of the government see Winkelbauer, *Ständefreiheit*, vol. 1, pp. 30–78, 465–76, 487–92; G. Ammerer, W. D. Godsey, Jr., M. Scheutz, P. Urbanitsch, A. S. Weiss, 'Die Stände in der Habsburgermonarchie. Eine Einleitung', in Ammerer et al. (eds), *Bündnispartner*, pp. 13–41.

12. Knittler, *Städte*, pp. 11–15.

13. G. Winner, 'Adeliger Stand und bürgerliche Hantierung. Die sieben landesfürstlichen Städte und die ständischen Gegensätze in Oberösterreich während des 16. Jahrhunderts', *Historisches Jahrbuch der Stadt Linz* (1959), pp. 57–92; L. Mákkai, 'Die Entstehung der gesellschaftlichen Basis des Absolutismus in den Ländern der österreichischen Habsburger', *Études historiques*, 1 (1960), pp. 627–68; A. Hoffmann, 'Die oberösterreichischen Städte und Märkte. Eine Übersicht ihrer Entwicklungs- und Rechtsgrundlagen', *Jahrbuch des Oberösterreichischen Musealvereins*, 84 (1932), pp. 63–213, on pp. 101–2.

14. For the complex problem of emigration see Winkelbauer, *Ständefreiheit*, vol. 1, pp. 55–78; A. Schunka, 'Emigration aus den Habsburgerländern nach Mitteldeutschland. Motive und soziale Konsequenzen', in R. Leeb, S. C. Pils and T. Winkelbauer (eds), *Staatsmacht und Seelenheil. Gegenreformation und Geheimprotestantismus in der Habsburgermonarchie* (Wien and München: Oldenbourg 2007), pp. 233–46; A. Stögmann, 'Die Gegenreformation in Wien. Formen und Folgen für die städtische Gesellschaft (1580–1660)', in ibid., pp. 273–88; A. Pühringer, '"Topographie der Gegenreformation" oder "Austrian Urban Renaissance?"', in ibid., pp. 289–310; M. Scheutz, 'Kammergut und/oder eigener Stand? Landesfürstliche Städte und Märkte und der "Zugriff" der Gegenreformation', in ibid., pp. 311–39. For example Vienna as the largest Austrian town lost economic power in a height of approximately 300,000 fl. A. Stögmann, 'Staat, Kirche und Bürgerschaft: Die katholische Konfessionalisierung und die Wiener Protestanten zwischen Widerstand und Anpassung (1580–1660)', in Weigl (ed.), *Wien*, pp. 482–564, on p. 536.

15. O. Brunner, *Die Finanzen der Stadt Wien von den Anfängen bis ins 16. Jahrhundert* (Wien: Deutscher Verlag für Jugend und Volk, 1929), pp. 46–9.

16. Stögmann, 'Staat', pp. 536–9.

17. H. Knittler, 'Städtelandschaften in Österreich im Spätmittelalter und in der Frühneuzeit', in Gräf and Keller (eds), *Städtelandschaft*, pp. 111–33, on pp. 132–3.

18. It is not possible to examine all towns in this paper, so I have tried to outline a general development and illustrate it using several examples. The sources analysed were the main accounts of sixteen towns in Lower and Upper Austria between 1550 and 1750, but it was only possible to analyse a few towns for the entire period, as many had a lack of sources. For more detailed information see A. Pühringer, *Contributionale, Oeconomicum und Politicum. Die Finanzen der landesfürstlichen Städte Nieder- und Oberösterreichs in der Frühneuzeit* (Wien and München: Verlag für Geschichte und Politik, 2002); for the larger sample Idem, 'Kleine Städte – große Schulden? Zur frühneuzeitlichen Finanzstruktur der landesfürstlichen Städte ob und unter der Enns', *Pro Civitate Austriae. Informationen zur Stadtgeschichtsforschung in Österreich*, NF 8 (2003), pp. 3–38; for Lower Austria idem, 'Ein Strukturvergleich niederösterreichischer Städte in der

frühen Neuzeit. Zur Konstellation kommunaler Finanzen vom Ende des 16. bis zur Mitte des 18. Jahrhunderts', in W. Rosner (ed.), *Die Städte und Märkte Niederösterreichs im Mittelalter und in der frühen Neuzeit* (St Pölten: Niederösterreichisches Institut für Landeskunde, 2005), pp. 102–33.

19. Following the theories about urbanization of P. Hohenberg and H. Lees, *The Making of Urban Europe 1000–1950* (Cambridge, MA: Harvard University Press, 1985) or J. de Vries, *European Urbanization 1500–1800* (Cambridge, MA: Harvard University Press, 1984), the hereditary lands would have been a region not worth analysing, because Vienna was the only large city. Generally the major part of the towns had about 2,000 inhabitants, about fifteen had 2,000–5,000 and only Steyr, Linz, Graz, Wiener Neustadt, Klagenfurt, Ljubljana, Innsbruck and Bolzano reached the peak of more than 10,000 inhabitants until the eighteenth century.

20. O. Brunner, *Die Rechtsquellen der Städte Krems und Stein* (Graz and Köln: Böhlau, 1954), pp. 272–98; Baltzarek, 'Beiträge', pp. 91–5.

21. O. Brunner, *Die Rechtsquellen der Städte Krems und Stein* (Graz and Köln: Böhlau, 1954), pp. 272–98; Baltzarek, 'Beiträge', pp. 91–5.

22. Taxes, funds, hospital and ecclesiastical concerns were separated in subordinated accounts. Baltzarek, 'Beiträge', p. 100.

23. For the Viennese financial system see Brunner, *Finanzen*; F. Baltzarek, *Das Steueramt der Stadt Wien 1526–1760* (Wien: Notring 1971).

24. Mean values generated over the entire period.

25. The towns had not only expenses for military purposes, but they got parts compensated by the estates or the prince.

26. This sample is owed to the quantity of sources.

27. The larger group consists of Steyr, Linz, Wels, Freistadt, Krems, Bruck/Leitha, Korneuburg and Baden, the smaller group of Hainburg, Laa/Thaya, Tulln, Eggenburg, Waidhofen/Thaya, Retz, Weitra and Drosendorf.

28. As a fact of the direct taxation the number of houses is relatively well known – in contrast to exact demographic rates.

29. Mensi, *Geschichte*, p. 9. The *Generallandtag* of Prague in 1541 was the first attempt to standardize property tax. Leasehold houses and facilities of trade and commerce were assessed by their earning power, other houses by their market value. A taxation rate was fixed, but still in the same year the princely ruler demanded other taxes. Shortly after this, in Styria, the rate of the towns was fixed and it was the first time, that the urban curia agreed paying a certain amount for a longer term. Ibid., pp. 49, 53.

30. W. Schulze, 'Reichstage und Reichssteuern im späten 16. Jahrhundert', *Zeitschrift für Historische Forschung*, 2 (1975), pp. 43–58.

31. It would lead to far to analyse in this paper the crucial role played by the estates within the entire early modern period. However for a good understanding of the urban finances, it had to be considered, because in the long term, the estates became more important for the specific situations of the towns than the princely ruler until the eighteenth century. Only at the end of the old regime, the central state replaced the estates more permanently, but this development differed from region to region.

32. Baltzarek, 'Beiträge', p. 79.

33. Ibid., p. 83.

34. Ibid., pp. 91–5. Still in the mid-eighteenth century the titles of the taxes were of wide range: taxes 'pro re fortificatoria', property tax, turk tax, poll tax etc. Beyond this, anticipa-

tions, 'dona gratuita et itineraria', payment in kind for military concerns were demanded. This all should be standardized, but only boarding quartered military was excluded.

35. In Steyr, the largest town of Upper Austria, there was a lack of sources.

36. K. Gerteis, 'Einleitung', in K. Gerteis (ed.), *Stadt und frühmoderner Staat. Beiträge zur städtischen Finanzgeschichte von Luxemburg, Lunéville, Mainz, Saarbrücken und Trier im 17. und 18. Jahrhundert* (Trier: THF, 1994), pp. 1–12; H. Potthoff, 'Der öffentliche Haushalt Hamburgs im 15. und 16. Jahrhundert', *Zeitschrift des Vereins für Hamburgische Geschichte*, 16 (1911), pp. 1–81, on pp. 60–3; D. Hohrath, '"Städtische" und "Staatliche" Kassen in der Stadt Mainz. Beobachtungen zum öffentlichen Finanzwesen in einer Haupt- und Residenzstadt um 1785', in Gerteis (ed.), *Stadt*, pp. 233–343, on p. 260; N. Ohler, 'Zum Haushalt der Stadt Freiburg im Breisgau im 16. und 17. Jahrhundert', *Schau-ins-Land* 94/95 (1976–7), pp. 253–89, on p. 277.

37. The academic discussion about excises and toll charges fills libraries, but meanwhile seems superfluous.

38. E. Klebel, 'Ungeld und Landgericht in Nieder- und Oberösterreich', *Mitteilungen des Instituts für Österreichische Geschichtsforschung*, 52 (1938), pp. 269–87; E. Hillbrand, 'Das Ungeld in Nieder- und Oberösterreich vom 13.–19. Jahrhundert mit besonderer Berücksichtigung der Zeit 1500–1700' (PhD dissertation, Universität Wien, 1953).

39. H. Hassinger, 'Ständische Vertretungen in den althabsburgischen Ländern und in Salzburg', in D. Gerhard (ed.), *Ständische Vertretungen in Europa im 17. und 18. Jahrhundert* (Göttingen: Vandenhoeck & Ruprecht, 1969), pp. 247–85, on pp. 273–4.

40. In some cases 'temporarily' meant over years or also decades. Particular levies on meat and livestock but also on luxury goods were the most usual.

41. Brunner, *Rechtsquellen*, p. 275.

42. P. Rauscher, 'Comparative Evolution of the Tax Systems in the Habsburg Monarchy, c. 1526–1740: The Austrian and the Bohemian Lands', in S. Cavaciocchi (ed.), *La Fiscalità nell'Economia Europea secc. XIII–XVIII – Fiscal Systems in the European economy from the 13th to the 18th centuries* (Florence: Firenze University Press, 2008), pp. 291–320, on pp. 310–11.

43. Unfortunately these subaccounts were maintained only in this town. A. Pühringer, 'Die Stadt Wels in der Frühneuzeit: Finanzen, Verwaltung und Politik zwischen Bauernkrieg, Gegenreformation und Einbindung in den frühmodernen Staat', *Jahrbuch des Musealvereines Wels*, 34 (2004–5), pp. 153–84, on pp. 180–4.

44. A. Pühringer, 'Finanzen und Kommunalbudget der Stadt Wels in der frühen Neuzeit', *Jahrbuch des Musealvereines Wels*, 30 (1993–5), pp. 133–55, on pp. 147–9, table 9, p. 154.

45. The accountancy of the estates can been seen in this context as a sort of highlight, because it administered the taxation for the princely ruler, the different excises for estates and rulers, and beyond this, managed their own credit system. It was a highly complex and sophisticated system of administration and survived like 'a state in a state' till the central administration prevailed. For a detailed analysis for Austria above the Enns see G. Putschögl, *Die landständische Behördenorganisation in Österreich ob der Enns vom Anfang des 16. bis zur Mitte des 18. Jahrhunderts. Ein Beitrag zur österreichischen Rechtsgeschichte* (Linz: Oberösterreichisches Landesarchiv, 1978), pp. 36–57.

46. Baltzarek, 'Beiträge', p. 99.

11 Fuhrmann, 'Taxation and Debt in Early Modern German Cities'

1. R. Bonney (ed.), *The Rise of the Fiscal State in Europe, c. 1200 – 1815* (Oxford: Oxford University Press, 1999). In the text the terms Holy Roman Empire, Empire, Reich and Germany are used interchangeably, despite the slight differences of meaning.
2. E. Maschke, J. Sydow, Vorwort, in Idem (eds), *Verwaltung und Gesellschaft in der südwestdeutschen Stadt des 17. und 18. Jahrhunderts* (Stuttgart, Kohlhammer, 1969), pp. 5–6, on p. 5.
3. E. Isenmann, 'Prinzipien, Formen und wirtschaftliche Auswirkungen von Besteuerung – Steuergerechtigkeit und Steuergleichheit im 15. Jahrhundert (Deutschland und Italien)', in *La Fiscalità nell'Economia Europea Secc. XIII–XVIII/Fiscal Systems in the European Economy from the 13th to the 18th Centuries* (Florence: Florence University Press, 2008), pp. 153–83, on p. 162–77.
4. F. Blaich, 'Die oberdeutsche Reichsstadt als Arbeitgeber vom 13. bis zum 16. Jahrhundert', in *Die Alte Stadt*, 9 (1982), pp. 1–18, on p. 12.
5. U. Dirlmeier, Stadt und Bürgertum. Zur Steuerpolitik und zum Stadt-Land-Verhältnis, in H. Buszello, P. Blickle, R. Endres (eds), *Der deutsche Bauernkrieg*, 3rd edn (Paderborn/München/Wien/Zürich, Ferdinand Schöningh, 1995), pp. 254–80, here p. 269.
6. Dirlmeier, 'Stadt und Bürgertum', pp. 268–9. With more examples U. Dirlmeier, *Untersuchungen zu Einkommensverhältnissen und Lebenshaltungskosten in oberdeutschen Städten des Spätmittelalters (Mitte 14. bis Anfang 16. Jahrhundert)* (Heidelberg: Carl Winter Universitätsverlag, 1978), pp. 61–6. C. T. Gemeiner, *Regensburgische Chronik* (München, C.H. Beck Verlag, 1971), vol. 3, p. 647 reported that rich citizens wanted to leave Regensburg in 1481, because they expected higher direct tax rates, since the reduction of the volume of trade would diminish the tax yield of indirect taxes.
7. Presumably at the time of the reorganization of the fiscal policy the Nuremberg council obtained the assent by Imperor Frederic III, that the 'Losunger' as the highest tax authorities had only to inform the council about incomes and expenditures; apart from that only the Roman King or the Emperor could examine the records; M. Diefenbacher (ed.), *Die Annalen der Reichsstadt Nürnberg von Johannes Müllner* (Nürnberg, Selbstverlag des Stadtarchivs Nürnberg, 2003), vol. 3, p. 31.
8. B. Fuhrmann, 'Die Bedeutung direkter und indirekter Steuern in ausgewählten Städten im Deutschen Reich (Römischen Reich) vom 14. bis ins 17. Jahrhundert', in *Fiscalità*, pp. 801–17, on pp. 806–8. P. Sander, *Die reichsstädtische Haushaltung Nürnbergs, dargestellt auf Grund ihres Zustandes von 1431 bis 1440* (Leipzig: Teubner Verlag, 1902), pp. 771–2, 784–5. B. Fuhrmann, 'Die Rentenverkäufe Nürnbergs vom Beginn der Überlieferung bis zur Mitte des 16. Jahrhunderts', to be published in *Mitteilungen des Vereins für Geschichte der Stadt Nürnberg*, 98 (2011).
9. Sander, *Haushaltung*, pp. 804–11, 823–33, 881–2.
10. R. Endres, 'Nürnberg in der Frühneuzei't, in Krüger, K. (ed.), *Europäische Städte im Zeitalter des Barock. Gestalt – Kultur – Sozialgefüge* (Köln/Wien, Böhlau Verlag, 1988), pp. 143–67, on pp. 145–7. J. Müller, 'Die Finanzpolitik des Nürnberger Rates in der zweiten Hälfte des 16. Jahrhunderts', *Vierteljahrsschrift für Social- und Wirtschaftsgeschichte*, 7 (1909), pp. 1–63.
11. W. Schwemmer, *Die Schulden der Reichsstadt Nürnberg und ihre Übernahme durch den bayerischen Staat* (Nürnberg: Selbstverlag der Stadtbibliothek, 1967), p. 13 (this sum was added by the relevant commission until the year 1810). M. Schieber, *Zinsen, Inflation, Schulden und Verschuldung in der Nürnberger Stadtgeschichte* (Nürnberg: Sandberg

Verlag, 2000), pp. 30–6. F. Buhl, 'Der Niedergang der reichsstädtischen Finanzwirtschaft und die kaiserliche Subdelegations-Kommission von 1797–1806', *Mitteilungen des Vereins für Geschichte der Stadt Nürnberg*, 26 (1926), pp. 111–278. H. Bingold, *Die reichsstädtische Haushaltung Nürnbergs während und nach dem Siebenjährigen Krieg (1756–1776)* (Nürnberg: Buch- und Kunstdruckerei Benedikt Hilz, 1911). W. Demel, *Reformen und sozialer Wandel, 1763–1806* (Stuttgart: Klett-Cotta, 2005), p. 207, estimates the debt in 1806 to 11,700,000 guilders.

12. P. Fleischmann, *Rat und Patriziat in Nürnberg. Die Herrschaft der Ratsgeschlechter vom 13. bis zum 18. Jahrhundert, Vol. 1: Der kleine Rat* (Neustadt a. d. Aisch, Verlagsdruckerei Schmidt, 2008), pp. 65, 187–203, 248–52.

13. Endres, 'Nürnberg', pp. 148–50.

14. B. Roeck, *Eine Stadt in Krieg und Frieden. Studien zur Geschichte der Reichsstadt Augsburg zwischen Kalenderstreit und Parität* (Göttingen: Vandenhoeck & Ruprecht, 1989), pp. 270–300. I. Bátori, 'Reichsstädtisches Regiment, Finanzen und bürgerliche Opposition', in G. Gottlieb et al. (eds), *Geschichte der Stadt Augsburg von der Römerzeit bis zur Gegenwart* (Stuttgart, Konrad Theiss Verlag, 1984), pp. 457–78. P. Fassl, *Konfession, Wirtschaft und Politik. Von der Reichsstadt zur Industriestadt, Augsburg 1750–1850* (Sigmaringen: Jan Thorbecke Verlag, 1988), pp. 171–89. I. Bátori, *Die Reichsstadt Augsburg im 18. Jahrhundert. Verfassung, Finanzen und Reformversuche* (Göttingen: Vandenhoeck & Ruprecht, 1969), pp. 97–105, 131, 196.

15. K. Rothe, *Das Finanzwesen der Reichsstadt Ulm im 18. Jahrhundert. Ein Beitrag zur Wirtschaftsgeschichte* (Ulm: Kommissionsverlag W. Kohlhammer, 1991), pp. 161, 180, 287, 358, 367–72, 448, 451.

16. T. Wolf, 'Memmingen im 17. Jahrhundert', in *Die Geschichte der Stadt Memmingen, 1: Von den Anfängen bis zum Ende der Reichsstadt* (Stuttgart: Konrad Theiss Verlag, 1997), pp. 541–676, on pp. 589–94. R. Huber-Sperl, 'Reichsstädtisches Wirtschaftsleben zwischen Tradition und Wandel', in ibid., pp. 679–782, on pp. 728–36.

17. H. Potthoff, *Der öffentliche Haushalt der Stadt Hamburg im 15. und 16. Jahrhundert*, in *Zeitschrift des Vereins für Hamburgische Geschichte XVI* (1911), pp. 1–85, on pp. 11, 29, 39, 43–4.

18. K. Zeiger, *Hamburgs Finanzen von 1563–1650* (Rostock: Carl Hinstorffs Verlag, 1936), pp. 29, 31, 63, 74, 89, 107–8, 123ff.

19. Bohnsack, H.-J., *Die Finanzverwaltung der Stadt Hamburg. Ihre Geschichte von den Anfängen bis zum Ersten Weltkrieg* (Hamburg: Verlag für Hamburgische Geschichte, 43, 1992), pp. 44–7. H. Reincke, 'Die alte Hamburger Stadtschuld der Hansezeit (1399–1563)', in *Städtewesen und Bürgertum als geschichtliche Kräfte, Gedächtnisschrift Fritz Rörig* (Lübeck: Verlag Max Schmidt-Römhild, 1953), pp. 489–511, on pp. 490, 510.

20. The last figures are calculated on the basis of H. Mauersberg, *Wirtschafts- und Sozialgeschichte zentraleuropäischer Städte in neuerer Zeit. Dargestellt an den Beispielen von Basel, Frankfurt a. M., Hamburg, Hannover und München* (Göttingen: Vandenhoeck & Ruprecht, 1960), pp. 462–3. In 1765–6 30.5 per cent of the revenue came from direct taxes, 16.7 per cent from indirect taxes, 9 per cent from customs revenue, and 19 per cent from repayments of loans. P. C. Hartmann, *Das Steuersystem der europäischen Staaten an Ende des Ancien Regime. Eine offizielle französische Enquete (1763–1769). Dokumente, Analyse und Auswertung. England und die Staaten Nord- und Mitteleuropas* (Zürich/München: Artemis Verlag, 1979), p. 144.

21. All data based on the following volumes: F. Bothe, *Die Entwicklung der direkten Besteuerung in der Reichsstadt Frankfurt bis zur Revolution 1612–1614* (Leipzig: Duncker

& Humblot, 1906). Mauersberg, *Wirtschafts- und Sozialgeschichte*, pp. 454–9. Fuhrmann, *Bedeutung*, pp. 810–11. W. Habich, *Das Weinungeld der Reichsstadt Frankfurt am Main. Die Entwicklungsgeschichte einer Getränkesteuer in Mittelalter und Neuzeit im Zusammenhang mit dem sogenannten Klingenheimer-Prozeß* (ND Aalen: Scientia Verlag, 1967). In the Swabian imperial cities the fiscal policy obviously damaged the lower classes; T. Wolf, *Reichsstädte in Kriegszeiten. Untersuchungen zur Verfassungs-Wirtschafts- und Sozialgeschichte von Isny, Lindau, Memmingen und Ravensburg im 17. Jahrhundert* (Memmingen: Verlag Memminger Zeitung, 1991), pp. 154, 160, 165, 214.

22. A. Dietz, *Frankfurter Handelsgeschichte* (Frankfurt/Main, 1925; ND Glashütten im Taunus: Verlag Detlev Auvermann, 1970), vol. 4, pt. 1, pp. 129–204. pt. 2, complete.

23. C. Looz-Corswarem, *Graf v., Das Finanzwesen der Stadt Köln im 18. Jahrhundert. Beitrag zur Verwaltungsgeschichte einer Reichsstadt* (Köln: Verlag der Buchhandlung Dr. H. Wamper GmbH, 1978), pp. 71–123, 128–55, 259–322. H.-W. Bergerhausen, *Köln in einem eisernen Zeitalter, 1610–1686* (Köln: Greven Verlag, 2010), pp. 269–87. On other demands for a reorganization of the finacial administration see U. Schmidt, *Südwestdeutschland im Zeichen der Französischen Revolution. Bürgeropposition in Ulm, Reutlingen und Esslingen* (Ulm: Kommissionsverlag W. Kohlhammer, 1993), pp. 100–6.

24. On legal treatment of the debt problem see C. Hattenhauer, 'Anmerkungen zur Regulierung der Staatschulden nach dem Dreißigjährigen Krieg', in G. Lingelbach (ed.), *Staatsfinanzen – Staatsverschuldung – Staatsbankrotte in der europäischen Staaten- und Rechtsgeschichte* (Köln/Weimar/Wien: Böhlau Verlag, 2000), pp. 123–44.

25. R. Hildebrandt, 'Zur Frage der reichsstädtischen Finanzen und Haushaltpolitik seit dem Westfälischen Frieden', in E. Maschke and J. Sydow (ed.), *Städtisches Haushalts- und Rechnungswesen* (Sigmaringen: Jan Thorbecke Verlag, 1977), pp. 91–107, on pp. 100–1. F. E. W. Tschaler, 'Die wirtschaftlichen, sozialen, kulturellen und politischen Folgen der Mediatisierung der Reichsstädte', in R. A. Müller, H. Flachenecker and R. Kammerl (eds), *Das Ende der kleinen Reichsstädte 1803 im süddeutschen Raum* (München: C. H. Beck Verlag, 2007), pp. 29–40, on pp. 32–5. W. Sponsel, 'Möchten wir das Glück der Ruhe, des dauerhaften Friedens und des Wohlstands'. Nördlingens Eingliederung in den bayerischen Staat 1802/03, in ibid., pp. 121–38, on pp. 124–5.

26. R. Schlögl, *Bauern, Krieg und Staat. Oberbayerische Bauernwirtschaft und frühmoderner Staat im 17. Jahrhundert* (Göttingen: Vandenhoeck & Ruprecht, 1988), p. 209. For the first in 1542 the Bavarian dukes reached a levy from indirect taxes on drinks, which in the following time could be administered without a consent with the estates, and which could be extended to other foodstuffs. At the beginning of the the seventeenth century these taxes come to more than 40 per cent of the official budget. D. Albrecht, 'Das Steuerwesen', in M. Spindler, *Max, Das alte Bayern. Der Territorialstaat vom Ausgang des 12. Jahrhunderts bis zum Ausgang des 18. Jahrhunderts* (München: C. H. Beck'sche Verlagsbuchhandlung, revised 1974), pp. 588–90, on p. 589.

27. M. Körner, 'Steuern und Abgaben in Theorie und Praxis im Mittelalter und in der frühen Neuzeit', in E. Schremmer (ed.), *Steuern, Abgaben und Dienste vom Mittelalter bis zur Gegenwart* (Stuttgart: Franz Steiner Verlag, 1994), pp. 53–76, on pp. 60–5. A. Schwennicke, *'Ohne Steuern kein Staat'. Zu Entwicklung und politischen Funktion des Steuerrechts in den Territorien des Heiligen Römischen Reichs* (Frankfurt a. M.: Vittorio Klostermann, 1983), pp. 73–103. H. Schulz, *Das System und die Prinzipien der Einkünfte im werdenden Staat der Neuzeit, dargestellt anhand der kameralwissenschaftlichen Literatur (1600–1835)* (Berlin: Duncker & Humblot, 1982), pp. 326–96.

28. Schremmer, E., Über 'Gerechte Steuern. Ein Blick zurück ins 19. Jahrhundert', in idem (ed.), Steuern, pp. 9–42.

29. J. Jenetzky, *System und Entwicklung des materiellen Steuerrechts in der wissenschaftlichen Literatur des Kameralismus von 1680 – 1840, dargestellt anhand der gedruckten zeitgenössischen Quellen* (Berlin: Duncker & Humblot, 1978), pp. 99–119.

30. P. Blickle, *Kommunalismus. Skizzen einer gesellschaftlichen Organisationsform*, 2 vols (München: Oldenbourg Wissenschaftsverlag, 2000), vol. 1, pp. 100–6, vol. 2, pp. 214–22. E. Isenmann, 'The Notion of the Common Good, the Concept of Politics, and Practical Policies in Late Medieval and Early Modern German Cities', in E. Lecuppre-Desjardin, A.-L. van Bruaene (eds), *De Bono Communi. The Discourse and Practise of the Common Good in the European City (13th–16th c.)/ Discours et pratique du Bien Communn dans les villes d'Europe (XIIIe au XVIe siècles)* (Turnhout: Brepols, 2010), pp. 107–48.

31. R. Bonney, 'Introduction', in idem (ed.), *Economic Systems and State Finance* (Oxford: Oxford University Press/Clarendon Press, 1995), pp. 1–18, on pp. 6, 13. In Prussia under Frederic II 75 per cent of the revenue or 82.4 per cent of verifiable expenditure were pumped into the military sector; W. Demel, *Europäische Geschichte des 18. Jahrhunderts. Ständische Gesellschaft und europäisches Mächtesystem im beschleunigten Wandel (1689/1700 – 1789/1800)* (Stuttgart/Berlin/Köln: Verlag W. Kohlhammer, 2000), p. 209.

32. W. Buchholz, *Geschichte der öffentlichen Finanzen in Europa in Spätmittelalter und Neuzeit. Darstellung – Analyse – Bibliographie* (Berlin: Akademie Verlag, 1996), pp. 17–8, 30.

33. V. Press, 'Der Merkantilismus und die Städte. Eine Einleitung', in idem (ed.), *Städtewesen und Merkantilismus in Europa* (Köln/Wien: Böhlau Verlag, 1983), pp. 1–14, on p. 3.

34. See E. Dittrich, *Die deutschen und österreichischen Kameralisten* (Darmstadt: Wissenschaftliche Buchgesellschaft, 1974). M. Sandl, *Ökonomie des Raumes. Der kameralistische Entwurf der Staatswirtschaft im 18. Jahrhundert* (Köln/Weimar/Wien: Böhlau Verlag, 1999).

35. M. Stolleis, *Geschichte des öffentlichen Rechts in Deutschland, Vol. I: Reichspublizistik und Policeywissenschaft 1600–1800* (München: C. H. Beck Verlag, 1988), pp. 378, 383.

36. Fuhrmann, *Bedeutung*, pp. 813–15. B. Fuhrmann, *Der Haushalt der Stadt Marburg in Spätmittelalter und Früher Neuzeit (1451/52 – 1622)* (St. Katharinen: Scripta Mercaturae Verlag, 1996), pp. 80–124, 237–9; K. Krüger, 'Entstehung und Ausbau des hessischen Steuerstaates vom 16. bis zum 18. Jahrhundert – Akten der Finanzverwaltung als frühneuzeitlicher Gesellschaftsspiegel', *Hessisches Jahrbuch für Landesgeschichte*, 32 (1982), pp. 103–25, on pp. 109, 112. K. Krüger, *Finanzstaat Hessen 1500–1567. Staatsbildung im Übergang vom Domänenstaat zum Steuerstaat* (Marburg, N. G. Elwert Verlag, 1980), pp. 279–84.

37. I. Schwab, 'Zeiten der Teuerung. Versorgungsprobleme in der zweiten Hälfte des 16. Jahrhunderts', in R. Bauer (ed.), *Geschichte der Stadt München* (München: C. H. Beck Verlag, 1992), pp. 167–88, on pp. 173, 176. M. P. Heimers, 'Die Strukturen einer barocken Residenzstadt. München zwischen Dreißigjährigem Krieg und dem Vorabend der Französischen Revolution', in ibid, pp. 211–43, on pp. 228, 234ff. Mauersberg, *Wirtschafts- und Sozialgeschichte*, pp. 470–1. Albrecht, *Steuerwesen*, p. 659. C. A. Hoffmann, *Landesherrliche Städte und Märkte im 17. und 18. Jahrhundert. Studien zu ihrer ökonomischen, rechtlichen und sozialen Entwicklung in Oberbayern* (Kallmünz/Opf., Verlag Michael Lassleben, 1997), pp. 407–16. C. A. Hoffmann, 'Integration in den frühneuzeitlichen Staat und Funktionsverlust – die altbayerischen Kleinstädte vom 16. bis

zum 18. Jahrhundert', in H. T. Gräf (ed.), *Kleine Städte im neuzeitlichen Europa* (Berlin: Berlin Verlag, 1997), pp. 83–109, on pp. 95–6.

38. H. H. v. Auer, *Das Finanzwesen der Stadt Freiburg von 1648 bis 1806, 1st pt. (1648–1700)* (Karlsruhe, Braunsche Hofbuchdruckerei, 1910), pp. 171–5, 185, 191.

39. K. Eiler, *Die kurtrierische Landstadt, in Geschichte der Stadt Koblenz, vol. 1: von den Anfängen bis zum Ende der kurfürstlichen Zeit* (Stuttgart: Konrad Theiss Verlag, 1992), pp. 137–61. M. Koelges, 'Handel und Gewerbe in der frühen Neuzeit', in ibid., pp. 333–47.

40. K. Müller, 'Unter pfalz-neuburgischer und pfalz-bayerischer Herrschaft (1614–1806)', in Weidenhaupt, H. (ed.), *Düsseldorf. Von den Ursprüngen bis ins 20. Jahrhundert, vol. 2: Von der Residenzstadt zur Beamtenstadt (1614–1900)* (Düsseldorf: Patmos Verlag, 1988), pp. 7–312, on pp. 102–7. H. Dinstühler, *Wein und Brot, Armut und Not. Wirtschaftskräfte und soziales Netz in der kleinen Stadt. Jülich im Spiegel vornehmlich kommunaler Haushaltsrechnungen des 16. und beginnenden 17. Jahrhunderts* (Jülich: Verlag der Joseph-Kuhl-Gesellschaft, 2001), pp. 44–115, 212–17. H. Engel, 'Finanzgeschichte des Herzogtums Jülich' (Diss. Bonn, 1958), pp. 70–82, 103–14.

41. P. Thomes, *Kommunale Wirtschaft und Verwaltung zwischen Mittelalter und Moderne. Bestandsaufnahme – Strukturen – Konjunkturen. Die Städte Saarbrücken und St. Johann im Rahmen der allgemeinen Entwicklung* (Stuttgart: Franz Steiner Verlag, 1995), pp. 121–71, tables 2–5, 9–13.

42. U. Wagner, 'Geschichte der Stadt zwischen Bergtheim 1400 und Bauernkrieg 1525', in idem (ed.), *Geschichte der Stadt Würzburg, here vol. 1: von den Anfängen bis zum Ausbruch des Bauernkriegs* (Stuttgart: Konrad Theiss Verlag, 2001), pp. 114–65. H.-P. Baum, 'Das konfessionelle Zeitalter (1525–1617)', in ibid., vol. 2: *Vom Bauernkrieg bis zum Übergang an das Königreich Bayern 1814* (Stuttgart: Konrad Theiss Verlag, 2004), pp. 50–100. H. Schott, 'Fürstlicher Absolutismus und barocke Stadt', in ibid., pp. 131–202.

43. All figures based on Mauersberg, *Wirtschafts- und Sozialgeschichte*, pp. 476–7. To the practice of credits in Hanover see B. Sturm, *'wat ich schuldich war' Privatkredit im frühneuzeitlichen Hannover (1550–1750)* (Stuttgart: Franz Steiner Verlag, 2009), pp. 104–13.

44. K. Schulz, 'Vom Herrschaftsantritt der Hohenzollern bis zum Ausbruch der Dreißigjährigen Krieges (1411/12–1618)', in W. Ribbe (ed.), *Geschichte Berlins, 1: Von der Frühgeschichte bis zur Industrialisierung*, 2nd edition (München: C. H. Beck Verlag, 1988), pp. 249–340, on pp. 262–3, 338. F. Escher, 'Die brandenburg-preußische Residenz und Hauptstadt Berlin im 17. und 18. Jahrhundert', in ibid., pp. 341–409, here pp. 349–59, 360–63, 381. W. Neugebauer, 'Brandenburg-Preußen in der Frühen Neuzeit', in idem (ed.), *Handbuch der Preußischen Geschichte, I: Das 17. und 18. Jahrhundert und Große Themen der Geschichte Preußens* (Berlin: Walter de Gruyter, 2009), pp. 113–407, here p. 201. I. Mieck, 'Preußen und Westeuropa', in ibid., pp. 411–851, on pp. 614ff.

WORKS CITED

Abadia, A., *La enajenación de las rentas señoriales en el reino de Aragón* (Saragossa: Institución Fernando el Católico, 1998).

Adla, F., 'L'endettement de la ville de Lyon au XVIIIe siècle', *Etudes et Documents*, 9 (1997), pp. 195–229.

Agnoletto, S., *Lo Stato di Milano al principio del Settecento. Finanza pubblica, sistema fiscale e interessi locali* (Milan: FrancoAngeli, 2000), pp. 287–90.

Agnoletto, S., 'The Spanish Heavy Tax-Regime: A Constraint on Capitalistic Moderniza-tion or a Matrix for Innovation? An Aspect of Accumulation in the "State of Milan" at the End of the Spanish Domination (1706)', in G. De Luca and G. Sabatini (eds), *In The Shadow of an Empire: How Spanish Colonialism Affected Economic Development in Europe and the World, 16th–18th Centuries* (Milan: FrancoAngeli, forthcoming).

Ago, R., *Carriere e clientele nella Roma barocca* (Bari: Laterza, 1990).

Ait, I., 'La dogana di S. Eustachio nel XV secolo', *Aspetti della vita economica e culturale a Roma nel Quattrocento* (Rome: Istituto di Studi Romani, 1981), pp. 81–147.

Albrecht, D., 'Das Steuerwesen', in M. Spindler, *Das alte Bayern. Der Territorialstaat vom Ausgang des 12. Jahrhunderts bis zum Ausgang des 18. Jahrhunderts* (Munich: C. H. Becksche Verlagsbuchhandlung, ed. revised 1974), pp. 588–90.

Alonso Mendizábal, C., *Blas de Lezo 'El Malquerido'* (Burgos: Dossoles, 2008).

Ammerer, G., 'Die Stände in der Habsburgermonarchie. Eine Einleitung', in G. Ammerer, W. D. Godsey, Jr., M. Scheutz, P. Urbanitsch and A. S. Weiß (eds), *Bündnispartner und Konkurrenten der Landesfürsten. Die Stände der Habsburgermonarchie* (Vienna and Munich: Oldenbourg 2006) pp. 13–41.

Andrés Ucendo, J. I., *La fiscalidad en Castilla en el siglo XVII. Los servicios de millones. 1601–1700* (Lejona: Universidad del País Vasco, 1999).

—, 'Castile's Tax System in the Seventeenth Century', *Journal of European Economic History*, 30:3 (2001), pp. 597–616.

—, 'Fiscalidad real y fiscalidad municipal en Castilla durante el siglo XVII: el caso de Madrid', *Investigaciones de Historia Económica*, 5 (2006), pp. 41–70.

—, 'Government Policies and the Development of the Financial Markets: The Case of Madrid in the Seventeenth Century', in F. Piola Caselli (ed.), *Government Debts and Financial Markets in Europe* (London: Pickering & Chatto, 2008), pp. 67–80.

—, '¿Quién pagó los impuestos en la Castilla del siglo XVII? El impacto de los tributos sobre el vino en Madrid', *Studia Historica. Historia Moderna*, 32 (2010), pp. 229–57.

Andrés Ucendo, J. I., and R. Lanza, 'Municipal Taxes, Prices and Real Wages in XVIIth Century Castile: the Case of Madrid', paper presented at the World Economic History Congress, Utrecht 2009, Session Q6: '*Urban Fiscal Systems and Economic Growth in Europe, 16th–18th Centuries*', <http://www.wehc-2009.org>.

Archer, I., 'The Burden of Taxation on Sixteenth-Century London', *The Historical Journal*, 44:3 (2001), pp. 599–621.

Ardant, G., *Historie de l'impôt* (Paris: Fayard, 1971).

Arnould, M. A., 'L'impôt dans l'histoire des peuples. Exposé introductive au colloque', L'impôt dans le cadre de la ville et de l'état. Colloque international, Spa, 6–9, LX, 1964, *Pro Civitate. Collection Histoire*, 8°, nr. 13 (1966), pp. 13–26.

Arnould, M. A., 'L'impot sur le capital en Belgique au XVIe siècle', *Le Hainaut économique* 1(1946), pp. 17–45.

Artola, M., *La Hacienda del Antiguo Régimen* (Madrid: Alianza, 1982).

Atienza, A., *Propiedad y señorío en Aragón* (Saragossa: Institución Fernando el Católico, 1993).

Atienza, A., Colás, G. Serrano, E., *El señorío de Aragón (1610–1640). Cartas de población* (Saragossa: Institución Fernando el Católico, 1998).

Auer, H. H. v., *Das Finanzwesen der Stadt Freiburg von 1648 bis 1806, 1st pt. (1648–1700)* (Karlsruhe: Braunsche Hofbuchdruckerei, 1910).

Bairoch, P., *Da Jericho a Mexico. Villes et economie dans l'histoire* (Paris: Gallimard, 1985).

Balen, M., *Beschrijvinge der stad Dordrecht, vervatende haar begin, opkomst, toeneming, en verdere stant*, 2 vols (Dordrecht: Symon Onder de Linde, 1677).

Baltzarek, F., 'Beiträge zur Geschichte des vierten Standes in Niederösterreich. Eine vergleichende Stadtgeschichtsuntersuchung mit besonderer Auswertung der Gaisruckschen Städteordnungen von 1745–1747', *Mitteilungen des Östesrreichen Staatsarchivs*, 23 (1970), pp. 64–104.

—, *Das Steueramt der Stadt Wien 1526–1760* (Vienna: Notring 1971).

Bangs, J. D., 'Holland's civic lijfrente loans (XVth century): some recurrent problems', *Publications du Centre Européen d'études Burgondo-médianes*, 23 (1983), pp. 75–82.

Barone, G., 'Mezzogiorno ed egemonie urbane', *Meridiana*, 5 (1989), pp. 13–47.

Bátori, I., *Die Reichsstadt Augsburg im 18. Jahrhundert. Verfassung, Finanzen und Reformversuche* (Göttingen: Vandenhoeck & Ruprecht, 1969).

—, 'Reichsstädtisches Regiment, Finanzen und bürgerliche Opposition', in G. Gottlieb et al. (eds), *Geschichte der Stadt Augsburg von der Römerzeit bis zur Gegenwart* (Stuttgart: Konrad Theiss Verlag, 1984), pp. 457–78.

Baum, H-P., 'Das konfessionelle Zeitalter (1525–1617)', in U. Wagner (ed.), *Geschichte der Stadt Würzburg, vol. II: Vom Bauernkrieg bis zum Übergang an das Königreich Bayern 1814* (Stuttgart: Konrad Theiss Verlag, 2004), pp. 50–100.

Bayard, F., *Le monde des financiers au XVIIe siècle* (Paris: Flammarion, 1988).

Beloch, K. J., *Bevölkerungsgeschichte Italiens* (Leipzig, De Gruyter & Co: 1961).

—, *Storia della popolazione italiana* (Florence: Casa Editrice Le Lettere, 1994).

Bérenger, J., *Finances et absolutism autrichien dans la seconde moitié du XVIIe siècle* (Paris: Champio, 1975).

Bergerhausen, H.-W., *Köln in einem eisernen Zeitalter, 1610–1686* (Cologne: Greven Verlag, 2010).

Bernal, A. M., *La financiación de la Carrera de Indias* (Sevilla-Madrid: Escuela de Estudios Hispanoamericanos, 1992).

Bertini, C. A., *La storia delle famiglie romane*, 2 vols (Rome: Collegio Araldico, 1914).

Bingold, H., *Die reichsstädtische Haushaltung Nürnbergs während und nach dem Siebenjährigen Krieg (1756–1776)* (Nürnberg: Buch und Kunstdruckerei Benedikt Hilz, 1911).

Blaich, F., 'Die oberdeutsche Reichsstadt als Arbeitgeber vom 13. bis zum 16. Jahrhundert', *Die Alte Stadt*, 9 (1982), pp. 1–18.

Blécourt, A.S. de and Fischer H.F.W.D., *Kort begrip van het Oud-Vaderlands Burgerlijk Recht*, 7th edn (Groningen: Wolters, 1959).

Blickle, P., *Kommunalismus. Skizzen einer gesellschaftlichen Organisationsform*, 2 vols (Munich: Oldenbourg Wissenschaftsverlag, 2000).

Blockmans, F., 'De stadsfinanciën', *Antwerpen in de XVIIIe eeuw, Instellingen, economie, cultuur* (Antwerpen: de Sikkel, 1952).

—, 'Finances publiques et inégalité sociale dans les pays-bas aux XIVe-XVIe siècles', in J.P. Genet and M. Le Mené (eds), *Genèse de l'état moderne: prélèvement at redistribution. Actes du colloque du Fontevraud* (Paris: CNRS, 1987), pp. 77–90.

—, 'Voracious States and Obstructing Cities: An Aspect of State Formation in Preindustrial Europe', *Theory and Society*, 18:5 (1989), pp. 733–56.

—, 'The Impact of Cities on State Formation: Three Contrasting Territories in the Low Countries, 1300–1500', in P. Blickle (ed.), *Resistance, Representation, and Community, part V. The Urban Belt and the Emerging Modern State* (Oxford: Oxford University Press, 1997), pp. 256–71.

Blondé, B., and J. Hanus, 'Beyond Building Cratsmen: Economic Growth and Living Standards in the Sixteenth-Century Low-Countries: The Case of 's-Hertogenbosch (1500–1560)', *European Review of Economic History*, 14 (2009), pp. 179–207.

Blok, P. J., *Geschiedenis eener Hollandsche stad*, 2 vols (The Hague: Martinus Nijhoff, 1910).

Bohnsack, H.-J., *Die Finanzverwaltung der Stadt Hamburg. Ihre Geschichte von den Anfängen bis zum Ersten Weltkrieg* (Hamburg: Verlag für Hamburgische Geschichte, 43, 1992).

Bonney, R., 'Introduction. Economic Systems and State Finance', in R. Bonney (ed.), *Economic Systems and State Finance* (Oxford: Clarendon Press, 1995).

—, *Economic Systems and State Finance* (Oxford: Clarendon Press, 1995).

— (ed.), *The Rise of the Fiscal State in Europe c. 1200–1815* (Oxford: Clarendon Press, 1999).

Bonney, R., and W. M. Ormrod, 'Introduction. Crises, Revolutions and Self-Sustained Growth: Towards a Conceptual Model of Change in Fiscal History', in W. M. Ormrod, R. Bonney and M. Bonney (eds), *Crises, Revolutions and Self-Sustained Growth* (Stanford: Shaun Tyas, 1999).

Boone, M., *Geld en macht. De Gentse stadsfinanciën en de Bourgondische staatsvorming (1384–1453)* (Ghent: Maatschappij voor Geschiedenis en Oudheidkunde, 1990).

—, '"Plus dueil que joie". Renteverkopen door de stad Gent in de Bourgondische periode: tussen private belangen en stedelijke financiën', *Gemeentekrediet van België: driemaandelijks tijdschrift*, 45 (1991–2), pp. 3–25.

Boone, M, D. Machteld and B. Reusens, *Immobiliënmarkt, fiscaliteit en sociale gelijkheid te Gent* (Kortrijk–Heule: UGA, 1983).

Boone, M., K. Davids and P. Janssens (eds), *Urban Public Debts. Urban Government and the Market for Annuities in Western Europe (14th–18th Centuries)* (Turnhout: Brepols 2003).

Boone, M, K. Davids and P. Janssens, 'Urban Public Debts from the 14th to the 18th Centuries: A New Approach', in M. Boone, K. Davids and P. Janssens (eds), *Urban Public Debts. Urban Goverment and the Market for Annuities in Western Europe (14th–18th Centuries)* (Turnhout: Brepols 2003).

Bordes, M., *La réforme municipale du contrôleur général Laverdy et son application (1764–1771)* (Toulouse: Fac. Lettres, 1968).

—, *L'administration provinciale et municipale en France au XVIIIe siècle* (Paris: SEDES, 1972).

Bos-Rops, J. A. M. Y., *Graven op zoek naar geld: de inkomsten van de graven van Holland en Zeeland, 1389–1433* (Hilversum: Verloren, 1993).

Bothe, F., *Die Entwicklung der direkten Besteuerung in der Reichsstadt Frankfurt bis zur Revolution 1612 – 1614* (Leipzig: Duncker & Humblot, 1906).

Boumans, R., 'Het verhandelen van stedelijke officiën te Antwerpen in de XVIIIe eeuw', *Bijdragen voor de geschiedenis der Nederlanden*, 3 (1948), pp. 42–68.

—, *Het Antwerps stadsbestuur voor en tijdens de Franse overheersing. Bijdrage tot de ontwikkelingsgeschiedenis van de stedelijke bestuursinstellingen in de Zuidelijke Nederlanden* (Brugge: de Tempel, 1965).

Bowsky, W. M., *The Finance of the Commune of Siena, 1287–1355* (Oxford: Clarendon Press, 1970).

Boyse, S., *An Historical Review of the Transactions of Europe from the Commencement of the War with Spain in 1739 to the Insurrection of Scotland in 1745* (Reading, 1747).

Braddick, M., *The Nerves of state, Taxation and the Financing of the English State, 1588–1714* (Manchester: Manchester University Press, 1996).

Braudel, F., 'Les emprunts de Charles-Quint sur la place d'Anvers', *Charles-Quint et son temps* (Paris, 1972), pp. 191–202.

Brunner, O., *Die Finanzen der Stadt Wien von den Anfängen bis ins 16. Jahrhundert* (Vienna: Deutscher Verlag für Jugend und Volk, 1929), pp. 46–9.

—, *Die Rechtsquellen der Städte Krems und Stein* (Graz and Cologne: Böhlau, 1954), pp. 272–98.

Buchholz, W., *Geschichte der öffentlichen Finanzen in Europa in Spätmittelalter und Neuzeit. Darstellung – Analyse – Bibliographie* (Berlin: Akademie Verlag, 1996).

Buhl, F., 'Der Niedergang der reichsstädtischen Finanzwirtschaft und die kaiserliche Subdelegations-Kommission von 1797–1806', *Mitteilungen des Vereins für Geschichte der Stadt Nürnberg*, 26 (1926), pp. 111–278.

Bulgarelli Lukacs, A., *L'imposta diretta nel regno di Napoli* (Milan: FrancoAngeli, 1993).

—, *Alla recerca del contribuente. Fisco, cadasto, gruppi di poteres, ceti emergenti nel Regno di Napoli del XVIII secolo* (Naples: Edizione Scientifiche Italiane, 2004).

—, 'Misurare l'imponibile. Le scelte dello Stato tra gruppi di pressione e ceti emergenti (Regno di Napoli, secolo XVIII)', in R. de Lorenzo, *Storia e misura. Indicatori sociali ed economici nel Mezzogiorno d'Italia* (Milan: FrancoAngeli, 2007), pp. 39–74.

—, 'Il debito pubblico in ambito municipale. Stato, comunità e creditori nel Regno di Napoli tra Seicento e Settecento', in G. De Luca and A. Moioli (eds), *Debito pubblico e mercati finanziari. Secoli XIII–XX* (Milan: FrancoAngeli, 2007), pp. 327–46.

—, 'The Fiscal System in the Kingdom of Naples: Tools for Comparison with the European Reality (13th–18th Centuries)', in S. Cavaciocchi (ed.) *La fiscalità nell'economia europea. Secc. XIII–XVIII. Fiscal Systems in the European Economy from the 13th to the 18th Centuries* (Florence: Olschki, 2008), pp. 241–57.

—, 'La popolazione del regno di Napoli nel Primo Seicento (1595–1648). Analisi differenziale degli effetti distributivi della crisi e ipotesi di quantificazione delle perdite demografiche', *Popolazione e Storia*, 1 (2009), pp. 77–113.

—, *La finanza locale sotto controllo. Il regno de Napoli di primo Seicento* (Venice: Marsilio, 2012).

Busolini, D., 'Il porto di Ripa Grande a Roma durante la prima metà del XVII secolo', *Studi Romani*, 42 (1994), pp. 249–73.

Canga Argüelles, J. de, *Diccionario de Hacienda con Aplicación a España* (1834) (Madrid: Instituto de Estudios Fiscales, 1968).

Capasso, B., *Catalogo ragionato dei libri, registri e scritturi esistenti nella sezione antica e prima serie dell'Archivio municipale di Napoli (1387–1806)*, I (Naples: Giannini, 1876).

Capra, C., 'The Italian States in the Early Modern Period', in R. Bonney (ed.), *The Rise of the Fiscal State in Europe, c. 1200–1815* (Oxford: Oxford University Press, 1999), pp. 417–42.

Caracciolo, F., *Sud, debiti e gabelle. Gravami, potere e società nel Mezzogiorno in etá moderna* (Naples: Edizione Scientifiche Italiane, 1983).

Carande, R., *Carlos V y sus banqueros* (Barcelona: Crítica, 1991).

Caravale, M., and A. Caracciolo, 'Lo Stato pontificio da Martino V a Pio IX', in G. Galasso (ed.), *Storia d'Italia*, vol. 14 (Turin: Utet, 1978).

Carbajo, M., *La población de la villa de Madrid desde finales del siglo XVI hasta mediados del siglo XIX* (Madrid: Alianza, 1987).

Cárceles de Gea, B., *Fraude y administración fiscal en Castilla. La Comisión de Millones (1632–1658): poder fiscal y privilegio jurídico-político.* (Madrid: Banco de España, 1994).

—, *Reforma y fraude fiscal en el reinado de Carlos II. La Sala de Millones* (Madrid: Banco de España, 1995).

Chaussinand-Nogaret, G., *Les financiers de Languedoc au XVIIIe siècle* (Paris: SEVPEN, 1972).

Chittolini, G., 'Notes sur la politique fiscale de Charles Quint dans le Duché de Milan: Le "nuovo catasto" et les rappots entre ville et campagne', in W. Blockmans, P. Mout and E. H. Nicolette (eds), *The World of Emperor Charles V* (Amsterdam: Royal Netherlands Academy of Arts and Sciences, 2004), pp. 143–60.

Cipolla, C. M., 'The Economic Decline of Italy', in B. Pullan (ed.), *Crisis and Change in the Venetian Economy* (London: Methuen, 1968), pp. 127–145.

Colas, G., *La bailía de Caspe en los siglos XVI y XVII* (Saragossa: Institución Fernando el Católico, 1979).

Colzi, F., *Il debito pubblico del Campidoglio. Finanza comunale e circolazione dei titoli a Roma fra Cinque e Seicento* (Naples: Edizioni Scientifiche Italiane, 1999).

Comín, F., *Hacienda y economía en la España contemporánea, 1800–1936* (Madrid: Instituto de Estudios Fiscales, 1988).

Coniglio, G., *Il viceregno di Napoli nel secolo XVII. Nuove notizia sulla vita commerciale e finanziaria tratte dagli archivi napoletani* (Naples: Edizioni di Storia e Letteratura, 1955).

Corritore, R. P., 'Il processo di "ruralizzazione" in Italia nei secoli XVII e XVIII', *Rivista di Storia Economica*, 2 (1993), pp. 353–86.

Cos-Gayón, F., *Historia de la administración pública en España (1851)* (Madrid: Instituto de Estudios Administrativos, 1987).

Courdurie, M., *La Dette des Collectivités Publiques de Marseille au XVIIIe siècle. Du débat sur le prêt à intérêt au financement par l'emprunt* (Marseille: Institut Historique de Provence, 1974).

Cova, A., *Il Banco di S. Ambrogio nell'economia milanese dei secoli XVII e XVIII* (Milan: Giuffrè, 1972).

Curtin, P., *The Atlantic Slave Trade: A Census* (Madison, WI: University of Wisconsin Press, 1969).

Dal Pane, L., *Lo Stato pontificio e il movimento riformatore del Settecento* (Milan: Giuffrè editore, 1959).

Dambruyne, J., *Mensen en centen. Het 16de-eeuwse Gent in demografisch en economisch perspectief* (Ghent: Maatschappij voor Geschiedenis en Oudheidkunde, 2001).

—, *Corporatieve middengroepen: aspiraties, relaties en transformaties in de 16e-eeuwse Gentse ambachtswereld* (Ghent: Academia Press, 2002).

D'Amico, S., 'Crisis and Transformation: Economic Reorganization and Social Structures in Milan, 1570–1610', *Social History*, 25 (2000), p. 1.

De Cupis, C., *Le vicende dell'agricoltura e della pastorizia nell'agro romano. L'annona di Roma giusta memorie, consuetudini e leggi desunte da documenti anche inediti. Sommario storico* (Rome: Tipografia nazionale di G. Bertero, 1911).

De Gennaro, G., *L'esperienza monetaria di Roma in età moderna (secc. XVI–XVIII). Tra stabilizzazione e inflazione* (Naples: Edizioni Scientifiche Italiane, 1980).

De Luca, G., *Commercio del denaro e crescita economica a Milano tra Cinquecento e Seicento* (Milan: Il Polifilo, 1996).

—, 'Mercanti imprenditori, élite artigiane e organizzazioni produttive: la definizione del sistema corporativo milanese (1568–1627)', in A. Guenzi, P. Massa and A. Moioli (eds),

Corporazioni e gruppi professionali nell'Italia moderna (Milan: FrancoAngeli, 1999), pp. 79–116.

—, 'Government Debt and Financial Markets: Exploring Pro-cycle Effects in Northern Italy during the Sixteenth and the Seventeenth Centuries', in F. Piola Caselli (ed.), *Government Debts and Financial Markets in Europe* (London: Pickering & Chatto, 2008), pp. 45–66.

Delumeau, J., *Vie économique et sociale de Rome dans la seconde moitié du XVIe siècle*, 2 vols (Paris: Boccard, 1957–59).

—, *Vita economica e sociale di Roma nel Cinquecento* (Florence: Sansoni Editore, 1979).

Demel, W., *Europäische Geschichte des 18. Jahrhunderts. Ständische Gesellschaft und europäisches Mächtesystem im beschleunigten Wandel (1689/1700–1789/1800)* (Stuttgart/ Berlin/Cologne: Verlag W. Kohlhammer, 2000).

—, *Reformen und sozialer Wandel, 1763–1806* (Stuttgart: Klett-Cotta, 2005).

Derijcke, L., 'The Public Annuity Market in Bruges at the End of the 15th Century', in M. Boone, K. Davids and P. Janssens (eds), *Urban Public Debts. Urban Goverment and the Market for Annuities in Western Europe (14th–18th Centuries)* (Turnhout: Brepols, 2003), pp. 165–81.

Dessert, D., *Argent, pouvoir et société au Grand Siècle* (Paris. Fayard, 1984).

Dickson, P. G. M., *The Financial Revolution in England: A Study in the Development of Public Credit, 1688–1756* (London: MacMillan, 1967).

Dickstein-Bernard, C., *La gestion financière d'une capitale à ses débuts: Bruxelles 1334–1467* (Brussels, 1977).

Diefenbacher, M., *Die Annalen der Reichsstadt Nürnberg von Johannes Müllner, vol. III* (Nürnberg: Selbstverlag des Stadtarchivs Nürnberg, 2003).

Dietz, A., *Frankfurter Handelsgeschichte*, vol. 4 (Frankfurt/Main 1925, ND Glashütten im Taunus: Verlag Detlev Auvermann, 1970).

Dinstühler, H., *Wein und Brot, Armut und Not. Wirtschaftskräfte und soziales Netz in der kleinen Stadt. Jülich im Spiegel vornehmlich kommunaler Haushaltsrechnungen des 16. und beginnenden 17. Jahrhunderts* (Jülich: Verlag der Joseph-Kuhl-Gesellschaft, 2001).

Dirk, H., *Hollands los- en lijfrenteleningen vóór 1672* (Schiedam: Roelants, 1950).

Dirlmeier, U., *Untersuchungen zu Einkommensverhältnissen und Lebenshaltungskosten in oberdeutschen Städten des Spätmittelalters. (Mitte 14. bis Anfang 16. Jahrhundert)* (Heidelberg: Carl Winter Universitätsverlag, 1978).

Dirlmeier, U., 'Stadt und Bürgertum. Zur Steuerpolitik und zum Stadt-Land-Verhältnis', in H. Buszello, P. Blickle and R. Endres (eds), *Der deutsche Bauernkrieg* (Paderborn/Munich/ Vienna/Zürich: Ferdinand Schöningh, 3. bibliographisch erg. Aufl, 1995), pp. 254–80.

Dittrich, E., *Die deutschen und österreichischen Kameralisten* (Darmstadt: Wissenschaftliche Buchgesellschaft, 1974).

Dokkum, H. W., and E. C Dijkhof, *Oude Dordtse lijfrenten. Stedelijke financiering in de vijftiende eeuw* (Amsterdam: Verloren, 1983).

Domínguez Ortiz, A., *Política y Hacienda de Felipe IV* (Madrid: Editorial de Derecho Financiero, 1960).

Dormer, D. J., *Discursos histórico-políticos* (Saragossa: l'Astral, 1989, facsimile of the original printed in 1684).

Durand, Y., *Les fermiers généraux au XVIIIe siècle* (Paris: Maisonneuve et Larose, 1997).

Durlauf S. N., and Blume L. E. (eds), *The New Palgrave Dictionary of Economics* (Palgrave: MacMillan, 2008, 2nd ed.).

Ebner, H., 'Zur Ideologie des mittelalterlichen Städtebürgertums aufgrund österreichischer Stadtrechte des späten Mittelalters', *Jahrbuch für Geschichte des Feudalismus*, 7 (1983), pp. 157–84.

Eiler, K., 'Die kurtrierische Landstadt', in *Geschichte der Stadt Koblenz, vol. 1: von den Anfängen bis zum Ende der kurfürstlichen Zeit* (Stuttgart: Konrad Theiss Verlag, 1992), pp. 137–61.

Emmanuelli, F.-X., *Un mythe de l'absolutisme bourbonien. L'intendance du milieu du XVIIe siècle à la fin du XVIIIe siècle (France, Espagne, Amérique)* (Aix-en-Provence: PUP, 1981).

Endres, R., 'Nürnberg in der Frühneuzeit', in K. Krüger (ed.), *Europäische Städte im Zeitalter des Barock. Gestalt –Kultur– Sozialgefüge* (Cologne/Vienna: Böhlau Verlag, 1988), pp. 143–67.

Engel, H., *Finanzgeschichte des Herzogtums Jülich* (Diss. Bonn 1958).

Esch, A., 'Immagine di Roma tra realtà religiosa e dimensione politica nel Quattro e Cinquecento', in L. Fiorani and A. Prosperi (eds), *Storia d'Italia. Annali 16. Roma la città del Papa. Vita civile e religiosa dal giubileo di Bonifacio VIII al giubileo di papa Wojtyla* (Turin: Einaudi, 2000).

—, 'Mercanti tedeschi e merci a Roma nella seconda metà del Quattrocento', *Archivi e Cultura*, 37 (2004), pp. 47–56.

Escher, F., 'Die brandenburg-preußische Residenz und Hauptstadt Berlin im 17. und 18. Jahrhundert', in W. Ribbe (ed.), *Geschichte Berlins, 1: Von der Frühgeschichte bis zur Industrialisierung*, controlled Ed. (Munich: C. H. Beck Verlag, 1988), pp. 341–409.

Escher, M., A. Haverkamp and F. G. Hirschmann (eds), *Städtelandschaft – Städtenetz – zentralörtliches Gefüge. Ansätze und Befunde zur Geschichte der Städte im hohen und späten Mittelalter* (Mainz: von Zabern, 2000).

Fassl, P., *Konfession, Wirtschaft und Politik. Von der Reichsstadt zur Industriestadt, Augsburg 1750 – 1850* (Sigmaringen: Jan Thorbecke Verlag, 1988).

Felix, J., *Economie et finances sous l'Ancien Régime. Guide du chercheur (1523–1789)* (Paris: 1994).

—, *Finances et politique au siècle des Lumières. Le ministère L'Averdy (1763–1768)* (Paris: CHEFF, 1999).

—, 'Les finances urbaines au lendemain de la guerre de Sept Ans', in F. Bayard (ed.), *Les finances en province sous l'Ancien Régime* (Paris: Comité pour l'histoire économique et financière de la France, 2000), pp. 179–228.

Felloni, G., 'Finanze statali, emissioni monetari ed alterazioni della moneta di conto in Italia nei secoli XVI–XVIII', *Atti della società ligure di storia patria*, 38 (1998), vol I.

Fernández de Pinedo, E., 'Coyuntura y política económicas', in M. Tuñón de Lara (ed.), *Historia de España. Vol VII. Centralismo, Ilustración y agonía del Antiguo Régimen (1715–1833)* (Barcelona: Labor, 1980), pp. 9–173.

Flachenecker, H., and R. Kiessling (eds), *Städtelandschaften in Altbayern, Franken und Schwaben. Studien zum Phänomen der Kleinstädte während des Spätmittelalters und der Frühen Neuzeit* (Munich: Beck, 1999).

Fleischmann, P., *Rat und Patriziat in Nürnberg. Die Herrschaft der Ratsgeschlechter vom 13. bis zum 18. Jahrhundert, Vol. 1: Der kleine Rat* (Neustadt a. d. Aisch: Verlagsdruckerei Schmidt, 2008).

Fortea, J. I., *Las Cortes de Castilla y León bajo los Austrias. Una interpretación histórica* (Valladolid: Junta de Castilla y León, 2008).

Fritschy, W., 'Three Centuries of Urban and Provincial Public Debt: Amsterdam and Holland', in M. Boone, K. Davids and P. Jenssens (eds), *Urban Public Debts. Urban Government and the Market for Annuities in Western Europe (14th–18th Centuries)* (Turnhout: Brepols, 2003), pp. 75–92.

Fritschy, W., 'Indirect taxes and Public Debt in the World of Islam', in S. Cavaciocchi (ed.) *La Fiscalità nell'economia europea, secc. XIII–XVIII* (Florence: Olschki, 2008), pp. 51–73.

Fuhrmann, B., *Der Haushalt der Stadt Marburg in Spätmittelalter und Früher Neuzeit (1451–52 – 1622)* (St Katharinen: Scripta Mercaturae Verlag, 1996).

—, 'Die Bedeutung direkter und indirekter Steuern in ausgewählten Städten im Deutschen Reich (Römischen Reich) vom 14. bis ins 17. Jahrhundert', in S. Cavaciocchi (ed.), *La Fiscalità nell'Economia Europea Secc. XIII–XVIII/Fiscal Systems in the European Economy from the 13th to the 18th Centuries* (Florence: Olschki, 2008), pp. 801–17.

—, 'Die Rentenverkäufe Nürnbergs vom Beginn der Überlieferung bis zur Mitte des 16. Jahrhunderts', will be published in *Mitteilungen des Vereins für Geschichte der Stadt Nürnberg*, 98 (2011).

Galasso, G., *Economia e società nella Calabria del Cinquecento* (Milan: Feltrinelli, 1975).

—, 'Puglia: tra provinzializzazione e modernità', in C. D. Fonseca (ed.), *La Puglia tra barocco e rococó. Civiltá e culture di Puglia* (Milan: Electra, 1982), vol. 4, pp. 373–86.

García Baquero, A., 'Las remesas de metales preciosos americanos en el siglo XVIII: una aritmética controvertida', *Hispania LVI/I* (1996), pp. 203–26.

García García, C., *La crisis de las Haciendas Locales. De la reforma administrativa a la reforma fiscal, 1743–1835* (Valladolid: Junta de Castilla y León, 1996).

García Lombardero, J., 'Algunos problemas de la administración y cobranza de las rentas provincials en la primera mitad del siglo XVIII', in A. de Otazu (ed.) *Dinero y crédito (siglos XVI al XIX)* (Madrid: Moneda y Crédito, 1978), pp, 63–87.

García Sanz, A., 'Repercusiones de la fiscalidad sobre la economía castellana en los siglos XVI y XVII', *Hacienda Pública Española*, 1 (1991), pp. 15–24.

Garnot, B., 'Les budgets de la ville de Chartres de 1727 à 1788', *Enquêtes et Documents* (Paris: CHEFF, 1993), vol. 5, pp. 79–98.

Gelabert González, J. E., 'Urbanization and De-Urbanization in Castile', in B. Yun and I. A. A. Thompson (eds), *The Castilian Crises of the Seventeenth Century* (Cambridge: Cambridge University Press, 1994).

Gelabert González, J. E., 'Cities, Towns and Small Towns in Castile', *Small Towns in Early Modern Europe* (Cambridge: Cambridge University Press, 1995).

Gelabert González, J. E., *La Bolsa del Rey* (Barcelona: Crítica, 1997).

Gelderblom, O., and J. Joonker, 'Public Finance and Economic Growth: The Case of Holland in the Seventeenth Century', *Journal of Economic History*, 71:1 (2011), pp. 1–38.

Gemeiner, C. T., *Regensburgische Chronik* (ND Munich: C.H. Beck Verlag, 1971).

Genet, J.-P., 'L'état moderne: un modèle opératorie?', in J.-P. Genet (ed.), *L'état moderne: genèse. Bilans et perspectives* (Paris: CNRS, 1990), pp. 261–81.

Gerard, P., 'Ethique d'une action. Les budgets municipaux à Nantes (quatre comptes entre 1663 et 1712)' (PhD dissertation, University of Nantes, 1994).

Gerteis, K., 'Einleitung', in K. Gerteis (ed.), *Stadt und frühmoderner Staat. Beiträge zur städtischen Finanzgeschichte von Luxemburg, Lunéville, Mainz, Saarbrücken und Trier im 17. und 18. Jahrhundert* (Trier: THF, 1994), pp. 1–12.

Giannini, M. C., 'Conflitti e compromessi. Il problema dell'esenzione fiscale del clero nella Città di Milano nella seconda metà del Cinquecento', *Trimestre*, 40 (2007), pp. 1–4.

Gómez Zorraquino, J. I., *Zaragoza y el capital comercial: la burguesía mercantil en el Aragón de la segunda mitad del siglo XVII* (Saragossa: Ayuntamiento, 1987).

Gräf, H. T., and Keller, K. (eds), *Städtelandschaft – Résau urbain – Urban network. Städte im regionalen Kontext in Spätmittelalter und früher Neuzeit* (Cologne and Vienna: Böhlau, 2004).

Groot, H. J. M. de, *Venle/Venlo. Hoe een stadje begon* (Zutphen: Walburg Pers, 2003).

Gross, H., *Rome in the Age of Enlightenment: The Post-Tridentine Syndrome and the Ancien Regime* (Cambridge: Cambridge University Press, 1990).

Guery, A., 'Les finances de la monarchie', *Annales, ESC* (March–April 1978), pp. 216–39.

—, 'Etat, classification sociale et compromis sous Louis XIV: la capitation de 1695', *Annales, ESC*, (September–October, 1986), pp. 1041–60.

Guignet, P., *Le pouvoir dans la ville au XVIIIe siècle. Pratiques politiques, notabilité et éthique sociale de part et d'autre de la frontière franco-belge* (Paris: EHESS, 1990).

—, 'Logiques financières, contraintes étatiques externes et fluctuations conjoncturelles : l'inégale originalité du modèle financier des grandes villes de la France du nord au XVI-IIe siècle', in F. Bayard, *Les finances en province sous l'Ancien Régime* (Paris: Comité pour l'histoire économique et financière de la France, 2000), pp. 229–57.

Gutiérrez Alonso, A., *Estudio sobre la decadencia de Castilla. La ciudad de Valladolid en el siglo XVII* (Valladolid: Universidad, 1989).

—, 'Ciudades y Monarquía. Las finanzas de los municipios castellanos en los siglos XVI y XVII', in L. Ribot and L. de Rosa (eds), *Ciudad y mundo urbano en la Época Moderna* (Madrid: Actas, 1997), pp. 353–86.

Guidi Bruscoli, F., *Benvenuto Olivieri, i 'mercatores' fiorentini e la Camera apostolica nella Roma di Paolo III Farnese (1534–1549)* (Florence: Leo S. Olschki, 2000).

Habich, W., *Das Weinungeld der Reichsstadt Frankfurt am Main. Die Entwicklungsgeschichte einer Getränkesteuer in Mittelalter und Neuzeit im Zusammenhang mit dem sogenannten Klingenheimer-Prozeß* (ND Aalen: Scientia Verlag, 1967).

Hamilton, E., 'The Decline of Spain', *Economic History Review*, 8 (1938), pp. 168–79.

—, *War and Prices in Spain, 1651–1800* (1947; New York: Russell, 1969).

Harding, V., 'The Crown, the City and the Orphans: The City of London and Its Finances, 1400–1700', in M. Boone, K. Davids and P. Jenssens (eds), *Urban Public Debts. Urban Government and the Market for Annuities in Western Europe (14th–18th Centuries)* (Turnhout: Brepols, 2003), pp. 51–60.

Harreld, D. J., *High Germans in the Low Countries: German Merchants and Commerce in Golden Age-Antwerp* (Leiden and Boston: Brill, 2004).

't Hart, M., 'In Quest for Funds: Warfare and State Formation in the Netherlands, 1620–1650' (PhD thesis, Leiden University, 1989).

—, 'Public Loans and Moneylenders in the Seventeenth Century Netherlands', *Economic and Social History in the Netherlands*, 1 (1989), pp. 119–39.

—, *The Making of a Bourgeois State: War, Politics and Finance during the Dutch Revolt* (Manchester: Manchester University Press, 1993).

—, 'Tussen kapitaal en belastingmonopolie. Interne grenzen aan staatsvorming in Nederland, 1580–1850', in H. Flap and M. H. D. van Leeuwen, *Op lange termijn. Verklaringen van trends in de geschiedenis van samenlevingen* (Hilversum: Verloren, 1994), pp. 129–46.

—, 'The Emergence and Consolidation of the Tax State: The Seventeenth Century', in R. Bonney (ed.) *Economic Systems and State Finance* (Oxford: Clarendon Press and European Science Foundation, 1995), pp. 281–94.

—, 'The Merits of a Financial Revolution: Public Finance, 1550–1700', in M. 't Hart, J. Jonker and J. L. van Zanden (eds), *A Financial History of The Netherlands* (Cambridge: Cambridge University Press, 1997), pp. 11–36.

't Hart, M., Jonker, J. and J. L. van Zanden, *A Financial History of the Netherlands* (Cambridge: Cambridge University Press, 1997).

't Hart, M., and M. van der Heijden, 'Het geld van de stad. Recent historiografische trends in het onderzoek naar stedelijke financien in der Nederlanden', *Tijdschrift voor Sociale en economische Geschiedenis*, 3:3 (2006), special issue: *Het geld van de stad*, pp. 3–35.

't Hart, M., and M. Limberger, 'Staatsmacht en stedelijke autonomie. Het geld van Antwerpen en Amsterdam (1500–1700)', *Tijdschrift voor Sociale en Economische Geschiedenis*, 3:3 (2006), special issue: *Het geld van de stad*, pp. 36–72.

Hartmann, P. C., *Das Steuersystem der europäischen Staaten an Ende des Ancien Regime. Eine offizielle französische Enquete (1763–1769). Dokumente, Analyse und Auswertung. England und die Staaten Nord- und Mitteleuropas* (Zürich/Munich: Artemis Verlag, 1979).

Hassinger, H., 'Ständische Vertretungen in den althabsburgischen Ländern und in Salzburg', in D. Gerhard (ed.), *Ständische Vertretungen in Europa im 17. und 18. Jahrhundert* (Göttingen: Vandenhoeck & Ruprecht, 1969), pp. 247–85.

Hattenhauer, C., 'Anmerkungen zur Regulierung der Staatsschulden nach dem Dreißigjährigen Krieg', in G. Lingelbach (ed.), *Staatsfinanzen – Staatsverschuldung – Staatsbankrotte in der europäischen Staaten- und Rechtsgeschichte* (Cologne/Weimar/Vienna: Böhlau Verlag, 2000), pp. 123–44.

Heimers, M. P., 'Die Strukturen einer barocken Residenzstadt. München zwischen Dreißigjährigem Krieg und dem Vorabend der Französischen Revolution', in R. Bauer (ed.), *Geschichte der Stadt München* (Munich: C. H. Beck Verlag, 1992), pp. 211–43.

Herborn, W., 'Kölner Verfassungswirklichkeit im Ancien Régime', in W. Ehbrecht (ed.), *Verwaltung und Politik in Städten Mitteleuropas. Beiträge zu Verfassungsnorm und Verfassungswirklichkeit in altständischer Zeit* (Cologne/Weimar/Vienna: Böhlau Verlag, 1994), pp. 85–113.

Hildebrandt, R., 'Zur Frage der reichsstädtischen Finanzen und Haushaltspolitik seit dem Westfälischen Frieden', in E. Maschke, J. Sydow (ed.), *Städtisches Haushalts- und Rechnungswesen* (Sigmaringen: Jan Thorbecke Verlag, 1977), pp. 91–107.

Hillbrand, E., 'Das Ungeld in Nieder- und Oberösterreich vom 13.–19. Jahrhundert mit besonderer Berücksichtigung der Zeit 1500–1700' (PhD dissertation, Universität Vienna, 1953).

Hocquet, J. C., 'City-State and Market Economy', in R. Bonney (ed.), *Economic Systems and State Finance, the Origins of the Modern State in Europe: 13th to 18th Century* (New York: Oxford University Press, 1995), pp. 81–100.

Hoffmann, A., 'Die oberösterreichischen Städte und Märkte. Eine Übersicht ihrer Entwicklungs- und Rechtsgrundlagen', *Jahrbuch des Oberösterreichischen Musealvereins*, 84 (1932), pp. 63–213.

—, 'Der oberösterreichische Städtebund im Mittelalter', *Jahrbuch des Oberösterreichischen Musealvereines*, 93 (1948).

Hoffmann, C. A., *Landesherrliche Städte und Märkte im 17. und 18. Jahrhundert. Studien zu ihrer ökonomischen, rechtlichen und sozialen Entwicklung in Oberbayern* (Kallmünz/Opf.: Verlag Michael Lassleben, 1997).

—, 'Integration in den frühneuzeitlichen Staat und Funktionsverlust – die altbayerischen Kleinstädte vom 16. bis zum 18. Jahrhundert', in H. T. Gräf (ed.), *Kleine Städte im neuzeitlichen Europa* (Berlin: Berlin Verlag, 1997), pp. 83–109.

Hoffman, P. T., G. Postel-Vinay and J.-L. Rosenthal., *Priceless Markets: The Political Economy of Credit in Paris, 1660–1726* (Chicago, IL: University of Chicago Press, 2000).

Hohenberg, P., and H. Lees, *The Making of Urban Europe 1000–1950* (Cambridge, MA: Harvard University Press, 1985).

Hohrath, D., '"Städtische" und "staatliche": Kassen in der Stadt Mainz. Beobachtungen zum öffentlichen Finanzwesen in einer Haupt- und Residenzstadt um 1785', in K. Gerteis (ed.), *Stadt und frühmoderner Staat. Beiträge zur städtischen Finanzgeschichte von Luxemburg, Lunéville, Mainz, Saarbrücken und Trier im 17. und 18. Jahrhundert* (Trier: THF, 1994), pp. 233–343.

Hourblin, X., *Les finances de Reims à la fin de l'Ancien Régime, 1765–1789* (Paris: CHEFF, 2008).

Hoz, C. de la., 'El sistema fiscal de Madrid en el Antiguo Régimen: las sisas', *Anales del Instituto de Estudios Madrileños*, 25 (1988), pp. 371–86.

—, 'Las reformas de la Hacienda Madrileña en la época de Carlos III', in equipo Madrid (ed.), *Carlos III, Madrid y la Ilustración. Contradicciones de un proyecto reformista* (Madrid: Alianza, 1988), pp. 77–101.

Huber-Sperl, R., 'Reichsstädtisches Wirtschaftsleben zwischen Tradition und Wandel', *Die Geschichte der Stadt Memmingen, 1: Von den Anfängen bis zum Ende der Reichsstadt* (Stuttgart: Konrad Theiss Verlag, 1997), pp. 679–782.

Inglada, J., 'Estudio de la estructura socio-económica de Huesca y su comarca en el siglo XVII' (graduate dissertation, Saragossa University, 1987).

Irsigler, F., 'Akzise', in R.-H. Bautier (ed.), *Lexikon des Mittelalters* (Munich: Deutscher Taschenbuch Verlag, 1997), vol. 1, col. 261.

Isenmann, E., 'Prinzipien, Formen und wirtschaftliche Auswirkungen von Besteuerung – Steuergerechtigkeit und Steuergleichheit im 15. Jahrhundert (Deutschland und Italien)', in S. Cavaciocchi (ed.), *La Fiscalità nell'Economia Europea Secc. XIII–XVIII/Fiscal Systems in the European Economy from the 13th to the 18th Centuries* (Florence: Olschki, 2008), pp.153–83.

—, 'The Notion of the Common Good, the Concept of Politics, and Practical Policies in Late Medieval and Early Modern German Cities', in E. Lecuppre-Desjardin and A.-L. van Bruaene (eds), *De Bono Communi. The Discourse and Practise of the Common Good in the European City (13th–16th c.)/ Discours et pratique du Bien Commun dans les villes d'Europe (XIIIe au XVIe siècles)* (Turnhout: Brepols, 2010), pp. 107–48.

Israel, J., *The Dutch Republi:. Its Rise, Greatness and Fall, 1477–1806* (Oxford: Oxford University Press, 1995).

Jenetzky, J., *System und Entwicklung des materiellen Steuerrechts in der wissenschaftlichen Literatur des Kameralismus von 1680 – 1840, dargestellt anhand der gedruckten zeitgenössischen Quellen* (Berlin: Duncker & Humblot, 1978).

Keene, D., 'Towns, Fiscality and the State. England, 700–1500', paper presented at the World Economic History Congress, Utrecht 2009, Session Q6: 'Urban Fuscal Systems and Economic Growth in Europe, 16th and 18th Centuries', <http://www.wehc2009.org>.

Kernkamp, J. H. (ed.), *Vijftiende-eeuwse rentebrieven van Noordnederlandse steden* (Groningen: Wolters, 1961).

Klebel, E., 'Ungeld und Landgericht in Nieder- und Oberösterreich', *Mitteilungen des Instituts für Österreichische Geschichtsforschung* 52 (1938), pp. 269–87.

Klein, K., 'Die Bevölkerung in Österreich vom Beginn des 16. Jahrhunderts bis zur Mitte des 18. Jahrhunderts', in H. Helczmanovszki (ed.), *Beiträge zur Bevölkerungs- und Sozialgeschichte Österreichs* (Vienna: Verlag für Geschichte und Politik, 1973), pp. 47–112.

—, *Daten zur Siedlungsgeschichte der österreichischen Länder bis zum 16. Jahrhundert* (Vienna: Verlag für Geschichte und Politik, 1980).

Knittler, H., *Städte und Märkte. Herrschaftsstruktur und Ständebildung* (Vienna: Verlag für Geschichte und Politik 1973), pp. 11–15.

Knittler, H., 'Städtelandschaften in Österreich im Spätmittelalter und in der Frühneuzeit', in Gräf and Keller (eds), *Städtelandschaft – Résau urbain – Urban network. Städte im regionalen Kontext in Spätmittelalter und früher Neuzeit* (Cologne and Vienna: Böhlau, 2004), pp. 111–33.

Koelges, M., 'Handel und Gewerbe in der frühen Neuzeit', *Geschichte der Stadt Koblenz, vol. 1: von den Anfängen bis zum Ende der kurfürstlichen Zeit* (Stuttgart: Konrad Theiss Verlag, 1992), pp. 333–47.

Körner, M., 'Steuern und Abgaben in Theorie und Praxis im Mittelalter und in der frühen Neuzeit', in E. Schremmer (ed.), *Steuern, Abgaben und Dienste vom Mittelalter bis zur Gegenwart* (Stuttgart: Franz Steiner Verlag, 1994), pp. 53–76.

Kreglinger, A., *Notice historique sur les impôts communaux de la ville d'Anvers* (Brussels, 1845).

Krüger, K., *Finanzstaat Hessen 1500–1567. Staatsbildung im Übergang vom Domänenstaat zum Steuerstaat* (Marburg: N. G. Elwert Verlag, 1980).

—, 'Entstehung und Ausbau des hessischen Steuerstaates vom 16. bis zum 18. Jahrhundert – Akten der Finanzverwaltung als frühneuzeitlicher Gesellschaftsspiegel', *Hessisches Jahrbuch für Landesgeschichte 32* (1982), pp. 103–25.

—, 'Public Finance and Modernization: The Change from Domain State to Tax State in Hesse in the Sixteenth and Seventeenth Centuries: A Case Study', in P. C. Witt (ed.), *Wealth and Taxation in Central Europe* (New York, 1987).

Lamarre, C., *Petites villes et fait urbain en France au XVIIIe siècle. Le cas bourguignon* (Dijon: EUD, 1993).

Lo Sardo, E., *Le gabelle e le dogane dei papi in età moderna. Inventario della serie Dogane della Miscellanea per materie* (Rome: Archivio di Stato di Roma, 1994).

Londei, L., 'La monetazione pontificia e la zecca di Roma in età moderna (secc. XVI–XVIII)', *Studi Romani*, 38 (1990), pp. 303–18.

Looz-Corswarem, C. Graf von, *Das Finanzwesen der Stadt Köln im 18. Jahrhundert. Beitrag zur Verwaltungsgeschichte einer Reichsstadt* (Cologne: Verlag der Buchhandlung Dr. H. Wamper GmbH, 1978).

López García, J. M. (ed.), *El impacto de la Corte en Castilla. Madrid y su territorio en la Época Moderna* (Madrid: Siglo XXI, 1998).

Llombart, V., 'A propósito de los intentos de reforma de la Hacienda castellana en el siglo XVIII: Campomanes frente al proyecto de la Única Contribución', *Hacienda Pública Española*, 38 (1976), pp. 123–32.

Macry, P., *Mercato e società nel Regno di Napoli. Commercio del grano e politica economica nel Settecento* (Naples: Guida, 1974).

Madoz, P., *Diccionario geográfico-histórico-estadístico de España y de sus posesiones de Ultramar* (1848) (Agualarga: Madrid, 1999).

Maiso, J., *La peste aragonesa de 1648 a 1654* (Saragossa: Universidad, 1982).

Maillard, J., 'Les ressources de la ville d'Angers au XVIIIe siècle', in F. Bayard (ed.), *Les finances en province sous l'Ancien Régime* (Paris: Comité pour l'histoire économique et financière de la France, 2000), pp. 169–77.

—, *Le pouvoir municipal à Angers de 1657 à 1789* (Angers: PU Angers, 1984).

Mákkai, L., 'Die Entstehung der gesellschaftlichen Basis des Absolutismus in den Ländern der österreichischen Habsburger', *Études historiques*, 1 (1960), pp. 627–68.

Malanima, P., *La decadenza di un'economia cittadina. L'industria a Firenze nei secoli XVI–XVIII* (Bologne: Il Mulino, 1982).

—, 'Italian Cities, 1300–1800: A Quantitative Approach', *Rivista di Storia Economica*, 16:2 (1988), pp. 91–126.

—, (1998), *La fine del primato. Crisi e reconversione nell'Italia del Seicento* (Milan: Mondadori, 1998).

—, *L'economia italiana. Dalla crescita medievale alla crescita contemporanea* (Bologne: Il Mulino, 2002).

Malatesta, S., *Statuti delle gabelle di Roma* (Rome: Tipografia della Pace, 1885).

Mantelli, R., *Burocrazia e finanze pubblichi nel Regno di Napoli* (Naples: Lucio Pironti, 1981).

Marcos Martín, A., 'Oligarquías urbanas y gobiernos ciudadanos en la España del siglo XVI', in E. Belenguer Cebrià (ed.), *Felipe II y el Mediterráneo, II. Los grupos sociales* (Madrid: Sociedad Estatal para la conmemoración de los Centenarios de Carlos V y Felipe II, 1999), pp. 265–93.

—, '¿Fue la fiscalidad regia un factor de crisis?', in G. Parker (ed.), *La crisis de la Monarquía de Felipe IV* (Barcelona: Crítica, 2006), pp. 173–253.

—, 'Deuda pública, fiscalidad y arbitrios en la Corona de Castilla durante los siglos XVI y XVII', in C. Sanz and B. J. García (eds), *Banca, crédito y capital. La Monarquía Hispánica y los antiguos Países bajos (1505–1700)* (Madrid: Fundación Carlos de Amberes, 2006), pp. 345–75.

Marqués de Santa Cruz de Mercenado, *Rapsodia económica política monárquica (1732)* (Oviedo: Universidad, 1984).

Marsilje, J. W., *Het financiële beleid van Leiden in de laat-Beierse en Bourgondische periode, 1390–1477* (Hilversum: Verloren, 1985).

Martínez Ruiz, J. I., 'Crédito Público y deudas municipales en España (siglos XV–XVIII)', in A. M. Bernal (ed.), *Dinero, Moneda y Crédito en la Monarquía Hispánica* (Madrid: Marcial Pons, 2000), pp. 863–77.

Maschke, E., and J. Sydow (eds), *Verwaltung und Gesellschaft in der südwestdeutschen Stadt des 17. und 18. Jahrhunderts* (Stuttgart: Kohlhammer, 1969), pp. 5–6.

Masini, R., *Il debito pubblico pontificio a fine Seicento. I monti camerali* (Città di Castello: Edimont, 2005).

Masure, T., 'De stadfinanciën van Antwerpen 1531–1571. Een poging tot reconstructie', 2 vols (PhD thesis, Ghent University, 1986).

Mateos, J. A., *Auge y decadencia de un municipio aragonés: el concejo de Daroca en los siglos XVI y XVII* (Daroca: Institución Fernando el Católico, 1997).

—, 'The Making of a New Landscape: Town Councils and Water in the Kingdom of Aragon during the Sixteenth Century' *Rural History*, 9:2 (1998), pp. 123–39.

—, 'Municipal Politics and Corporate Protectionism: Town Councils and Guilds in the Kingdom of Aragon during the Sixteenth and Seventeenth Centuries', in B. Blondé, E. Vanhaute and M. Galand (eds), *Labour and Labour Markets between Town and Countryside (Middle Ages–Nineteenth Century)* (Turnhout: Brepols, 2001), pp. 178–97.

—, 'La hacienda municipal de Albarracín en el siglo XVII: crisis, endeudamiento y negociación', *Teruel*, 88–89:2 (2000–2002), pp. 171–212.

—, 'Propios, arbitrios y comunales: la hacienda municipal en el reino de Aragón durante los siglos XVI y XVII', *Revista de Historia Económica*, 21:1 (2003), pp. 51–77.

—, 'Control público, hacienda municipal y mercado agrario en Aragón durante los siglos XVI y XVII', *Hispania*, 66:223 (2006), pp. 547–82.

—, 'La política municipal de abastos en Aragón durante los siglos XVI y XVII: fiscalidad y mercado preindustrial', *Revista de Historia de la Economía y de la Empresa*, 4 (2010), pp. 321–50.

Matilla Tascón, A., *La única contribución y el catastro de la Ensenada* (Madrid: Ministerio de Hacienda, 1947).

Mauersberg, H., *Wirtschafts-und Sozialgeschichte zentraleuropäischer Städte in neuerer Zeit. Dargestellt an den Beispielen von Basel, Frankfurt A.M., Hamburg, Hannover und München* (Göttingen: Vandenhoeck & Ruprecht, 1960).

McCloskey, D., 'A Mismeasurement of the Incidence of Taxation in Britain and France, 1715–1780', *Journal of European Economic History*, 7:1 (1978), pp. 209–10.

Medeiros, F., 'Espaces ruraux et dynamiques sociales en Europe du Sud', *Annales ESC, 5* (1988), pp. 1081–107.

Mensi, F., *Geschichte der direkten Steuern in Steiermark bis zum Regierungsantritt Maria Theresias* (Graz and Vienna: Styria, 1921), vol. 3.

Meyer, J., and J.-P. Pousseau, *Etudes sur les villes françaises. Milieu du XVIIe siècle à la veille de la Révolution française* (Paris: SEDES, 1995).

Mieck, I., 'Preußen und Westeuropa', in W. Neugebauer (ed.), *Handbuch der Preußischen Geschichte, I: Das 17. und 18. Jahrhundert und Große Themen der Geschichte Preußens* (Berlin/New York: Walter de Gruyter, 2009), pp. 411–851.

Molho, A., *Florentine public finances in the early Renaissance, 1400–1433* (Cambridge, Mass.: Harvard University Press, 1971).

Moncada, S. de., *Restauración de la Abundancia de España* (1619), ed. J. Vilar (Madrid: Instituto de Estudios Fiscales, 1974).

Monsoriu, B. de, *Summa de todos los fueros y observancias del reyno de Aragon y determinaciones de micer Miguel del Molino* (Saragossa: Colegio de abogados, 1982, facsimile of the original printed in 1589).

Morineau, M., 'Budgets de l'Etat et gestion des finances royales en France au XVIIIe siècle', *Revue historique*, 264 (1980), pp. 289–336.

—, *Incroyables, gazettes et fabuleaux metaux. Les retours des trésors americains d'après les gazettes hollandaises (XVIe–XVIIIe siècles)* (Paris: Cambridge University Press and Maison des Sciences de l'Homme, 1985).

—, 'Panorama de l'Ancien Régime fiscal en France', in F. Bayard (ed.), *Les finances en province sous l'Ancien Régime* (Paris: Comité pour l'histoire économique et financière de la France, 2000), pp. 305–38.

Müller, J., 'Die Finanzpolitik des Nürnberger Rates in der zweiten Hälfte des 16. Jahrhunderts', *Vierteljahrsschrift für Social-und Wirtschaftsgeschichte 7* (1909), pp. 1–63.

Müller, K., 'Unter pfalz-neuburgischer und pfalz-bayerischer Herrschaft (1614–1806)', in H. Weidenhaupt (ed.), *Düsseldorf. Von den Ursprüngen bis ins 20. Jahrhundert, vol. 2: Von der Residenzstadt zur Beamtenstadt (1614–1900)* (Düsseldorf: Patmos Verlag, 1988), pp. 7–312.

Musi, A (ed.), *Le città nel Mezzogiorno nell'etè moderna* (Naples: Guida, 2006).

—, *Il territorio sghembo. Forme e dinamiche degli sapzi umani in etá moderna* (Bari: Edipuglia, 2006).

Muto, G., 'The Spanish System: Centre and Periphery', in R. Bonney (ed.), *Economic Systems and State Finance* (Oxford: Oxford University Press, 1995).

Neal, L., *The Rise of Financial Capitalism: International Capital Markets in the Age of Reason* (Cambridge: Cambridge University Press, 1990).

Neri, P., *Relazione dello stato in cui si trova l'opera del censimento universale del Ducato di Milano nel mese di maggio dell'anno 1750* (Milan: G. R. Malatesta, 1750), p. 16.

Neugebauer, W., 'Brandenburg-Preußen in der Frühen Neuzeit', in W. Neugebauer (ed.), *Handbuch der Preußischen Geschichte, I: Das 17. und 18. Jahrhundert und Große Themen der Geschichte Preußens* (Berlin/New York: Walter de Gruyter, 2009), pp. 113–407.

Nussdorfer, L., *Civic politics in the Rome of Urban VIII* (Princeton, NJ: Princeton University Press, 1992).

O'Brien, P. K., and P. Hunt, 'The Rise of a Fiscal State in England, 1485–1815', *Historical Research*, 66 (1993), pp. 129–76.

Ohler, N., 'Zum Haushalt der Stadt Freiburg im Breisgau im 16. und 17. Jahrhundert', *Schau-ins-Land*, 94–5 (1976–7), pp. 253–89.

Olivo, J., 'La evolución de la hacienda municipal de Calatayud durante el siglo XVII', *Jerónimo Zurita*, 76–7 (2002), pp. 221–40.

Ormrod, W. M., 'England in the Middle Ages', in R. Bonney (ed.), *The Rise of the Fiscal State in Europe c. 1200–1815* (Cambridge: Cambridge University Press, 1999), pp. 19–56.

Ostoni, M., *Il tesoro del re. Uomini e istituzioni della finanza pubblica milanese fra Cinquecento e Seicento* (Naples: Istituto Italiano per gli Studi Filosofici, 2010).

Otero, F., *La vila de Fraga al segle XVII*, 2 vols (Calaceite: Institut d'Estudis del Baix Cinca, 1994).

Outhwaite, R. B., 'The Trials of Foreign Borrowing: The English Crown and the Antwerp Money Market in the Mid-Sixteenth Century', *Economic History Review*, 19 (1966), pp. 289–305.

Outhwaite, R. B., 'Royal Borrowing in the Reign of Elizabeth I: The Aftermath of Antwerp', *English Historical Review*, 86 (1971), pp. 251–63.

Palermo, L., 'L'economia', in A. Pinelli (ed.), *Storia di Roma dall'antichità ad oggi. Roma del Rinascimento* (Bari: Gius. Laterza & figli, 2001), pp. 46–68.

Parigino, G. V., *Il bilancio pontificio del 1657* (Naples: Edizione Scientifiche Italiane, 1999).

Partner, P., *Renaissance Rome 1500–1559. A Portrait of a Society* (Berkeley, CA: University of California Press, 1976).

—, 'The Papacy and the Papal States', in R. Bonney (ed.), *The Rise of the Fiscal State in Europe 1200–1815* (Oxford: Oxford University Press, 1999), pp. 359–38.

Parziale, L., *Nutrire la città. Produzione e commercio a Milano tra Cinque e Seicento* (Milan: FrancoAngeli, 2009).

Peiró, A., *Zaragoza y el capital comercial: la burguesía mercantil en el Aragón de la segunda mitad del siglo XVII* (Barcelona: Crítica, 2002).

Persson, K. G., *An Economic History of Europe. Knowledge, Institutions and Growth, 600 to the Present* (Cambridge: Cambridge University Press, 2010).

Petrocchi, M., *Roma nel Seicento* (Bologne: Cappelli, 1970).

Pezzolo, L., *L'Oro dello Stato. Societá, finanza e fisco nella Reppublica Veneta del secondo '500* (Venice: Il Cardo, 1991).

—, 'The Venetian government debt, 1350–1650', in M. Boone, K. Davids and P. Janssens (eds), *Urban Public Debts. Urban Government and the Market for Annuities in Western Europe (14th–18th Centuries)* (Turnhout: Brepols 2003), pp. 61–74.

Piola Caselli, F., 'Merci per dogana e consumi alimentari a Roma nel Seicento', *La popolazione italiana nel Seicento* (Bologne: Clueb, 1999), pp. 387–409.

—, 'Public Debt, State Revenue and Town Consumption in Rome (16th–18th Centuries)', in M. Boone, K. Davids and P. Jansenns (eds), *Urban Public Debt. Urban Government and the Market for Annuities in Western Europe (14th–18th Centuries)* (Turnhout: Brepols, 2003), pp. 93–105.

—, 'Public Debt in the Papal States: Financial Market and Government Strategies in the Long Run', in F. Piola Caselli (ed.), *Government Debts and Financial Markets in Europe* (London: Pickering & Chatto, 2008), pp. 105–19.

Potthoff, H., 'Der öffentliche Haushalt Hamburgs im 15. und 16. Jahrhundert', *Zeitschrift des Vereins für Hamburgische Geschichte*, 16 (1911), pp. 1–81.

Potter, M., and J. L. Rosenthal, 'Politics and Public Finance in France: The Estates of Burgundy, 1660–1790', *Journal of Interdisciplinary History*, 27: 4 (1997), pp. 577–612.

Prak, M., *Gezeten burgers. De elite van een Hollandse stad, Leiden 1700–1748* (Hilversum: Verloren, 1985).

Prak, M., and J. L van Zanden, 'Tax Morale and Citizenship in the Dutch Republic', in O. Gelderblom (ed.), *The Political Economy of the Dutch Republic* (Bodmin: Ashgate, 2009), pp. 143–66.

Press, V., 'Der Merkantilismus und die Städte. Eine Einleitung', in V. Press (ed.), *Städtewesen und Merkantilismus in Europa* (Cologne/Vienna: Böhlau Verlag, 1983), pp. 1–14.

Přibram, A. F., 'Die niederösterreichischen Stände und die Krone in der Zeit Kaiser Leopolds I.', *Mitteilungen des Instituts für Österreichische Geschichtsforschung* 14 (1893), pp. 589–652, on p. 598.

Prins, I., *Het faillissement der Hollandsche steden: Amsterdam, Dordrecht, Leiden en Haarlem in het jaar 1494, uit de wordingsgeschiedenis van den Nederlandschen Staat* (Amsterdam: Van Looy, 1922).

Pugliese, S., *Condizioni economiche e finanziarie della Lombardia nella prima metà del secolo XVIII* (Turin: Fratelli Bocca, 1924).

Pühringer, A., 'Finanzen und Kommunalbudget der Stadt Wels in der frühen Neuzeit', *Jahrbuch des Musealvereines Wels* 30 (1993/94/95), pp. 133–55.

—, *Contributionale, Oeconomicum und Politicum. Die Finanzen der landesfürstlichen Städte Nieder- und Oberösterreichs in der Frühneuzeit* (Vienna and Munich: Verlag für Geschichte und Politik, 2002).

—, 'Kleine Städte – große Schulden? Zur frühneuzeitlichen Finanzstruktur der landesfürstlichen Städte ob und unter der Enns', *Pro Civitate Austriae. Informationen zur Stadtgeschichtsforschung in Österreich* NF 8 (2003), pp. 3–38.

—, A., 'Die landesfürstlichen Städte ob und unter der Enns. Funktionale Städtelandschaften?', in H. T. Gräf and K. Keller (eds), *Städtelandschaft, – Résau urbain – Urban network. Städte im regionalen Kontext in Spätmittelalter und früher Neuzeit* (Cologne and Vienna: Böhlau, 2004).

—, 'Die Stadt Wels in der Frühneuzeit: Finanzen, Verwaltung und Politik zwischen Bauernkrieg, Gegenreformation und Einbindung in den frühmodernen Staat', *Jahrbuch des Musealvereines Wels*, 34 (2004/05), pp. 153–84.

—, 'Ein Strukturvergleich niederösterreichischer Städte in der frühen Neuzeit. Zur Konstellation kommunaler Finanzen vom Ende des 16. bis zur Mitte des 18. Jahrhunderts', in W. Rosner (ed.), *Die Städte und Märkte Niederösterreichs im Mittelalter und in der frühen Neuzeit* (St Pölten: Niederösterreichisches Institut für Landeskunde, 2005), pp. 102–33.

—, '"Mitleiden" ohne "Mitsprache"? Die landesfürstlichen Städte Österreichs als Vierter Stand', in G. Ammerer, W. D. Godsey, Jr., M. Scheutz, P. Urbanitsch and A. S. Weiß (eds), *Bündnispartner und Konkurrenten der Landesfürsten. Die Stände der Habsburgermonarchie* (Vienna and Munich: Oldenbourg 2006).

—, A., '"Topographie der Gegenreformation" oder "Austrian Urban Renaissance"?', in R. Leeb, S. C. Pils and T. Winkelbauer (eds), *Staatsmacht und Seelenheil. Gegenreformation und Geheimprotestantismus in der Habsburgermonarchie* (Vienna and Munich: Oldenbourg 2007), pp. 289–310.

Putschögl, G., *Die landständische Behördenorganisation in Österreich ob der Enns vom Anfang des 16. bis zur Mitte des 18. Jahrhunderts. Ein Beitrag zur österreichischen Rechtsgeschichte* (Linz: Oberösterreichisches Landesarchiv, 1978), pp. 36–57.

Rapp, R., *Industry and Economic Decline in Seventeenth-Century Venice* (Cambridge, MA: Harvard University Press, 1976).

Rauscher, P., 'Comparative Evolution of the Tax Systems in the Habsburg Monarchy, c. 1526–1740: The Austrian and the Bohemian Lands', in S. Cavaciocchi (ed.), *La Fiscalità nell'Economia Europea secc. XIII–XVIII – Fiscal Systems in the European economy from the 13th to the 18th centuries* (Florence: Olschki, 2008), pp. 291–320.

Redondo, G., *Las corporaciones de artesanos de Zaragoza en el siglo XVII* (Saragossa: Institución Fernando el Católico, 1982).

—, 'Las relaciones comerciales de Aragón-Francia en la Edad Moderna: datos para su estudio en el siglo XVII', *Estudios*, 85–6 (1985), pp. 123–54.

Reese, T. R., 'Georgia in Anglo-Spanish Diplomacy, 1736–1739', *William and Mary Quarterly*, 15:2 (1958), pp. 168–90.

Reese, T. R., *Colonial Georgia: A Study in British Imperial Policy in the Eighteenth Century* (Athens, GA: University of Georgia Press, 1963).

Reincke, H., 'Die alte Hamburger Stadtschuld der Hansezeit (1399–1563)', in *Städtewesen und Bürgertum als geschichtliche Kräfte, Gedächtnisschrift Fritz Rörig* (Lübeck: Verlag Max Schmidt-Römhild, 1953), pp. 489–511.

Reinhardt, V., 'Annona and Bread Supply in Rome', in P. van Kessel and E. Schulte (eds), *Rome and Amsterdam: Two Growing Cities in Seventeenth Century Europe* (Amsterdam: Amsterdam University Press, 1997), pp. 209–20.

Reinhard, W., *Papstfinanz und Nepotismus unter Paul V. (1605–1621), Studien und Quellen zur Struktur und zu quantitativen Aspekten des päpstliche Herrschaftssystems*, 2 vols (Stuttgart: Anton Hiersemann, 1974).

Reitsma, R., *Centrifugal and Centripetal Forces in the Early Dutch Republic: The States of Overijssel 1566–1600* (Amsterdam: Rodopi, 1982).

Rey Castelao, O., 'Mutaciones sociales en una sociedad immutable: el Reino de Galicia en el reinado de Felipe V', in E. Serrano (ed.), *Felipe V y su tiempo* (Saragossa: Fernando el Católico, 2004), pp. 343–74.

Ribot García, L., 'Las reformas militares y navales en tiempos de Felipe V', in E. Maza Zorrilla and M de la C. Marcos del Olmo (coord.), *Estudios de Historia. Homenaje al professor Jesús María Palomares* (Valladolid: Universidad de Valladolid, 2006), pp. 129–62.

Ringrose, D., *Madrid y la economía española* (Madrid: Alianza, 1985).

Rodríguez, J. M., *Blas de Lezo. El vasco que salvo al Imperio Español* (Barcelona: Altera, 2008).

Rodríguez Villa, A., *Patiño y Campillo: reseña histórico-biográfica de estos dos ministros de Felipe V* (Madrid: Establecimiento tipográfico de los sucesores de Rivadeneyra, 1882).

Roeck, B., *Eine Stadt in Krieg und Frieden. Studien zur Geschichte der Reichsstadt Augsburg zwischen Kalenderstreit und Parität* (Göttingen: Vandenhoeck & Ruprecht, 1989).

Romano, R., *Prezzi, salari e servizi a Napoli nel seccolo XVIII. 1734–1806* (Milan: Banca Commerciale Italiana, 1965).

Rothe, K., *Das Finanzwesen der Reichsstadt Ulm im 18. Jahrhundert. Ein Beitrag zur Wirtschaftsgeschichte* (Ulm: Kommissionsverlag, W. Kohlhammer, 1991).

Ruiz Martín, F., 'Procedimientos crediticios para la recaudación de los tributos fiscales en las ciudades castellanas durante los siglos XVI y XVII. El caso de Valladolid', in A. de Otazu (ed.), *Dinero y crédito* (Madrid: 1978), pp. 37–47.

Sabatini, G., *Proprietà e proprietari a L'Aquila e nel contado. Le rilevazioni catastali in età spagnola* (Naples: Edizioni Scientifiche Italiane, 1995).

Salas, J. A., 'La evolución demográfica aragonesa en los siglos XVI y XVII', in J. Nadal (ed.), *La evolución demográfica bajo los Austrias* (Alicante: Instituto Juan Gil Albert, 1992), pp. 169–79.

—, 'Las haciendas concejiles aragonesas en los siglos XVI y XVII. De la euforia a la quiebra', in *Poder político e instituciones en la España Moderna* (Alicante: Instituto Juan Gil Albert, 1992), pp. 11–66.

Salomoni, A. (ed.), *Memorie storico-diplomatiche degli Ambasciatori, Incaricati d'affari, Corrispondenti, e Delegati, che la città di Milano inviò a diversi suoi principi dal 1500 al 1796* (Milan: Tipografia Pulini al Bocchetto, 1806).

Salvemini, B., 'Sui presupposti materiali dell'identità locale in antico regime: le città della Pugli centrale fra XVI e XVIII secolo', in A. Musi (ed.), *Le città nel Mezzogiorno nell'età moderna* (Naples: Guida, 2006).

Sander, P., *Die reichsstädtische Haushaltung Nürnbergs, dargestellt auf Grund ihres Zustandes von 1431 bis 1440* (Leipzig: Teubner Verlag, 1902).

Sandl, M., *Ökonomie des Raumes. Der kameralistische Entwurf der Staatswirtschaft im 18. Jahrhundert* (Cologne/Weimar/Vienna: Böhlau Verlag), 1999.

Sardá, J., 'La política monetaria y las fluctuaciones de la economía española en el siglo XIX', in R. Ortega (ed.) *Escritos (1948–80)* (Madrid: Banco de España, 1987), pp. 65–283.

Saupin, G., 'Les octrois de Nantes de la création de la municipalité à 1732', in P. Haudrere (ed.), *Pour une histoire sociale des villes* (Rennes: PU, 2006) pp. 43–57.

—, 'Les octrois de la ville de Nantes à la fin de l'Ancien Régime', in D. Le Page (ed.), *Usages et images de l'argent dans l'Ouest atlantique aux Temps modernes, Enquêtes et Documents* (Rennes: PU, 2007), pp. 211–29.

Scheutz, M., 'Kammergut und/oder eigener Stand? Landesfürstliche Städte und Märkte und der "Zugriff" der Gegenreformation', in R. Leeb, S. C. Pils and T. Winkelbauer (eds), *Staatsmacht und Seelenheil. Gegenreformation und Geheimprotestantismus in der Habsburgermonarchie* (Vienna and Munich: Oldenbourg 2007), pp. 311–39.

Schieber, M., *Zinsen, Inflation, Schulden und Verschuldung in der Nürnberger Stadtgeschichte* (Nürnberg: Sandberg Verlag, 2000).

Schlögl, R., *Bauern, Krieg und Staat. Oberbayerische Bauernwirtschaft und frühmoderner Staat im 17. Jahrhundert* (Göttingen: Vandenhoeck & Ruprecht, 1988).

Schmidt, U., *Südwestdeutschland im Zeichen der Französischen Revolution. Bürgeropposition in Ulm, Reutlingen und Esslingen* (Ulm: Kommissionsverlag W. Kohlhammer, 1993).

Schott, H., 'Fürstlicher Absolutismus und barocke Stadt', in U. Wagner (ed.), *Geschichte der Stadt Würzburg, vol. 2: Vom Bauernkrieg bis zum Übergang an das Königreich Bayern 1814* (Stuttgart: Konrad Theiss Verlag, 2004), pp. 131–202.

Schremmer, E., 'Über Gerechte Steuern. Ein Blick zurück ins 19. Jahrhundert', in E. Schremmer (ed.), *Steuern, Abgaben und Dienste vom Mittelalter bis zur Gegenwart* (Stuttgart: Franz Steiner Verlag, 1994), pp. 9–42.

Schulze, W., 'Reichstage und Reichssteuern im späten 16. Jahrhundert', *Zeitschrift für Historische Forschung*, 2 (1975), pp. 43–58.

—, *Reich und Türkengefahr* (Munich: Beck, 1978).

Schulz, H., *Das System und die Prinzipien der Einkünfte im werdenden Staat der Neuzeit, dargestellt anhand der kameralwissenschaftlichen Literatur (1600–1835)* (Berlin: Duncker & Humblot, 1982).

Schulz, K., 'Vom Herrschaftsantritt der Hohenzollern bis zum Ausbruch der Dreißigjährigen Krieges (1411/12–1618)', in W. Ribbe (ed.), *Geschichte Berlins, 1: Von der Frühgeschichte bis zur Industrialisierung* (Munich: C. H. Beck Verlag, 1988), pp. 249–340.

Schunka, A., 'Emigration aus den Habsburgerländern nach Mitteldeutschland. Motive und soziale Konsequenzen', in R. Leeb, S. C. Pils and T. Winkelbauer (eds), *Staatsmacht und Seelenheil. Gegenreformation und Geheimprotestantismus in der Habsburgermonarchie* (Vienna and Munich: Oldenbourg 2007), pp. 233–46.

Schwab, I., 'Zeiten der Teuerung. Versorgungsprobleme in der zweiten Hälfte des 16. Jahrhunderts', in R. Bauer (ed.), *Geschichte der Stadt München* (Munich: C. H. Beck Verlag, 1992), pp. 167–88.

Schwemmer, W., *Die Schulden der Reichsstadt Nürnberg und ihre Übernahme durch den bayerischen Staat* (Nürnberg: Selbstverlag der Stadtbibliothek, 1967).

Schwennicke, A., *'Ohne Steuern kein Staat'. Zu Entwicklung und politischen Funktion des Steuerrechts in den Territorien des Heiligen Römischen Reichs* (Frankfurt A. M.: Vittorio Klostermann, 1983).

Sebastián Marín, M., and Vela Santamaria, F. J. 'Hacienda Real y Presión Fiscal en Castilla a comienzos del reinado de Felipe IV', in J. I. Fortea Pérez and M. C. Cremades Griñán (eds), *Política y Hacienda en el Antiguo Régimen* (Murcia: Universidad de Murcia, 1998), pp. 553–67.

Sella, D., *Crisis and Continuity: The Economy of Spanish Lombardy in the Seventeenth Century* (Cambridge, MA: Harvard University Press, 1979).

—, *Italy in the Seventeenth Century* (London: Longman, 1997).

Sella, S., *Salari e lavoro nell'edilizia lombarda durante il secolo XVII* (Pavia: Editrice Succ. Fusi, 1968).

Sewalt, E. L. M., 'Atterminatie ende staet. De rol van het landsheerlijke gezag bij de ondercurarelestellling van de stad Haerlem in de late Middeleeuwen' (unpublished MA thesis: Leiden University, 1994).

Signorotto, G., 'Aperture e pregiudizi nella storiografia italiana del XIX secolo. Interpretazioni della Lombardia "spagnola"', *Archivio Storico Lombardo*, 126 (2000), pp. 513–60.

Sivori, G., 'Il tramonto dell'industria serica genovese', *Revista Historica Italiana*, 84 (1972), pp. 897–997.

Slack, P., *The English Poor Law*, 1531–1782 (Cambridge: Cambridge University Press, 1990).

Smith, A. *The Wealth of the Nations* (1776), ed. K. Sutherland (Oxford: Oxford University Press, 2008).

Soly, H., 'Fortificaties, belastingen en corruptie te Antwerpen in het midden der 16e eeuw', *Bijdragen tot de Geschiedenis*, 53 (1970), pp. 191–210.

—, *Urbanisme en kapitalisme te Antwerpen in de 16de eeuw: de stedebouwkundige en industriële ondernemingen van Gilbert van Schoonbeke* (Brussels: Gemeentekrediet van België, 1977).

Sonnino, and Traina, R., 'La peste del 1656–57 a Roma: organizzazione sanitaria e mortalità', *La demografia storica delle città italiane* (Bologna: S.I.D.E.S., 1982), pp. 430–58.

Sponsel, W., 'Möchten wir das Glück der Ruhe, des dauerhaften Friedens und des Wohlstands'. Nördlingens Eingliederung in den bayerischen Staat 1802/03', in R. A. Müller, H. Flachenecker, R. Kammerl (eds), *Das Ende der kleinen Reichsstädte 1803 im süddeutschen Raum* (Munich: C. H. Beck Verlag, 2007), pp. 121–38.

Stabel, P., *Dwarfs Among Giants: The Flemish Urban Network in the Late Middle Ages* (Leuven: Garant, 1997).

Stabel, P., and J. Haemers, 'From Bruges to Antwerp: International Commercial Firms and Government's Credit in the Late 15th and Early 16th Century', in C. Sanz Ayan and B. J. Garcia Garcia, *Banca, crédito y capital : la Monarquía Hispánica y los antiguos Países Bajos (1505–1700)*(Madrid: Fundación Carlos de Amberes, 2006), pp. 21–37.

Stamhuis, I. H., 'De ontwikkeling van de actuariële theorie tot de zeventiende- en achttiende eeuw', in J. van Gerwen and M. van Leeuwen (eds), *Studies over zekerheidsarrangementen: risico's, risicobestrijding en verzekeringen in Nederland vanaf de Middeleeuwen* (Amsterdam: NEHA, 1998), pp. 157–74.

—, 'Levensverzekeringen 1500–1800', in J. van Gerwen and M. van Leeuwen (eds), *Studies over zekerheidsarrangementen: risico's, risicobestrijding en verzekeringen in Nederland vanaf de Middeleeuwen* (Amsterdam: NEHA, 1998), pp. 141–56.

Stögmann, A., 'Staat, Kirche und Bürgerschaft: Die katholische Konfessionalisierung und die Wiener Protestanten zwischen Widerstand und Anpassung (1580–1660)', in A. Weigl (ed.), *Wien im Dreißigjährigen Krieg. Bevölkerung – Gesellschaft – Kultur – Konfession* (Vienna and Cologne: Böhlau, 2001), pp. 482–564.

—, 'Die Gegenreformation in Wien. Formen und Folgen für die städtische Gesellschaft (1580–1660)', in R. Leeb, S. C. Pils and T. Winkelbauer (eds), *Staatsmacht und Seelenheil. Gegenreformation und Geheimprotestantismus in der Habsburgermonarchie* (Vienna and Munich: Oldenbourg 2007), pp. 273–88.

Stolleis, M., *Geschichte des öffentlichen Rechts in Deutschland, Vol. I: Reichspublizistik und Policeywissenschaft 1600–1800* (Munich: C. H. Beck Verlag, 1988).

Strangio, D., *Crisi alimentari e politica annonaria a Roma nel Settecento* (Rome: Istituto Nazionale di Studi Romani, 1999).

—, 'Debito pubblico e sistema fiscale a Roma e nello Stato pontificio tra '600 e '700', in S. Cavaciocchi (ed.), *Fiscal Systems in the European Economy from the 13th to the 18th Centuries: atti della 'Trentanovesima settimana di studi'*, vol. 1 (Florence: Olschki, 2008), pp. 499–508.

Streng, J. C., *'Stemme in staat': de bestuurlijke elite in de stadsrepubliek Zwolle 1579–1795* (Hilversum: Verloren, 1997).

Stumpo, E., *Il capitale finanziario a Roma fra Cinque e Seicento. Contributo alla storia della fiscalità pontificia in età moderna (1570–1660)* (Milan: Cedam, 1985).

Sturm, B., *'Wat ich schuldich war' Privatkredit im frühneuzeitlichen Hannover (1550–1750)* (Stuttgart: Franz Steiner Verlag, 2009).

Tabacchi, S., 'Il controllo sulle finanze delle comunità negli antichi Stati italiani', *Storia Amministrazione Costituzione*, 4 (1996), pp. 96–8.

Téllez Alarcia, D., 'La independencia de los EEUU en el marco de la "Guerra Colonial" del siglo XVIII (1739–1783)', *Tiempos Modernos: Revista Electrónica de Historia Moderna*, (2001), vol 2.

Thomes, P., *Kommunale Wirtschaft und Verwaltung zwischen Mittelalter und Moderne. Bestandsaufnahme – Strukturen – Konjunkturen. Die Städte Saarbrücken und St. Johann im Rahmen der allgemeinen Entwicklung* (Stuttgart: Franz Steiner Verlag, 1995).

Thompson, I. A. A., 'Taxation, Military Spending and Domestic Economy in Castile in the Later Sixteenth Century', *War and Society in Habsburg Spain: Selected Essays* (Aldershot: Ashgate, 1992).

Tilly, C., 'Cities and States in Europe', *Theory and Society*, 18 (1989), pp. 563–84, on p. 570.

—, *Coercion, Capital and European States, AD 990–1990*, revised paperback edn (Oxford: Blackwell Publishing, 1992).

—, 'Citizenship, Identity and Social History', *International Review of Social History*, 40 (1995), pp. 1–49.

Touzery, M., *L'invention de l'impôt sur le revenu. La taille tarifée, 1715–1789* (Paris: Comité pour l'histoire économique et financière de la France, 1994).

—, *Atlas de la généralité de Paris au XVIIIe siècle* (Paris: CHEFF, 1995).

— (ed.), *De l'estime au cadastre en Europe. L'époque moderne* (Paris: CHEFF, 2007).

Tracy, J. D., *A Financial Revolution in the Habsburg Netherlands: Renten and Renteniers in the County of Holland, 1515–1565* (Berkely, CA and Los Angeles, CA: University of California Press, 1985).

Travaglini, C. M., 'The Roman Guilds System in the Early Eighteenth Century', in A. Guenzi, P. Massa and F. Piola Caselli (eds), *Guilds, Markets and Work Regulations in Italy, 16th–19th Centuries* (Aldershot:Ashgate, 1998).

Tschaler, F. E. W., 'Die wirtschaftlichen, sozialen, kulturellen und politischen Folgen der Mediatisierung der Reichsstädte', in R. A. Müller, H. Flachenecker, R. Kammerl (eds), *Das Ende der kleinen Reichsstädte 1803 im süddeutschen Raum* (Munich: C. H. Beck Verlag, 2007), pp. 29–40.

Unger, J. H. W., and W. Besemer, *De oudste stadsrekeningen van Rotterdam* (Rotterdam: Gemeentelijke Archiefdienst, 1899).

Uztáriz, G. de., *Teoría y práctica de comercio y de marina* (1724), ed. G. Franco (Madrid: Aguilar, 1968).

van der Burg, M., 'Burgers en bestuurders. Rotterdams stadsfinanciën in de tweede helft van de zeventiende eeuw', *Rotterdams Jaarboekje*, 11:1 (2003), pp. 106–30.

—, *Tot laste der Stadt Rotterdam. De verkoop van lijfrenten en de Rotterdamse renteniers (1653–1690)* (MA thesis, University of Amsterdam, 2002).

van der Burg, M., and M. 't Hart, 'Renteniers and the Recovery of Amsterdam's Credit (1578–1605)', in M. Boone, K. Davids and P. Janssens (eds), *Urban Public Debts. Urban Government and the Market for Annuities in Western Europe (14th–18th Centuries)* (Turnhout: Brepols, 2003), pp. 197–218.

van der Heijden, M., 'Stadsrekeningen, stedelijke financiën en historisch onderzoek', *NEHA. Bulletin voor de economische geschiedenis* 14:2 (1999), pp. 129–66.

—, 'Renteniers and the Public Debt of Dordrecht (1555–1572)', in M. Boone, K. Davids and P. Janssens (eds), *Urban Public Debts. Urban Government and the Market for Annuities in Western Europe (14th–18th Centuries)* (Turnhout: Brepols, 2003), pp. 183–96.

—, *Geldschieters van de stad. Financiële relaties tussen burgers, stad en overheden 1550–1650* (Amsterdam: Bert Bakker, 2006).

—, 'State Formation and Urban Finances in Sixteenth and Seventeenth-Century Holland', *Journal of Urban History*, 32:3 (2006), pp. 429–50.

van der Heijden, M., and M. 't Hart, 'Recente historiografische trends in het onderzoek naar stedelijke financiën in de Nederlanden', *Tijdschrift voor Sociale en Economische Geschiedenis*, 3: 3 (2006), pp. 3–35.

van der Heijden, M., E. van Nederveen Meerkerk, G. Vermeesch and M. van der Burg (eds), *Serving the Urban Community: The Rise of Public Facilities in the Low Countries* (Amsterdam: Aksant, 2009).

van Honacker, K., *Lokaal verzet en oproer in de 17de en 18de eeuw: collectieve acties tegen het centraal gezag in Brussel, Antwerpen en Leuven* (Heule: UGA 1994).

van Schaïk, R., *Belasting, bevolking en bezit in Gelre en Zutphen (1350–1550)* (Hilversum: Verloren, 1987).

—, 'The Sale of Annuities and Financial Politics in a Town in the Eastern Netherlands Zutphen, 1400–1600', in M. Boone, K. Davids, P. Janssens (eds), *Urban Public Debts: Urban*

Government and the Market for Annuities in Western Europe (14th–18th Centuries) (Turnhout: Brepols 2003), pp. 109–26.

Van Uytven, R., *Stadsfinanciën en stadsekonomie te Leuven van de XIIe tot het einde der XVIe eeuw* (Brussels, 1961).

—, 'Vorst, adel en steden: een driehoeksverhouding in Brabant van de twaalfde tot de zestiende eeuw', *Bijdragen tot de Geschiedenis*, 59 (1976), pp. 93–122.

van der Wee, H., *The Growth of the Antwerp Market and the European Economy, 14th–16th Centuries*, 3 vols (The Hague: Nijhoff 1963).

van Werveke, H., *De Gentse stadsfinanciën in de Middeleeuwen* (Brussels: 1934).

van Zanden, J. L., and M. Prak, 'State Formation and Citizenship: The Dutch Republic between Medieval Communes and Modern Nation States', in J. L. van Zanden, *The Long Road to Industrial Revolution: The European Economy in a Global Perspective, 1000–1800* (Leiden-Boston: Brill, 2009), pp. 205–32.

Vela, F. J., 'Las obras públicas en la Castilla del siglo XVII: un gravamen oneroso y desconocido', *Studia Historica. Historia Moderna*, 32 (2010), pp. 125–77.

Vigo, G., *Finanza pubblica e pressione fiscale nello Stato di Milano durante il secolo XVI* (Milan: Banca Commerciale Italiana, 1977).

—, 'Real Wages of the Working Class in Italy. Building Workers' Wages (14th to 18th Century)', *Journal of European Economic History*, 3:2 (1974), pp. 379–99.

—, *Fisco e società nella Lombardia del Cinquecento* (Bologne: Il Mulino, 1979).

—, 'Alle origini dello stato moderno: fiscalità e classi sociali nella Lombardia di Filippo II', *Studi in memoria di Mario Abrate* (Turin: Università di Torino, 1986), vol. 2, pp. 765–75.

Vijlder, N., De, 'De publieke rentenmarkt van Antwerpen, een sociaal-economische analyse 1630–1709' (PhD thesis, Ghent University, 2010).

Vries, J. de, *European Urbanization 1500–1800* (Cambridge, MA: Harvard University Press, 1984).

Vries J. de and A. van der Woude, *The First Modern Economy: Success, Failure and Perseverance of the Dutch Economy, 1500–1815* (Cambridge: Cambridge University Press, 1997).

Wagner, U., 'Geschichte der Stadt zwischen Bergtheim 1400 und Bauernkrieg 1525', in U. Wagner (ed.), *Geschichte der Stadt Würzburg, vol. I: von den Anfängen bis zum Ausbruch des Bauernkriegs* (Stuttgart: Konrad Theiss Verlag, 2001), pp. 114–65.

Weigl, A., 'Residenz, Bastion und Konsumptionsstadt: Stadtwachstum und demographische Entwicklung einer werdenden Metropole', in A. Weigl (ed.), *Wien im Dreißigjährigen Krieg. Bevölkerung – Gesellschaft – Kultur – Konfession* (Vienna and Cologne: Böhlau, 2001), pp. 31–105.

Wijsenbeek-Olthuis, T., *Achter de gevels van Delft : bezit en bestaan van rijk en arm in een periode van achteruitgang (1700–1800)* (Hilversum: Verloren, 1987).

Wilson, C., 'Taxation and the Decline of Empires. An Unfashionable Theme', *Bijdragen en Mededelingen van Historisch Genootschap*, 77 (1963), pp. 10–26.

Winkelbauer, T., *Ständfreiheit und Fürstenmacht. Länder and Untertanen des Hauses Habsburg im konfessionellen Zeitalter* (Vienna: Ueberreuter, 2003), vol. 1.

Winner, G., 'Adeliger Stand und bürgerliche Hantierung. Die sieben landesfürstlichen Städte und die ständischen Gegensätze in Oberösterreich während des 16. Jahrhunderts', *Historisches Jahrbuch der Stadt Linz* (1959), pp. 57–92.

Witt, J. de., *Waerdye van lyf-rente naer proportie van los-renten* ('s-Gravenhage: Jacobus Scheltus, 1671).

Wolf, T., *Reichsstädte in Kriegszeiten. Untersuchungen zur Verfassungs- Wirtschafts- und Sozialgeschichte von Isny, Lindau, Memmingen und Ravensburg im 17. Jahrhundert* (Memmingen: Verlag Memminger Zeitung, 1991).

—, *Memmingen im 17. Jahrhundert, in: Die Geschichte der Stadt Memmingen, 1: Von den Anfängen bis zum Ende der Reichsstadt* (Stuttgart: Konrad Theiss Verlag, 1997), pp. 541–671.

Yun Casalilla, Bartolomé, 'Mal avenidos pero juntos. Corona y oligarquías urbanas en Castilla en el siglo XVI', *Vivir el siglo de Oro. Poder, cultura e historia en la época moderna: estudios en homenaje al profesor Ángel Rodríguez Sánchez* (Salamanca: Universidad, 2003), pp. 61–75.

Zapatero, J. M., *La Guerra del Caribe en el siglo XVIII* (Madrid: Servicio Histórico Militar y Museo del Ejército, 1990).

Zeiger, K., *Hamburgs Finanzen von 1563–1650* (Rostock: Carl Hinstorffs Verlag, 1936).

Zuijderduijn. J., 'The emergence of provincial debt in the county of Holland (thirteenth-sixteenth centuries)', *European Review of Economic History*, 14 (2010), pp. 335–59.

INDEX